A Journey to Purchasing and Naming The Brown Hill Cemetery

A Journey to Purchasing and Naming The Brown Hill Cemetery

Sam Barber

Library of Congress Control Number:		2014908138
ISBN:	Hardcover	978-1-4931-8827-7
	Softcover	978-1-4931-8828-4
	eBook	978-1-4931-8826-0

Print information available on the last page.

Rev. date: 10/01/2015

To order additional copies of this book, contact:
Xlibris
1-888-795-4274
www.Xlibris.com
Orders@Xlibris.com
551358

CONTENTS

DEDICATION

JULIA MARION BROWN JONES, 1917 ...

*To God, to family, especially my Aunt Julia Marion Brown Jones,
to the good folks of Trenton, NC, and to the many, many participants
who so unselfishly provided spiritual and intellectual stability and nourishment.*

ACKNOWLEDGMENTS

An unfeigned debt of gratitude is offered to all of the individuals and institutions who contributed so graciously to aid in the successful completion of this project.

Special recognition is offered to the librarians and graduate students in the Carolina Room at the Joyner Library of the East Carolina University, Greenville, NC; to Dr. John Lawrence, department chair; to Ms. Susan Holland, assistant librarian; and an extra special tribute to Mr. Fred Harrison, staff assistant, for his tireless, cooperative, invaluable, and unrelenting support; and to a special graduate student, Ms. Jennifer Jones. The support and rich knowledge of the subject matter shared by the Carolina Room librarians and helpers were crucial in bringing this project to a successful conclusion.

For their untiring support, a tribute is offered to Mrs. Martha Elmore, manuscript archivist, Mr. Dale Sauter, manuscript curator and Mr. Arthur Carlson, university library specialist with university archives of the Special Collection Department at the Joyner Library at East Carolina University, Greenville, NC. Thanks to Dr. Lathan Turner, associate dean of students, East Carolina University, Greenville, NC, for his support. Special appreciation is offered to the clerks at City Hall, Mrs. Pat Suggs and Ms. Polly Jones. Ms. Jones's experience as a former secretary for the cemetery section of the city clerk's office for the City of Greenville was an invaluable source of inspiration and knowledge. She, too, worked tirelessly in providing City Aldermen *Minutes* and answers to a plethora of relevant inquiries.

Credit is due to Mr. Christian Lockamy of the city's planning and mapping department for the book cover design and map creations; to Ms. Karen Gilkey, planner ll, city's housing division; to Mr. Merrill Flood of the city community planning commission; to Mrs. Colleen Sicley, secretary of the cemetery department at public works; to Mr. Wesley B. Anderson, former director of public works; to Mr. Kevin Heifferon, supervisor of building and grounds and to Mr. Johnny Grimsley, retired former supervisor of cemetery grounds at the public works department, Greenville, NC. Also, to Mr. Phil Dickerson, head engineer, and Mr. Willie Freeman, deceased, head technician, management information systems for Pitt County, Greenville, NC.

Additional credits are given to Mr. Paul Harris, former executive director of the North Carolina Board of Funeral Directors; Mr. Peter M. Burke, executive director of the North Carolina Board of Funeral Directors, Raleigh, NC; and to Mr. Jim Walker, president, Mr. David Period and Mr. Patrick Hartman of reprographics, production and purchasing services of Rivers and Associates, Inc. Engineering Company, Greenville, NC. Incalculable credit is extended to Ms. Elizabeth Hayden, librarian, State Library at North Carolina History and Museum at the North Carolina Archives; to Ms. Delia Little, information center supervisor, Wake County Register of Deeds, Wake County Justice Center, Ms. Sandra R. Croops, branch manager, Olivia Raney Library, all of Raleigh, NC. Also, much credit is offered to Mr. Matt Torri, manuscripts research librarian, Ms. Carol Tobin, research and instructional staff and Mr. Tim Gilmore, all of the Wilson Library, University of North Carolina, Chapel Hill, NC. A tribute of gratitude is given to the following: Mr. Vincent Jones, special collection librarian at the Kellenburger Room, Craven County Public Library, New Bern, NC; Mr. Stan Little, administrative assistant, Mr. John P. Wood, restoration specialists of the Eastern Office, State Historic Preservation Office, Greenville, NC; Mr. Bryan Evans, supervisor, and Mr. Paul J. Andrews, resource conservation specialist and watershed technician of the Pitt County Soil and Conservation Center, Greenville, NC; Mr. Derrick Stevens, reference librarian of the Sheppard Library, Greenville, NC; and Mrs. Ethelene Hardy-Stover, convention service manager for the Convention and Visitors Bureau, Greenville, NC, for their support of this project. To Mr. Anthony Miller, director of the gas systems division, and Ms. Lisa Johnson, administrative assistant of the Greenville Utilities Commission, Greenville, NC, a special thanks of gratitude is offered for sharing valuable Utilities Commission documents.

Without the knowledge and support of some very special local and regional individuals, the project would have been devoid of authenticity. So to Mr. Charles Gatlin, member of the Sycamore Hill Missionary Baptist Church and caterer; Ms. Ellis Brown, member of the Sycamore Hill Missionary Baptist Church and retired director of the W. E. Flanagan Funeral Home; Mrs. Lucille Hines, deceased former member of the Sycamore Hill Missionary Baptist Church; Mrs. Audrinee Harvey-Tyson, member and secretary of the Sycamore Hill Missionary Baptist Church; Mr. D. D. Garrett, deceased real estate agent and activist; Mr. Donovan Phillips, director of the Donovan-Phillips Funeral Home; Mr. Larry Bardlavens, agent, Nationwide Insurance Company; Mr. Roger Kammerer and Mr. William Kittrell, historians; Mrs. Crystal Meador, office manager, Pinewood Memorial Park; Mr. James Albert Miller and Deaconess Connie Morris; members of the Sycamore Hill Missionary Baptist Church and researchers, Mr. Jesse Holliday, former downtown resident; Mr. Alton Harris, member of the Sycamore Hill Missionary Baptist Church and a retired employee of Burroughs Wellcome Pharmaceutical company and Mrs. Ella Harris, also a member of the Sycamore Hill Missionary Baptist Church, is a retired assistant Principal of Rose High School; Mrs. Nancy Howell, reader, retired human relations assistant, Dupont-Chemical Company, Kinston, NC, all of Greenville, NC; to Mr. Charles G. Irving, Jr., deceased book publisher, Irving-Swain Press of Raleigh, NC; Timothy Collins, Ph.D., Assistant Director, Illinois Institute for Rural Affairs, Western Illinois University, Macomb, IL, and proprietor, Then and Now Media, primary reader; Mrs. Louise Russell and sister Mrs. Blanchie Morgan, owners of In Us You Trust Home Health Care, and Mrs. Christine Sutton Gray, home maker, of Kinston, NC; Mr. Elliott Futrell, owner of Evergreen Memorial Park of Goldsboro, NC; and Mrs. Mona Reynolds Jones, International Compass Testing Coordinator of Saudi Arabia, King Faisal University, Al-Ahassa, Saudia Arabia, for their generous support and unselfish cooperation.

INTRODUCTION

"Remember the days of old, consider the years of many generations: ask thy Father, and he will show thee; thy elders, and they will tell thee,"[1] are the final passionate farewell instructions Moses spoke to the new generation of Israelites waiting with anxious anticipation to enter into the Promised Land. (Moses was divinely inspired by God to alert and remind his people by both oral and visual communications to remember their past. Many years later, this history was collected, codified, and written down for the entire world to see. And today, people all over the world have the wonderful opportunity to read and to be inspired by these glorious stories of the Israelites' experiences.)

From 1771, when Greenville, NC was established as a town, to 1885, there was evidence of only one historical marker (headstone) of a black citizen buried in the city, namely, Mrs. Laura B., Wife of Alfred Cully, Nov. 7, 1847-July 15, 1885, buried at the Cherry Hill Cemetery, Greenville's integrated cemetery. Other than that one historical marker, there is no evidence of any positive landmarks and only limited evidence of a historical presence of blacks in the City.

A dearth of historical information about the Brown Hill Cemetery, the City's public black cemetery designated for burying its black citizens, precludes any real discussion about black deceased citizens. This lack resulted in a search to consult Kittrell, *Survey of Cemeteries in Pitt County, North Carolina*.[2] Kittrell cites Mrs. Mollie Brown's headstone as the oldest in the collection. The citation reads, Mollie Brown, Wife of Andrew Brown, b. November 4, 1868, d. November 30, 1887.

---

[1]   Thomas Nelson, ed. *Holy Bible*. Nashville, TN: Thomas Nelson Publishers, 1988, p. 350.

[2]   William "Bill" Kittrell. *Cemetery Survey of Pitt County, North Carolina*. Greenville, NC: Pitt County Historical Society, 2007, p. 326-362.

Figure 1. Mrs. Mollie Brown's headstone

Mrs. Mollie Brown's headstone in Brown Hill Cemetery is the oldest found in Kittrell's Survey.

Immediately, the dates suggested that a Slave Burying Ground existed before the Brown Hill Cemetery. I conjectured that for Mr. Brown to purchase a headstone for his wife, he was a loyal former slave or a free slave or a frugal sharecropper and a man of influence and of some means. If he were a former slave, physical evidence shows that the headstone was separated from the main Slave Burying Ground, perhaps suggesting that Mr. and Mrs. Brown were a highly favored couple.

Further research, however, suggested my initial theory was inaccurate. Compelling evidence in a conversation with Deaconess Connie Morris, member of the Sycamore Hill Missionary Baptist Church (SHMBC), and Mr. Johnny Grimsley, former director of the Brown Hill Cemetery department and now supervisor of grounds,[3] revealed that Mrs. Brown was initially buried at the Sycamore Hill Baptist Church Cemetery and moved to the Brown Hill Cemetery during the Shore Drive Rehabilitation Project of Urban Renewal in

---

[3]   Sam Barber. Connie Morris. Interview during meeting with Johnny Grimsley. Greenville, NC, May 8, 2012.

1969. (See Appendices 1 and 2 for more details.) This move was confirmed by a contemporary report in the DAILY REFLECTOR, the local newspaper, on September 5, 1969, by Rev. B. B. Felder. He stated: "Following preparation of a map of the grounds and identification of the sites, when possible, a number of the markers will be moved to the Brown Hill Cemetery."[4]

> In addition, a 1969 memorandum from Harry Hagerty, City Manager, stated:

> It is further agreed that this letter [to the Sycamore Hill Missionary Baptist Church congregation] be accompanied by a plot plan of the existing cemetery [Sycamore Hill Baptist Church Cemetery] showing the identification of the remains contained thereon and the present position in the existing cemetery.[5]

On October 9, 1969, because the Shore Drive Rehabilitation Project had caused serious racial tensions and mistrust between City officials and the Negro community, the City agreed ". . . to convey to the (SHMBC) gratis grave lots numbers 41 through 70 of Section CC of The Brown Hill Cemetery . . . for the purpose of receiving the remains which are presently located in the said Sycamore Hill Church Cemetery."[6] There were 42 identified bodies, 23 known and 19 unknown, to be moved.[7]

However, Rev. J. A. Nimmo, pastor of SHBC from 1928 to 1961, stated "... two hundred and more of their bodies (members) now sleep on this same spot, which they landmarked for the coming generations to serve God and

---

[4] "Larger Job of Locating Old Gravesite Remains." THE DAILY REFLECTOR, September 5, 1969, p. 6.

[5] Harry E. Hagerty, City Manager, Memorandum, "Relocation of the Sycamore Hill Baptist Church Cemetery." *Minutes of City Council*, Greenville, NC, August 6, 1969, p. 1.

[6] Frank M. Wooten, Mayor. "Agreement." *Minutes of City Council*, Greenville, NC, October 9, 1969, p. 2.

[7] Lester E. Turnage, Jr. "Appraisal of the Property of Sycamore Hill Baptist Church Cemetery Parcel 4-6." *Minutes of City Council*, Greenville, NC, February 23, 1969, Preliminary Inventory of the The Greenville Urban Renewal Files, 1969-1977, p. 1; Pitt County Register of Deeds, "Certificate for Removal of Graves." Deed Book V-38, October 9, 1969, p. 53 (Manuscript Collection #647) http:// digital.lib.ecu. edu/special/ead/findingaids/0674A1.

---

maintain their homes in this area of the city."[8] An Agreement (Contract No 97) by the City and the SHMBC ". . . approved the removal of all identified bodies from the SHBC Cemetery to the Brown Hill Cemetery with contributions in the amount of $5,000.00."[9] The question may be raised as to what happened to the remaining bodies. Confirmation that the identified bodies were moved to the Brown Hill Cemetery culminated in an agreement signed by City officials, by Rev. B. B. Felder, pastor of SHMBC, by Mr. Leroy James, Chairman of the Trustee Board of the church and by Mr. W. E. Flanagan, Operator and Owner of the Flanagan Funeral Home on October 9, 1969.[10]

Dead at the age of 19, Mrs. Mollie Brown perhaps succumbed to childbirth, and Andrew wanted to memorialize his young wife and perhaps child's death in perpetuity. Fortunately for Mrs. Brown and the black community, she was buried with a headstone at the Sycamore Hill Baptist Church Cemetery. Regrettably, the Cherry Hill Cemetery and the Sycamore Hill Baptist Church Cemetery were the only cemeteries for the burial of colored citizens. With no other identified Negro cemeteries with headstones in the city, Negro bodies were apparently buried without headstones or thrown in the Tar River, holes, ditches, lakes, ponds or wooded areas to be consumed by wild animals, buzzards and insects. In the early 20th century, Kammerer reports that ". . . black bodies of paupers were seen along railroad tracks and unidentified bodies of paupers and executed criminals have been reported."[11]

Because of this neglect for human life, generations of Greenville's black history have been forever lost. Fortunately for history and the black community, along with Mrs. Molly Brown's headstone, Mr. Grimsley remembers moving Mr. Wiley Clark, 1857-1929, Mr. S. P. Humphrey, 1847-1912, Ms. Jane Latham, 1841-1921, a founding member of the Sycamore Hill Baptist Church, Mrs. Zelma (no last name), 1809-1910, an unnamed stone, 1854-1925, Mr. Rosher Johns, 1909—, and a broken unnamed stone, 1854-1925, from the Sycamore Hill Baptist Church Cemetery to the Brown Hill Cemetery. According to Death Certificates, other headstones moved from the Sycamore Hill Baptist Church Cemetery but unknown to Mr. Grimsley included the following:

---

8   "This House of God Will Be Destroyed Under Urban Redevelopment." THE DAILY REFLECTOR, Greenville, NC, April 29, 1961, p. 7.
9   Wooten, Ibid, 1968.
10 Pitt County Register of Deeds. "Certificate for Removal of Graves." Ibid.
11 Roger Kammerer. "Undertakers and Funeral Homes in Greenville." GREENVILLE TIMES, Greenville, NC, October 18-21, 2009; Kittrell, 2007, Appendix B, p. 5.

Table 1. On-Site Grave Inspections

Name	Birth Date*	Death Date
Clark, Hettie	1866	1913
Clark, Willie	1857	1920
Latham, Mollie	11/08/1873	08/06/1942
(Ukn.), Rhonda	09/12/1815	03/20/1899
Sutton, Julia	06/30/1876	07/03/1893
Sutton, Julia	11/15/1890	11/01/1929
Wooten, Cynthia	12/21/1852	09/20/1918

Dates in tables are in mm/dd/yy format.

Mrs. Mollie Latham was originally buried at the Brown Hill Cemetery. Mrs. Catherine Knox, (D.C. Vol. 5. # 342) b. Nov. 1, 1837-d. Jan. 30, 1917; Mrs. Jane Hardy, (D.C. Vol. 6. # 449) b. (ukn.)-d. Aug. 28, 1917; and Mrs. Mary Harris, (D.C. Vol. 7. # 95) b. (ukn.)-d. Aug. 10, 1919, age about 105, were founding members of the Sycamore Hill Baptist Church and were buried at the church cemetery but not mentioned in the move. Noteworthy, Ms. Lena Harris, b. (ukn.)-d. Nov. 11, 1917, about 59 years old, was a founding member of the SHBC. She was originally buried at the Cooper Field Cemetery by the J. I. Ormond Funeral Home. The S. G. Wilkerson Funeral Home buried Mrs. Jane Hardy, Ms. Lena Harris and Mrs. Mary Harris at the SHBC Cemetery.

A close examination of plots 41-70 assigned by City officials to entomb the re-interred bodies from the Sycamore Hill Baptist Church Cemetery to the Brown Hill Cemetery shows they are not logically arranged. On-site grave inspections revealed that of the 42 re-interred bodies, those with current stones show they are scattered throughout the assigned area. Mr. Grimsley stated that the Public Works Department played no part in this arrangement. The arrangement choice was made by Deacon Matthew Lewis and Ms. Ellis Brown.[12] For easier identification, a preferred logical arrangement would have been to place all identified bodies together and all unidentified ones together. On-site ground inspections revealed a pattern of juxtaposed headstones between older and newer ones. For example, Mrs. Carrie Lee Gatlin, a longtime member of the Sycamore Hill Missionary Baptist Church buried in 2004, was buried only four plots south of Mrs. Mollie Brown.

---

[12] Sam Barber. Johnny Grimsley. Interview about arrangement of graves from the Sycamore Hill Baptist Church Cemetery, Greenville, NC, November 29, 2012.

Greenville's black population has only a few memorials with which to celebrate and no state historical markers or national records of historical places or, in fact, any official historical sites listed at the Greenville Visitors and Convention Bureau. With the 250th Anniversary Celebration of the city's founding rapidly approaching, a proactive City Council has the opportunity to shatter the myth of "illusion of inclusion"[13] by erecting and strategically placing statues and historical markers of selected Afro-Americans throughout the city. The historic Bell Tower of the former Sycamore Hill Baptist Church—torched by an arsonist on February 13, 1969[14]—would be an auspicious start and make a very powerful statement. A marker presently exists, but a huge shrub blocks it from public view. Also, historical markers could be placed at the sites of the Colored School, located at Flemming Street,[15] the Colored Christian College, Third and South Street,[16] later renamed the Tar River Industrial and Collegiate Institute,[17] and the Town Common, First and Greene Streets.

Noteworthy, despite a beautifully well-placed marker at the Town Common site, there is no historical information, nor any mention of a black presence on the marker.

Former Downtown residents recall that for many, many years, the Town Common was the area the City fathers consigned as that part of town where blacks lived, worked, died, and buried their dead. The Town Common was permanently shut down and laid waste when the citizens were forced to move during the Shore Drive Rehabilitation Project of Urban Renewal during the mid-1960s. It is now a park located on the banks of the Tar River. In spite of grandiose plans by City officials to develop the area with businesses, municipal buildings and residential quarters, thousands of dollars were spent planning, designing, displacing and moving citizens from their homes, contributing to huge sums of wasted tax payers' dollars for the Shore Drive Project. Unfortunately, this project never reached the optimistic plans envisioned by the City fathers.

---

13 Marguerite Ross Barnett; James A. Hefner. *Public Policy for the Black Community*. New York: Alfred Publishing Company, 1976, p. xii.

14 "Old Sycamore Hill Church Burns; Arson Suspected in Costly Loss." THE DAILY REFLECTOR, Greenville, NC, February, 13, 1969, sec. 1, p. 1.

15 Pitt County Register of Deeds. "Higgs Bros to Col School Dist No 46." Deed Book F-6, May 12, 1897, p. 190.

16 Pitt County Register of Deeds. "Colored Christian College." Deed Book M-8, January 17, 1907, p. 447.

17 Pitt County Register of Deeds. "Tar River Industrial and Collegiate Institute Certificate of Incorporation." Book 2, 1910; and 1914, Book A-11, p. 376 and Book R-9, p. 415.

After more than 30 years of inaction, however, only recently has there been any discussion by City Council to revisit the area.

Several historical churches for possible consideration for markers could include:

- Colored Episcopal Church, 522 Bonner Lane;
- Cornerstone Baptist Church, 1301 Railroad Street;
- Disciples Church, 208 W. 13th Street;
- Free Will Baptist Church, Greene Extension-Mill Town;
- Free Will Baptist Church, Riverdale;
- Hemby's Chapel, 605 Sheppard Street;
- Holiness Church, 1104 Douglas Street;
- Mt. Cavalry, 500 Hudson Street;
- Primitive Baptist, 415 Third Street;
- Shiloh Primitive Baptist Church, Third Street near the ACLR crossing;
- Sycamore Hill Baptist Church, First and Greene Streets;
- York Memorial AME Zion Church, 304 Albemarle Street.[18]

Presently, the Brown Hill Cemetery is one of four historical sites that could qualify for state and local historical markers in Greenville.

---

[18] Ernest H. Miller, ed. *The Greenville North Carolina City Directory*. Ashville, NC: The Piedmont Press, 1916-1917.

Figure 2. Greenville Town Common

The marker at the Town Common site contains no historical information, nor any mention of a black presence.

Now that the city has committed itself to invest about $33,690 to upgrade Norris Street, a short contiguous street to Skinner and the Brown Hill Cemetery, it is conceivable that this area might survive.[19] The true value and meaning of this historic area will remain forever unknown unless significant movement is garnered immediately to preserve this historic site. Also, almost half a century after the city spent thousands of taxpayer dollars to upgrade the Town Common area, it is now being revisited by private developers to upgrade it to a commercial and residential district.

Three other sites are the Greenville Elementary School built in 1950 (now the South Greenville School, Figure 3);[20] the playground across the street from the Cooper Field Cemetery established in 1937 (now the location of the South

---

19 Wayne Bowers, Director of Public Works. "Ervin Mills Memorandum." Greenville, NC, February 17, 2012.

20 J. H. Rose. "School Ready for Occupancy." *Board of Education Minutes*. Greenville, NC, April 27, 1950, p. 259.

Side Gymnasium built in 1957);[21] including all contiguous properties on Howell Street; and the Town Common area on the banks of the Tar River, established from the beginning of the town.

Figure 3. Views of South Greenville School

The South Greenville School was built in 1950 on the site of what is now known as the Brown Hill Cemetery.

---

[21] South Side Gymnasium Plaque, 1957.

Other than the SHBC Cemetery, an early educational monument in the black community was a "Colored School" on Fleming Street established by Trustees Moses King, Samuel Cherry, and John P. Norcott in 1897.[22]

The Greene Place, located outside of the city limits, may be credited for the location of Greenville's most memorable memorials, the Colored Cemetery and The Colored Christian College, later named the Tar River Industrial and Collegiate Institute. The Tar River Industrial and Collegiate Institute offered both a high school and a college curriculum. The Institute had the authority by its Certificate of Incorporation to ". . . confer the degree of A.B., A.M., D.D., and the Ph.D. and other degrees as the said trustees and their successors may desire . . . .[23] Foreclosure proceedings in 1937[24] ultimately led to neglect and the razing of the buildings, destroying forever a significant historical landmark. The Colored Cemetery—with a name change to Cooper Field circa 1912-1913 and now a part of the Brown Hill Cemetery—ranks as the only well-known historical site for the black community. And although Brown Hill Cemetery honors generations of Browns, a white humanitarian family, it is the one memorial that all Greenvillians should instill with great pride and celebrate for its longevity.

From as early as 1887 to the present, black families of all generations, including slaves, ex-slaves, preachers, teachers, lawyers, doctors, politicians, military personnel of all wars, and just plain ordinary citizens, have been buried or re-interred on the property now known as the Brown Hill Cemetery. Table 2 lists an impressive number of veterans buried at the Brown Hill Cemetery who served, fought courageously and bravely and died in all wars for the sake of democracy.

---

[22] Pitt County Register of Deeds. "Higgs Bros to Col School District No. 46." May 12, 1897, Book F-6, p. 190.

[23] Pitt County Register of Deeds, Records of Incorporation. "Certificate of Incorporation #13378." May 19, 1915, Book 2, p. 447.

[24] [24] Pitt County Register of Deeds. "Foreclosure Deed." Deed Book X-21, January 11, 1937, p. 331.

Table 2: Honor Roll List of Veterans Buried at the Brown Hill Cemetery

World War I

Brown, Jessie C., NC PVT 365 INF 92 DIV WW I b. May 12, 1896-d. August 28, 1951

Daniel, Russell Early, PVT US Army WW I b. February 28, 1898-d. October 29, 1976

Daniels, Charlie, NC PVT US Army WW I b. April 9, 1892-d. April 3, 1966

Darden, Tony, PFC US Army WW I b. November 12, 1895-d. January 28, 1973

Davis, Charles Z., NC PVT 19 FA REPL DRAFT WW I b. August 7, 1896-d. November 6, 1948

Forbes, Thaddeus J., NC CPL 323 LABOR BN OMC WW I b. March 12, 1889-d. April 12, 1952

Hardy, Clint, US Army WW I b. November 17, 1896-d. September 26, 1976

Jones, Moses, NC PVT HQ CO 365 INF 92 DIV WW I b. November 3, 1896-d. March 30, 1957

Langley, William Holden, US Army WW I b. November 13, 1893-d. February 14, 1984

Lucas, John Wesley, NC PFC US Army WW I b. April 16, 1900-d. December 11, 1969

Marshmond, Arthur, NC PVT II CO 161 DEPOT BRIGADE WW I b. May 6, 1896-d. April 4, 1963

Moore, Alexander, NC PVT 349 LABOR BN OMC WW I b. May 26, 1897-d. March 1, 1950

Moye, Heber, PVT US Army WW I b. July 4, 1894-d. April 14, 1974

Owens, John, NC PVT US Army WW I b. October 4, 1898-d. December 23, 1946

Rogers, Jousha, NC PVT US Army WW I b. August 10, 1891-d. August 12, 1959

Ruffin, John, MC CPL US Army WW I b. January 18, 1893,-d. January 7, 1960

Savage, Solomon, PVT US Army WW I b.—, 1894-d.— 1978

Smith, Bernard, NC PVT 365 INF 92 CIV WW I b. March 16, 1896-d. November 25, 1948

Smith, Charlie, NC PVT US Army WW I b.—1896-d.—1956

Smith, James M., NC PVT US Army WW I b. January 10, 1896-d. July 27, 1969

Tucker, John, NC PVT SANHARY CORPS WW I b. June 15, 1889-d. February 1, 1948

White, Nep, NC PVT CO C 514 SVC BN ENG CORPS WW I b. July 15, 1886-d.—

Wiggins, John A., NC PVT US Army WW I b. March 26, 1895-d.—, 1970

Winston, John Henry, Sr., NC SGT CO D 330 LABOR BN OMC WW I b. January 1, 1890-d. February 21, 1969

World War II

Adams, Moses, VIRGINIA TEC5 147 PORT CO TC WW II b. October 17, 1924-d. July 16, 1977

Adams, Thomas, Jr., NC SSGT 4510 AIR BASE GP AF WW II & KOREA, b. March 14, 1919-d. November 17, 1958

Anderson, Bert, NC PFC US Army WW II b. August 8, 1912-d. June 20, 1969

Anderson, Kelly Douglas, NC PFC US Marine Corps WW II b. March-, 1929-d.—

Atkinson, George A., NC PFC 1458 SVC COMD UNIT WW II b. March 12, 1909-d. January 20, 1967

Banks, Travis Lee, NC 2nd LT 7 CV INF 1 CAV DIV INF WW II & KOREA b. January 7, 1927-d. October 3, 1951

Barnes, David L., Virginia PVT US Army WW II b. March 19, 1906-d. November 2, 1973

Barnes, James, NC PVT US Army WW II b. August 20, 1911-d. January 27, 1964

Barnes, Joshua I., NC PVT TRP B9 CAVALRY WW II b. August 11, 1916-d. January 2, 1954

Barnes, Leroy, NC CORP US Army WW II b. November 8, 1905-d. March 25, 1962

Barnes, Willie Lee, TN US Navy WW II b. June 10, 1929-d. November 22, 1986

Barnett, William Henry, NC PFC US Army WW II b. June 27, 1914-d. May 9 (8), 1968

Barnhill, Alfred Benjamin, Jr., US Army WW II b.— 1919-d.— 1979

Bernard, George, Jr., NC TEC5 US Army WW II b. September 5, 1913-d. April 12, 1957

Blount, James E., NC PVT US Army WW II b. March 9, 1919-d. August 8, 1960

Bradley, William E., US Army WW II b. February 19, 1910-d. September 30, 1976

Briley, Earl, NC PVT US Marine Corps WW II b. January 17, 1925-d. December 25, 1944

Brown, James H., NC PVT CO C 29 QM TRK REGT WW II b. June 9, 1905-d. February 11, 1970

Carney, Christopher Columbus, NC S USNR WW II b. December 3, 1923-d. May 19, 1963

Clark, Robert L., CPL US Army WW II b. February 15, 1924-d. November 23, 1971

Clark, William B., NC SGT US Army WW II b. December 23, 1920-d. March 1, 1956

Daniels, Percy L., NC SGT US Army WW II b. May 26, 1922-d. October 25, 1962

Darden, Alex, US Army WW II b. December 10, 1923-d. March 19, 1989

Ebron, William L., NC TECH 5 US Army WW II b. February 19, 1920-d. March 16, 1964

Edwards, Claude E., NC MASTER SGT WORD DEPT WW II b. October 28, 1914-d. January 4, 1949

Ellis, Ada G., MS2 US Navy WW II b. February 13, 1957-d. November 23, 1982

Filmore, Douglas Lee, NC STM3 US Navy WW II b. January 24, 1925-d. June 24, 1963

Foreman, Merrion Frank, CP2 US Army WW II b.—1921-d—1980

Gardner, Ernest, PVT US Army WW II b. October 12 (17), 1902-d. August 5, 1965 (66)

Godette, Thomas Hulynn, NC CPL 384 AAF AVIATION SQ WW II b. August 15, 1913-d. April 21, 1952

Gorham, Ernest Douglas, CPL US Army WW II b.—1923-d.—1977

Grimes, Lemon, NC PFC 125 PORT CO TC WW II b. June 10, 1914-d. October 19, 1968

Harris, Chester E., NC PVT US Army WW II b. June 2, 1901 d. July 31, 1956

Hill, Albert Clinton, Jr., TECH 5 US Army WW II b.—1921- d.—1979

Hopkins, Nelson, PVT US Army WW II b. June 20, 1927-d. January 26, 1985

James, Earl, DC PFC 2621 AAE BASE UNIT WW II b. April 2, 1922-d. February 4, 1950

Jenkins, Charlie James, NC TEC5 ENGINEERS WW II b. March 18, 1921-d. August 16, 1951

Johnson, Howard, PVT US Army WW II b. September 19, 1923 – d. November 27, 1993

Johnson, Rosher E., NC SSGT US Army WW II b. September 7, 1909-d. February 28, 1972

Jones, Andrew, NC PFC TRANSP CORPS WW II b. January 3, 1920-d. July 11, 1949

Jones, Clem, Jr., PVT US Army WW II b. August 12, 1921-d. June 21, 1986

Jones, Elbert Nathaniel, PVT US Army WW II b.—1926-d.—1978

Joyner, Samuel, NC PVT 294 BAS UNIT AAF WW II b. July 22, 1921-d. May 5, 1953

King, Sylvester, NC STM1 US Navy WW II b. August 23, 1924-d. February 14, 1973

Knox, Louis, US Navy WW II b. January 2, 1926-d. June 30, 1982

Lofton, Willie, PFC US Army WW II b. June 1, 1922-d. February 13, 1983

Mills, Amos T., Jr., TEC5 US Army WW II b. July 1, 1910-d. May 10, 1985

Norcutt, Arthur Lee, TEC3 US Army WW II b. June 2, 1908-d. October 3, 1975

Pierce, William R., NC PFC US Army WW II b. June 12, 1923-d. December 15, 1956

Pitt, Ned D., Jr., PVT US Army WW II b. August 7, 1907-d. April 3, 1992

Rasberry, Peter Elijah, S1 US Navy WW II b. January 17, 1919-d. May 24, 1973

Reid, James, NC PFC US Army WW II b. December 26 (21), 1921-d. January 19, 1974

Robinson, Benjamin, US Army WW II b. June 3, 1923-d. January 12, 1976

Roland, Sidney N., NC PFC US Army WW II b. April 12, 1922-d. June 14, 1972

Sherrod, William Wright, TSGT US Army WW II b. December 20, 1926-d. October 18, 1978

Shiver, William D., Jr., SPC US Army WW II b. April 17, 1922-d. July 16, 1977

Siders, Leon P., NC TEC4 753 OM CO WW II b.—d.—

Smith, James N., PVT US Army WW II b. September 22, 1901-d. November 18, 1970

Stancil, Rufus William, TEC4 US Army WW II b. April 23, 1921-d. January 22, 1984

Stokes, Robert L., CPL US Air Force WW II b. August 14, 1927-d. March 15, 1981

Suggs, Charlie, Jr., NC STM 30 USNR WW II b. December 25, 1917-d. August 28, 194-

Teel, James, PVT US Army WW II b. November 5, 1919-d. August 17, 1992

Tucker, Robert Lee, Jr., NC S1 WW II b. May 9, 1925-d. March 25, 1953

Well, Walter, OM SVC CO WW II b. April 7, 1924 (26)-d. July 18, 1969 (68)

Wells, John C., NC PFC 3225 OM SVC CO WW II b. April 7, 1924 (26)-d. July 18, 1969

Williams, Lyman, NC STM1 USNR WW II b. October 30, 1925-d. February 4, 1964

Willoughby, Bennie V., NC ODC US Army WW II b. March 25, 1917-d. September 23, 196-

Wilson, James R., NC PVT CAC WW II b. January 20, 1920-d. June 3, 1944

Wilson, Randolph O. C., NC TEC 4 42 SIG HV CONS BN WW II b. August 28, 1912-d. May 24, 1949

Woodward, Otis, NC PFC 86 OM RAILHEAD CO WW II b. July 30, 1914-d. February 14, 1950

Wooten, Arthur, Jr., NC STM2 US Army WW II b. August 8, 1917-d. December 16, 1973

Korea

Anderson, Winzer Earl, CPL US Army KOREA b. April 28, 1918-d. December 18, 1978

Howard, Roosevelt, NC PFC US Army KOREA b. December 17, 1933-d. July 2, 1973

Smith, David Lee, SSGT US Air Force KOREA, b. May 18, 1931-d. January 30, 1984

Taft, James Junie, NC PVT CO L 2 CALVALRY REGT KOREA b. July 24, 1927-d. May 26, 1957

Vietnam and Others Not Specified on Headstones

Atkinson, Ricky Nelson, 2nd Lt US Army b. October 4, 1957-d. July 31, 1980

Barnhill, Hinton D., US Army b. June 30, 1890-d. January 5, 1975

Briley, George, NC PVT 353 FIELD ARTY b. June 4, 1917-d. August 25, 1941

Bryant, William, US Army b. July 6, 1898-d. January 20, 1975

Cox, Gary Donte, SP4 US Army b. March 10, 1961-d. December 29, 1981

Ebron, Joseph, PVT US Army b. July 4, 1912-d. July 11, 1974

Evans, Albert, A2C US Air Force b. December 25, 1932-d. July 18, 1961

Evans, Malachi Lewis, PFC US Army b.—1957-d.—1979

Everett, A. Thomas, SGT b. December 29, 1944-d. September 27, 1968

Farmer, Henry Lee, NC CP2 SIGNAL CORPS b. April 21, 1924-d. November 30, 1959

Fenner, Carr, NC PVT 161 DEPOT BRIG b. May 19, 1939-d.—

Garrett, Louico M., PVT US Army b. May 16, 1915-d. June 27, 1974

Gaylord, George, Jr., NJ PVT 366 INF (September 1)

Gray, Brownie Edward, NC PVT 1CL OM CORPS b. December 26, 1912-d. February 8, 1945

Gray, Reginald Hill, A1C US Air Force b.—1940-d.—1978

Grimes, Slade, CO K 14 US OLD HV ARTY b.—d.—

Harris, John Arthur, NC SP3 US Army b. March 20, 1926-d. September 10, 1969

Hopkins, Elisha, NC PVT CO C 344 SERVICE BN OMC b.—d.—

Johnson, Johnnie J., PVT US Army b.—1923-d.—1979

Jones, Alton R., SP4 US Army b. July 3, 1951-d. November 29, 1974

Jones, Leland, PV2 US Army VIETNAM b. August 16, 1947-d. February 25, 1975

Joyner, William E., PFC US Army b. September 1, 1927-d. July 12, 1974

Langley, Alonzy, VIRGINIA FARRIER VET HOSPITAL b. August 31, 1893-d. November 15, 1943

Langley, James, US Army b.—1909-d.—1974

Linsey, Larry, PVT US Army b. January 22, 1896-d. September 6, 1974

Moore, James Calvin, SP4 US Army b. December 3, 1953-d. June 10, 1982

Morris, Rawlin, DOC PVT US Army b. August 5, 1935-d. May 28, 1972

Parker, Jarvis, PVT US Army b. July 4, 1896-d. July 2, 1974

Speights, Lawrence A., NC SGT b. February 23, 1932-d. August 3, 1962

Taylor, Anthony, LCPL CO D 4 MAR3 MAR DIV VIETNAM PH b. November 9, 1946-d. May 1, 1969

Teele, Willie Henry, NC PVT 1 CL 41 ENGRS, November 28, 1941 (only date shown)

Thomas, Lee, FLORIDA PVT 344 SERV BN QMC b. April 17, 1937-d.—

Watts, Danny Earl, US Army VIETNAM b. March 8, 1948-d. February 7, 1982

White, Raymond, PVT US Army b. August 18, 1923-d. September 10, 1974

Williams, Johnnie, Jr., US Army b.-20, 1912-d. September 22, 1974

Williams, Murry J., PVT US Army b. March 26, 1896-d. August 25, 1958

Wilson, Woodrow, Jr., SSGT US Air Force VIETNAM b. August 1, 1942-d. July 11, 1971

Woodward, James, NC PVT 933 CO TRANS CORP, b. April 13, 1934-d.—

Wooten, James Aloysius, SP4 US Army b. February 2, 1954-d. April 26, 1995

By Kittrell's count from 1913 to 1940, more than 1,600 bodies were buried on the Brown Hill Cemetery site. Given the limited space in the three Greenville cemeteries where black folk were buried—Brown Hill, Cherry Hill, and Sycamore Hill—reviewing the population of Greenville from 1771 to 1940, one could certainly call into question the disposition of many bodies of Greenville's black citizens before this public cemetery.

When one remembers that memorials are sanctioned by Scripture, all Americans, but especially black Americans, should never forget to be obedient to God's will and calling. In everything we do, we should pay homage to all of our ancestors so that we, too, don't run the risk of becoming rootless generations.

Again, to all Greenvillians, but especially its black citizens, it is worth noting that Greenville's 250th Anniversary Celebration is rapidly approaching. Certainly, the black community will want to do its part by showcasing a representative sampling of important historical markers, historical register identifications, official historical sites, and other memorials. It is imperative, then, that the few existing memorials from the past be preserved while, at the same time, working exceptionally hard to build future ones.

To participate in and to make a valuable contribution to the 250th anniversary will be a once-in-a-lifetime experience. The journey will not be easy and will require much energy, time, effort and even some personal expense. But in the end, to experience the pride of preserving memorials for now and for future generations will be one of the most pleasurable, rewarding, and enjoyable moments of your lives. Discovery can be exciting, profitable, and yet intensely challenging. Seniors, this is your moment: A mind is a terrible thing to waste. Get on board and enjoy the journey.

PURPOSE OF THE STUDY

The purpose of this project is not only to discover and to share information about the past, but to encourage senior citizens and others to participate fully in an activity that will benefit themselves, as well as future generations. Death is certain, and for environmental and aesthetic purposes, surely folks will want to be secure in the knowledge that their final resting place will be perpetually maintained.

I discovered the historic Greenville Brown Hill Cemetery while preparing a presentation for the Southside Senior Group, Ms. Ethel Lytle, president, with intense encouragement from colleagues Mrs. Ernestine Hasclrig (late) and Mr. John Dixon, on February 7, 2011, at the Eppes Cultural Center, 400 Nash Street, Greenville, NC. Previous experience with cemetery restoration for the Greenwood Cemetery in New Bern, NC, under the directorship of Mrs. Mary Peterkin, guided my vision to simply encourage the Southside Senior Group to partner with the Public Works Department in an effort to improve the cosmetic, environmental and aesthetic appeal of the Brown Hill Cemetery.

The Brown Hill Cemetery is the oldest city-owned cemetery set aside for the burial of black citizens. The City purchased the property from the William B. Brown heirs in 1939. Before this purchase, a few Greenville blacks with influence and means were buried in the City-owned integrated Cherry Hill Cemetery or the privately owned Sycamore Hill Baptist Church Cemetery. The Cherry Hill Cemetery was donated to the city in 1872 by Mr. T. R. Cherry and Mrs. Sally Cherry. The SHBC had, as most churches of the day, an adjoining cemetery on the church ground especially for its members. Four other cemeteries in Greenville designated white only were the Methodist Cemetery, the Episcopalian Cemetery, the Memorial Baptist Church Cemetery and the Evans Cemetery. In 1924, the city purchased the Greenwood Cemetery as an expansion cemetery for its white citizens and in 2003 the Homestead Cemetery as an expansion cemetery for all citizens.

Armed with limited or no historical records, the journey to discover the origin of the Cooper Field Cemetery and to learn more about the history of the Brown Hill Cemetery was, indeed, a challenge of unparalleled dimensions.

CHAPTER 1

Preliminary Inquiries

The initial approach to discovering information about the Brown Hill Cemetery involved a representative sampling of inquiries from knowledgeable or longtime Greenville residents, most of whom were unaware of the name Colored Cemetery. They only knew about the Cooper Field Cemetery. But when queried about the origin, the age, the deceased, the plots of prominent citizens, the size of the cemetery, the name change and the quality of maintenance at the Cooper Field Cemetery, most respondents became mutes. A few respondents, however, knew legends concerning Cooper Field. One longtime prominent Greenville resident said it was named after a Mr. Charlie Cooper who lived at 1028 Mack Street. Others had heard this story, too. Another person suggested it was named for a Charlie Cooper who lived at 515 Shepard Street. Yet another suggested that it might have been named for a Charlie "Tom" Cooper who lived at Route 1, Box 85A, Greenville. Upon examining death certificates of these individuals, none seemed to be a prime candidate for the honor. Kittrell's *Survey* includes Mr. Charlie Cooper, 515 Shepard Street, as the only named individual buried in 1978 at the Brown Hill Cemetery.

Except for the few black folks buried at the Sycamore Hill Baptist Church Cemetery and the Cherry Hill Cemetery, other respondents stated that the name Cooper Field was always commonly known within the black community as the cemetery designated by City officials to bury Greenville's black citizens. The origin or the name was of very little or no concern. The cemetery had been called Cooper Field for as long as they could remember. One individual stated that a Mr. Louis G. Cooper, a prominent white Greenville attorney, might have donated land and the cemetery named in his honor. An examination of his papers in the

Special Collection room at the East Carolina University Library did not reveal a charitable spirit toward the support for a colored cemetery.[25]

A powerful and eureka moment on this journey would have been to discover documented evidence of the Greene's, the Brown's, the Dial's , and other major plantation landowners exercising a humanitarian spirit, as did Mr. T. R. Cherry and wife, Mrs. Sally Cherry, by providing a burial ground for colored citizens. Even though Mr. Cherry was a "Negro Trader,"[26] his donation of a colored section in the all-white Cherry Hill Cemetery in 1872 spoke volumes to his humanitarian spirit. His quest for justice for all mankind trumped the attitudes of his relatives, friends, neighbors and others. As a publicly owned integrated cemetery, it is an important landmark in the history of Greenville.

Figure 1.1. Cherry Hill Cemetery.

Preserved memorials show a number of influential colored citizens of means buried at the Cherry Hill cemetery.[27]

---

25   Lewis Cooper. "Lewis G. Cooper Papers, 1922-1950." http//digital.lib.ecu.edu. special/ead/review.aspx/id=0304&q-cooper. L.G. Cooper Files. File Folder.

26   United States Census. June, 5, 1860. Washington, DC, U.S. Govt. Printing Office, p. 8.

27   Elizabeth Ross. "The Cherry Hill Cemetery Gravestone Inscriptions." 1990. www. rootsweb.ancestry.com/~ncpcfr/pChrHill.htm.

Rather than showing compassion for the slaves, numerous landowners' deeds and land division documents attest to the custom of selling slaves as property for money. For example, a Lanier Daniel transcript states,

> ... I have sold unto the said John Cherry a certain Negro girl named Charity about the age of two years and six months old and I ... Lanier Daniel do warrant and forever defend this said negro Charity into the said John Cherry his heirs as .... [28]

Another reference records the following account:

> Know all men by these present that J. Benjamin Forbes have this day Bargained and sold a certain Negro man ... to Hardy Smith for a quality of four hundred and fifty dollars which Negro I will warrant and defend the right and title of two Negro(es) unto the said Hardee Smith .... [29]

Mrs. Laura B. Cully, Nov. 7, 1847-July 15, 1885, has the distinction of being the first identified black person buried at Cherry Hill; Edmonds, Henry, Apr. 11, 1826-Feb. 1, 1892, is the second. From 1913 to 1939, Ms. Ross identifies 24 memorials of colored citizens buried at the Cherry Hill Cemetery, while between 1913 and 1940, there are 129 official death certificates recorded at the Pitt County Courthouse of colored citizens buried at the cemetery. Many empty spaces, no headstones, broken and illegible headstones might account for this difference.

Preserved memorials show a number of influential colored citizens of means buried at the Cherry Hill Cemetery. [30]

Two tremendously useful and valuable lists are offered to citizens interested in researching the genealogy of colored citizens buried at the Cherry Hill Cemetery from 1872 to 1940 (Tables 1.1 and 1.2).

---

[28] Pitt County Clerk of Court, Wills and Testimonies. "Sale of Negro Girl." Superior Court, Greenville, NC, Vol. R, 1810, p. 366.

[29] Pitt County Clerk of Court, Wills and Testimonies. "Sale of Negro Man." Superior Court, Greenville, NC, Vol. R, 1809, p. 224.

[30] Ross, Ibid, p. 1-3.

Table 1.1. Black Citizens Buried in Cherry Hill Cemetery, 1872-1913.

Barnes, Dennis, Died Mar. 20, 1904, Age 41 Years

Barnhill, Rosa, Nov. 1881 or 1890-Oct. 15, 1908

Bullock, Alex, May 2, 1877-Aug. 17, 1907

Cherry, Alonza B., Aug. 4, 1854-Apr. 12, 1906

Cully, Laura B., Nov. 7, 1847-July 15, 1885

Eaton, John H., Sept. 15, 1914-Oct. 6, 1896

Edmonds, Henry, Apr. 11, 1826-Feb. 1, 1892

Elks, Jennie, Nov. 14, 1847-Nov. 8, 1911

Jackson, Nathan, Jan. 15, 1884-Jan. 9, 1900

King, Moses, Died Oct. 11, 1909, Age 56 Yrs.

No Name,—12, 1905

Norcott, Sallie H., Nov. 8, 1905-Apr. 1, 1908

Norcott, Wallace T. F., Feb 10, 1900-Jan. 27, 1901

Norcott, Wiley P., Feb. 10, 1833-Dec. 30, 1909

Plummer, Delia, Feb. 15, 1866-Jan. 20, 1908

Russell, Jacob Raspers, Mar. 4, 1881-Oct. 7, 1908

Stewart, Benjamin, Col., Dec. 29, 1879-Aug. 31, 1909

Sutton, Lillian B., Sept. 25, 1887-May 3, 1907

Taft, Annie, Apr. 13, 1881-Jan. 6, 1911

Wooten, Arthur, Aug. 6, 1888-Aug. 17, 1906

Table 1.2. Black Citizens Buried in Cherry Hill Cemetery, 1913-1940.

Name	Vol	Death Certificate Number
Anderson, Luke	1, 2, 3	457
Atkinson, Herbert	12	453
Baker, Nixon	8	568
Barbour, William	6	506
Barlow, Patricia	25	368
Barnes, Louise	8	400
Barnhill, Frenando	22	387
Barnhill, Nellie	23-24	272
Bass, Moremma	8	354
Best, Artis Lee	21	603

Beverly, Sally	13	451
Brown, Bobby L.	24	472
Brown, Bobby L.	24	521
Canadi, Seger	8	422
Cherry, Mamie Larethia	6	433
Cherry, O. C.	11	473
Cherry, Samuel	12	481
Clark, Emiley	8	344
Clark, Reubin	1, 2, 3	463
Clarke, Hillaird	7	114
Daniel, John	11	529
Daniels, Zeno	1, 2, 3	415
Davis, William	9	390
Dial, Rivers	11	473
Dixon, Tempie	7	279
Dudley, Charity	11	534
Duff, Mary	8	390
Eaton, Mary Ethel	6	471
Edmonds, Herbert	6	500
Edwards, Claudine	1, 2, 3	449
Ehoree, James B. Titus	21	585
Evans, Arnold	13	441
Evans, Millissa	25	301
Evans, William	25	301
Exum, Kate Cherry	21	504
Fleming, Frank	1, 2, 3	473
Fleming, Joseph	6	583
Fleming, Lettis	6	496
Forbes, Julia	6	551
Foreman, Vernon	6	430
Foreman, Vivian	4	557
Gorham, Dianah	7	64
Gorham, Jimmie	1, 2, 3	481
Graham, Herolene	13	525

Grant, Harriett	1, 2, 3	464
Gray, Arthur	24	581
Gray, Olivia Ellen	7	59
Harris, George William	12	437
Haskins, Delia	13	442
Henderson, Rogers	23	437
Huff, Henry	8	390
Humphrey, William	12	542
Infant	15	431
Infant	21	611
Infant	25	425
Jackson, Clide	12	532
Jackson, Harriett	6	591
Jackson, Hattie	13	476
James, Frances Funedell	4	564
James, Ormond Wilson	15	450
Jenkins, Francis	4	564
Johnson, Eddie Porter	21	616
Johnson, Harriett	6	591
Johnson, William	20	393
Jones, Whitt	6	432
Joyner, Johnson Roosevelt	23	419
King, Daniel	9	357
King, Francis E.	9	392
King, Jackson	9	373
King, Virginia	16	513
King, Warren	9	483
Lang, James H.	12	516
Latham, Dortha M.	24	453
Latham, Eva McCall	11	478
Latham, Peton Wells	13	452
Latham, Peton Willie	13	499
Lathem, Jacob	7	70
Laytham, Herbert	12	536

Little, William J.	9	379
Locke, Junnie	23	332
Long, James H.	12	516
Malyeo, Francis	1, 2, 3	439
May, Nora	11	530
Moore, Mabel	21	570
Mooring, Dezora	11	466
No Name	1, 2, 3	442
No Name	1, 2, 3	443
No Name	6	558
No Name	8	431
No Name	9	371
No Name	11	562
No Name	13	500
No Name	15	450
No Name	17	443
No Name	20	317
No Name	25	432
Parker, Aaron	24	346
Parker, Caroline	7	134
Parker, Henry Lee	6	533
Parle, Henry	21	624
Patrick, Cyndia	7	63
Patrick, Lucyndia	7	67
Phine, Lincoln	8	585
Price, Redmond	6	491
Randon, Bettie	9	559
Rhodes, Francis	7	130
Rhodman, Rock	6	517
Rivers, Henry	6	481
Rogers, Henderson	1, 2, 3	437
Ross, Morenema	8	354
Ruffin, Mary	12	478
Ruffin, Robert	4	550

Slaughter, Pearl	11	532
Smith, Anna	25	362
Smith, Bettie	6	518
Smith, Elizabeth	9	417
Smith, Mary Anne Phillips	19	486
Smith, Virginia Bea	19	487
Starkey, Caroline	11	429
Staton, Frances	25	310
Stillborn	6	447
Stillborn	13	452
Stillborn	17	482
Stillborn	21	624
Sugg, Charlie Junior	21	614
Thorne, Maggie	25	270
Tucker, James A.	11	500
Webb, Charlie, Jr.	11	524
Webster, Hanah	7	97
Williams, Carity	24	446
Williams, Edith	8	349
Williams, Fannie	8	393
Williams, Hazel	6	534
Williams, Jane	6	512
Wilson, Edith	8	349
Wooten, Clarice	11	541
Wooten, John Henry	13	555
Wooten, Willie B.	11	461[31]

---

[31]   Ross, Ibid, p. 4-5.

Ms. Ross acknowledges, however, that "... many of the stones are broken, missing, or simply illegible."[32]

Monetary restraints perhaps precluded many blacks from buying burial plots at the Cherry Hill Cemetery. Plots ranged from $10 for single graves; 10-ft. x 20-ft. plots for four graves were $35 each for inside plots and $45 for corner plots; and a 20-ft. x 20-ft. plot for four or more graves cost $125 each for inside or corner plots.[33]

The progressive humanitarian spirit of the Cherry family undermines any notion of an unequal status for some Negroes in Greenville and deserves a special debt of gratitude. The Cherry Deed clearly outlines specific instructions regarding the participation, use, and maintenance of the Cherry Hill Cemetery:

> . . . for the uses and purposes of public burial grounds for the population or people of said Town of Greenville and for no other use or purpose—that is to say, that all that portion of said plot of ground lying North of dividing line beginning at the dividing line of the pieces or parcels of land known in the plot of said Town of Greenville as Lots Number (3 & 4) three and four, running North 78° West. 17 poles to a sweet gum tree, shall be held by the said parties of the second part and their succession, exclusively for burial purposes for the colored population of said Town and all that portion lying South of said dividing line, shall be by them held exclusively for burial purposes for the white population of said Town— . . . .

> Provided, further, that the said parties of the Second part and their succession shall appoint annually two discreet citizens of said Town one Colored and one white to take charge of their respective burial grounds, to Superintend the same and see that burial[s] are made on their respective grounds with order and regularity.

> Provided that nothing in this Deed shall operate to prevent the parties of the second part and their successors from permitting persons not citizens or inhabitants of Said Town from burying in said graves.

> . . . the said parties of the first part have herewith set their hands and seals to day and year first above written.

---

[32] Ross, Ibid, p. 1.
[33] J. O. Duval, City Clerk. "Price of Lots for the New Colored Cemetery." *Minutes of City Council*, Greenville, NC, Book 6, June 6, 1940, p. 194.

Signed Sealed and Delivered in presence of U. S. Rev. 50 cts.

T. R. Cherry, Seal
Sallie A. Cherry, Seal

State of North Carolina, Pitt County in the Probate Court: April 5th 1872[34]

Contrary to the Cherry Deed and apparently in defiance of the Cherry family's wishes, "The first reference to the Cherry Hill Cemetery in the *City Minutes* appeared August 4, 1898: The committee for the white cemetery shall have control and supervision of that part of Cherry Hill Cemetery set aside for the burial of colored persons."[35]

---

[34] Pitt County Register of Deeds. "Colored Section of Cherry Hill Cemetery." Deed Book V, April 5, 1872, p. 59-61.

[35] Kittrell. Ibid, Vol. 2, Appendix B, 2007, p. 4.

CHAPTER 2

The Colored Cemetery

For contemporary citizens who can retrieve tomes of information at the click of a button, frustration over the paucity of published documents about the beginning of the Colored Cemetery might rattle one's sensitivity. For generations, the culture of neglect by the press and media when chronicling information for and about Negro citizens and their contributions are legendary. Greenville Negroes had no local newspaper coverage before THE "M' VOICE in 1987,[36]" and not until the *Wings Over Jordan Choir*[37] radio program after the late 1930s did Negroes have a voice on radio that addressed and promoted the needs and interests of Negro citizens.

The only quasi-positive thing Negroes heard on radio was "Negro" music. Broadcasts reflecting Negro interests consisted basically of a steady diet of Ragtime, New Orleans syncopated tunes, Blues, Folk Music, to include spirituals on Sunday mornings, and entertainment shows such as the *Amos and Andy* variety, often performed by whites. Many Negro listeners considered much of this entertainment to be primarily of the minstrel-type and performed in a demeaning and burlesque manner. Greenville's main source of news was published in regional newspapers, especially the NORFOLK JOURNAL AND GUIDE of Norfolk, VA. That news basically focused on religious and social activities. However, selected deaths and horrific crimes about black citizens appeared regularly in local archival newspapers.

For many Negroes, accounts of vital information such as births, deaths, marriages, and divorce dates were recorded in family Bibles, in free fertilizer

---

[36] "African American Newspapers in North Carolina," prepared by Russell Michalak, August 2005, and updated by Susan Everhardt, May 2009. http:/www.lib.unc.edu/ ncc/ref/study/africanamericannewspapers.

[37] Sam Barber. "*The Choral Style of the Wings Over Jordan Choir.*" DMA Dissertation. University of Cincinnati, 1978, p. 13.

---

notepads, on loose leaf notebook paper, in spiral notebooks, and on brown paper bags, etc., and spread verbally via oral communications. Poor record keeping, lost Bibles, temporary records, and fading memories contributed significantly to the loss of valuable family histories. The few official records that might have been preserved were destroyed by fire when three Pitt County Courthouses burned by 1858. It was not until 1877 that a fourth Courthouse was completed. The fourth Courthouse and more records were destroyed by fire on February 24, 1910.[38] Local and state official record keeping of vital statistics began in 1913. Much credit is due to the dedicated early public servants at the Pitt County Courthouse for their excellent service in preserving the valuable contemporary records we use today.

Other than the Cherry Hill Cemetery (Table 1.2) and the Sycamore Hill Baptist Church Cemetery (Table 2.2), evidence shows that most colored citizens, following the Biblical example of undesirables, were buried on the Greene Place located outside of the city limits. The Greene Place is cited in several documents as an industrial zone that included lumber companies, cotton gins, brick companies, and even the Oak City Live Stock Company, Inc.[39] Noteworthy is that several deeds, official documents and archival sources reference the Greene Place as the location where many colored citizens lived, worked, and died. Although black bodies were spotted in other locations, limited resources or no means precluded them from being buried in either the Cherry Hill or the Sycamore Hill Baptist Church Cemeteries. As referenced earlier, the Colored Cemetery on the Greene Place was the designated location for burying Greenville's colored citizens. Expressions of surprise and even jubilation would have been greeted by a victorious shout to discover documented evidence verifying the existence of a Slave Burying Ground or a Colored Cemetery on or near the Greene Place or in some other location within the City.

As cited earlier, one report described two other places, including West Fifth Street (at the railroad tracks), where several skeletons were found. It was reported that part of town was used to bury black paupers.[40] That same report accounts for "... a graveyard ... known as 'Buzzard's Roost,' on Reade Street, extending from Fourth Street to south of Fifth Street, is said to be the final resting place of paupers and criminals who had been executed."[41] It is highly probable that most of the unidentified individuals were colored citizens.

---

[38] Angelfire. "Interesting Tidbits about the Pitt County Courthouse, *1858-1910.*" *www.angelfire.com/art2/1910courthouse/court.html.*

[39] Pitt County Register of Deeds. "Oak City Live Stock Company, Inc." Book W 14, November 21, 1923, p. 124.

[40] Kittrell. Ibid, Vol. 2. Appendix B. 2007, p. 5.

[41] Kittrell. Ibid, 2007.

The Pitt County Register of Deeds chronicles 23 burials at the Sycamore Hill Baptist Church Cemetery between 1913 and 1951 (Table 2.1).

Table 2.1. Sycamore Hill Baptist Church Cemetery from 1913-1951.

Name/Age	Vol.	Death Cert.	Birth & Death*	Occupation	Dr.	Undertaker
Austin, Harry, 66	11	531	b. 1851-d. 10/24/1923	Day Laborer	Battle	Flanagan & Cherry
Clark, Martha	5	339				
Emmett, Nancy, 81	8	409	b. 1840-d. 10/17/1921	Domestic	Battle	C. A. Albritton
Fuenches, C. P., 4 M	8	593	d. 4/16/1922	Infant		C. A. Albritton
Hardy, Jane, 74	6	449	b. 1843 d. 8/28/17	Domestic		Sam Short
Harris, Mary	7	95	b. 1814 d. 9/10/1919	Widow		S. G. Wilkerson
Isler, Rhoda Mary	1-3	478	b. c. 1865 d. 4/28/1914			J. T. I. Boyd
James, Lynell	13	528	b. 8/10/1926 d. 1/1/1927			Flanagan & Cherry
Knox, Cathrine	5	342	b. 11/1/1837 d. 1/30/1917	Nurse,	Widow	J. F. Ormond
Latham, Jane, 80	11	540	b. c.1843 d. 11/8/1923	Domestic		Flanagan & Cherry
No Name, 8 D	6	466	b. 10/19/1917 d. 10/26/1917	Infant		S. G. Wilkerson
Savage, Martha	5	338	b. 12/1/1914 d. 1/1/1917			J. F. Ormond
Simpson, James Albert	8	509	b. 3/23/1921 d. 4/30/1921			S. G. Wilkerson
Whitley, Della, 65	9	362	b. c. 1857 d. 5/31/1922	Domestic	Capehart	Jenkins & Smith
Williams, George, 74	6	537	b. 3/4/1844 d. 5/18/1918	Painter		Sam Short
Williams, Mary E., 69	12	487	b. 9/11/1854 d. 6/19/1925		Williams	Cherry
Wooten, Lucindy, 65	6	550	b. 12/21/1852 d. 9/20/1918		Capehart	S. G. Wilkerson
VOL 26 (1940)						
Basemore, George Clinton, 57	26	468	b.—d. 10/24/1940	Grocery Store		Flanagan & Parker
VOL 27 (1941)						
Cherry, LaLue, 3M 2D	27	420	b.—d. 9/1/1941		T.M. Watson	Flanagan
Whitley, William, 87	27	354	b.—d. 10/30/1939	Painter	Smith	Flanagan & Parker
VOL 28 (1942)						
Latham, Mollie, 55	28	340	b. 11/8/1858 d. 8/6/1942	Domestic	Capehart	Flanagan & Parker
VOL 30 (1944)						
Couston, Lula, 67	30	270	b.—d. 3/28/1944	Domestic	Capehart	Flanagan & Parker
VOL 36 (1950-51)						
Ebron, Georgina, stillborn	36	867	d. 11/20/1951		Midwife	Family

*Dates in tables are in mm/dd/yy format.

Before 1907, deeds at the Office of the Pitt County Register of Deeds reveal the description of land contiguous to the Colored Cemetery owned by Mr. William H. Dial, Jr., Mr. J. J. Perkins, Mr. A. C. Perkins, Mr. Guy T. Evans, and Mr. Benjamin E. Moye, but make no mention of a Colored Cemetery. However, "A Notice of Public Renting of Farm Land" states that the land of W. H. Dial, Guy T. Evans and the Greenville Cotton Mills are cited in deeds for property adjacent to the Colored Cemetery. Other early industries in the area such as the Greenville Knitting Co., 1903, the Greenville Lumber Company, the Greenville Lumber and Veneer Company, 1903, the Atlantic Coast Line Railroad Company, and the Norfolk and Southern Railroad Company make no reference to a cemetery on or near the Greene Place.[42]

It is not inconceivable, therefore, that the humanitarian spirit exercised by Mr. Charles Greene ignored or abandoned legal and social custom and attitudes, as well as land distribution practices to insure a protected cemetery for Christian burials on his plantation for his slave inhabitants. Mr. Greene, a wealthy landowner, conveyed much of his property to Nancy Greene Brown, his daughter and the wife of William B. Brown, a noted doctor during this period. Apparently this humanitarian spirit of compassion was kept alive by Dr. Brown and wife, Nancy. This conclusion might lead one to be secure in knowing that Mr. Greene did indeed provide a Slave Burying Ground on his plantation for his slaves. Under normal circumstances, property does not shrink, change or move. Therefore, given that the Brown property was contiguous to the Colored Cemetery, to know the true ownership of the Colored Cemetery property could provide a reliable link to a Slave Burying Ground and ultimately to the origin of the Colored Cemetery. Such action, however, might require a search by professional Title Search attorneys to make a definitive determination of ownership.

Based on preserved headstones, it is highly probable that a Slave Burying Ground or a Negro cemetery existed long before the name Colored was attached. References to a Colored Cemetery on the Greene Place surfaced with regularity beginning around 1907. During and after 1907, there are three references citing the location of a Colored Cemetery. The earliest known is a reference on the Greene Place in a deed conveyed by the Browns to the Colored Christian College.[43] The

[42] J. O. Duval, City Clerk. "Notice of Public Renting of Farm Land." *Minutes of City Aldermen, Greenville,* NC, December 5, 1940, Book 6, p. 252; Ernest H. Miller, ed. *The Greenville North Carolina City Directory.* Ashville, NC: The Piedmont Press, 1916-1917, p. 182.

[43] Pitt County Register of Deeds. "Colored Christian College." Deed Book R—9, October 17, 1910, p. 415.

second reference cites the conveyance of property to the Old Eastern Missionary Baptist Association for the Tar River Industrial and Collegiate Institute.[44] The location shows that the Tar River Industrial and Collegiate Institute replaced the Colored Christian College. Therefore, it is conceivable that the Colored Christian College might have been the precursor to the Tar River Industrial and Collegiate Institute. And the third citation references the Colored Cemetery as being on the Greene Place in the Deed of Sale by the City when purchasing the Brown Hill Cemetery.[45]

Reminiscent of Biblical practices for undesirables, the Greene Plantation was located outside of the city limits and generally the location for burying colored citizens. Therefore, it is highly conceivable that the Colored Cemetery might have initially been a gratis Slave Burying Ground carved out of a parcel of land donated by the Greenes or Browns and operated autonomously by trustworthy slaves, ex-slaves, freed slaves, and sharecroppers who lived and worked on the plantation. The Greene Plantation apparently consisted of hundreds of acres of land. In one case, Mr. Charles Greene gifted his daughter, Nancy, the wife of Dr. William M. B. Brown, with 700 additional acres of land which was later conveyed to Dr. Brown.[46] A contemporary map and on-site grave inspections of the cemetery property show that the Colored Cemetery is approximately 5.6 acres and was perhaps located in a wooded and hilly area on the south bank of a tributary flowing into the Green Mill Run.[47]

As early as October 30, 1946, the Long Acres Subdivision map shows the western part of a cemetery near the Greenville Spinners, Inc.[48] at Howell, Brown (now Skinner), and Norris streets. It has yet to be confirmed if this parcel labeled cemetery has been officially attached to the Brown Hill Cemetery. And according to a map prepared by the City engineer[49] outlining the boundaries of the Colored Cemetery, the above cited cemetery property is contiguous to the Colored Cemetery. And as late as June 9, 1966, evidence shows that "Cooperfield

---

[44] Pitt County Register of Deeds. "The Tar River Industrial and Collegiate Institute." Deed Book A-11, 1910, p. 376; Deed Book R—9, 1914, p. 415.

[45] J. O. Duval. "Purchase of the Brown Hill Cemetery." *Minutes of City Aldermen.* Greenville, NC, October 5, 1939. Book IV, p. 136; Pitt County Register of Deeds. "Bessie R. Brown." Deed Book V-22, October 12, 1939, p. 556.

[46] Pitt County Register of Deeds. "George Greene to Charles Greene Bill of Sale." Book CC, November 25, 1923, p. 129.

[47] *Insurance Maps of Greenville, N.C.* "Green Mill Run." New York: Sanborn, 1916.

[48] W. C. Rodman. "Property of Greenville Spinners, Inc." Map. Greenville, NC, October, 30, 1946.

[49] Henry Rivers. "Colored Cemetery Map." Greenville, NC, 1941.

is a private cemetery located adjacent to the Brownhill Cemetery on land now owned by the City."[50] And if it were City property, the Cooperfield Cemetery had been so poorly maintained that the:

> City Manager advised that a petition with approximately 64 signatures [unavailable] has been received by Mr. C. K. Beatty requesting that the City of Greenville's Street Department clean and clear Coopersfield Cemetery of all debris, paper, weeds and rubbish which is now defacing the beautification of Cooperfield Cemetery.[51]

The implication here suggests that the City owns the Cooperfield property, as did a request made by Mr. Boston Boyd's daughter, Francis, in 1943. Yet the previous statement cites the cemetery as a private cemetery even though the earlier statement says:

> Cooperfield Cemetery is a private cemetery located adjacent to the Brownhill Cemetery on land now owned by the City . . . . Motion was made by Councilman Brimley to authorize the City to clean up and maintain that portion of Cooperfield on city property adjacent to Brownhill Cemetery and to take steps to make it a part of Brownhill Cemetery.[52]

The language of a private cemetery or annexation of Cooperfield is contradictory and thoroughly confusing at best. Requests to the Public Works Department to furnish verification of annexation as a City-owned cemetery were never answered.

With the dawn of the 20th century, several factors perhaps prompted and awakened many colored citizens to the realization that the Greene Plantation was, indeed, the place where family members, friends, and others lived, worked, died and were buried. Accordingly, acute lingering memories of deceased loved ones buried at the Greene Place, along with the sightings of raised or depressed earth patterns, unmarked graves, and even a few preserved headstones, undoubtedly validated the existence of a Slave Burying Ground on the Greene Plantation worthy of further investigation. Obviously, further investigation inspired an impassioned desire within the community to trace ancestral roots. It is most likely these positive

---

[50]   Harry E. Hagerty, City Manager. "Cooper Field Cemetery." *Minutes of City Council.* Greenville, NC, June 9, 1966, Book 11, p. 37.

[51]   Hagerty, Ibid.

[52]   Hagerty. Ibid.

signs sparked further investigation into the burial practices of family members which undoubtedly led to an organized effort to resurrect, restore, and preserve the Slave Burial Grounds, which ultimately evolved into a formal recognition of the Colored Cemetery.

Documentation accounts for at least three preserved headstones at the Brown Hill Cemetery before the turn of the 20th century and four headstones before 1910. Four headstones are referenced in Kittrell's colored cemetery survey as: one unknown headstone, b. September 12, 1847 -d. March 20, 1899; Ransom Brown, b. June 12, 1828-d. September 25, 1905; John Marable, b. May 8, 1871 -d. August 17, 1905; and Sarah Tucker, b. February 26, 1882-d. June 6, 1908. On-site grave inspection accounts for two additional headstones: Julia Sutton, b. June 30, 1876-d. July 3, 1893, and Rhonda, (no last name given), -d. April 20, 1899. Julia Sutton's name appears twice in Section CC of bodies moved from the Sycamore Hill Baptist Church Cemetery in 1969. Mr. Ernest L. Denton, in a document compiled for the *Historical Records of North Carolina*, lists two individuals in a Works Projects Administration (WPA) report.[53] They are George V. Donaldson, b. February 3, 1892-d. January 5, 1909, and John Marable, b. May 8, 1871-d. August 17, 1905 (also cited by Kittrell). Although an arrow on Mrs. Mollie Brown's headstone pointing to the left might suggest that her husband may have been buried next to her at the SHBC Cemetery, there is no identified headstone at the Brown Hill Cemetery to suggest this. Perhaps Mr. Brown's might be one of the 19 unmarked graves now located at the Brown Hill Cemetery. Of interest and perhaps growing out of a curiosity for a rationale for the scattered locations of the re-interred graves, is that Mrs. Mollie Brown is buried only four plots north of Mrs. Carrie Lee Gatlin, b. February 19, 1908-d. January 9, 2005, a longtime member of the SHMBC, along with two of her sons, Mr. Eddie Boy Gatlin, b. September 10, 1937-d. November 15, 2005, and Mr. Calvin Gatlin, b. August 15, 1940-d. September 29, 1995. Mr. Willie Clark, b.—1857-d.—1920 is buried next to Mrs. Brown to the south. Mr. Ronald Brown, b. July 5, 1953-d. May 6, 1999, is buried next to Mrs. Brown to the north. The juxtaposition of these grave sites is unusual and gives us no organized clue about the arrangement or location of the re-interred bodies from The Sycamore Hill Baptist Church Cemetery.

Although due diligence prevailed in the search to trace the origin of the Colored Cemetery, to date, some details remain unresolved. The experience of interviewing local citizens, researching pristine maps, reviewing deeds and land distribution documents, reviewing wills and testimonies, reviewing a variety of archival sources, and conducting on-site cemetery inspections, etc., far outweighed and exceeded any expected outcomes that might have resulted from this investigation. The results were astounding, producing a treasure trove

---

[53]   Ernest L. Denton. *Cooper Field Cemetery.* Raleigh, N.C., 1940, p. 1.

of information about a diverse cross-section of Greenville's citizenry. This experience provided a window of opportunity into the minds, hearts, character, and spirit of many of Greenville's diverse citizens.

Albeit evidence to date does not confirm the presence of any public preserved colored cemeteries within or circling the city limits of Greenville, and with no identified cemeteries, legends tell us that many Negro bodies were disposed of along roadsides or thrown into ditches, lakes, holes, or dumped in the Tar River or in open fields or wooded area where wild beasts, insects, and birds consumed them. Social and cultural practices of the time let us know that it is not unreasonable to assume that city draymen such as Mr. Sam Short and others just might have buried some bodies illegally within the city limits. The case for such bodies has been cited earlier. *Minutes* of City Aldermen reference the use of lime on several occasions for the prevention of diseases within city limits.[54] Some observers state that blacks might have been taken back to the country for burial. That theory is highly suspect in that without property, most likely white property owners might not look too favorably on burying black city folks on their property.

Death is certain and it has no face. All must experience death and cross the Jordan River when our appointed time comes. The assurance of quality and perpetual cemetery care should give us comfort in knowing that in death we will rest in eternal peace. At the same time, such cemetery care is beneficial to our present environmental and cultural health. Public works employees agree that the Brown Hill Cemetery is better maintained today than at any time during its 73-year history. Improvements and recommendations are always welcomed and appreciated, and the Public Works Department would be more than overjoyed to welcome the Southside Senior Group to partner with them to help maintain, beautify, and map the Brown Hill Cemetery. To make this ignoble cemetery a cherished and honored site would be a great memorial beneficial to all Greenville citizens, but especially its black ones.

The lack of maintenance at the Brown Hill Cemetery has been and continued to be problematic from as early as the 1940s until well into the 1970s. Ms. Francis Boyd—daughter of Mr. Boston Bonaparte Napoleon Boyd, the first black City Alderman for the City of Greenville—recognized as early as 1943 the importance of the disparity of care and maintenance at the Brown Hill Cemetery. She petitioned the City to allow her to assume personal responsibility

---

[54]   J. C. Tyson. *Ordinances of the Town of Greenville, North Carolina.* Greenville, NC: THE REFLECTOR COMPANY, Publishers, 1910, p. 32.

for maintaining the cemetery.[55] The record does not show the results of her appeal. The petition gives the impression that the Colored Cemetery property belonged to the City of Greenville. However, the Rodman citation in 1968 states that the Colored Cemetery was private. But the petition submitted by Mr. C. K. Beatty perhaps confirms the City's ownership provisions. In August, 1973, Mr. W. H. Carstarphan, City Manager, was so troubled over the deteriorating maintenance at the Brown Hill Cemetery that he sent a formal complaint to the Mayor and City Council making recommendations noting that the maintenance policies (do not apply uniformly to all City cemeteries.) The letter reads in part:

> . . . in effect, there is very little control on the operation of Brownhill. Vault location, grave depths, and maintenance policies are poorly defined. As a result, the general appearance of Brownhill is distorted and the Cemetery Division is handicapped in its effort to maintain the good appearance of the facility.[56]

If the City fathers perhaps thought with time the Brown Hill Cemetery problem would just go away, that was not the case. On March 31, 1978, a letter from Mr. Donovan Phillips to Mayor Percy R. Cox, expressed great concern about the Brown Hill Cemetery:

> Dear Mayor Cox:
>
> Several problems have surfaced concerning the use and disposition of dead human remains in the Brown Hill Cemetery: including duplicity of sales of plots. This has contributed to confusion between the City and funeral directors, as well as animosity.
>
> We were promised approximately, one and half years ago, the designation of a Cemetery Commission; so far this action or promise has not been ratified by the present or past City Council. This Commission is desperately needed to correct, control, and protect cemetery usage in the past, present, and future of this city.

---

[55] J. O. Duval, City Clerk, "Request from Boston Boyd's Daughter to Take Over Maintenance of the Cooper Field Cemetery." *Minutes of City Council*, Greenville, NC, September 2, 1943, Book 6, p. 508.

[56] W. H. Carstarphen, City Manager. "Mayor and Council." Greenville, NC, August 7, 1973.

Hoping to hear from you in the most immediate future.

Respectfully yours,
Signed
Donovan Phillips, Co-Owner
Phillips Brothers Mortuary[57]

On April 11, 1978, Mayor Cox responded:

Dear Donovan:

I am in receipt of your letter concerning Brownhill Cemetery and the creation of a Cemetery Commission.

After a review of the present operations concerning the sale of cemetery plots and the maintenance of Brownhill Cemetery, it is my opinion we have not had duplicate sales of lots recently and Mr. Mayo Allen, Director of Public Works Department has done an excellent job in maintaining all cemeteries. Therefore, I do not feel the creation of a Cemetery Commission is needed at this time. Should you have problems concerning the cemetery, please contact Mr. Allen and I am confident he will do all possible to resolve the matter.

Your interest in our City is sincerely appreciated.

Yours very truly,
Signed
Percy R. Cox, Mayor[58]

As with most problems, the Mayor viewed this problem only in the eyes of the beholder.

Already referenced is the Petition signed by 64 citizens requesting improvements within the Brown Hill Cemetery.

To cite the U.S. Bureau of Census for Greenville from 1850 to 1940 is instructive (Table 2.2). Although no numbers are available for African Americans between 1850 and 1890, sources such as the *North Carolina*

---

[57] Donovan Phillips, Co-Owner, Phillips Brothers Mortuary. "Mayor Percy R. Cox." Greenville, NC, March 31, 1978.

[58] Percy R. Cox, Mayor. "Mr. Donovan Phillips." Greenville, NC, April 11, 1978.

Yearbook[59] and *Branson's North Carolina Business Directory*[60] tell us that colored folks outnumbered white folks during the early years of Greenville's history.[61] And between 1930 and 1940, one can assume that Negroes were in no small numbers. Therefore, the disposition of Negro bodies cited earlier becomes a troubling matter.

Table 2.2. U.S. Census of Population Counts for Greenville, 1850-1940.

YEAR	WHITES	AFRICAN AMERICANS
1850	1,893	
1860	823	
1870	601	
1880	912	
1890	1,937	
1900	2,565	1,472
1910	4,101	2,221
1920	5,772	2,827
1930	9,194	
1940	12,674[62]	

The Colored Cemetery and the Sycamore Hill Baptist Church Cemeteries were relatively small. The Colored Cemetery was only about 5.68 acres and Sycamore Hill only an acre. Knowledge of this Colored Cemetery should not be seen as an anomaly, but as a milestone development and a memorial to be cherished and honored. Even though only a few headstones for Negroes have been preserved, that does not preclude the presence of markers at unmarked graves. From Colonial times to the present, Americans have always been very careful to honor and respect our deceased brothers and sisters and to provide, whenever possible, a Christian burial.

---

[59] *North Carolina Year Book and Business Directory*. Raleigh, NC: THE NEWS AND OBSERVER, 1902-1941.

[60] Branson, Levi. *Branson's North Carolina Business Directory*. Raleigh, NC: Levi Branson, 1867/68-1897.

[61] Thomas W. Young, Staff Correspondent. "Greenville's Spirit of Community Enterprise Has Counter-Part Among Negroes in Hub of Eastern Carolina." JOURNAL AND GUIDE, Norfolk, VA, August, 10, 1929, p. 9.

[62] Michael Cotter, ed. "The Architectural Heritage of Greenville, N.C." Greenville, NC: The Greenville Area Preservation Association, 1988, p. 170.

Today, we witness the careful excavation and preservation of Indian Mounds and Slave Burial Grounds. Cemetery properties are protected by law. In North Carolina, a law as early as 1840-1841 was drafted and ratified by the General Assembly on January 12, 1841. This law, designed to protect cemeteries, was a landmark decision by state officials.[63]

History tells us that wherever colored folks were buried, respect for the dead with a Christian burial was expressed in creative ways by temporary markers such as wooden crosses, hand-carved wooden headpieces, metal headpieces, glass jars, whole or broken bottles, twigs, tin cans or other temporary head devices. In time, these temporary markers deteriorated or were just simply destroyed, with devastating consequences. With no headstones or any identification markings, generations of history were lost forever.

Kittrell's *Survey of Cemeteries in Pitt County North Carolina* is an extraordinary collection and a valuable resource needed for this journey. The Kittrell lists, plus on-site grave inspections of the Brown Hill Cemetery, provided the link to a possible Slave Burying Ground and the origin of the Colored Cemetery. For example, the headstone for Mrs. Mollie Brown, entombed in Greenville as early as 1887, although in a private cemetery, provided incontrovertible evidence of an organized effort to establish Christian burials for colored citizens.

Reflecting on the humanitarian spirit displayed by the Cherry family to provide a designated section of the integrated Cherry Hill Cemetery to bury selected Negroes as early as 1872, it is truly unfortunate that this Christian expression of human dignity did not manifest itself widely in other landowners. For the many contributions and sacrifices the colored race was making and made to develop the city into what it has become today, contemporary documents suggest that deeply rooted segregationist practices precluded land owners from embracing Christian principles to mitigate the Southern scourge by donating land for a Slave Burying Ground or a public colored cemetery.

In addition, and from a historical perspective, to applaud Kittrell's ground-breaking *Survey* is an understatement. In 2007, however, by the time Kittrell's *Survey* was published, official death certificates were being collected and codified by the state. The four earlier Pitt County Courthouse fires, plus a fifth one on February 10, 1910, resulted in the loss of many official death certificates.[64]

A number of the early death certificates are sometimes illegible and lack sequential organization, perhaps due to age and delayed filings. Death certificates

---

[63] North Carolina General Assembly. "Churches." Raleigh, NC: W. R. Gales, printer to the Legislature (Office of the Raleigh Register), January 12, 1841, p. 10-11.

[64] Roger Kammerer. "Pitt County's Five Courthouses." Greenville, NC, GREENVILLE-TIMES, September 18-October 1, 1985, p. 5.

beginning in 1913 are an excellent and rich vein of family history. Individuals with a serious interest in genealogy can glean from these certificates such valuable information as full name, place of birth, date of birth, date of death, education level, occupation, parents' name, cause of death, place of death, attending physician, length of illness, residence, time at residence, citizenship, gender, military affiliation, race, marital status, date of burial, place of burial, location of cemetery, name of funeral director, certification by the coroner, etc.

For example, the death certificate for Moring Adams, who died February 8, 1914, age c. 36, is perhaps the earliest identified individual burial in the Cooper Field Cemetery. Sarah J. Walker, who died December 14, 1914, is perhaps the earliest identified individual with a Greenville death certificate. Both certificates are recorded in Vol. 1-3, 1913, 1914, and 1915 of *Vital Statistics* in the Register of Deeds Office in the Pitt County Courthouse. As stated, by 1939, when the City of Greenville purchased the Brown Hill Cemetery, only about 130 confirmed headstones were accounted for at the Cooper Field Cemetery.[65] By 2007, when Kittrell's collection was published, there were about 1,494 extant headstones. However, due to the many unmarked graves, illegible stones, and many empty spots, Kittrell admits that there might have been many more burials. In fact, according to the boundaries of the original Brown Hill Cemetery map, all 451 names listed on death certificates as being buried in Greenville or the City were actually buried in that cemetery. While there may be issues with the accuracy of death certificates, they remain the best records available for data on deceased members of Pitt County's African American community.

---

[65]   Kittrell, 2007, Ibid.

CHAPTER 3

Origin of Cooper Field

Names establish and form the foundation within societies' culture. Biblical names of people and places, for example, were prayerfully chosen to represent God's will and blessings. Further, names give both credibility and legitimacy to people, places, and things. Additionally, names honor, recognize, acknowledge, and accentuate special gifts, talents, or contributions.

Map 3.1 "Colored Cemetery" Rendering by Henry Rivers, Greenville City Engineer.

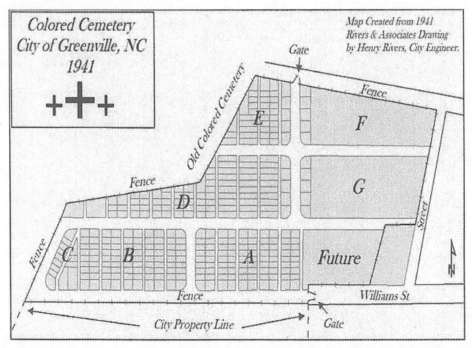

1941 map shows layout of Cooper Field.

By 1907, deeds of the Brown's, Dial's, and the Greenville Cotton Gin clearly identify and establish the name and the presence of a Colored Cemetery. From 1910 to 1913 before the name Cooper Field (Map 3.1) was established and death certificates recorded at the Pitt County Courthouse, Kittrell accounts for 12 preserved headstones at what became Cooper Field. These headstones clearly established the presence of a Colored Cemetery. The list includes Table 3.1:

Table 3.1. Headstones at what became Cooper Field. Kittrell's Account

NAME	BIRTH*	DEATH
Clark, Hettie	1866	1913
Donalson, Eva	09/19/1909	07/15/1910
Dudley, George E.	07/09/1870	04/23/1910
Hardy, Little Susan	1844	11/14/1911
Humphery, S. P.	05/05/1847	02/29/1912
Keel, William Jessie	10/07/1890	12/07/1910
Sheppard, Maggie	01/03/1899	09/27/1911
Taft, Zelma	1909	12/05/1910
Unknown	1899	03/20/1899
Wells, Eva	(ukn.)	04/22/1912
Whitchurst, Heber	05/25/1901	10/16/1910
Whitker, Irine	02/13/1867	08/05/1911

On-site grave inspections account for three more

Clark, Heith	1866	1913
Humphery, S. P.	05/05/1847	02/27/1912
Thelma Link	1909	1910

Denton, the WPA worker, accounts for eight more

Donalson, Eva	09/12/1909	07/16/1910
Dudley, Geo. V.	07/09/1870	04/23/1910
Harrington, Joe	1846	12/12/1910
Sheppard, Henretta	1909	1911
Sheppard, Maggie	01/03/1899	08/27/1911
Sheppard, Jennie	1911	1911
Wells, Levi	1880	04/22/1912
Whitaker, Lewis	02/13/1867	08/05/1911

Dates in tables are in mm/dd/yy format.

After 1913, however, the populations of Milltown, the location of an all-black community and later named Cooper Field, coupled with the surrounding areas and the establishment of new industries in the area, account for a noticeable increase in burial activity at the Colored Cemetery. From 1913 to 1940, Kittrell accounts for 130 headstones, while death certificates document 682 bodies buried at Brown Hill. Mr. Kittrell admits that the empty spaces, lack of headstones and broken headstones, suggest that more bodies were buried at the Colored Cemetery than have been counted.

The names Cooper Field, along with Milltown,[66] were derived from the workplace and the location where the workers and their families lived. The workers, called "coopers" were employed at the Greenville Cooperage and Lumber Company. Because the "coopers," were isolated in company camps or settlements away from the main community, they bonded into a close-knit community for survival. The Greenville Cooperage and Lumber Company, a subsidiary of the Norfolk Lumber Company, was located in southwest Pitt County, just outside Greenville's city limits. It was in an open field contiguous to the Atlantic Coastline Railroad tracks and the Norfolk and Southern Railroad tracks. Because the area was characterized as an industrial zone, it is included in Sanborn's insurance maps.[67]

During the last quarter of the nineteenth and first quarter of the twentieth centuries, the continuing Industrial Revolution ushered in dramatic shifts in working conditions, moving people from farming into factories. Eastern Carolina was rich in resources with land and trees for both cotton mills and lumber companies. Both types of industries sprang up everywhere. The companies, in a paternalistic effort to supervise and control the lives of their workers, built company settlements. Tradition provides evidence that the Greenville Cooperage and Lumber Company settlement included shanties, a commissary, a mail drop, a barbershop, a school for rudimentary education for the children, and either a church or a local minister to provide weekly religious services.[68] Total control of these wage-slave settlements included both matters of life and death.

In 1912, The Greenville Cooperage and Lumber Company set up a plant in Greenville's industrial zone to meet the rapidly growing demands of the lumber

[66] Ernest H. Miller, ed. *The City of Greenville, North Carolina, City Directory.* Ashville, NC: The Piedmont Press, 1916-1917, p. 199.
[67] *Insurance Maps of Greenville, North Carolina.* New York: Sanborn Maps, 1916.
[68] A. Johnson. "Life in a Southern Mill Village." 2005, p. 1-5. www.ecu.edu/cs-lib/reference/instruction/millvillages.cmf.

industry.[69] Several other companies targeted Greenville for its human and natural resources. Resources were plentiful, and labor was cheap. The Greenville Cooperage and Lumber Company was noted for all kinds of wood products, but it was especially distinguished for its production of staves and cooper's stock for barrels.

Documents verify that the Greenville Cooperage and Lumber Company greatly benefited the financial health of Greenville. The *Twenty-Sixth Annual Report of the Department of Labor and Printing of the State of North Carolina* in 1912, recognized "...the Greenville Cooperage and Lumber Company as having the most Capital Stock in Pitt County, with the Cabinet Veneer Company a very close second."[70] Its capital stock was worth $75,000 with an estimated plant value of $25,000. Some plant characteristics included a 300-horsepower steam-powered engine, a ten-hour workday, a sixty-hour workweek, and a total workforce of 120 people. The 1912 *Minutes of the Greenville Water and Light Company* give further evidence of the company's presence in Greenville. The November 1912 *Minutes* stated that "The Greenville Cooperage and Lumber Company made a request to be connected to the City's Light Plant . . . for a minimum charge to be not less than $10.00 per month & .10 cts per K.W. Hour)."[71] While the *North Carolina Department of Labor and Printing Report*[72] does not list the Greenville Cooperage and Lumber Company in 1916, the *City Directory* of 1916-1917 lists it on pages 126 and 199 respectively. Deeds continue to show the company purchased property in Greenville until as late as 1920. Table 3.2.

Table 3.2. List of Property Deeds from the County Recorder's Office by the Greenville Cooperage and Lumber Company, 1912-1920.

BOOK	PAGE	YEAR
B 10	435	1912
I 10	505	1913
B 11	282	1913

---

[69] James C. Tyson. "Provide Lights to the Greenville Cooperage and Lumber Company." *Minutes of the Greenville Utility Commission*, November 12, 1912, p. 102, 107, 109; M. L. Shipman; Geo. B. Justice. *Twenty-Sixth Annual Report of the Department of Labor and Printing of the State of North Carolina.* Raleigh, NC: Edwards and Broughton Printers and Binders, 1912, p. 77.

[70] Tyson. Ibid, p. 77.

[71] Tyson. Ibid, 1912, p. 102, 107, 109; Shipman and Justice. Ibid, 1912, p. 77.

[72] Shipman. Ibid, 1916.

B 11	141	1914
V 11	157	1916
H 12	172	1917
H 12	408	1917
H 13	95	1919
L 13	194	1919
B 20	507	1920
S 13	70	1920

Without doubt, the presence of the Greenville Cooperage and Lumber Company in Greenville can be credited with the rapid economic growth that made Greenville a desirable city to work and live.

As most workers at the Greenville Cooperage and Lumber Company were ex-slaves or ex-tenant farmers or otherwise unemployed or underemployed, they were mostly illiterate. The perceived stability of a wage job in a segregated community that provided a bare minimum of amenities motivated these "coopers" to leave the farm or to leave the ranks of the unemployed or underemployed. By doing so, it enabled them to seek and secure regular employment on the local economy. Since hard work, long hours, and little pay were already the norm for these workers, employment at the Greenville Cooperage and Lumber Company provided an opportunity for them to provide a better quality of life for themselves and a brighter future for their children. The pay scale in 1914 ranged from $1 to $3 dollars per week.[73] Many work days extended well beyond twelve-hour shifts, and conditions were not only hard, but hazardous.

To survive these harsh and hazardous working and living conditions, workers were compelled to bond into a close-knit community. Being isolated beyond the city limits evoked a strong desire to survive. In a spirit of unity, they called themselves the Cooper Field workers. This bond strengthened their resolve to thrive and survive. All types of wood products were made at the plant for sale and distribution. So when a "cooper" or a family member died, the company supervisor provided the casket and arranged to bury the member at the Colored Cemetery. As no administrative burial practices have surfaced, it is difficult to know the procedures for funeral arrangements in burying these workers. The Colored Cemetery was located less than a quarter of a mile across the railroad tracks from the company town.

With time, the cemetery became known as the Cooper Field Cemetery, and the name Colored Cemetery was dropped. The euphonious timbre of the name Cooper Field spread quickly beyond the settlement, and in short order,

---

[73] Shipman. Ibid, 1914, p. 54, 112.

Cooper Field and the Cooper Field Cemetery became household names within the Greenville community. By attaching the workplace name "cooper" to the cemetery and settlement in which the "coopers" lived, worked, and died, this ignoble and humble name ultimately gained cultural and official legitimacy, giving rise to one of Greenville's earliest and most prominent and cherished Negro memorials, namely, the Brown Hill Cemetery. By late 1913 and early 1914, for example, the name Cooper Field gained such wide currency that it was placed on all official death certificates of black folks at the Pitt County Courthouse and the state office of vital statistics in Raleigh.

While the Cooper Field settlement is listed in the 1916-1917 *City Directory*,[74] events of WW I and the absence of press coverage between 1918 and 1925 perhaps precluded publishing copies of the directories. During those years, Cooper Field apparently became a recognized name in city government. By 1926 or 1927, the name Cooper Field entered into the *City Directory's* permanent lexicon as "a colored settlement w of Railroad Ave."[75] A November 21, 1923, deed cites the name Cooper's Field in a property land sale by Redrick D. and Cora Brown to the Oak City Live Stock Company Corporation.[76] The 1937-1938 *City Directory* lists Cooper Field with a population of 216;[77] the 1938-1939 *City Directory* cites Cooper Field as ". . . a colored section southwest of junction ACL RR and N-S RR. pop 223,"[78] while the 1944-45 edition cites Cooper Field as ". . . a colored Settlement at junction ACLR & NSRS at the end of 16th Street."[79] Additionally, by 1939, the *Minutes* of the City Aldermen cited the name Cooper Field officially along with the name Greene Place when purchasing the Brown Hill Cemetery property from the Brown heirs.[80] The Citation reads in part: "The following land lying and being immediately southwest of the City of Greenville in what is known as the Greene Place,

---

[74]   Miller. Ibid, 1916-1917, p. 182.

[75]   Miller. Ibid, 1926-1927, p. 240.

[76]   Pitt County Register of Deeds, "Oak City Live Stock Company, Inc." Deed Book W14, November 21, 1923, p. 124.

[77]   Miller. Ibid, 1937-1938, p. 240.

[78]   Miller. Ibid, 1937-1938, p. 394.

[79]   Miller. Ibid, 1944-1945, p. 324.

[80]   Pitt County Register of Deeds. "Purchase of the Cemetery known as Greene Place or Cooper Field." Deed Book V-22, October, 12, 1939, p. 556.

sometimes called Cooper Field"[81] (or the cemetery known as Greene Place or Cooper Field).[82]

Throughout our history, Americans have, for the most part, respected and honored the dead and the cemeteries or places that entombed their bodies. Today, Indian Mounds and Slave Burying Grounds are protected by state laws. When the need arises, they are carefully excavated. To protect the deceased and to ensure proper care for the dead, state laws have been established and professional embalmers and funeral home directors are entrusted to provide transparency and accountability to grieving families. Without embalmers, undertakers and funeral directors, cemeteries could not have become established and thriving institutions.

From the evidence, white undertakers buried black folks at the Cooper Field Cemetery during the first quarter of the twentieth century in no small numbers. Black funeral practitioners and embalmers were in short supply or non-existent. Mr. Sam Short, credited as being the first official black embalmer and undertaker in the City of Greenville, did a brisk business in burying blacks at Cooper Field during the late teens of the 20th century. Even though no official record exists at the North Carolina State Board of Funeral Directors confirming a license for Mr. Short, he is listed in the *City Directory* of 1916-1917 as a drayman. In the Fourteenth U.S. Census Report of 1920, he is listed as an embalmer and undertaker.[83]

By March 1921, Kammerer reported that "Rives & Smith, 'colored undertakers and licensed embalmers,'...bought Short's undertaking business... In March 1921, F. G. Williams & Co, undertakers and embalmers, opened an undertaking business."[84] No records exist at the North Carolina State Board of Funeral Directors showing the above cited persons were granted an embalmers' license. Most funeral directors/embalming practitioners in Greenville were obviously practicing without a license. North Carolina required embalmers to

[81]   J. O. Duval, City Clerk. "Purchase of Colored Cemetery." *Minutes of City Aldermen.* Greenville, NC, July 6, 1939, Book VI, p. 94.

[82]   [84] Pitt County Register of Deeds. "W. B. Brown and Nancy Lee." June 8, 1914, Book 11, p. 332.

[83]   United States. Bureau of the Census. "Fourteenth U.S. Census Report of 1920 State of North Carolina, Greenville Township, Sheet No. 8, Enumeration District No. 52. Washington, DC.

[84]   Roger Kammerer. "Undertakers and Funeral Homes in Greenville." GREENVILLE TIMES, Greenville, NC, October 18-21, 2009. Appendix 2 contains an extended discussion of the undertaking business in the area.

get a license as early as 1901,[85] but funeral directors' licenses were not required before 1941. Mr. E. G. Flanagan (white) is credited as being the first licensed embalmer in Greenville.[86]

Mr. John Flanagan of the John Flanagan Buggy Co., along with his brother, Mr. E. G. Flanagan, established themselves early as the leading undertakers in Greenville. John Flanagan soon invested his time, interest and money in other pursuits, while E. G. Flanagan later followed and sold the undertaking business to Mr. Stephen G. Wilkerson. Wilkerson's funeral business eclipsed all funeral businesses in Greenville and remains the leader to this day.

Between 1913 and 1940, there were more than 40 undertakers or their surrogates providing funeral services and burying black folks at the Cooper Field Cemetery. Death certificates allow us to track the burial practices of blacks not only at Cooper Field, but also in Pitt and surrounding counties.

Table 3.3. *Tracking Charts of Burials* **at the Cooper Field Cemetery.**

CERTIFICATE NUMBER	NAME	FUNERAL HOME	DATE OF DEATH	DATE OF BURIAL	AGE
Vol. 1-2-3, **1913-1915**					
396	Moring Adams	Ormond & Jenkins	02/08/14	02/08/14	None
408	Infant	Ormond & Jenkins	07/08/14	07/09/14	4M 4D
414	Christine Nobles	Ormond & Jenkins	08/04/17	08/05/14	1
421	Patsie Taylor	Ormond Bro	01/20/15	01/23/15	60
429	Dinah Taft	Ormond & Jenkins	02/23/15	02/24/15	102
430	L. W. Williams	Ormond Bro	02/12/15	02/13/15	54
431	Alexander Jones	Ormond & Jenkins	03/13/15	03/14/15	None
432	Lucy B. Poindexter	Ormond Bro	04/01/15	04/02/15	37
435	Infant	Charles Freeman	04/18/15	04/19/15	80
438	John Shivers	Ormond Bro	05/06/15	05/07/15	36
466	Eva Hopkins	Ormond & Jenkins	03/15/14	03/16/14	None
468	Ella Socks	Ormond & Jenkins	03/26/14	03/27/14	26
472	Straywood Spell	Ormond & Jenkins	03/27/14	03/30/14	52

---

[85]   North Carolina State Board of Embalmers. *Meeting of State Board of Embalmers.* Raleigh, NC, September 23, 1901, p. 1.

[86]   Ibid, p. 4.

489	Mallone Forbes	Ormond & Jenkins	06/10/14	06/11/14	None
508	Celia Edwards	Ormond & Jenkins	09/10/14	09/11/14	4
510	Anthony Vines	Ormond & Jenkins	09/12/14	09/13/14	50
515	Clifton Briley	Ormond & Jenkins	10/19/14	10/19/14	1M-11D
517	Leslie Carr	Ormond & Jenkins	10/31/14	11/01/14	1M-10D
518	Virginia Lee Teel	John Flanagan	11/04/14	11/04/14	None

Vol. 4, 1916

418	Claude Brown	Willis Jenkins	06/25/16	06/26/16	None
509	Esther Langley	Willis Jenkins	06/02/16	06/03/16	57
517	Preston Price	S. G. Wilkerson	08/30/16	08/31/16	24
518	Louisa Holland	S. G. Wilkerson	09/08/16	09/09/16	30
520	Feneby Rena Shivers	Ormond & Jenkins	11/29/14	11/30/14	23
530	John Mitchell	S. G. Wilkerson	11/18/16	11/19/16	52
545	Jessie May Fleming	Willis Jenkins	06/18/16	06/18/16	None
547	Unknown	Willis Jenkins	07/02/16	07/03/16	None
490	Lucille Gerrigan	Sam Short	01/24/16	01/25/16	21
553	Willie Hemby	J. F. Ormond	10/23/16	10/23/16	1
570	James Earl Ruffin	J. F. Ormond	12/14/16	12/15/16	None

Vol. 5, 1917

340	Nannie May Walker	J. F. Ormond	01/19/17	01/19/17	6
351	Albert Mayers	S. G. Wilkerson	02/23/17	02/24/17	5
352	Minnie Hester	S. G. Wilkerson	02/26/17	02/27/17	16
354	Johnnie Blount	S. G. Wilkerson	03/18/17	03/09/17	13
355	Lois Whitaker	S. G. Wilkerson	03/14/17	03/15/17	69
357	Ed Forbes	Sam Short	03/02/17	None	22
459	O. Daniel	Sam Short	03/11/17	03/12/17	1
360	Margaret Bryant	S. G. Wilkerson	04/09/19	04/10/17	13
362	Annie Fleming	J. F. Ormond	04/06/17	04/08/17	16
364	Charles Henry Dozier	J. F. Ormond	03/31/17	04/01/17	3M
367	Cleophus Jenkins	S. G. Wilkerson	04/26/17	04/27/17	13
372	Oscar Highsmith	J. F. Ormond	05/15/17	05/16/17	1
373	Henry Daniel	S. G. Wilkerson	05/10/17	05/11/17	65
374	Neel Brown	S. G. Wilkerson	05/17/17	05/18/17	38
376	Minnie Jones	S. G. Wilkerson	05/28/17	05/29/17	14

377	Charlie May	S. G. Wilkerson	05/28/17	05/29/17	24
378	Clarence Eden Whichard	S. G. Wilkerson	06/15/17	06/16/17	None
381	Julious Johnson	S. G. Wilkerson	06/13/17	06/14/17	3
382	Georgia Lee Huggins	S. G. Wilkerson	06/18/17	06/18/17	1
383	John King	S. G. Wilkerson	06/19/17	06/20/17	47
384	James Nathaniel Edwards	J. F. Ormond	07/04/17	07/08/17	None
385	Laura Maye	Sam Short	06/04/17	06/05/17	50
386	Pluny Brown	Sam Short	06/01/17	06/02/17	70
387	Wadell Evans	Sam Short	06/14/17	06/15/17	None
392	William Howard Moore	S. G. Wilkerson	01/17/17	01/18/17	25
399	Lonza Daniel	S. G. Wilkerson	02/12/17	02/13/17	None
404	Matthew Peterson	S. G. Wilkerson	03/16/17	03/17/17	6M8D
433	Major Pollock	S. G. Wilkerson	10/26/17	10/28/17	70
434	John Jordan, Jr.	S. G. Wilkerson	10/24/17	10/24/17	1M-5D

Vol. 6, July 1917-1918

429	Mary Harris	Sam Short	07/05/17	07/06/17	28
431	Mary Alice Flowers	J. F. Ormond	07/21/17	07/21/17	5D
437	Willie Atkinson	S. G. Wilkerson	—	07/31/17	None
439	Silva May	Sam Short	07/18/17	07/19/17	55
441	Joseph Sheilds	Sam Short	07/31/17	08/01/17	12M-26D
446	Lura May Yarborough	S. G. Wilkerson	08/28/17	08/29/17	2
448	Shade Gray, Jr.	S. G. Wilkerson	09/19/17	09/20/17	60
451	Rufus Howell	S. G. Wilkerson	08/22/17	08/23/17	None
453	James Authur Carr	S. G. Wilkerson	09/28/17	09/29/17	None
454	Emma Artis	S. G. Wilkerson	09/13/17	09/14/17	13
455	Richard Whitehead, Sr.	S. G. Wilkerson	09/30/17	10/01/17	76
456	Herbert Little	Sam Short	08/23/17	08/24/17	Few Hours
457	Norton Edward Clarke	Sam Short	09/22/17	09/23/17	2
460	Russ Harrington	S. G. Wilkerson	10/14/17	10/15/17	65
468	Emily Nobles	S. G. Wilkerson	11/18/17	11/19/17	13
470	Olie Gertrude Peyton	J. F. Ormond	11/09/17	11/14/17	11
472	Lena Harris	S. G. Wilkerson	11/11/17	11/13/17	58
478	Young Richmond	S. G. Wilkerson	12/08/17	12/09/17	63

480	Mary May	Sam Short	02/14/18	02/15/18	3M
482	Geo Lee Grant	Sam Short	02/07/18	02/08/18	37
484	Annie Lee Moore	S. G. Wilkerson	02/01/18	02/02/18	2
494	Stillborn	S. G. Wilkerson	03/23/18	03/23/16	Stillborn
495	Simon Harris	S. G. Wilkerson	03/28/18	03/29/18	6M 3D
497	Ralph Alexander Roberts	S. G. Wilkerson	06/02/16	06/03/18	None
498	Lewis Allen	S. G. Wilkerson	06/01/18	06/01/18	69
499	Pheobia Tucker	S. G. Wilkerson	03/21/18	03/22/18	8
501	Henry Sheppard	S. G. Wilkerson	05/14/18	05/15/18	80
502	Julious Terry	S. G. Wilkerson	05/11/18	05/17/18	None
507	Lewis Hopkins	S. G. Wilkerson	04/05/18	04/06/18	None
509	Rachell Gaskins	S. G. Wilkerson	06/11/18	06/12/18	48
513	Luveina Clarke	Sam Short	04/30/18	05/01/18	20
516	Infant	S. G. Wilkerson	06/07/18	06/07/18	7M
520	Alice Gorham	S. G. Wilkerson	07/03/18	07/04/18	None
523	Cora Bell May	S. G. Wilkerson	07/18/18	07/19/18	14
524	Lewis Carey, Jr.	S. G. Wilkerson	07/19/18	07/20/18	1
527	Alexander Peyton	S. G. Wilkerson	07/30/18	07/31/18	2
528	Rosa Watson	S. G. Wilkerson	08/01/18	08/02/18	C17
529	Clifton Jones	S. G. Wilkerson	08/01/18	08/02/18	1 Hour
530	Luvernia Harris	Sam Short	08/01/18	08/02/18	6M-10D
531	Mattie Lee Eaton	S. G. Wilkerson	08/03/18	08/04/18	9M-15D
535	Bing F. Lienberger	Sam Short	08/08/18	08/09/18	60
539	Annie May Grandy	S. G. Wilkerson	08/26/18	08/27/18	5
541	Willie Ford Boone	S. G. Wilkerson	09/02/18	09/03/18	10
545	Margaret Shiver	S. G. Wilkerson	09/11/18	09/12/18	11
552	Malsen Pryar	S. G. Wilkerson	10/10/18	10/11/18	70
553	Charles Jones	S. G. Wilkerson	10/15/18	10/15/18	5
554	Ida Foreman	S. G. Wilkerson	10/15/18	10/16/18	14
555	Lula James	Sam Short	10/15/18	10/15/18	33
556	Lucille Earnel	S. G. Wilkerson	11/16/18	11/17/18	C22
557	Bertha Vines	S. G. Wilkerson	10/16/18	10/16/18	27
559	Mattie M. Williams	S. G. Wilkerson	10/20/18	10/20/18	18M
560	Mary Bailey	S. G. Wilkerson	10/20/18	10/21/18	11
561	Will Webb	S. G. Wilkerson	10/21/18	10/22/18	37
562	Unknown	S. G. Wilkerson	10/21/18	11/05/18	26
564	Loradu Cherry	S. G. Wilkerson	10/22/18	10/24/18	5

565	Carrie Pollard	S. G. Wilkerson	10/24/18	10/25/18	24
566	Jasper Forbes	S. G. Wilkerson	10/24/18	19/25/18	5
567	Jesse Bradley	S. G. Wilkerson	10/24/18	10/25/18	C30
568	Lewis Fleming	S. G. Wilkerson	10/25/18	10/26/18	6
570	Louisa Gray	Sam Short	10/28/18	10/29/18	26
573	Hattie Emmis	S. G. Wilkerson	11/03/18	11/04/18	31
575	Gertrude Green	S. G. Wilkerson	10/03/18	10/04/18	26
576	Fannie Carr	S. G. Wilkerson	10/17/18	10/18/18	25
584	A. B. Williams	Sam Short	11/29/18	11/30/18	71
586	Alfred Barnhill	Sam Short	12/06/18	12/07/18	None
590	Mandy Maneys	Sam Short	11/25/18	11/26/18	79
592	Maggie Fleming	Sam Short	12/07/18	12/08/18	None
594	No Name	Sam Short	12/03/18	12/04/18	None
595	Robert Williams	Sam Short	10/04/18	10/05/18	18
596	Alex Bailey, Jr.	Sam Short	11/14/18	11/15/18	11M
598	William Washington Jenkins	S. G. Wilkerson	12/28/18	12/29/18	C8
602	George Nobles	S. G. Wilkerson	12/18/18	12/19/18	None
603	Samuel Shivers	S. G. Wilkerson	12/31/18	01/01/19	37
616	Nettie Euborn	S. G. Wilkerson	11/14/17	11/15/17	18
626	Richard Edward Williams	S. G. Wilkerson	12/21/17	12/22/17	11M-15D
627	James R. Mayo	S. G. Wilkerson	01/22/18	01/22/18	54
658	Lucinda Brown	S. G. Wilkerson	04/08/18	04/09/18	36
664	Arden Evans	S. G. Wilkerson	05/17/18	05/17/18	50
603	Margaret Shine Burton	S. G. Wilkerson	09/11/18	09/12/18	15
695	Heneretta D. Carr	S. G. Wilkerson	09/18/18	09/19/18	4M-6D
717	Mary Becton	Sam Short	10/25/19	10/26/18	34
734	Edna Carr	S. G. Wilkerson	10/14/18	10/15/18	C36

Vol. 7, 1919

245	Infant	S. G. Wilkerson	01/18/19	01/18/19	None
275	Edward Killbrew	S. G. Wilkerson	07/18/19	07/19/19	8
278	Redmond Fleming	S. G. Wilkerson	07/03/19	07/04/19	51
288	Alla Barnes	Sam Short	10/05/19	10/06/19	60
296	Harriett Thompson	Jenkins & Co	02/20/20	02/21/20	110
299	Sam P. Johnson	Sam Short	10/04/19	10/05/19	48

Vol. 7, 1920

65	Mamie Wahab	Sam Short	01/15/19	01/16/19	35
66	Laura N. Brown	S. G. Wilkerson	01/21/19	01/22/19	3
68	Abram Mills	S. G. Wilkerson	02/05/19	02/06/19	80
71	Lucy Davis	S. G. Wilkerson	02/13/19	02/14/19	55
73	Rodgers Rossie Rhodes	Sam Short	03/11/19	03/12/19	27
74	Aaron Briley	Sam Short	03/13/19	03/14/19	31
77	Verna Mae Webb	S. G. Wilkerson	07/03/19	07/04/19	4M-8D
80	Laura Hemby	S. G. Wilkerson	05/30/19	05/31/19	None
82	Lillian Williams	Sam Short	04/20/19	04/21/19	6
83	Pheobie Belcher	S. G. Wilkerson	04/01/19	04/02/19	68
85	Africa Brown	S. G. Wilkerson	05/05/19	05/05/19	65
86	Mamie Ruth Hall	S. G. Wilkerson	05/21/19	05/22/19	None
87	John Albritton	S. G. Wilkerson	04/23/19	04/24/19	None
94	Henry Harding	S. G. Wilkerson	08/16/19	08/17/19	82
96	Francis Mariah Blount	S. G. Wilkerson	09/09/19	09/09/19	None
98	Edward Harris	Sam Short	06/11/19	06/12/19	51
99	Charlotte Turner	S. G. Wilkerson	08/05/19	08/06/19	61
104	Della Randolph	S. G. Wilkerson	08/31/19	09/01/19	C 42
105	Sarah Grayham	S. G. Wilkerson	08/23/19	08/24/19	42
108	Ferby Forbes	S. G. Wilkerson	08/06/19	08/07/19	None
113	Jennette Rogers	Sam Short	12/08/19	12/09/19	None
117	John Dickens	S. G. Wilkerson	11/13/19	11/14/19	50
118	Auston Bernard	Sam Short	01/08/20	01/09/20	28
119	Hardison Farmer	S. G. Wilkerson	01/09/20	01/11/20	None
120	Miles Moye	Sam Short	12/29/19	12/30/19	36
122	Ellen Harris	S. G. Wilkerson	01/28/20	01/30/20	54
128	Mary Brown	S. G. Wilkerson	01/08/19	01/09/19	C 85 or C 90
129	Maggie Bell	S. G. Wilkerson	01/06/19	01/08/19	58
132	Milton Taft	S. G. Wilkerson	12/20/19	12/20/19	26
135	No Name	Jenkins & Harris	05/09/20	05/09/20	None
136	Nettie Lee Forks	Jenkins & Harris	05/16/20	05/17/20	5
139	Daisy Jenkins	S. G. Wilkerson	03/19/20	03/21/20	21
142	No Name	Jenkins & Harris	06/13/20	06/14/20	Two Hours
143	No Name	Jenkins & Harris	06/14/20	06/15/20	1D 2Hours

148	Mary Foreman	Jenkins & Harris	01/27/20	01/28/20	41
149	Edward Brown	Jenkins & Harris	01/28/20	01/29/20	None
152	Jannie Tucker	S. G. Wilkerson	07/12/20	07/13/20	None

Vol. 8, 1921

336	Emma Daniel	S. G. Wilkerson	07/25/20	07/25/20	22
337	Sarah Williams	Jenkins & Harris	07/29/20	07/30/20	72
338	Stillborn	Hand Made Box	06/05/20	06/05/20	None
339	Stillborn	Nixon Reed	06/04/20	06/04/20	1. 11. 20
341	John Arthur Smith	S. G. Wilkerson	08/03/20	08/03/20	None
343	Willie May Evans	Jenkins & Harris	08/24/20	08/25/20	8M
345	Mary L. James	Sam Short	07/22/20	07/23/20	6M 2D
346	Eleanor Forbes	S. G. Wilkerson	09/02/20	09/03/20	36
347	Nelson Bender	S. G. Wilkerson	08/31/20	08/31/20	None
348	Bessie Galloway	S. G. Wilkerson	09/25/20	09/26/20	C24
350	Chrispus F. Atkins	S. G. Wilkerson	09/19/20	09/20/20	None
353	Julia Barton	Jenkins & Harris	12/12/20	12/15/20	C 37
355	Janis Haskins	S. G. Wilkerson	11/29/20	12/01/20	C 60
358	Elizabeth Forbes	S. G. Wilkerson	01/05/21	01/07/21	41
359	Sarah Evans	Jenkins & Harris	11/22/20	11/23/20	55
361	Mary Lock	Jenkins & Harris	01/10/21	01/11/21	40
368	Jackson Harris	S. G. Wilkerson	03/20/21	03/21/21	80
372	Clarke Cherry	S. G. Wilkerson	04/24/21	04/24/21	36
374	Clara Fleming	F. G. Williams	04/10/21	04/01/21	19
377	Hariett Hopkins	Sam Short	04/26/21	04/27/21	54
378	Infant	Home Made Box	03/01/21	03/01/21	Stillborn
379	Infant, Stillborn	Home Made Box	02/26/21	02/26/21	Stillborn
380	Bessie House	S. G. Wilkerson	03/11/21	03/12/21	3M
381	Charles Ashley Harper	Home Made Box	10/16/21	10/16/21	Baby
382	James Williams	F. G. Williams	05/27/21	05/28/21	None
384	Sanda Johnson	F. G. Williams	06/14/21	06/16/21	41
385	Stillborn	F. G. Williams	06/06/21	06/07/21	Stillborn
387	Stillborn	S. G. Wilkerson	05/28/21	05/28/21	Stillborn
391	George Neal	Sam Short	06/08/21	06/09/21	C 62
392	Luziana Ebron	S. G. Wilkerson	04/04/21	14/05/21	C 52
394	Will Royester	Rives & Small	07/24/21	07/25/21	C 50

| 396 | Martha Foreman | George Williams | 07/28/21 | 07/29/21 | 23 |
| 398 | Charlie G. Smith | S. G. Wilkerson | 08/02/21 | 08/05/21 | 27 |

Vol. 8,1921

401	Thomas Rich	Jenkins & Britt	08/29/21	08/30/21	69
402	Gerald Spell	Jenkins & Britt	08/31/21	09/01/21	65
403	Jane Mayo	Jenkins & Britt	08/31/21	09/01/21	60
405	Everett Swindell Bradley	S. G. Wilkerson	09/11/21	09/12/21	None
408	Francis Dell Hemby	S. G. Wilkerson	10/17/21	10/18/21	7M
410	Sam McClinton	Jenkins & Britt	10/19/21	10/21/21	8M 20D
411	Jesse B. Shield	S. G. Wilkerson	10/26/21	10/27/21	8D
412	Coner Wilson	C. A. Albritton	11/14/21	11/16/21	20
413	Jerry Best, Jr.	F. G. Williams	11/29/21	11/30/21	4
414	Walter Hemby	Jenkins & Britt	11/21/21	11/22/21	6M 6D
419	Sarah Robinson	C. A. Albritton	12/11/21	12/18/21	19
421	Rosa Dixon	Jenkins & Britt	12/31/21	01/01/22	45
424	Sam Price, Jr.	S. G. Wilkerson	10/01/21	10/02/21	None
425	Alice Williams	F. G. Williams	01/12/22	01/13/22	57
439	Joe Clegg Smith	Jenkins & Harris	04/10/20	04/11/20	C 45
440	Porter Smith	Jenkins & Harris	03/29/20	03/30/20	None
465	Stillborn	Home Made Box	06/07/20	06/07/20	Stillborn
517	John May	F. G. Williams	04/23/21	04/24/21	50
536	Samuel Hall	Jenkins & Britt	10/08/21	10/10/21	42
537	Mary O. Hegan	Jenkins & Britt	10/13/21	10/14/21	5
539	Jane Wilkerson	C. A. Albritton	10/04/21	None	40
541	Alonza Foreman	S. G. Wilkerson	11/08/21	11/09/21	29
552	Mary Benton	S. G. Wilkerson	01/05/22	01/06/22	C 18
560	Clara Donelson	S. G. Wilkerson	02/23/22	02/24/22	20
572	Laurence Moore	Jenkins & Britt	03/24/22	03/25/22	38
576	John Smith	S. G. Wilkerson	04/28/22	04/28/22	Stillborn
592	Infant	S. G. Wilkerson	05/08/22	05/09/22	None
597	Ida Davis	C. A. Albritton	05/10/22	05/12/22	47
601	Ed Braxton	S. G. Wilkerson	05/27/22	05/28/22	78
613	Katie Spell	Wilkerson & Co	01/16/22	01/17/22	68

Vol. 9, 1922

344	Fannie Williams	S. G. Wilkerson	01/04/22	01/05/22	77
347	No Name	F. G. Williams	01/29/22	01/30/22	Premature
352	Willie Frank Stafford	F. G. Williams	02/08/22	02/09/22	None
356	Tom Williams	Jenkins & Britt	03/09/22	03/10/22	60
358	Mary Lizer McConnell	Jenkins & Britt	02/28/22	03/01/22	38
361	Eliza Cooper	C. A. Albritton	05/27/22	05/29/22	59
364	Virginia Moore	S. G. Wilkerson	05/26/22	05/26/22	2M 14D
374	Bradshaw Burton	S. G. Wilkerson	06/08/22	06/09/22	24
377	Nursey Judge	S. G. Wilkerson	02/13/22	02/14/22	34
380	Mary Lee Johnson	Home Made Box	07/07/22	07/08/22	None
381	Jesse Johnson, Jr.	Home Made Box	07/07/22	07/08/22	None
382	Mary E. Tearle	Frank Williams	07/19/22	07/20/22	None
386	Rosetti Shepard	Jenkins & Britt	08/17/22	08/08/22	C 36
387	Lottie B. Wilks	C. A. Albritton	08/20/22	08/22/22	19
389	Jack Brown, Jr.	S. G. Wilkerson	09/03/22	09/03/22	4
391	Alice Lee Pender	S. G. Wilkerson	09/11/22	09/12/22	None
396	Infant	S. G. Wilkerson	09/05/22	09/06/22	None
403	Julia Lewis	C. A. Albritton	09/29/22	10/01/22	45
404	John Price	S. G. Wilkerson	10/05/22	10/06/22	28
405	Emma Burnell	S. G. Wilkerson	09/21/22	09/22/22	3M 14D
406	Estella Maulshy	C. A. Albritton	10/10/22	10/12/22	20
408	Lydia Tucker	S. G. Wilkerson	09/30/22	10/01/22	60
410	William J. Gardner	W. E. Flanagan	11/05/22	11/06/22	None
413	Harry F. Daniel	W. E. Flanagan	11/28/22	11/29/22	3M 6D
415	Stillborn	S. G. Wilkerson	11/17/22	11/17/22	Stillborn
416	Infant	S. G. Wilkerson	11/17/22	11/18/22	None
418	Haywood Tucker	W. E. Flanagan	12/31/22	01/01/23	49
420	Mary Hunter	W. E. Flanagan	01/01/23	01/02/23	47
423	Hazel Beaman	S. G. Wilkerson	12/12/22	12/12/22	C 47
433	Terilia Roberson	S. G. Wilkerson	06/17/22	06/18/22	C 40
450	Christine Patrick	Jenkins & Britt	03/02/22	03/03/22	91
451	James Edwards	C. A. Albritton	08/30/22	09/03/22	28
456	Caesar Vines	S. G. Wilkerson	09/23/22	09/24/22	C 61
459	Ray Atkinson	S. G. Wilkerson	01/01/22	01/02/22	Stillborn

464	Easter Brown	S. G. Wilkerson	10/10/22	10/11/22	48
480	John Reddick	S. G. Wilkerson	09/15/22	09/15/22	None
481	James Moore, Jr.	F. G. Williams	12/26/21	12/26/21	None
482	Nixon Reeves	W. E. Flanagan	12/14/22	12/16/22	76
484	Clara Williams	S. G. Wilkerson	12/06/22	12/07/22	22

Vol. 10, 1923   None

Vol. 11, 1924

371	Pearl Royster	Flanagan & Cherry	02/20/24	02/21/24	49
373	James Henry Graham	S. G. Wilkerson	05/01/24	05/02/24	8
376	Annie Carr	S. G. Wilkerson	04/27/24	04/28/24	C 40
387	Annie May Bell	S. G. Wilkerson	05/11/24	05/12/24	1M 21D
388	Hill McGown	Flanagan & Cherry	05/12/24	05/13/24	C 34
393	Walter Smith	Flanagan & Cherry	03/16/24	03/17/24	41
401	Ada George	Flanagan & Co	07/15/24	07/18/24	C 47
402	Joseph Harris	Flanagan & Co	07/19/24	07/20/14	36
405	Alfred Slaughter	Flanagan & Cherry	08/05/24	08/07/24	23
411	Mack Williams	Flanagan & Cherry	08/29/24	08/31/24	C 75
413	Festus Harris	S. G. Wilkerson	10/17/24	10/18/24	C 26
414	Willie Ray Shivers	S. G. Wilkerson	10/27/24	10/28/24	5
415	Leo Bynum	S. G. Wilkerson	10/16/24	10/17/24	69
419	Winnie Waen	J. I. Baker & Co	10/04/24	10/05/24	19
421	Laura Staton	Jenkins Co	10/04/24	10/05/24	68
427	Mary Blount	S. G. Wilkerson	11/21/24	11/23/24	C 28
428	Haywood Barnhill	Flanagan & Cherry	11/16/24	11/17/24	C 61
433	Sarah Spruill	Flanagan & Cherry	10/19/24	10/20/24	None
434	Lucindy Parker	S. G. Wilkerson	10/04/24	10/05/24	C 62
435	Linda Cannon	Flanagan & Cherry	10/22/24	10/26/24	C 53
336	Lena Clarke	S. G. Wilkerson	11/26/24	11/27/24	C 18
437	Roxie Reeves	S. G. Wilkerson	10/18/24	11/23/24	C 54
438	Hazeltine Pratt	J. I. Baker	12/08/24	12/09/24	2M 10D
440	Clara Mills	S. G. Wilkerson	12/12/24	12/13/24	26
446	Irvin Joyner	S. G. Wilkerson	11/18/24	11/19/24	72
447	Lee Anna Freeman	S. G. Wilkrson	11/24/24	11/25/24	18
448	Susan Allen	J. I. Baker & Co	12/13/24	12/17/24	73

449	Isaac Carr	Flanagan & Cherry	12/22/24	12/26/24	56
453	Charles H. Griffin	W. E. Flanagan	01/23/23	01/24/23	1 1M
455	Danwood Richardson	W. E. Flanagan	02/08/23	02/11/23	47
456	Dempsy Ruffin	S. G. Wilkerson	12/28/23	11/29/23	59
459	Denwood Richardson	W. E. Flanagan	02/08/23	02/11/23	47
460	Glardeen McDaniels	S. G. Wilkerson	02/12/23	02/13/23	77
467	Mary Jackson	W. E. Flanagan	03/17/23	03/19/23	29
468	Moses Belcher	W. E. Flanagan	03/10/23	03/11/23	50
472	Carror Coward	W. E. Flanagan	04/02/23	04/03/23	18
474	Mattie Robinson	S. G. Wilkerson	03/14/23	03/15/23	None
475	James Thomas Williams	S. G. Wilkerson	03/20/23	03/21/23	None
476	Willie Hooper	S. G. Wilkerson	04/02/23	04/03/23	21
480	Moses Dixon	W. E. Flanagan	04/10/23	04/11/23	45
481	Joyner R. Graham	W. E. Flanagan	04/14/23	04/15/23	1
492	Eddu Dudley	S. G. Wilkerson	06/21/23	06/22/23	2M 27D
494	Manda Daniel	W. E. Flanagan	05/28/23	05/29/23	69
496	No Name	S. G. Wilkerson	06/22/23	06/23/23	None
499	Maynard Spill	W. E. Flanagan	06/28/23	06/30/23	16
504	Carrie Alexander	W. E. Flanagan	07/16/23	07/17/23	29
509	James Braxton	W. E. Flanagan	07/23/23	07/24/23	39
514	Theodore Pender	S. G. Wilkerson	11/13/23	11/14/23	8
526	Bertie Langley	S. G. Wilkerson	10/23/23	10/24/23	23
533	Albert Williams	W. E. Flanagan	10/07/23	10/08/23	65
537	Charity Coward	Flanagan & Cherry	11/01/23	11/02/23	C 5
544	Julian Little	Flanagan & Cherry	12/09/23	12/12/23	C 5
548	Lamb B. Whitehurst	Flanagan & Cherry	12/13/24	12/16/24	28
550	Willie McArthur Joyner	S. G. Wilkerson	02/21/24	02/22/24	9M
551	William J. Little	S. G. Wilkerson	02/07/24	02/08/24	None
552	Ned Kittrell	Flanagan & Cherry	02/01/24	02/03/24	C 39
555	Everhurst Foreman	Flanagan & Cherry	01/04/24	01/06/24	22
556	Ida Reaves	S. G. Wilkerson	02/11/24	02/03/24	None
576	David Webester Foreman	S. G. Wilkerson	01/25/23	01/26/23	50
588	Minerva Lovett	W. E. Flanagan & Co	04/03/23	04/04/23	38
592	Wilson Right Clark	W. E. Flanagan & Co	05/17/23	05/18/23	39

593	Stanley Hopkins	W. E. Flanagan & Co	05/15/23	05/16/23	65
596	Mary Reaves	S. G. Wilkerson	04/14/23	04/15/23	34
622	Clarence Earl Bass	S. G. Wilkerson	06/15/23	06/16/23	6
634	Mary Smith	S. G. Wilkerson	07/04/23	07/05/23	63
640	Stillborn	S. G. Wilkerson	08/04/23	08/04/23	Stillborn
654	Mary McMillan	S. G. Wilkerson	08/02/23	08/03/23	24
660	Stillborn	S. G. Wilkerson	03/11/23	03/11/23	Stillborn
682	Herbert Brown, Jr.	S. G. Wilkerson	11/24/23	11/24/23	None
726	Minnie Hardy	S. G. Wilkerson	03/26/24	03/27/24	45
748	James E. Spear	S. G. Wilkerson	06/03/24	06/04/24	1
778	William Waldrop	S. G. Wilkerson	12/04/24	12/05/24	59

Vol. 12, 1925

435	Bettie Wilson	J. I. Baker	01/08/25	01/10/25	57
442	Major Best, Jr.	S. G. Wilkerson	01/19/25	01/20/25	1M 18D
444	Stillborn	S. G. Wilkerson	06/16/25	06/17/25	Stillborn
445	Jane Wright	Flanagan & Cherry	01/30/25	02/01/25	45
454	Eleanor Wing Howell	J. I. Baker & Co	02/05/25	02/06/25	C33
457	Reed Gorham	Flanagan & Cherry	02/20/25	02/22/25	C 47
467	Lillie Teel	Wilkerson & Williams	04/01/25	04/02/25	C 27
469	Joseph Earl Ruffin	Flanagan & Cherry	03/25/25	03/26/25	None
470	Stillborn	Home Made Box	12/06/24	12/07/24	Stillborn
471	James Williams	Home Made Box	12/11/23	12/11/23	None
475	Bertha Wills	J. I. Baker	05/27/25	05/28/25	10M 8D
477	Leonard Weston	Wilkerson & Williams	05/26/25	05/28/25	21
482	Lany Pope	J. I. Baker	06/01/25	06/03/25	55
485	Lizzy Smith	J. I. Baker	06/18/25	06/19/25	6
486	Euginia Daniels	L. C. Cherry	06/17/25	06/18/25	C35
492	Nathaniel Harris	K. T. Futrell	06/28/25	06/29/25	C35
493	Flora Albritton	Wilkerson & Williams	07/02/25	07/03/25	70
499	Mayer Forbes	W. E. Flanagan	07/19/25	07/20/25	C51
503	General Bryant	W. E. Flanagan	06/29/25	06/30/25	C51
504	Samuel Obby	W. E. Flanagan	07/06/25	07/08/25	C43
510	Carry Elizabeth Stokes	J. I. Baker	08/03/25	08/04/25	2M 3D

512	Stillborn	Wilkerson & Williams	08/06/25	08/07/25	Stillborn
518	Lena Dixon	Wilkerson & Williams	08/24/25	08/25/25	33
521	Moses Grayham, Jr.	Wilkerson & Williams	08/03/25	08/04/25	None
522	Fred Warren	L. C. Cherry	08/27/25	08/28/25	C37
525	Eller Daniel	J. I. Baker	08/31/25	09/02/25	C23
530	Nina Dupree	W. E. Flanagan	09/28/25	09/29/25	18
533	Mary Malison Watson	W. E. Flanagan	06/23/25	06/24/25	1M 3D
534	Alexander Gully	W. E. Flanagan	07/13/25	07/14/25	80
546	Nettie Dayton	W. E. Flanagan	10/12/23	10/14/23	50
447	Irene Jones	Wilkerson & Williams	10/09/25	10/11/25	C21
548	Alton Wilcox	W. E. Flanagan	09/20/25	09/27/25	36
549	Ellen Wright	W. E. Flanagan	12/03/25	12/06/25	C16
560	Infant	Home Made Box	06/10/24	06/11/24	Stillborn
576	No Name	Wilkerson & Williams	02/15/25	02/16/25	None
590	Ameondell Forbes	S. G. Wilkerson	05/30/25	05/31/25	6M 5D
592	Spelman Gray	J. I. Baker	06/27/25	06/28/25	63
594	Premature Baby	Wilkerson & Williams	06/13/25	06/13/25	Premature
605	Hurley Gay	W. E. Flanagan	06/06/25	06/06/25	2M

Vol. 13, 1926

449	Stillborn	Wilkerson & Williams	08/02/26	08/03/26	Stillborn
467	Edith May Harris	W. E. Flanagan	03/06/26	03/07/26	9M
468	Rosie Foreman	W. E. Flanagan	04/06/26	04/07/26	C 20
475	Lillian Spell	W. E. Flanagan	04/23/26	04/24/26	C 16
482	Ida Mae Giles	Home Made Box	05/18/26	05/19/26	1M
486	Hattie Jergan	W. E. Flanagan	06/05/26	06/07/26	17
489	George Dixon	Wilkerson & Williams	06/08/26	06/09/26	C 25
497	Jenina May	W. E. Flanagan	07/26/26	07/26/26	C 60
498	Richard Forbes	W. E. Flanagan	07/25/26	07/26/26	C 69
500	No Name	W. E. Flanagan	05/29/26	05/30/26	10M 9D
501	No Name	Home Made Box	08/07/26	08/07/26	9M

503	Edward Fleming	Wilkerson & Williams	07/01/26	07/02/26	2
508	Abraham Jenkins	W. E. Flanagan	05/28/26	05/30/26	Unknown
510	Stillborn	Wilkerson & Williams	08/05/26	08/05/26	Stillborn
512	Evelyn Green	W. E. Flanagan	07/30/26	08/01/26	C80
513	Dora Wiggens	W. E. Flanagan	08/13/26	08/14/26	C21
516	Willie Harris	Wilkerson & Williams	09/25/26	09/26/26	C62
523	Ernest Gorham	W. E. Flanagan	09/30/26	10/03/26	C35
527	Rose Killbrew	W. E. Flanagan	08/02/26	08/03/26	C80
529	Stillborn	Wilkerson & Williams	09/24/26	09/24/26	Stillborn
531	Wesley Foreman	John R. Joyner	07/18/26	07/18/26	C50
532	Ellen Hardy	W. E. Flanagan	11/03/26	11/05/26	C40
533	Helen Joyner	W. E. Flanagan	10/27/26	10/28/26	6M 24D
534	Nathan Lewis	W. E. Flanagan	10/25/26	10/26/26	C60
535	John Foreman	Ernest A. Byron	06/12/26	06/13/26	45
552	Stillborn	Wilkerson & Williams	04/12/26	04/13/26	Stillborn
580	Josephine Barnhill	W. E. Flanagan	06/05/26	06/06/26	C27
615	Ruth Stokes	John Lipscomb	07/05/26	07/05/26	No Name
583	Harriett John Coward	W. E. Flanagan	07/25/26	07/25/26	Stillborn

Vol. 14, 1927

374	No Name	E. S. Williams	04/27/27	04/27/27	None
377	Carolina Shivers	W. E. Flanagan	02/12/27	02/13/27	C80
379	Harry Farmer	W. E. Flanagan	01/30/27	01/31/27	C57
381	Rendy Carr	W. E. Flanagan	02/05/27	02/07/27	C80
382	Hoyt Cannon	W. E. Flanagan	04/28/27	04/30/27	C56
383	Wilma Wright	W. E. Flanagan	05/03/27	05/05/27	C15
385	Lenora Dupree	W. E. Flanagan	04/24/27	04/24/27	C17
401	Stillborn	W. E. Flanagan	05/23/27	05/24/27	Stillborn

Vol. 15, 1928

397	Frank McNeill	Williams Fun. Home	05/27/28	05/28/28	27
427	Stillborn	Home Made Box	02/20/27	02/20/27	Stillborn
428	Dock Applewhite	W. E. Flanagan	01/20/27	01/21/27	None
429	Ada V. May	J. I. Baker	03/15/27	03/16/27	None
433	Lovely Cherry	J. I. Baker	03/13/27	03/15/27	53
436	Willie D. Davis	W. E. Flanagan	02/25/27	02/27/27	C 22
437	Stillborn	Pitt Co.	02/12/27	02/12/27	Stillborn
444	Tommie Equiella Bartlette	J. I. Baker	04/23/27	04/24/27	1M 10 D
445	Carrie Jones	J. I. Baker	04/17/17	04/18/27	46
446	Mary T. Suggs	J. I. Baker	11/22/27	11/23/27	4M 2D
447	Rhone Carr	W. E. Flanagan	03/29/27	04/03/27	C47
449	Ertma Mayo	W. E. Flanagan	05/09/27	05/10/27	C 80
452	Heron Bruce Barnhill	J. I. Baker	05/05/27	05/06/27	3M 13D
453	David Thomas Parks	J. I. Baker	05/25/27	05/27/27	16
460	Pennie Davis	E. S. Williams	06/01/27	06/02/27	C 20
467	Pauline Fleming	W. E. Flanagan	06/09/27	06/12/27	54
468	Robert Mayo	W. E. Flanagan	07/03/27	07/04/27	22
469	John H. House	W. E. Flanagan	06/30/27	07/04/27	22
478	Floyd Edwards	J. I. Baker	08/09/27	08/09/27	14D
480	Hattie Barnhill	W. E. Flanagan	05/06/27	05/08/27	C 48
481	Daisy May Lee	E. S. Williams	06/11/27	06/12/27	1-19D
486	John Jordan	W. F. Flanagan	08/30/27	09/04/27	62
497	Stillborn	Home Made Box	10/20/27	10/21/27	Stillborn
503	Stillborn	Sam Jones, Acting	08/24/27	08/24/27	Stillborn
543	Lucy Carr Murphy	Willie Jenkins, Acting	03/22/28	03/25/28	41
546	James Killebrew	Williams Fun. Parlor	04/05/28	04/06/28	39
574	Sarah Whitley	Johnson Fun. Parlor	06/23/28	06/24/28	72
585	Stillborn	J. L. King, Acting	08/02/28	08/02/28	Stillborn
586	Stillborn	J. I. Baker	08/20/28	08/20/28	Stillborn
587	Stillborn	J. L. King, Acting	08/21/28	08/21/28	Stillborn
593	Stillborn	E. S. Williams	09/07/28	09/07/28	Stillborn

602	Freeman Hewly, Jr.	J. I. Baker	10/20/28	10/26/28	44
609	Stillborn	Willie Jenkins, Acting	12/18/28	12/19/28	Stillborn
611	Robert Watson	E. S. Williams	10/21/28	10/21/28	22
618	Stillborn	J. L. King, Acting	10/16/28	10/16/28	Stillborn
622	Stillborn	W. E. Flanagan	07/11/28	07/12/28	Stillborn

Vol. 16, 1929

402	Fred Foreman, Jr.	E. S. Williams	12/09/28	12/13/28	22
430	Thomas Williams	Flanagan & Parker	02/18/29	02/19/29	53
451	Haywood Nettles	Williams Fun. Parlor	06/05/29	06/06/29	81
461	Samuel Bryant	J. I. Baker	06/17/29	06/18/29	30
487	Phoebe Foreman	J. I. Baker	10/17/29	10/20/29	68
509	Della McGowan	J. I. Baker	01/16/29	01/17/29	70
511	Ida Bell Dupree	J. I. Baker	02/08/29	02/09/29	3
512	Ethel Crandall	J. I. Baker	02/09/29	02/10/29	20
531	Stillborn	Flanagan & Parker	10/29/29	10/29/29	Stillborn
532	Stillborn	J. I. Baker	10/30/29	10/31/29	Stillborn
534	Stillborn	Flanagan & Parker	03/14/29	03/15/29	Stillborn

Vol. 17, 1930

434	Charlie R. Tyson	J. I. Baker	01/20/30	01/21/30	7M 17 D
440	Unnamed	Ellis Langley, Acting	02/11/30	02/12/30	7M
445	Novella Lee Jones	Ellis Langley, Acting	02/28/30	02/28/30	2M
452	Fannie Albert Moore	Ellis Langley, Acting	03/02/30	03/03/30	3M 7D
456	Stillborn	Ellis Langley, Acting	02/25/30	02/25/30	Stillborn
470	Carrie Eliz Stewart	Ellis Langley, Acting	03/16/30	03/17/30	1D-9 Hrs
472	Infant	Jim Davis, Acting	03/28/30	03/29/30	9M
478	Stillborn	Ellis Langley, Acting	04/04/30	04/05/30	Stillborn
480	Stillborn	Ellis Langley, Acting	03/22/30	03/22/30	Stillborn

481	Infant	Ellis Langley, Acting	04/09/30	04/10/30	1-9M
484	Albert Lambert, Jr.	J. I. Baker	03/31/30	04/01/30	14
487	James A. May	Williams Fun. Parlor	04/12/30	04/14/30	7M
491	Stillborn	Ellis Langley, Acting	05/21/30	05/21/30	Stillborn
495	Willie Lee Bryant	Ellis Langley, Acting	05/30/30	05/31/30	7M-2D
504	Fannie Lee Green	Ellis Langley, Acting	06/01/30	06/14/30	22 D
505	Dora E. Atkinson	Flanagan & Parker	06/14/30	06/15/30	4-9M 11D
511	Sudie O'Neal	Williams Fun. Parlor	06/16/30	06/18/30	25
514	Stillborn	Ellis Langley, Acting	07/14/30	07/15/30	Stillborn
518	Hoyt Hardee	Co. Welfare Office	07/14/30	07/14/30	C 80
519	William Dock Daniels	Ellis Langley, Acting	07/24/30	07/24/30	Premature
524	Larry Jas Knight	Ellis Langley, Acting	07/30/30	07/30/30	3-7M 2D
525	Eliz Gay	Ellis Langley, Acting	08/14/30	08/15/30	3M-3D
536	Ernestine Ruby	Ellis Langley, Acting	08/21/30	08/21/30	1M 12D
536	Infant	Ellis Langley, Acting	08/21/30	08/21/30	Infant
552	Elnora Barnes	Ellis Langley, Acting	09/01/30	09/02/30	1-6M-25D
554	Roy Lee Rouse	Ellis Langley, Acting	10/22/30	10/23/30	5M 24D
556	Jessie Jas Morris	Ellis Langley, Acting	11/01/30	11/03/30	1-4M
571	Maxine Barnes	J. I. Baker	10/07/30	10/08/30	18
573	Stillborn	Ellis Langley, Acting	11/22/30	11/23/30	Stillborn
584	Ben Portis	J. I. Baker	11/27/30	11/28/30	86
592	Stillborn	Ellis Langley, Acting	07/12/30	07/12/30	Stillborn
599	Stillborn	Ellis Langley, Acting	01/08/31	01/08/31	Stillborn
614	Wiliam Moore, Jr.	Williams Fun. Parlor	05/14/30	05/15/30	14M

Vol. 18, 1931

369	Clarence Earl Jones	Williams Fun. Parlor	05/27/30	05/28/30	3
373	Sarah Moore	J. I. Baker	05/09/29	05/10/29	45
375	Willar Dean Sumrell	Ellis Langley, Acting	01/29/31	01/30/31	7M 29D
397	John Wilkins Coy	Pitt Co. Welfare	02/26/31	02/27/31	7M 5D
399	Toney Evans	Flanagan & Parker	09/03/29	09/08/29	62
402	Infant	Ellis Langley, Acting	03/10/31	03/11/31	Infant
415	Unkn.	Unkn.	03/10/31	None	22D
427	Stillborn	Ellis Langley, Acting	04/12/31	04/13/31	Stillborn
429	Therman Earl Langley	Ellis Langley, Acting	04/14/31	04/16/31	8D
432	Louise Lumford	Ellis Langley, Acting	04/26/31	04/27/31	29D
463	Stillborn	Baker Fun. Home	07/10/31	07/10/31	Stillborn
464	James A. Smith	Baker Fun. Home	07/11/31	07/12/31	18D
468	Premature	Baker Fun. Home	06/11/31	06/12/31	Premature
469	Frank Venters	Baker Fun. Home	11/11/30	11/12/30	11M-19D
470	Owen Goin Kinsey	J. I. Baker	12/13/31	12/16/31	3M-2D
471	Steward Knox	J. I. Baker	12/17/30	12/19/30	77
473	Jordan Moore	J. I. Baker	04/03/30	04/06/30	Unk.
475	Helen Joyce Harper	J. I. Baker	06/30/30	07/01/30	10D
496	Stillborn	Ellis Langley, Acting	09/17/31	09/18/31	Stillborn
497	Stillborn	Unkn	10/02/31	10/03/31	Stillborn
507	Stillborn	Ellis Langley, Acting	11/24/31	11/24/31	Stillborn
512	Sam'l Hugh Worthington	Ellis Langley, Acting	10/10/31	10/11/31	2D
513	Paul Grives	Ellis Langley, Acting	10/21/31	10/22/31	1D-13 Hours
514	Silas Grives	Ellis Langley, Acting	10/21/31	10/22/31	1D-15 Hours
518	Louisteen Jackson	Ellis Langley, Acting	12/12/31	12/13/31	3D

551	Stillborn	Ellis Langley, Acting	01/17/32	01/18/32	Stillborn
557	Stillborn	Ellis Langley, Acting	01/30/32	01/30/32	Stillborn
558	Stillborn	Ellis Langley, Acting	01/30/32	01/30/32	Stillborn

Vol. 19, 1932

405	Horace Moore Brady	Ellis Langley, Acting	02/26/32	02/26/32	2M 3D
407	Effie Ree House	Flanagan & Parker	02/26/32	02/28/32	20
417	Stillborn	Ellis Langley, Acting	03/22/32	02/23/32	Stillborn
420	Stillborn	Herman Tyson, Acting	04/18/32	04/19/32	Stillborn
421	Franza Moore	Ellis Langley, Acting	04/10/32	04/11/32	2 1/2 D
435	Lillian McDonald	Neal Bradley, Acting	04/27/32	04/28/32	4D
436	James McDonald	Neal Bradley, Acting	04/29/32	04/30/32	6D
440	Stillborn	Ellis Langley, Acting	05/28/32	05/28/32	Stillborn
454	Bobby Lewis Grives	Baker Fun. Parlor	05/20/32	05/21/32	8M 15D
467	Stillborn	Ellis Langley, Acting	07/13/32	07/13/32	Stillborn
481	Dorothy Mae Tyson	Ellis Langley, Acting	08/07/32	08/08/32	1M-14D
488	Stillborn	Ellis Langley, Acting	08/23/32	08/23/32	Stillborn
492	Unnamed	Claude Cox, Acting	09/10/32	09/10/32	Less Than 10 Hours
494	Stillborn	Andrew Langley, Acting	08/28/32	08/29/32	Stillborn
496	Infant	Andrew Langley, Acting	09/12/32	09/13/32	5 Minutes
499	Stillborn	Andrew Langley, Acting	09/21/32	09/22/32	Stillborn
502	Stillborn	Andrew Langley, Acting	10/04/32	10/04/32	Stillborn
508	Stillborn	Andrew Langley, Acting	10/23/32	10/24/32	Stillborn

523	Henerritta Bernard	Williams Fun. Parlor	09/09/32	09/10/32	48
524	Stillborn	Andrew Langley, Acting	07/08/32	07/09/32	Stillborn
525	Ora Eliz Dixon	Co. Welfare Dept	09/25/32	09/26/32	27
526	Willie Jas Dixon	Co. Welfare Dept	10/16/32	10/17/32	Infant
530	Mary Lee Langley	Andrew Langley, Acting	12/07/32	12/08/32	Stillborn
540	Lou Raven	K. T. Futrell	12/04/32	12/05/32	Stillborn
550	Stillborn	Andrew Langley, Acting	12/04/32	12/05/32	Stillborn

Vol. 20, 1933

281	Herbert Whichard, Jr.	Williams Fun. Parlor	01/12/33	01/12/33	11M
282	Jane Ross	Williams Fun. Parlor	01/15/33	01/16/33	41
283	Meliza Richards	Williams Fun. Parlor	01/17/33	01/18/33	54
297	Unkn.	Andrew Langley, Acting	01/27/33	01/28/33	7D
306	Lizzo Mae Holland	Williams Fun. Parlor	04/16/33	04/17/33	7M-6D
312	Infant	Andrew Langley, Acting	06/06/33	06/07/33	17D
330	Infant	Andrew Langley, Acting	07/09/33	07/10/33	22 Hours
337	Susan Ann Sinette	Flanagan & Parker	09/14/33	09/17/33	54
344	Rosa Lee Belcher	Williams Fun. Parlor	09/11/33	09/12/33	24
355	Mary Jenkins	Andrew Langley, Acting	10/24/33	10/25/33	19 Hours
356	Martha Jenkins	Andrew Langley, Acting	10/24/33	10/25/33	1 Hour
360	Doris Holland	Williams Fun. Parlor	11/12/33	11/13/33	3M 6D
368	No Name	Andrew Langley, Acting	11/26/33	11/27/33	1 Hour
371	Mary Gayther	S. G. Wilkerson & Sons	10/17/33	10/18/33	38
372	Robert Lee Hemby, Infant	Andrew Langley, Acting	11/29/33	11/30/33	15D

| 374 | Lucy McCoy | Andrew Langley, Acting | 12/01/33 | 12/01/33 | 12D |

Vol. 21, 1934

470	Nat Worrell	R. Thigpen, Acting	01/16/34	01/17/34	None
474	Green Parker	Wms Fun. Home	01/20/34	01/21/34	None
494	Douglas Dupree	J. I. Baker	01/09/34	01/10/34	25
528	Edward Love	Wms Fun. Home	06/15/34	06/16/34	1M 8D
550	Nicole Hines	Wms Fun. Home	07/28/34	07/29/34	21
559	Neal Nobles, Jr.	Flanagan & Parker	08/02/34	08/05/34	29
580	Carlton J. Cherry	J. I. Baker	11/02/34	11/03/34	5M
601	Lutrell Shivers	Andrew Langley, Acting	12/12/34	12/12/34	1 1/2 D
602	Betty Joe McDaniel	Andrew Langley, Acting	07/27/34	07/27/34	15D
605	Pauline Tucker	Flanagan & Parker	11/23/34	11/28/34	82
606	Annie Brown	Flanagan & Parker	11/24/34	11/27/34	46
610	Edna Carl Sheppard	Andrew Langley, Acting	12/11/34	12/11/34	14D
615	Stillborn	Andrew Langley, Acting	03/22/34	03/23/34	Stillborn
617	Artie J. Briley	Andrew Langley, Acting	04/10/34	04/10/34	Stillborn
618	Stillborn	Andrew Langley, Acting	05/02/34	05/02/34	Stillborn
619	Stillborn	Andrew Langley, Acting	05/21/34	05/21/34	Stillborn
622	Stillborn	Andrew Langley, Acting	05/21/34	05/21/34	Stillborn
623	Stillborn	Andrew Langley, Acting	06/06/34	06/06/34	Stillborn
625	Stillborn	Charlie Parker (Father)	09/17/34	09/17/34	Stillborn
626	Stillborn	Andrew Langley, Acting	11/12/34	11/12/34	Stillborn
627	Stillborn	Andrew Langley, Acting	10/16/34	10/16/34	Stillborn
628	Stillborn	Andrew Langley, Acting	10/14/34	10/15/34	Stillborn
629	Stillborn	Andrew Langley, Acting	10/26/34	10/26/34	Stillborn

| 632 | Stillborn | Andrew Langley, Acting | 12/06/34 | 12/06/34 | Stillborn |
| 633 | Stillborn | Andrew Langley, Acting | 11/19/34 | 11/19/34 | Stillborn |

Vol. 22, **1935**

350	Sarde F. Gray	Andrew Langley, Acting	06/28/35	06/29/35	3D
377	Martha L. Peyton	Flanagan & Parker	05/31/35	06/01/35	5
417	Ann Lee Carman	Flanagan & Parker	10/01/35	10/03/35	16
421	Laurence H. Roberts	Andrew Langley, Acting	08/01/35	08/01/35	3 Hours

Vol. 23–24, **1936-1937**

327	Dora Lee Dawson	S. G. Wilkerson	01/14/36	01/15/36	71
371	Anna Wilson	Flanagan & Parker	03/04/36	03/06/36	56
383	William Forbes	Flanagan & Parker	04/24/36	05/01/36	52
402	Jane Graham	Flanagan & Parker	06/26/36	06/28/36	73
410	Alberta Norman	Flanagan & Parker	06/28/39	06/29/39	1
429	Henry Juilcious	Andrew Langley, Acting	11/19/36	11/20/36	6 Hours
363	Evelyn P. C. Langley	Flanagan & Parker	09/28/37	09/29/37	7M
387	David F. Turner	Flanagan & Parker	11/20/37	11/23/37	75

Vol. 24, **1938**

316	Henry Evans	Flanagan & Parker	01/21/38	01/23/38	58
324	Rheubea McCullum	Flanagan & Parker	01/17/38	01/21/38	58
369	Lillie P. Hines	Flanagan & Parker	05/07/38	05/09/38	13M-21D
380	Frances Whitaker	Flanagan & Parker	05/27/38	05/29/38	38
390	Flaura Cherry	Flanagan & Parker	04/17/38	04/19/38	38
493	Infant, Unnamed	Andrew Langley, Acting	07/03/38	07/03/38	Infant
394	Infant, Unnamed	Andrew Langley, Acting	06/21/38	06/26/38	Infant
499	Julia Smith	Flanagan & Parker	06/19/38	06/23/38	80
403	John Speight	R. W. Lock	07/14/38	07/15/38	75
418	James Hemby	R. W. Lock	07/23/38	07/23/38	11M-5D

419	Henry Moore, Jr.	Andrew Langley, Acting	08/11/38	08/12/38	Premature
429	Mozelle Waters	Flanagan & Parker	08/12/38	08/14/38	44
447	Willie James Clemmons	Andrew Langley, Acting	10/04/38	10/04/38	1M-3D
450	Dock Perkins	Flanagan & Parker	10/22/38	10/24/38	49
454	Jordan Whitehurst	R. W. Lock	11/27/38	11/29/38	61
466	Odessa Perkins	Flanagan & Parker	10/12/38	10/13/38	1
470	Mary Eliza Tucker	Flanagan & Parker	10/17/38	10/19/38	66
490	Lula Tucker	Flanagan & Parker	11/07/38	11/09/38	45
491	Slabell Carr	Flanagan & Parker	08/26/38	08/28/38	31
492	Russell T. Hemby	Flanagan & Parker	10/03/38	10/04/38	2
580	Rufus Fleming	Andrew Langley, Acting	05/20/38	05/21/38	2
582	No Name	Andrew Langley, Acting	10/03/38	10/03/38	None
583	Wm. Underwood	Andrew Langley, Acting	12/21/38	12/22/38	No Name
584	John Shivers	Andrew Langley, Acting	08/01/38	08/01/38	Stillborn
566	Stillborn	J. I. Baker	01/28/38	01/28/38	Stillborn
567	Stillborn	Andrew Langley, Acting	03/21/38	03/21/38	Stillborn
569	Stillborn	Andrew Langley, Acting	01/12/38	01/13/38	Stillborn
570	Stillborn	Andrew Langley, Acting	04/03/38	04/04/38	Stillborn
575	Infant	Andrew Langley, Acting	07/17/38	07/17/38	Stillborn
576	Stillborn	Andrew Langley, Acting	04/03/38	04/03/78	Stillborn
580	Stillborn	Andrew Langley, Acting	05/20/38	05/21/38	Stillborn
582	Stillborn	Andrew Langley, Acting	10/03/38	10/03/38	Stillborn
583	Stillborn	Andrew Langley, Acting	12/21/38	12/22/38	Stillborn
584	Stillborn	Andrew Langley, Acting	08/01/38	08/01/38	Stillborn

Vol. 25, 1939

270	Imogene Green	S. G. Wilkerson	10/25/39	10/26/39	6M 10D
281	Sterling Edwards	Flanagan & Parker	01/08/40	01/11/40	3D
291	Carrie Waldrop	R. W. Lock	01/08/39	01/11/39	64
295	Ernest Nobles	R. W. Lock	02/07/39	02/09/39	38
307	Viola Thorne	Flanagan & Parker	02/21/39	02/22/39	87
309	Charity Forbes	Flanagan & Parker	02/02/39	02/05/39	None
311	Francis Barrett	Flanagan & Parker	03/08/39	03/09/39	27
319	Joe Johnson, Jr.	Andrew Langley, Acting	05/01/39	05/01/39	18 Hours
321	Ed Hardy	Joseph May	08/29/39	08/30/39	45
328	Funier Carr	Flanagan & Parker	05/19/39	05/22/39	47
331	Samuel H. Ward	Flanagan & Parker	05/25/39	05/27/39	7M
334	Elaira Forbes Smith	Flanagan & Parker	04/13/39	04/16/39	None
335	Emma Watson	Flanagan & Parker	06/02/39	06/03/39	16
342	Nancy Shepard	Flanagan & Parker	04/10/30	04/12/39	75
343	Elmore Price	Flanagan & Parker	06/11/39	06/13/39	28
350	James Hardee	Flanagan & Parker	05/24/39	05/26/39	21
357	Martha Jones Evans	Flanagan & Parker	07/04/39	07/06/39	63
363	Sifox Fleming	Flanagan & Parker	08/08/39	08/13/39	73
366	Mary Bryant	Flanagan & Parker	06/28/39	06/29/39	66
372	Bessie Stocks	Flanagan & Parker	08/25/39	08/27/39	37
382	Abraham Cobb, Jr.	Andrew Langley, Acting	08/04/39	08/04/39	41/2M
384	Fred Taft	Flanagan & Parker	09/13/39	09/15/39	40
388	Delzora L. Gibbs	Flanagan & Parker	08/28/39	08/30/39	45
391	Lula Kittrell Bennett	Phillip Bros.	08/23/39	08/27/39	25
395	Ivory Watson, Jr.	Andrew Langley, Acting	09/14/39	09/15/39	1D
398	Edward Bland	Flanagan & Parker	09/21/39	09/23/39	32
399	Thomas Sheppard	Flanagan & Parker	05/24/39	05/28/39	24
411	Johnnie & Auth Pettifore	Andrew Langley, Acting	09/20/39	09/20/39	1 1/2D
413	Delsora Gray	Phillip Bros.	None	10/25/39	1 1M 18D
415	Nancy Fleming	Phillip Bros.	10/19/39	10/21/39	56

425	Laura Bell Parker	Flanagan & Parker	10/25/39	10/27/39	3
431	Lula Bell Bennett	Phillip Bros.	12/07/39	12/09/39	3M 14D
444	Louise Moore	Flanagan & Parker	10/20/39	10/22/39	9

TABLE 3.4 A LIST OF UNDERTAKERS WHO BURIED FOLKS AT COOPER FIELD CEMETERY FROM 1913 - 1939

	1913-1915	1916	1917	1918	1919	1920	1921	1922	1923	1924	1925	1926	1927	1928	1929	1930	1931	1932	1933	1934	1935	1936-1937	1938	1939
ALBRITTON							3	6																
BAKER FUNERAL HOME										3	8		8	2	7	4	5				2		1	
BAKER, J.I.																	3	1						
BRADLEY, NEAL, ACTING																		2						
CHERRY, L.C.											2	1												
COX, CLAUDE, ACTING																1		1						
DAVIS, JIM, ACTING																								
FLANAGAN AND CHERRY										17	12	16	16											
FLANAGAN AND PARKER														1	4	1		1	1	4	2	5	13	40
FLANAGAN, JOHN BUGGY CO.	1													1										
FLANAGAN CO	1							3	2	2	3		2											
FREEMAN, CHARLIE	1																							
HOME MADE BOX						2	3																	
JENKINS AND BRITT							7	6																
JENKINS AND HARRIS				2	2	10																		
JENKINS COMPANY		1								1														

TABLE 3.4 A LIST OF UNDERTAKERS WHO BURIED FOLKS AT COOPER FIELD CEMETERY FROM 1913 - 1939

	1913-1915	1916	1917	1918	1919	1920	1921	1922	1923	1924	1925	1926	1927	1928	1929	1930	1931	1932	1933	1934	1935	1936-1937	1938	1939
JENKINS, WILLIE		3											1	1										
JOHNSON FUNERAL HOME														1										
JONES, GEORGE														1										
JONES, SAM																								
JOYNER, JOHN R.												1	1											
KING, J.L.														3										
LANGLEY, ANDREW, ACTING																			8	4	2	37	11	40
LANGLEY, ELLIS, ACTING																	20	12	8					
LIPSCOMB, JOHN												1												
LOCK, RON W.																							3	2
MAY, W. JOSEPH																								1
ORMOND AND JENKINS																								
ORMOND, J.F.	16	2	7	1																				
PARKER, WM. F.															1									
PHILLIP BROTHERS																								4

TABLE 3.4 A LIST OF UNDERTAKERS WHO BURIED FOLKS AT COOPER FIELD CEMETERY FROM 1913 - 1939

	1913-1915	1916	1917	1918	1919	1920	1921	1922	1923	1924	1925	1926	1927	1928	1929	1930	1931	1932	1933	1934	1935	1936-1937	1938	1939
REED, NIXON						1																		
RIVES AND SMITH							1																	
SHORT, SAM		1	11	9	20	2		2					4	5										
THIGPEN																					1			
TYSON, HERMAN, ACTING																			1					
W & W											1	1												
WELFARE											1	1				1	1							
WILKERSON AND WILLIAMS		2	6								6	3	1		1	4	1	3						
WILKERSON, S. G.	3	3	48	50	22	13	12	23																
WILKERSON, S. G. AND SON									17	20	5	4												
WILLIAMS, E. S.						1	3				3		2	1										
WILLIAMS, FRANK							1																	
WILLIAMS FUNERAL HOME														2						1	1	1		
WILLIAMS FUNERAL PARLOR								1						1	1	4			1	5	3			
WILLIAMS, GEORGE							1	1																

Dates in tables are in mm/dd/yy format.

90

Chapter 4

The Brown Hill Cemetery

Many magical and exhilarating moments transpired on this uncharted yet concerted and harmonious journey to discover the origin and history of the Brown Hill Cemetery. Although many, many hours were spent searching page by page through the *Minutes of City Aldermen* from 1924 to 1939 to find a rationale for purchasing a colored cemetery, none was found. However, the opportunity to review pristine maps and plats, to read archival newspapers, wills and testaments, deeds, and other documents, to copy death certificates data, to make on-site grave inspections, and most importantly, to interview a myriad of individuals, provided a most fascinating excursion and a vital link into the culture and character of a host of Greenville citizens.

Given the culture of the time or at any time, in fact, to use taxpayer's money without a justifiable rationale is unlawful. And even though no rationale was found, there was no official recorded movement toward purchasing a Colored Cemetery until February and April of 1939. The search, however, unearthed several fascinating and startling observations about a lack of transparency and accountability by City Aldermen and the tight control the Board exercised over its Negro citizens during this time of enforced segregation. It is no surprise, then, that both the Aldermen and the press were reticent about the purchase of a colored cemetery. Fortunately, within the Negro community, quiet, diplomatic strategies were at work and uppermost on the minds of parents, teachers, and the community to counteract these injustices by educating and empowering their children to ". . . press toward the mark for the prize of the high calling" [87] and to prepare them to face future challenges.

The most surprising observation was the complete control City Aldermen exercised over the movement and events of its Negro citizens. The attitude to control tightly the events and activities of the city might have been inspired from

---

[87]   Nelson. *Philippians 3:14,* p. 1855.

the residue of what Gov. Thomas J. Jarvis viewed as the *Negroized take over of Greenville* in 1885.[88] Evidence shows that between 1924 and 1939, it was a rarity for even a Negro to attend council meetings much less to submit a petition. Between the dates cited, only two petitions and two appeals were observed: a petition for the support of a library and another for a playground near Cooper Field. An appeal from the Pastor of York Methodist Church for the City to help with noise control for a Sunday night's service and an appeal from Mr. F. B. Barnhill ". . . who asked permission to have the North Carolina State Colored Firemen's Convention to convene in Greenville in August, 1924. Mr. Barnhill asked for and received a $300.00 donation for the Convention."[89]

---

[88] "Negroized take over of Greenville." THE EASTERN REFLECTOR, Greenville, NC, November 18, 1898, p. 2.

[89] J. O. Duval, City Clerk. "Black Fireman's Petition." *Minutes of Aldermen*, Greenville, NC, February 7, 1924, Book III, p. 379.

Map 4.1. Brown Hill Cemetery.

Brown Hill Cemetery is outlined in black in this aerial view. The South Greenville school complex is in the middle of the outlined area.

Frequent requests, however, were made for permission to hold dances and to establish or move pool halls. A request to permit a Negro gentleman to sell peanuts from his front porch was an example of a defining moment of total control. The request was granted. There was never a request or petition from a colored citizen to petition the City Aldermen to purchase, annex, or maintain the Cooper Field Cemetery or to purchase a City-owned independent cemetery for the colored race (Map 4.1.).

Evidence shows, however, that conversations for purchasing a Colored Cemetery were being held in committee. Before the plan was presented to Council, Dr. N. Thomas Ennett informed the City Aldermen that:

> I have secured a tracing showing a location and area of the proposed Colored Cemetery site constituting 18.89 acres, having a frontage of 516.6 [feet] on Highway #43 and extending back to the Tar River . . . . He reported to the Board that a proposed tract of land west of the City on Highway NC 43 had been approved by State standards for a 'Negro Cemetery.'[90]

With knowledge of the city's plan to purchase a Colored Cemetery and at a later meeting, Dr. J. A. Battle appeared before Council and stated ". . . that his race was in full accord with the idea of the Town in purchasing this land (Cooper Field) and developing it into a Cemetery for the Colored people."[91]

During these discussions, Dr. William B. Brown died, and the city moved with dispatch to purchase a Colored Cemetery. Brown, one of Greenville's most prominent, respected, and influential citizens, died suddenly on April 16, 1938.[92] He was buried on April 18.[93] On July 6, 1939, financial distress compelled Ms. Bessie R. Brown, administratrix of the Brown Estate, to petition the court to sell property to make assets for the Brown Estate.[94]

---

[90] J. O. Duval, City Clerk. "Purchase of Brown Hill Cemetery." *Minutes Of City Council*, Greenville, NC, April 6, 1939, Book 6, p. 32.

[91] J. O. Duval, City Clerk. "Dr. Battle's Approval of Brown Hill Cemetery." *Minutes, of City Council*, Greenville, NC, June, 1, 1939, Book 6, p. 51.

[92] "Death Claims Noted Citizen." THE DAILY REFLECTOR, Greenville, NC, April 16, 1938, p. 1.

[93] "Final Rites Held for W. B. Brown." THE DAILY REFLECTOR, Greenville, NC, April 18, 1938, p. 1.

[94] Pitt County Clerk of Courts. "Special Proceedings Document: Bessie Brown." *Superior Court*, 1939, BOOK 6, p. 468.

Aldermen learned the location of the Cooper Field property in 1924 when purchasing the property for the Greenwood Cemetery.[95] A diminishing Negro population, coupled with other social and financial influences, perhaps motivated city officials to move with dispatch to consider purchasing a colored cemetery. Even though the record does not show any discussion in chambers for purchasing a Colored Cemetery until February 1939, the Cemetery Committee had already located a State-approved property.[96] Informal discussions about the City's plans to purchase a Colored Cemetery circulated outside of chambers. With that knowledge, Ms. Jesse Rountree Moye, a highly respected and influential citizen, along with others, protested and blocked the move to put a Negro cemetery at the entrance to the City based on the rationale that they did not want a colored cemetery at the gateway to the City.[97]

The Cooper Field Cemetery was located outside of the City limits and was the burial ground for many of Greenville's less affluent colored citizens. Already established is solid evidence of the lack of funds for less affluent citizens to be buried in the two established cemeteries, Cherry Hill and the Sycamore Hill Baptist Church: "It was reported in 1902, while workmen were digging down the hill for the extension of West Fifth Street (at the railroad tracks), that several skeletons were found. It was reported then that that part of town was used to bury black paupers. In 1903, that part of town called "Buzzard's Roost," ... it was said to be the final resting pace of paupers and criminals who had been executed (most likely the victims were black).[98]

In the search for cemetery property, Mr. J. E. Winslow offered to sell the City some property for a cemetery in West Greenville for $33,000 (acreage not cited). He later offered to reduce the price to $27,000. A proposal was made that if the City refused to purchase the land, the owners would develop a private cemetery.[99] As this property was being offered during the time a search was

---

[95]   J. O. Duval, City Clerk. "Promissory Note to James and Elvira Brown." *Minutes of City Aldermen,* Greenville, NC, November 8, 1924, Book III, p. 451.

[96]   J. O. Duval, City Clerk. "Proposed Colored Cemetery." *Minutes of City Aldermen,* Greenville, NC, April 6, 1939, Book 6, p. 32.

[97]   J. O. Duval, City Clerk. "Blocked Proposed Colored Cemetery." *Minutes of City Aldermen,* Greenville, NC, April 26, 1939, Book 6, p. 38.

[98]   Kitrell, Ibid.

[99]   J. O. Duval, City Clerk, "Developing a Cemetery in West Greenville." *Minutes of City Aldermen,* Greenville, NC, April 1, 1926, Book 6, p. 546.

being conducted for a colored cemetery and in West Greenville, we can surmise the offer was for a colored cemetery.

Knowing that the Brown property was available and located in a highly industrialized area with little or no commercial use or residential value, the City Aldermen perhaps calculated that they could accomplish a three-fold mission by (1) purchasing the property at less than fair market value; (2) gaining favor with a declining colored population that was rapidly leaving Greenville and moving to northern cities; and (3) thwarting any embarrassment to the Brown heirs, perhaps the most urgent issue. Consequently, the Aldermen acted with dispatch to purchase the Brown property adjoining the Cooper Field Cemetery at less than fair market value.

To the Aldermen's credit, they exercised transparency and accountability when purchasing the Greenwood Cemetery,[100] an expansion cemetery purchased for the burial of white citizens. State statutes and guidelines were followed, and three bids were submitted to Council as required by North Carolina law for discussion and approval. These practices were violated when purchasing the Brown property for a Colored Cemetery. Mr. Harry Brown, attorney for the Brown heirs, submitted the only formal and comprehensive bid before Council to purchase the Brown property. His bid was for $3,000 for 19.09 acres (Map 4.1) with a 3 percent per annum interest rate.[101] The City countered by offering the heirs $2,000.[102] The Brown heirs made a counter offer, and the City accepted a final offer of $2863.50 with a 6 percent per annum interest rate.[103] In the final analysis, the intense negotiations resulted in a negligible net gain for the City.

Transparency and accountability exercised by the City Aldermen when purchasing the Greenwood Cemetery in 1924 highlight several aberrations in the purchase of the Brown property for a colored cemetery. With Greenwood, City Aldermen exercised caution and executed their duties in an efficient and professional manner. That process was described as ". . . it is hereby certified and recited, that each and every act, condition, and thing required to be done, to have happened, and to be performed, precedent to and in the issuance of this note, has been done, has happened, and has been performed in full and strict compliance

---

[100] J. O. Duval, City Clerk. "Purchasing the Greenwood Cemetery." *Minutes of City Aldermen*, Greenville, NC, April 1, 1924, Book III, p. 546.

[101] J. O. Duval, City Clerk. "Sale of Brown Land for Colored Cemetery." *Minutes of City Aldermen*, Greenville, NC, June 1, 1939, Book 6, p. 53.

[102] Duval. Ibid, June 22, 1939, p. 71.

[103] Duval. Ibid, October 5, 1939, p. 136.

with the Constitution and Laws of the State of North Carolina."[104] The Cemetery Committee operated systematically and responsibly to find suitable properties to present to Council for discussion and consideration. Afterward, the Cemetery Committee presented comprehensive bids to Mayor D. M. Clark and the Aldermen. All bids were transparent and accountable, following the guidelines below:

1. Three proposals of prospective properties were presented.
2. The names and addresses of property owners were submitted.
3. The number of acres of the property was cited.
4. Explanations of any encumbrances were explained and discussed.
5. Property prices were quoted.
6. Methods of payments were explained and summarized.
7. Suggested closing dates were offered.
8. Blank bank notes for payment were prepared and discussed.

To strengthen the Cemetery Committee's report of transparency and accountability, the committee even arranged a reconnaissance trip for all of the Aldermen one Saturday morning to visit and review the properties.

In contrast to purchasing the Brown property for a colored cemetery, the City Aldermen—some of whom were on the Greenwood Cemetery search committee and who were familiar with State statues, policies and practices—abdicated their responsibility and violated North Carolina laws when purchasing the Brown property. Haste was no excuse for ignoring the law. But it is important to note in this context that the purchase of a colored cemetery ignited inflammatory passions and a movement to stop the plan led by Ms. Jesse Moye.[105]

Fortunately, for future historians, the *Minutes of City Aldermen*, Book VI and Book VII, chronicle a detailed account of the process and procedures employed by the Aldermen when purchasing the Brown property for the colored cemetery. Those guidelines have been reconstructed here in a complete timeline for instruction and illumination (Table 4.1).

---

[104] J. O. Duval, City Clerk. "Greenwood Cemetery." *Minutes of City Aldermen*, Greenville, NC, November 8, 1924, Book III, p. 421.

[105] Elizabeth H. Copeland. *Chronicles Of Pitt County North Carolina*. Winston-Salem, NC: Hunter Publishing Company, 1982, p. 542-543.

Table 4.1. Timeline for the Purchase and Naming of the Brown Hill Cemetery. (A true copy of the *Minutes* of City Council, Greenville, NC)

February 2, 1939, p. 14, par. 1

The question of proposed colored cemetery being placed on the water shed was taken up and discussed, and order passed that this be investigated.

March 8, 1939, p. 22, par. 1, 2, & 3

The Clerk then read the following report from Dr. N. Thomas Ennett relative to the Colored Cemetery which matter was left open for further investigation by the Cemetery Committee.

Greenville, N.C.
March 2, 1939

Mr. J. O. Duval
City Clerk
Greenville, N.C.

My dear Mr. Duval:

In Re: New Colored Cemetery West of City on Falkland Highway
In reply to your inquiry, I wish to advise you that the location of the above mentioned cemetery meets the conditions of the State Statute requiring that cemeteries be not less than 500 yards from the source of a municipal water supply.
Attached hereto is a copy of a certificate furnished this office by J. Hicks Corey.

Yours very truly,
N. Thomas Ennett, M.D.
Pitt County Health Officer

Nte/mbh
3/2/39

Mr. Rivers, following instructions of the Finance Committee, made a report on Brown property for Colored Cemetery in what is known as Cooper Field.

April 6, 1939, p. 32, par. 5 & 10

I have secured a tracing showing a location and area of the proposed Colored cemetery Site 18.98 Acres, having a frontage of 516.6 [feet] on Highway #43, and extending back to the Tar River.

The matter of the Colored Cemetery on the Falkland Highway was again taken up and referred to the Cemetery Committee.

April 18, 1939, p. 38, par. 6

Miss Jessie Moye came before the Board with reference to the proposed Colored Cemetery on the Falkland Highway or 5th Street extended, and protested against the Town or anyone else putting a cemetery at this location due to the spoiling the approach to the Town, Mayor Blount informed Miss. Moye that her protest would be considered.

May 4, 1939, p. 44, par. 1

The matter of Colored cemetery in what is known as Cooper Field was discussed and Harry Brown, Attorney for the W. B. Brown, Est. stated that they had approximately 17.5 acres of land that they would sell to the City at the price of $3,000.00 but would prefer a cash deal. As no recent survey had been made of this property and that one strip of land was claimed by the Greenville Cotton Mills, this matter was referred back to Mr. Harry Brown and Mr. R. Lee to investigate and endeavor to have the property lines located.

June 1, 1939 p. 51, par. 3

Rev. W. A. Ryan came before the Board and read a communication relative to appointing a City Planning Committee, Park and Recreational Committee and a Cemetery Committee, this petition embodied in another one, appearing later in these Minutes.

p. 52, par. 1 & 2

Alderman Spain, Chairman of the Cemetery Committee of the Board of Aldermen, reported to the Board and recommended that the Town offer the W. B. Brown Heirs $2,000.00 for the 19.08 acres of land adjoin[ing] the Cooperfield Cemetery and the recommendation by the Cemetery Committee was accepted by the Board.

Dr. J. A. Battle then arose and stated that his race was in full accord with the idea of the Town in purchasing this land and developing it into a Cemetery for the Colored People.

p. 53, par. 5, p. 54, par. 1 & 2

The following letter from Attorney Harry M. Brown, Representative of the W. B. Brown Heirs, with reference to the Colored Cemetery was read:

May 23, 1939

The Mayor and the Board of Aldermen
City of Greenville
Greenville, N.C.

Gentlemen:

The Estate of W. B Brown, deceased, hereby offers to the City of Greenville the following real property:

The W. B. Brown land, lying southwest of the City of Greenville, bounded by the present Colored Cemetery., and Greenville Cotton Mill, Guy T. Evans, W. H. Dial, and others, containing 19.09 acres by actual survey made by W. C. Dresback, C. E. on May 11 and 12, 1939, as appears on a plat made by said Dresback now on file in the office of J. O. Duval, City Clerk.

The above-described land is offered on the following terms: $3,000. due and payable $600.00 1, 2, 3, 4, and 5 years from the date of the closing of the transaction, with interest from date at the rate of 3 per cent per annum.

Respectively submitted,
Harry M. Brown, Atty. for Bessie R. Brown, Administratrix
of the Estate of W. B. Brown

Mrs. J. H. B. Moore, President of the Woman's Club, stated the purpose of the meeting: To request the Mayor and Board of Aldermen to take such steps as would insure an adequate and long-range planning for the City of Greenville, both in meeting the present needs of our growing community and provide such work should be done are-General City Planning, including Zoning Regulations; Public Parks; Recreation Centers, including Playgrounds; Cemetery Planning.

p. 55, Par. 3

That a Cemetery Committee be and the same is hereby created, composed of five members, to be appointed by the Board of Aldermen, whose terms of office shall be: two members for five years, two members for three years, and one member for two years, whose duties shall be to act as an advisory committee to the Board of Aldermen with reference to the maintenance and future expansion of the Cemeteries of the City of Greenville. The committee to serve without compensation or remuneration.

June 22, 1939, p. 71, par. 3 & 4

The Cemetery Committee reported that the Brown Heirs has rejected the offer of $2,000.00 made on March 1st, 1939, for the 19.09 acres of land wanted for the Colored Cemetery in what is known as Cooperfield. Motion was made by Alderman Watson, seconded by Alderman Fleming that the matter of buying this property be placed in the Cemetery Committee's hands with the power to act; the purchase price not to exceed $3,000.00. (Land purchased by Committee for $2,863.50).

Motion by Alderman Fleming, seconded by Alderman Spain, that Alderman Burnette, Chairman of the Committee of Sanitation and Health, take up with Dr. N. Thomas Ennett and the North

Carolina State Board of Health the advisability of having a Cemetery placed on the Water Shed. Motion was voted on and carried.

June 29, 1939, p. 74, par. 8 & 9, p. 75, par. 9

A proposed Contract for the sale of Cemetery lots to the colored people in the new Cemetery for this race was read and approved, with possibly some minor changes to be made later and the Cemetery Committee was instructed to look into the matter of having a survey made and lots laid off:

NORTH CAROLINA-PITT COUNTY

This CONTRACT made and entered into this the _____ day of 1939___ by the payment of $_____ this day made by the party of the second part,

WITNESSETH:

That the party of the first part, for and in consideration of the payment of $_____ this day made by the party of the second part, the receipt of which is admitted, and of the payment of _____ on the _____ day of each and every month hereafter until the full sum of $_____, including the amount this day paid, shall have been paid in full, does hereby contract and agree to convey to the party of the second part, heirs or assigns, at any time after all payments to the party of the first part as herein above set forth have been made, a good and indefeasible fee simple title with full covenants and warranty to a certain lot or parcel of land located with full covenants and warranty to a certain lot or parcel of land located in said County and State, near the Town of Greenville, in _____ Cemetery, and being Unit Lot No. ___ in said cemetery as shown on Map Book N. ___ in the office of the Register of Deeds of Pitt County, to which map reference is hereby made.

Provided, and upon condition, nevertheless, that said lot shall be used only for the purpose of burying the remains of colored persons therein, but that the remains of no person shall be buried therein until after a deed of conveyance has been executed and delivered to the party of the second part for said lot.

Provided further, that in the event the said party of the second part shall fail to make any payment to the party of the first part on said lot as herein above provided, the said party of the second part shall have a grace period of thirty days after the maturity date of any payment on which to pay the same, but if the said party of the second part shall fail to make the payments as herein provided when due, or within the grace period of thirty days thereafter, then and in that event the party of the second part shall forfeit to the party of the first part any sum or sums that may have been under the provisions of this contract as liquidated damages, and the contract shall thereupon be terminated.

IN WITNESS THEREOF the party of the first part has caused these presents to be signed in its name by its Mayor, and its corporate seal to be affixed and attested by its Clerk, all by authority of the Board of Aldermen duly given, this the day and year first above written.

TOWN OF GREENVILLE
BY: _____ Mayor

Attest :
J. O. Duval
Clerk

SEE PROBATION FORM WHICH HAS BEEN OMITTED, p. 79.
PROBATION FORM OMITTED IN THE COPYING OF THE MINUTES WHICH IS TO BE ATTACHED TO CONTRACT ON SALE OF LOTS AT COLORED CEMETERY

NORTH CAROLINA-PITT COUNTY

I _____, a notary public in and for the County of Pitt and State of North Carolina so thereby certify that _____ personally appeared before me this day, who being by me duly sworn says that he is Mayor of the Town of Greenville, a municipal corporation, and that the seal affixed to the foregoing instrument in writing is the corporate seal of said municipal corporation; that said writing was signed and sealed by him, and was attested by J. O. Duval, Clerk, in behalf of said municipal Corporation and by its authority duly govern; and the said _____ acknowledged the said writing to be the act and deed of said municipal corporation.

Witness my hand and official seal this the _____ day of _____ 19_____.

_____
Notary Public

My Commission expires: _____

July 6, 1939, p. 83, par. 2

Mr. W. Robert Derrick, Landscape Architect, of Raleigh, North Carolina, came before the Board with reference to planning Cemeteries. This matter was referred to the Cemetery Committee.

p. 94, par. 5

The following Cemetery Resolution was read and approved, subject to the approval of the Local Government Commission.

RESOLUTION

WHEREAS, the Board of Aldermen of the City of Greenville in regular session on the 22 day of June, 1939 authorized and empowered the Cemetery Committee of said Board to purchase a site for a Negro Cemetery from the heirs of W. B. Brown for a price not to exceed $3,000.00, and

WHEREAS, on the 23rd day of June, 1939 the Cemetery Committee reached an agreement with the Administratrix of the Estate of W. B. Brown to purchase 19.09 acres of land situate in the Greene Place, sometimes called Cooper Field, at a price of $2,863.50, the purchase price to be represented by five bonds of the City of Greenville each on the sum of $572.70, due 1, 2, 3, 4, & 5 years, respectively, from date, with interest at the rate of three per cent per annum.

WHEREAS, after being duly authorized in a proceeding brought for the purpose, Bessie R. Brown, Administratrix of the Estate of W. B. Brown, has executed to the City of Greenville a deed in fee simple for said 19.09 acres of land;

NOW THEREFORE, BE IT RESOLVED by the Board of Aldermen of the City of Greenville in regular session on the 6th day of July 1939: That the City of Greenville, by its Mayor, Jack Spain, to be certified by J. O. Duval, City Clerk, execute to Bessie R. Brown, Administratrix of the Estate of W. B. Brown, five bonds, each in the sum of $572.70, due and payable 1, 2, 3, 4, & 5 years, respectively, from date, with interest at the rate of three per cent per annum.

Jack Spain
Mayor

I, J. O. Duval, City Clerk of the City of Greenville, North Carolina do hereby certify that the foregoing is a true and correct copy of a Resolution passed by the Board of Aldermen of the City of Greenville, North Carolina on the 6th day of July, 1939.

J. O. Duval
City Clerk

(Seal)

July 10, 1939, p. 98, par. 5

Mayor Spain then appointed the following Aldermen to serve on the Various Committees of the City for the ensuing term.

Cemetery Committe
Collins, J. A. Chairman
Fleming, L. B.
Taft, Jos. M.

August 3, 1939, p. 103, par. 2 & 3

Mr. W. F. Pollard came before the Board with reference to selling the City a Power Lawn Mower to be used for the Mowing of grass at the Cemeteries, Athletic Field and other lots of the City and quoted a five (5) H. P. Mower at the price of $388.30 less 15% discount, making a net price of $330.06. Motion made by Alderman Collins, seconded by Alderman Sellers that the City purchase this machine, provided the machine would be delivered f. o. b. Greenville, N.C. Motion voted on and carried.

Alderman Collins then recommended that the Cemetery Department be taken out of the Street Department and a full-time man be employed as keeper of the Cemeteries and Parks, including the Baseball Park. Alderman Collins also recommended that Mr. J. K. Hester be employed at a salary of $100.00 per month to do this work. Mr. Hester to furnish his own car, gasoline and Trailer for the removal of grass and other rubbish, that might accumulate on these sites, and transportation of all equipment from one place to another and Mr. Hester begin work as soon as the new Power Mower arrived in Greenville. This motion was seconded by Alderman Sellers, voted on and carried.

August 3, 1939, p. 104, par. 1

On motion of Alderman Fleming, which was duly seconded and carried, the Mayor and Clerk were instructed to go to Raleigh on August 8th, 1939 and appear before the Local Government Commission with reference to issuing notes and payment of the Colored Cemetery Property and then revert back from Raleigh in due time to attend a District Meeting of the Institute of Government, which is to be held in Windsor, North Carolina in the afternoon of the same date.

September 7, 1939, p. 124, par. 6

Mr. Harry M. Brown came before the Board with reference to the colored cemetery matter and offered to let the Town have the land on an open account since the Local Government Commission did not approve the issuing of Notes to pay for this land. After some discussion, this matter was referred to the Cemetery Committee.

October 5, 1939, p. 136, par. 2

Mr. Harry Brown, Attorney for the W. B. Brown Heirs, came before the Board and made another proposition relative to the City purchasing what is known as the Cooper Field for colored cemetery. Motion was made by Alderman Collins, seconded by Alderman Sellers that the Board accept Mr. Brown's offer and the following resolution was passed and ordered spread on the minutes.

RESOLUTION

WHEREAS, the Board of Aldermen of the City of Greenville has agreed to purchase a site for a Negro Cemetery from the Heirs of W. B. Brown, deceased, for the price of $2,863.50, payable $500.00 in cash at the delivery of the deed, balance July 1. 1940, with interest at the rate of six per cent per annum from October 1. 1939, and

WHEREAS, after being duly authorized in a proceeding brought for the purpose, Bessie R. Brown, Administratrix of the Estate of W. B. Brown, has executed to the City of Greenville a deed in fee simple for the land agreed upon, to wit: 19.09 acres situate in Greene Place, sometimes called Cooper Field;

NOW THEREFORE, BE IT RESOLVED by the Board of Aldermen of the City of Greenville in regular Session on the 5th day of October, 1939 that the City of Greenville obligates to pay to Bessie R. Brown, Administratrix, the sum of $2,863.50, payable $500.00 in cash and balance with interest at the rate of six per cent per annum from October 1, 1939 on July 1, 1940; and J. O. Duval, City Clerk is hereby authorized to pay over to said Bessie R. Brown, Administratrix, on the 10th day of October, 1939 the sum of $500.00 and to receive the deed for said land.

Jack Spain
Mayor

_____   _____

_____   _____

_____   _____

Members of the Board   Members of the Board

November 22, 1939, p. 138, par. 2

On motion of Alderman Fleming, the clerk was instructed not to sell any Cemetery Lots until the cash was paid and that he be instructed to use every possible means of collecting what had been sold and not paid for.

November 22, 1939, p. 152, par. 2

On motion by Alderman Collins, Mr. Rivers was instructed to go to Williamston and see about getting the W. P. A. [to] sponsor a project whereby they would render some assistance to the City of Greenville in getting the property, which they recently purchased for a Colored Cemetery, cleared up.

On motion by Alderman Taft, the Board then adjourned.

J. O. Duval
Clerk

Approved:
Jack Spain, Mayor

December 7, 1939, p. 155, par. 2

A motion was made, seconded and carried that the matter of getting up a Map of the Colored Cemetery property was put in the hands of the Cemetery Committee and Mr. Henry L. Rivers, City Engineer, with power to act.

February 8, 1940, p. 164, par. 5

Engineer H. L. Rivers made a report on the Colored Cemetery property and presented to the Board a Map, which had been made of the property, and informed the members that an application had been made with the WPA for common labor to help develop this property but he had not, as yet, heard from the WPA authorities.

April 2, 1940, p. 183, par. 2

Mr. Moore, Local Manager of the WPA, was before the Board with Docket NC-C-74-41344, which Docket is for the newly acquired Colored Cemetery. Motion by Alderman Watson, seconded by Alderman Fleming that the Cemetery Committee and Street Committee cooperate with Mr. Moore toward starting this work. Mr. Moore advised the Board that this project would start early in May.

May 2, 1940, p. 186, par. 6

Motion made, seconded and carried that the Cemetery Committee, the Mayor and Engineer work out prices on lots at the new colored cemetery and report to the Board at the next regular meeting.

June 6, 1940, p. 194, par. 3, 4, & 5

The report of the Cemetery Committee was read to the Board, as follows:

Greenville, N.C.
May 20, 1940

The Cemetery Committee composed of J. A. Collins, L. B. Fleming and Joseph M. Taft, of the City of Greenville, N.C. met in the City Clerk's Office on the above named date and the following were present:

Mayor Jack Spain, J. O. Duval, City Clerk, Henry L. Rivers, City Engineer and Mr. Moore, Superintendent of the Works Progress Administration.

The matter of buying a fence for the new Colored Cemetery was gone into with Mr. G. E. Cherry, Jr., Representative of the Stewart Iron Works and it was learned at this meeting that the City would have to purchase the Post for this fence, as the WPA allotment was insufficient to buy the post and also wire for this fence. These Posts were purchased the following day by the Committee at a price of $647.00.

The Committee then went into the price of lots for the new Colored Cemetery and named the following prices:

Single Graves	10.00 each
10 ft x 20 ft-four grave sections	35.00 each for inside lots
	45.00 each for corner lots
20ft x 20ft-more than four grave sections	100.00 each for inside lots and also corner lots.

There being no further business to be transacted, the meeting adjourned.

J. O. Duval
City Clerk

This Report was accepted by the Board.

Motion was then made, seconded and carried that the City agree to furnish sand to be used in putting down the fence referred to in the above and at the suggestion of Alderman Collins, Chairman of the Cemetery Committee, the Board voted not to fence any of the old Colored Cemetery property and only fence the property recently purchased and owned by the City.

August 1, 1940, p. 217, par. 1

Alderman J. A. Collins, Chairman of the Cemetery Committee read the following report of his Committee:

Greenville, N.C.
July 29, 1940

The Cemetery Committee of the City of Greenville met at the City Clerk's office on the night of the above date, the following being present:

Mayor Jack Spain	L. B. Fleming
J. A. Collins	J. D. Simpson

Mr. S. G. Wilkerson, Undertaker, and Mr. Henry L. Rivers, Engineer, were called before the Committee and the Cemetery situation was gone into very thoroughly.

GREENWOOD CEMETERY

Due to needed repairs and improvements at the Greenwood Cemetery, the Committee recommends to the Board that circular lot #5 in section "A" be sold to Mr. Louis G. Cooper at a price of $175.00 and that individual lots #s 9 and 12, in section "A" be sold to Mr. S. G. Wilkerson at a price of $250.00.

That the balance of the unsold unit lots in sections "A," "B" and "C" be put on the market and sold at a price of $80.00 per unit.

That the Driveway beyond Sections "E" and "F" be changed from eight foot Driveway to a sixteen foot Driveway and the individual squares, south of the proposed circle, in section "F" and "G" be laid off into units sections to conform with sections "D" and "E."

That the rest of the unsold individual lots that are now laid off in Section "A," "B" and "C" said lots being 20 ft by 20 ft, be sold at $150.00 each.

The Committee further recommends to build a temporary fence just east of where the circle will be from the farm road on the south of the Cemetery to the driveway just north of the proposed circle. Also beginning at the present fence, including gate, up to the northern edge of the last Driveway, as shown on the Map, then east to connect with the temporary fence beyond the proposed circle.

Engineer Rivers was instructed to make another map of the Single Grave Section of Greenwood Cemetery so that the numbers will correspond.

That two single graves be sold to one person, but only two, unless approved by the Board.

COLORED CEMETERY

The Committee recommends to this Board that Curb and Gutter be put down on both sides of the 20 foot driveway in the Colored Cemetery, from Williams Street to driveway running east and west approximately 354 feet on both sides.

J. A. Collins, Chairman

Attest: J. O. Duval, City Clerk

August 1, 1940, p. 218, par. 1 & 2

A motion was made by Alderman Fleming requesting that the Street Department be authorized to repair the entrance street to the Colored Cemetery, work to be done under the supervision of Engineer Rivers. Motion voted on and carried.

Following the adoption of the report of the Cemetery Committee, motion was made by Alderman Simpson that the money from the sale of lots to Mr. Louis G. Cooper and Mr. S. G. Wilkerson be earmarked and used in building a fence around Greenwood Cemetery. The motion was amended to include that the amount spent should not exceed $425.00. Also amending ordinance relative to placing 40% of the sale of lots in the Special Fund but this amendment is to apply only to these two sales.

November 7, 1940, p. 242, par. 1, 2, & 13

Alderman Collins, Chairman of the Cemetery Committee, reported that Engineer Rivers had made a new Map of the Colored Cemetery, which Map was presented to the Board and accepted and Blueprints ordered to be made.

The Cemetery Committee was also ordered to put certain Curbing at the Colored Cemetery by the Street Employees under the supervision of the Cemetery Committee.

The advertisement of rent of the Greenwood Cemetery land and the balance of the Hardee Farm was read to the Board. At the request of Mr. J. H. Rose, the Clerk was instructed not to advertise for rent the balance of the land at the Hardee Farm but on motion of Alderman Collins, an advertisement was ordered drawn to advertise the rent of the 14 acres of cleared land adjacent to the Colored Cemetery and what is known as Cooper Field.

December 5, 1940, p. 252, par. 2 & 3

As no Bids had been received on the renting of the fourteen acres of land adjacent to the Colored Cemetery, as per copy of advertisement below, motion was made, seconded, noted on and carried that this land not be rented for the year 1941 but be turned over to the colored people of Greenville for a Playground and that they be so notified.

NOTICE OF PUBLIC RENTING OF FARM LAND

Sealed bids will be received by the City of Greenville up to 12 o'clock noon, on December 2, 1940, for the rental for the year 1941 of the following described farm lands:

All the cleared land (except that portion now being developed by the City of Greenville, N.C. in what is known as the Colored Cemetery) lying and being southwest of Greenville, lying and being in what is known as Cooper Field, bound on the north by Wyatt Street on the east by Third and Ames Streets and the land of W. H. Dial and Guy T. Evans, and on the west by the land of the Greenville Cotton Mills, deeded by the W. B. Brown Heirs to the City of Greenville on the 4th day of October 1939 on Deed recorded in the Pitt County Courthouse in Book V-22, page 556, containing 14 acres more or less.

Any and all persons interested in renting said land for agricultural purposes for the year 1941 will please file their bids with the City Clerk at the Municipal Building, in Greenville, N.C. within the time specified.

The successful bidder will be required to pay the rent in cash equal to the amount of his bid on September 15, 1941.

The lessor reserved the right to accept or reject any and all bids.

This the ____ day of November, 1940

City of Greenville, N.C.

By J. O. Duval

City Clerk

January 9, 1941, p. 260, par. 1

The first matter taken up was the recognition of Mrs. J. H. B. Moore and Mrs. W. E. Hooker, who were present in the interest of General City Planning for the City of Greenville and Mrs. Moore introduced Alderman L. B. Fleming, Chairman of the Planning Committee, who made the following recommendations of Committee appointments:

CEMETERY COMMITTEE

Mrs. H. S. Ragsdale	3 years term
Mr. Withers Harvey	3 years term
Mr. Bancroft Moseley	2 years term
Mrs. Tom Rivers	2 years term
Dr. S. M. Crisp	3 years term
Mr. S. G. Wilkerson	5 years term
Mrs. R. C. Deal	5 years term

January 9, 1941, p. 264, par. 2

Alderman Collins reported on the Curbing being placed at the Colored Cemetery and quoted Engineer Rivers in the cost so far figured as being 22.8 cents per lineal foot against a previous price made for this call of work of 40 cents. Motion was then made, seconded and carried that the Cemetery Committee continue this work until 2,000 feet of this curbing was laid.

February 6, 1941, p. 271, par. 5

Alderman Collins reported on the Curb and Gutter recently put in at the Colored Cemetery and stated that, according to the figures of Engineer Rivers, they had put down 2398 feet of Curbing and the cost of same was 18 cents per foot.

October 3, 1941, p. 360, par. 4

Alderman Collins, Chairman of the Cemetery Committee, asked permission to put in some additional curbing at the Colored Cemetery and Mr. Henry Rivers stated that this could be done at a cost of about $50.00 and it was so ordered.

September 3, 1942, p. 422, par. 7

Mr. Henry L. Rivers, City Engineer presented a sketch to the Board showing the different approaches to the Colored Cemetery. This matter was referred to the Cemetery Committee and Street Committee to take up with Mr. Mat Long and see what arrangements could be made about the approach through his property.

October 6, 1942, p. 426, par. 5

Alderman Collins then read a report on the Curb and Gutter completed at the New Colored Cemetery on this request:

1750 feet of 6 × 12 concrete curb has been constructed, developing 108 lots. Cost of the 1750 feet of curbing was $341.20 or 19.5 cents per foot. Grading and leveling lots amounted to $45.00.

Total spent for curb and grading $386.20

October 8, 1942, p. 427, par. 1

The Mayor was requested to write each of the colored Undertakes and call their attention to having some bodies in the Cemetery too shallow and request that they follow the State Law in making these burials.

January 21, 1943, p. 440, par. 3

The Cemetery situation was taken up and the Clerk informed the Board that he had taken up with Miss Bessie Brown the matter of naming the new colored cemetery and she stated that the W. B. Brown Estate would raise no objection whatsoever in using the name of "Brown" on naming this cemetery and it was decided, at present to name the colored cemetery "Brownhill Cemetery" and if no objections was raised at the February 6th meeting, the Clerk would have Deeds printed so they could be delivered for lots sold. The matter of curbing additional unit lot section for Greenwood Cemetery and also curbing more space for single graves was referred to the Cemetery Committee with power to act.

The meeting then adjourned.

J. O. Duval
Clerk

Approved:
Bob Sugg
  Mayor

March 4, 1943, p. 450, par. 9, 10 & 11

The Clerk then informed the Board that Mr. L. W. Cherry from the American Legion had reported that the County Commissioners had agreed to pay $200.00 on the plot of land in Greenwood Cemetery designated for the burial of War Veterans and the matter of drawing Deed and completing this transaction was left with the City Attorney and the Mayor.

The Clerk informed the Board that the New section has been completed in Greenwood Cemetery and that he had let the two lots out on deposit at a price of $75.00 each and asked the Board to set the price per lot in that section and on motion by Alderman Watson the price was set at $80.00

The Clerk took up several matters pertaining to the Colored Cemetery and this was referred to the Cemetery Committee.

March 11, 1943, p. 453, par. 1

Mayor Sugg called on the persons present and Prof. Davenport, Principal of the Colored Schools, came before the Board and asked permission to use the cleared land adjacent to the Colored Cemetery for gardens for the Colored people. Motion by Alderman Bostic, which was duly seconded, that this request be granted and Engineer Rivers was instructed to work with Professor Davenport in staking off various lots of different sizes for the different families.

September 2, 1943, p. 508, par. 5

The request from Boston Boyd's daughter for the City to clean up and take over the maintenance of the Cooper Field Cemetery was taken up and discussed and referred to the Cemetery Committee to investigate.[106] No response reported.

The Naming of the Brown Hill Cemetery

Names define people, places, and things. Animate names honor while inanimate ones define locations. Therefore, then, the etiology of the Brown Hill Cemetery originated from the owners of the property on which the cemetery is located. The Hill part of the name was designated by the elevation of its topography. The elevation at the Brown Hill Cemetery is about 60 feet above sea level in contrast to the elevation of the Cherry Hill Cemetery which is about 50 feet, Sycamore Hill Baptist Church Cemetery is about 48 feet above sea level.[107] Additionally, the designated name Hill is sequential and in conformity with the names of the Sycamore Hill Baptist Church and the Cherry Hill Cemeteries (Table 4.2).

Albeit Ms. Bessie Brown stated that the "W. B. Brown Estate would raise no objections whatsoever in using the name of 'Brown' in naming this cemetery, the city decided . . . to name the colored cemetery BROWNHILL."[108] Brown Hill is a two-part word and should be represented as such. The decision to spell the name of the cemetery "Brownhill" perhaps misrepresents and dishonors the intent of the Brown family.

---

[106] J. O. Duval, City Clerk, "Request from Boston Boyd's Daughter to Take Over Maintenance of the Cooper Field Cemetery." *Minutes of City Council*, Greenville, NC, September 2, 1943, Book 6, p. 508.

[107] Sam Barber. Christian Lockamy. Interviews, 2011-2012.

[108] J. O. Duval, City Clerk. "Naming of the Brown Hill Cemetery." *Minutes of City Council*, Greenville, NC, January 31, 1943, Book 6, p. 440.

Table 4.2. Alphabetized List of Citizens Buried at the Brown Hill Cemetery, 1913-1939.

NAME	VOL.	DEATH CERT. NO.
Adams, John Henry	1, 2, 3	482
Adams, Morning	1, 2, 3	396
Albritton, Flora	12	493
Albritton, John	7	87
Alexander, Carrie	11	504
Allen, Lewis	6	498
Allen, Susan	11	448
Applewhite, Dock	15	428
Artis, Emma	6	454
Atkins, Chrispus F.	8	350
Atkinson, Dora E.	17	505
Atkinson, Ray	9	459
Atkinson, Willie	6	437
Bailey, Alex, Jr.	7	596
Bailey, Mary	6	560
Bailey, Mary	6	563
Barnes, Alla	7	288
Barnes, Elnora	17	552
Barnes, Maxine	17	571
Barnhill, Alfred	6	586
Barnhill, Hattic	15	480
Barnhill, Haywood	11	428
Barnhill, Heron Bruce	15	452
Barnhill, Josephine	13	580
Barrett, Francis	25	311
Barrett, Fred Long	25	359
Bartlette, Tommie Equiella	15	444
Barton, Julia	8	353
Bass, Clarence Earl	11	622
Beaman, Hazel	9	423
Becton, Mary	6	717
Belcher, Moses	11	468
Belcher, Pheobie	7	83
Belcher, Rosa Lee	20	344
Bell, Annie May	11	387
Bell, Maggie	7	129

Bender, Nelson	8	347
Bennett, Lula Bell	25	390
Bennett, Lula Lee	25	431
Benton, Mary	8	552
Bernard, Auston	7	113
Bernard, Henerritta	19	523
Best, Jerry, Jr.	8	413
Best, Major, Jr.	11	442
Bland, Edward	25	398
Blount, Francis Mariah	7	96
Blount, Johnnie	5	354
Blount, Mary	11	427
Boone, Willie Ford	6	541
Boston, Julia	8	353
Bradley, Everett Swindell	8	405
Bradley, Jesse	6	567
Brady, Horace Moore	19	405
Braxton, Ed	8	601
Braxton, James	11	509
Briley, Aaron	7	74
Briley, Artie J.	21	617
Briley, Clifton	1, 2, 3	515
Brown, Africa	7	85
Brown, Annie	21	606
Brown, Claude	2	418
Brown, Danny	6	386
Brown, Easter	9	464
Brown, Edward	7	149
Brown, Herbert, Jr.	11	682
Brown, Jack, Jr.	9	389
Brown, Laura N.	7	66
Brown, Lucinda	7	6
Brown, Mary	7	128
Brown, Neel	5	374
Brown, Penny	6	404
Brown, Pluny	5	386
Bryant, General	12	503
Bryant, Margaret	5	360
Bryant, Mary	25	366
Bryant, Samuel	16	461
Bryant, Willie Lee	17	495

Burnell, Emma	9	405
Burton, Bradshaw	9	374
Burton, Margaret Shine	6	693
Bynum, Leo	11	415
Cannon, Hoyt	14	382
Cannon, Linda	11	435
Carey, Lewis, Jr.	6	524
Carman, Annie	22	417
Carr, Annie	11	376
Carr, Edna	6	734
Carr, Fannie	6	576
Carr, Funier	25	328
Carr, Heneretta D.	6	695
Carr, Issac	11	449
Carr, James Authur	6	453
Carr, Leslie	1, 2, 3	517
Carr, Rendy	14	381
Carr, Rhone	15	447
Carr, Slabell	24	491
Cherry, Carlton J.	2	1
Cherry, Clarke	8	372
Cherry, Flaura	24	390
Cherry, Loradu	6	564
Cherry, Lovely	15	433
Clark, Wilson Right	11	592
Clarke, Lena	11	436
Clarke, Luvernia	6	513
Clarke, Norton Edward	6	457
Clemmons, Willie James	24	447
Cobb, Abraham, Jr.	25	382
Cooper, Eliza	9	361
Cowan, Ann Lee	22	417
Coward, Carror	11	472
Coward, Charity	11	537
Coward, Harriett	13	583
Coy, Lucy Mae	20	374
Crandall, Ethel	16	512
Daniel, Eller	12	525
Daniel, Emma	8	336
Daniel, Emma	8	479
Daniel, Harry F.	9	413

Daniel, Henry	5	373
Daniel, Lonza	5	399
Daniel, Manda	11	494
Daniel, O.	5	359
Daniels, Euginia	12	486
Davis, Ida	8	597
Davis, Lucy	7	71
Davis, Pennie	15	460
Davis, Willie D.	15	436
Dawson, Dora Lee	23	327
Dayton, Nettie	12	546
Dickens, John	7	117
Dixon, George	13	489
Dixon, Lena	12	518
Dixon, Moses	11	480
Dixon, Ora Eliz	19	525
Dixon, Rosa	8	421
Dixon, Sudie May	11	492
Dixon, Will Jas	19	526
Donelson, Clara	8	560
Dozier, Charles Henry	5	364
Dudley, Eddu	11	492
Dupree, Douglas	21	494
Dupree, Ida Bell	16	511
Dupree, Lenora	14	385
Dupree, Nina	12	530
Earnel, Lucille	6	556
Eaton, Mattie Lee	6	531
Ebron, Luzianna	8	392
Edwards, Celia	1, 2, 3	508
Edwards, Floyd	15	478
Edwards, James	9	451
Edwards, James Nathaniel	5	384
Edwards, Sterling	25	281
Emmis, Hattie	6	573
Eubron, Nettie	6	616
Evans, Arden	6	664
Evans, Henry	24	316
Evans, Martha Jane	25	357
Evans, Sarah	8	359
Evans, Toney	18	399

Evans, Wadell	5	387
Evans, Willie May	8	343
Farmer, Hardison	7	119
Farmer, Hardy	14	379
Fleming, Annie	5	362
Fleming, Clara	8	374
Fleming, Edward	13	503
Fleming, Jessie May	2	545
Fleming, Lewis	6	568
Fleming, Maggie	6	592
Fleming, Nancy	25	415
Fleming, Pauline	15	467
Fleming, Redmond	7	278
Fleming, Rufus	24	580
Fleming, Sifox	25	363
Flowers, Alice Mary	6	431
Forbes, Ameondell	12	590
Forbes, Charity	25	309
Forbes, Ed	3	357
Forbes, Eleanor	8	346
Forbes, Eli	5	457
Forbes, Elizabeth	8	358
Forbes, Ferby	7	108
Forbes, Jasper	6	566
Forbes, Mallone	1, 2, 3	508
Forbes, Mayer	12	499
Forbes, Nettie Lee	7	136
Forbes, Richard	13	498
Forbes, William	23	383
Foreman, Alonza	8	541
Foreman, David Webester	1	576
Foreman, Everhurst	11	555
Foreman, Fred, Jr.	16	402
Foreman, Ida	6	554
Foreman, John	13	535
Foreman, Martha	8	396
Foreman, Mary	7	148
Foreman, Phoebe	16	487
Foreman, Rosie	13	468
Foreman, Wesley	13	531
Forks, Nettie Lee	7	136

Freeman, Lee Ann	11	447
Galloway, Bessie	8	348
Gally, Alexander	12	534
Gardner, William J.	9	410
Gaskins, Rachell	6	509
Gather, Mary	20	371
Gay, Eliz	17	525
George, Ada	11	401
Gerrigan, Lucille	2	490
Gibbs, Debora L.	25	388
Giles, Ida Mae	13	482
Gorham, Alice	6	520
Gorham, Ernest	13	523
Gorham, Reed	11	457
Graham, James Henry	11	373
Graham, Jane	23	402
Graham, Joyner R.	11	481
Grandy, Annie May	6	539
Grant, Geo Lee	6	482
Gray, Delsora	25	413
Gray, Hurley	12	605
Gray, Louisa	6	570
Gray, Sarde F.	22	350
Gray, Shade, Jr.	6	448
Gray, Spelman	12	592
Grayham, Moses, Jr.	12	521
Grayham, Sarah	7	105
Green, Evelyn	13	512
Green, Fannie Lee	17	504
Green, Gertrude	6	575
Green, Imogene	25	270
Griffin, Charles H.	11	453
Grives, Bobby Lewis	19	454
Grives, Paul	18	513
Grives, Silas	18	514
Gully, Alexander	12	534
Hall, Mamie Ruth	7	86
Hall, Samuel	8	536
Hardee, Hoyt	17	518
Hardee, James	25	350
Harding, Henry	7	94

Hardy, Ed	25	321
Hardy, Ellen	13	532
Hardy, Minnie	11	726
Harper, Charlie Ashley	8	381
Harper, Helen Joyce	18	475
Harrington, Russ	6	460
Harris, Edith May	13	467
Harris, Edward	7	98
Harris, Ellen	7	122
Harris, Festus	11	413
Harris, Jackson	8	368
Harris, Joseph	11	402
Harris, Lena	6	472
Harris, Luvernia	6	530
Harris, Mary	6	429
Harris, Nathaniel	12	492
Harris, Simon	6	495
Harris, Van Ray	6	596
Harris, Willie	13	516
Haskins, Janis	8	355
Hayes, Stillborn	17	573
Hegan, Mary O.	8	537
Hemby, Francis Dell	8	408
Hemby, Freeman, Jr.	15	602
Hemby, James	24	418
Hemby, Laura	7	80
Hemby, Robert lee	20	372
Hemby, Russell T.	24	492
Hemby, Walter	8	414
Hemby, Willie	4	553
Hester, Minnie	5	352
Hewly, Freeman, Jr.	15	602
Highsmith, Oscar	5	372
Hines, Lillie P.	24	369
Hines, Nicole	21	550
Holland, Doris	20	360
Holland, Lizzo Mae	20	306
Holland, Louisa	2	518
Home Made Box	8	338
Hooper, Willie	11	476
Hopkins, Eva	1, 2, 3	466

Hopkins, Hariett	8	377
Hopkins, Lewis	6	507
Hopkins, Stanley	11	593
House, Bessie (Infant)	8	380
House, Effie Ree	19	407
House, John H.	15	469
Howell, Eleanor Wing	11	454
Howell, Rufus	6	451
Huggins, Georgia Lee	5	382
Hunter, Mary	9	420
Infant	1, 2, 3	408
Infant	1, 2, 3	414
Infant	1, 2, 3	435
Infant	6	516
Infant	7	245
Infant	8	592
Infant	9	396
Infant	9	416
Infant	12	560
Infant	15	427
Infant	17	472
Infant	17	481
Infant	17	536
Infant	18	402
Infant	19	481
Infant	19	496
Infant	19	526
Infant	20	312
Infant	20	330
Infant	20	368
Infant	24	393
Infant	24	575
Jackson, Louisteen	18	518
Jackson, Mary	11	467
James, Lula	6	555
James, Mary L.	8	345
Jenkins, Abraham	13	508
Jenkins, Cleophus	5	367
Jenkins, Daisey	7	139
Jenkins, Dockery	7	139
Jenkins, Martha	20	356

Jenkins, Mary	20	355
Jenkins, William Washington	6	598
Jerrigan, Hattie	13	486
Johnson, Jesse, Jr.	9	381
Johnson, Joe, Jr.	25	319
Johnson, Julious	5	381
Johnson, Mary Lee	9	380
Johnson, Sam P.	7	299
Johnson, Sandy	8	384
Jones, Alexander	1, 2, 3	431
Jones, Carrie	15	445
Jones, Charles	6	553
Jones, Clarence Earl	18	369
Jones, Clifton	6	529
Jones, Irene	12	547
Jones, Lula	6	555
Jones, Mary L	8	345
Jones, Minnie	6	376
Jones, Novella Lee	17	445
Jordan, John	15	486
Jordan, John, Jr.	5	434
Joyner, Helen	13	533
Joyner, Irvin	11	446
Joyner, Willie McArthur	11	550
Judge, Nursey	9	377
Juilcious, Henry	23	479
Killbrew, Edward	7	275
Killbrew, James	15	546
Killbrew, Rose	13	527
King, John	5	383
Kinsey, Owen Goin	18	470
Kittrell, Ned	11	552
Knight, Larry Jas	17	524
Knox, Stewart	18	471
Lambert, Albert, Jr.	17	484
Langley, Bertie	11	526
Langley, Esther	2	509
Langley, Evelyn P. C.	23	363
Langley, Thomas Earl	18	429
Lee, Daisy May	15	481
Lewis, Julia	9	403

Lewis, Nathan	13	534
Lienberger, Bing, F.	6	535
Little, Herbert	6	546
Little, Julian	11	544
Little, William J.	11	551
Lock, Mary	8	361
Love, Edward	21	528
Lovett, Minerva	11	588
Loy, John Wilkins	18	397
Lumford, Louise	18	432
Maneys, Mandy	6	590
Maulsby, Estella	9	406
May, Ada V.	15	429
May, Charlie	5	377
May, Cora Bell	6	523
May, James A.	17	487
May, Jenia	13	497
May, John	8	517
May, Mary	6	480
May, Silva	6	439
Maye, Laura	5	385
Maye, Miles	7	120
Mayo, Ertma	15	449
Mayo, James R.	6	627
Mayo, Jane	8	403
Mayo, Robert	15	468
McClinton, Sam	8	410
McConnell, Mary Lizer	9	358
McCullum, Rheubea	24	324
McDaniel, Betty Joe	21	602
McDaniels, Glardeen	11	460
McDonald, James	19	436
McDonald, Lillian	19	435
McGown, Della	16	509
McGown, Hill	11	388
McMillan, Mary	11	654
McNeill, Frank	15	397
Meyers, Albert	5	340
Mills, Abram	7	68
Mills, Bertha	11	475
Mills, Clara	11	440

Mitchell, John	2	530
Moore, Annie Lee	6	484
Moore, Fannie Albert	17	452
Moore, Franza	19	421
Moore, Henry, Jr.	24	419
Moore, James, Jr.	9	481
Moore, Jordan	18	473
Moore, Laurence	8	572
Moore, Louise	25	444
Moore, Sarah	18	373
Moore, Virginia	9	364
Moore, William Howard	5	392
Moore, William, Jr.	17	614
Morris, Jas Jessie	17	556
Moye, Miles	7	120
Murphy, Lucy Carr	15	543
Myers, Albert	4	351
Neal, George	8	391
Nettles, Haywood	16	451
Nobles, Christine	1, 2, 3	414
Nobles, Emily	6	468
Nobles, Ernest	25	295
Nobles, George	6	602
Nobles, Neal, Jr.	21	558
Norman, Alberta	23	410
No Name	2	54
No Name	6	562
No Name	6	594
No Name	7	135
No Name	7	142
No Name	7	143
No Name	9	347
No Name	11	496
No Name	12	576
No Name	13	500
No Name	13	501
No Name	13	518
No Name	14	374
No Name	17	415
No Name	17	440
No Name	19	492

No Name	20	297
No Name	21	470
No Name	21	525
No Name	24	394
No Name	24	582
Obby, Samuel	12	504
O'Neil, Sudie	17	511
Parker, Green	21	474
Parker, Laura Bell	25	425
Parker, Lucindy	11	434
Parks, David Thomas	15	453
Patrick, Christine	9	456
Pelleman, Matthew	6	404
Pender, Alice Lee	9	391
Pender, Theodore	11	514
Perkins, Dock	24	450
Perkins, Odessa	24	466
Peterson, Matthew	5	404
Pettifore, Johnnie and Auth	25	411
Peyton, Alexander	6	527
Peyton, Martha L.	22	377
Peyton, Olie Gertrude	6	470
Poindexter, Lucy B.	1, 2, 3	432
Pollard, Carrie	6	565
Pollock, Major	5	433
Pope, Lany	11	482
Portis, Ben	17	584
Post, Pearl	11	371
Pratt, Hazeltine	11	438
Premature	9	347
Premature	12	494
Premature	17	519
Premature	18	468
Price, Elmore	25	343
Price, John	9	404
Price, Preston	2	517
Price, Sam, Jr.	8	424
Pryar, Malsen	6	552
Raffie, Dempsy	11	456
Randolph, Della	7	104
Raven, Lou	19	540

Reaves, Ida	11	556
Reaves, Mary	11	596
Reddick, John	9	480
Reeves, Nixon	9	482
Reeves, Roxie	11	437
Rena, Fenely	1, 2, 3	570
Rich, Thomas	8	401
Richards, Meliza	20	283
Richardson, Danwood	11	455
Richardson, Denwood	11	456
Richmond, Young	6	478
Roberson, Terila	9	433
Roberts, Laurence H.	22	421
Roberts, Ralph Alexander	6	497
Roberts, Rossie	7	73
Robinson, Mattie	11	474
Robinson, Sarah	8	419
Rogers, Jennette	7	113
Ross, Jane	20	282
Royester, Will	8	394
Ruby, Ernestine	17	536
Ruffin, Dempsy	11	456
Ruffin, James Earl	4	570
Ruffin, Joseph Earl	11	469
Shepard, Nancy	25	342
Shepard, Rosetti	9	386
Sheppard, Edna Carl	21	610
Sheppard, Henry	6	501
Sheppard, Thomas	25	399
Shield, Jesse B.	8	411
Shields, Joseph	6	441
Shiver, Margaret	6	545
Shivers, Beverly Rena	1, 2, 3	520
Shivers, Carolina	13	377
Shivers, Fenely Rena	1, 2, 3	520
Shivers, John	24	584
Shivers, Lutrell	21	601
Shivers, Samuel	6	603
Shivers, Willie Ray	11	414
Sinette, Susan Ann	20	337
Slaughter, Alfred	11	405

Smith, Charlie G.	8	398
Smith, Elaira Forbes	25	334
Smith, James A.	18	462
Smith, Joe Clegg	8	439
Smith, John	8	576
Smith, John Arthur	8	341
Smith, Julia	24	399
Smith, Lizzy	12	485
Smith, Mary	11	634
Smith, Porter	8	440
Smith, Walter	11	393
Socks, Ella	1, 2, 3	468
Spear, James E.	11	748
Speight, John	24	403
Spell, Gerald	8	402
Spell, Katie	8	613
Spell, Lillian	13	475
Spell, Straywood	1, 2, 3	472
Spill, Mayrard	11	499
Spruill, Sarah	11	433
Stafford, Willie Frank	9	352
Staton, Laura	11	421
Stewart, Carrie Eliz	17	470
Stocks, Bessie	25	372
Stillborn	6	494
Stillborn	8	338
Stillborn	8	339
Stillborn	8	378
Stillborn	8	379
Stillborn	8	385
Stillborn	8	387
Stillborn	8	465
Stillborn	9	415
Stillborn	11	640
Stillborn	11	660
Stillborn	11	444
Stillborn	11	470
Stillborn	12	512
Stillborn	13	449
Stillborn	13	510
Stillborn	13	529

Stillborn	13	552
Stillborn	14	401
Stillborn	15	427
Stillborn	15	437
Stillborn	15	585
Stillborn	15	586
Stillborn	15	587
Stillborn	15	593
Stillborn	15	609
Stillborn	15	618
Stillborn	15	622
Stillborn	15	428
Stillborn	15	497
Stillborn	15	503
Stillborn	16	531
Stillborn	16	532
Stillborn	16	534
Stillborn	17	456
Stillborn	17	478
Stillborn	17	480
Stillborn	17	491
Stillborn	17	514
Stillborn	17	573
Stillborn	17	592
Stillborn	17	599
Stillborn	18	427
Stillborn	18	461
Stillborn	18	463
Stillborn	18	468
Stillborn	18	496
Stillborn	18	497
Stillborn	18	506
Stillborn	18	507
Stillborn	18	551
Stillborn	18	557
Stillborn	18	558
Stillborn	19	417
Stillborn	19	420
Stillborn	19	440
Stillborn	19	467
Stillborn	19	488

Stillborn	19	494
Stillborn	19	499
Stillborn	19	502
Stillborn	19	508
Stillborn	19	523
Stillborn	19	524
Stillborn	19	530
Stillborn	19	550
Stillborn	21	615
Stillborn	21	618
Stillborn	21	619
Stillborn	21	622
Stillborn	21	623
Stillborn	21	625
Stillborn	21	626
Stillborn	21	627
Stillborn	21	628
Stillborn	21	629
Stillborn	21	632
Stillborn	21	633
Stillborn	24	566
Stillborn	24	567
Stillborn	24	569
Stillborn	24	570
Stillborn	24	576
Stillborn	24	580
Stillborn	24	582
Stillborn	24	583
Stillborn	24	584
Stokes, Carry Elizabeth	12	510
Stokes, Ruth	13	615
Suggs, Mary T.	15	446
Summrell, Willar Dean	18	375
Taft, Dinah	1, 2, 3	429
Taft, Fred	25	384
Taft, Milton	7	132
Taylor, Patsie	1, 2, 3	421
Tearle, Mary E.	9	382
Teel, Lillie	11	462
Teel, Virginia Lee	1, 2, 3	518
Terry, Julious	6	502

Thompson, Harriett	7	296
Thorne, Viola	25	307
Tucker, Haywood	9	418
Tucker, Jannie	7	152
Tucker, Lula	24	490
Tucker, Lydia	9	408
Tucker, (Male Infant)	15	497
Tucker, Mary Eliza	24	470
Tucker, Pauline	21	605
Tucker, Pheobia	6	499
Turner, Charlotte	7	99
Turner, David F.	23	387
Tyson, Charlie R.	17	434
Underwood, Wm.	24	583
Unknown	6	562
Unknown	18	415
Venters, Frank	18	469
Vines, Anthony	1, 2, 3	510
Vines, Bertha	6	557
Vines, Ceasar	9	456
Vines, Cliffie	19	472
Wahab, Mamie	7	65
Waldrop, Carrie	25	291
Waldrop, William	11	778
Walker, Nannie May	5	340
Walters, Mozella	24	429
Ward, Samuel H.	25	331
Warn, Winnie	11	419
Warren, Fred	12	522
Watson, Emma	25	335
Watson, Ivory, Jr.	25	395
Watson, Mary Malison	12	533
Watson, Robert	15	611
Watson, Rosa	6	528
Webb, Verna Mae	7	77
Webb, Will	6	561
Weston, Leonard	11	477
Whichard, Clarence Edward	5	378
Whichard, Herbert, Jr.	20	281
Whitaker, Frances	24	380
Whitaker, Louis	5	355

Whitehead, Richard, Sr.	6	455
Whitehurst, Jordan	24	454
Whitehurst, Lamb B.	11	548
Whitley, Sarah	15	574
Wiggins, Dora	13	513
Wilcox, Alton	12	548
Wilkerson, Jane	8	539
Wilks, Lottie B	9	387
Williams, A. B.	6	584
Williams, Albert	11	533
Williams, Alice	8	425
Williams, Clara	9	484
Williams, Fannie	9	344
Williams, Festus	11	413
Williams, James	8	386
Williams, James	11	471
Williams, James Thomas	11	475
Williams, Lillian	7	82
Williams, L. W.	1, 2, 3	430
Williams, Mack	11	411
Williams, Mattie M.	6	559
Williams, Richard Edward	6	626
Williams, Robert	6	595
Williams, Sarah	8	337
Williams, Thomas	16	430
Williams, Tom	9	356
Wilson, Anna	23	371
Wilson, Bettie	12	435
Wilson, Coner	8	412
Winslow, Betty	11	435
Worell, Nat	21	470
Worthington, Sam'l Hugh	18	512
Wright, Ellen	12	549
Wright, Jane	11	445
Wright, Wilma	14	383
Yarborough, Lula May	6	446

Hard evidence to show that the Greenville black community established or operated an independent cemetery in Greenville or an adjacent one to the Slave Burying Ground or old Colored Cemetery is all but nonexistent. Two hundred and fifty grave plots adjoining the Cooper Field Cemetery were initially unaccounted tor by the Public Works Division. Mrs. Colleen Sicley in a memo on April 24, 2012, stated, "We would have no information on them [the estimated 250 grave plots on the 1941 Colored Cemetery Map] because the city didn't own or operate the cemetery until October 1939."[109] However, evidence shows that by 1914 black citizens were being buried in what Mr. Henry Rivers, City of Greenville engineer, describes as the Colored Cemetery later known as the Cooper Field Cemetery in contrast to what might be characterized as an unknown Slave Burying Ground. (See Map 3.1 by Henry Rivers,[110] City of Greenville engineer, and Table 4.3 and Table 4.4). Of the approximately 451 death certificates listed in the Register of Deeds office at the Pitt County Courthouse, 149 of these bodies were buried at Cooper Field. From the evidence, one could conclude that the remaining bodies listed on the official death certificates as buried in Greenville or the City cemeteries could very well be buried at Cooper Field. It is highly possible that there were no preserved headstones for many of these graves and, over time, contemporary markers were destroyed or removed. This section of the cemetery could very well be called the Cooper Field Cemetery.

Table 4.3. Death Certificates of Individuals Buried in the Greenville or City Cemetery.

CERT NO.	NAME	FUNERAL HOME	DEATH DATE

Vols. 1, 2, 3, 1913–1915

CERT NO.	NAME	FUNERAL HOME	DEATH DATE
447	Sarah J. Walker	John Flanagan	05/28/14
483	Sally Taft	John Flanagan	05/28/14
496	Mamie R. Dupree	John Flanagan	05/28/14
497	Robert Daniel	John Flanagan	05/28/14
498	Marion Obey	John Flanagan	05/28/14
499	Fannie Barnard	John Flanagan	05/28/14
423	Moses Williams	John Flanagan	05/28/14
434	No Name	John Flanagan	05/28/14
452	Carmella Williams	Ormond Jenkins	05/28/14
486	Almyra Patrick	John Flanagan	05/28/14
440	Silver Bell Branch	No Undertaker	05/28/14

---

109 Colleen Sicley, Secretary of the Brown Hill Cemetery Department. "Memorandum: Cooper Field Cemetery." Greenville, NC, April 24, 2012.
110 Rivers. Map 1941.

444	Eliza Edmonds	John Flanagan	05/25/15
449	Pennia Brown	John Flanagan	06/14/15
450	Cherry Braxton	Boyd Furniture Co.	09/16/15
451	No Name	John Flanagan	08/31/15
452	Jackson Johnson	John Flanagan	09/09/15
453	James Williams	John Flanagan	07/13/15

Vol. 4, 1916

416	Mattie Greene	S. G. Wilkerson	06/20/16
463	Edmond Fomas	Sam Short	04/09/16
465	Jimmie Barber	Sam Short	04/18/16
478	Paulette Bryant	Elder Coke	10/31/15
479	Gilbert Gart	W. S. Moye	11/05/15
485	Martha Scott	John Flanagan	12/23/15
492	Chas. Edwards	Sam Short	01/29/16
494	Queen Dupree	John Flanagan	02/03/16
499	Alifort Green	Sam Short	03/11/16
500	Celia Cooper	Sam Short	03/13/16
501	John S. Foreman	John Flanagan	03/30/16
503	Tom May	Sam Short	04/12/16
505	Iva Beatrice Simons	Sam Short	04/18/16
506	Viola Hines	John Flanagan	04/19/16
507	Augustus Fleming	John Flanagan	05/02/16
510	Ed Braxton	Sam Short	05/12/16
512	Mary Collins	Sam Short	06/17/16
542	Noah Hardy	Sam Short	06/10/16
543	Gladys Carr	Sam Short	06/16/16
565	James Latham	Sam Short	11/03/16
566	Caesar Blount	Sam Short	11/07/16
567	Annabell Thompson	Sam Short	11/10/16
568	Dorsie Johnston	Sam Short	11/29/16

Vol. 5, 1916

346	Harrriet James	Sam Short	02/14/17
347	Josephine May	Sam Short	02/16/17
348	Hattie Hemby	Sam Short	02/22/17
366	Violette Herohan	Sam Short	04/16/17

Vol. 6, 1917-1918

| 720 | Moses Lumsford | S. G. Wilkerson | 10/29/18 |

Vol. 7, 1920

| 102 | Annie Lee Jackson | S. G. Wilkerson | 10/28/19 |

Vol. 8, 1921

| 467 | No Name | S. G. Wilkerson | 08/14/20 |
| 611 | James Hardee | S. G. Wilkerson | 06/10/22 |

Vol. 9, 1922

| 376 | Infant | Home Made Box | 06/14/22 |
| 384 | Helen D. Wooten | C. A. Albritton | 08/09/22 |

Vol. 10, 1923

None

Vol. 11, 1924

None

Vol. 12, 1925

| 561 | Infant, Stillborn | S. G. Wilkerson | 03/23/24 |

Vol. 13, 1926

None

Vol. 14, 1927

None

Vol. 15, 1928

454	Stillborn Girl	Homemade Box	04/16/27
473	Wm. Ernest Mooring	W. E. Flanagan	07/25/27
495	Linnie Johnson	W. E. Flanagan	10/14/27
539	Maria Moore	W. E. Flanagan	01/15/28
540	William Griffin	Flanagan & Parker	03/13/28
553	Andrew Small	Flanagan & Parker	01/06/28
554	Mary Wilson	Flanagan & Parker	04/10/28
555	Ruth Gorham	Flanagan & Parker	04/28/28
556	John F. Green	Flanagan & Parker	04/29/28
557	Dink Johnson	Flanagan & Parker	05/01/28
562	Hattie Boyd	Flanagan & Parker	05/19/28
563	Edward Blount	Flanagan & Parker	02/12/28
567	Cherry Forbes	Flanagan & Parker	05/24/28
590	Claud Forbes	W. E. Flanagan	08/29/28
598	Emma Gray	W. E. Flanagan	09/08/28
623	Stillborn	J. I. Baker	07/22/28

Vol. 16, 1929

389	Ernestine Swittle	Flanagan & Parker	11/17/28
390	Lillie Wooten	Flanagan & Parker	12/02/28
391	Lillie Mae Moore	Flanagan & Parker	12/11/29
392	Baby Barnhill	Flanagan & Parker	01/16/29
393	Elizabeth Braxton	Flanagan & Parker	12/08/29
395	Olivia Norcott	Flanagan & Parker	10/04/28
397	Mardecia Anderson	Flanagan & Parker	01/10/29
404	Julia Sutton	Flanagan & Parker	11/01/28
405	Eugene Watts	Flanagan & Parker	11/22/28
410	Jennie Hopkins	Flanagan & Parker	12/18/28
411	Hattie Mayo	Flanagan & Parker	01/29/29
419	Dora Williams	Flanagan & Parker	02/15/29
420	Cordena Garfield	Flanagan & Parker	05/23/29
421	Charlie Jackson	Flanagan & Parker	10/07/28
422	David Payton	Flanagan & Parker	11/21/28
425	Amos Edwards	Flanagan & Parker	12/02/28
433	Laura Parker	Flanagan & Parker	04/15/29
441	Celia Davis	Flanagan & Parker	04/21/29
443	Dora Cherry	C. A. Albritton	05/22/29
445	Mamie Langley	Flanagan & Parker	03/13/29

454	Oscar Sutton	Flanagan & Parker	06/17/29
462	Peter Latham	W. E. Flanagan	06/08/29
465	No Name	E. S. Williams	07/20/29
473	James Staton	Flanagan & Parker	04/20/19
474	Mable Adams	Flanagan & Parker	04/26/29
476	Annie G. Pender	J. I. Baker	06/19/29
491	Ella Humphrey	W. E. Flanagan	07/27/29
492	Charlie Patrick	W. E. Flanagan	07/24/29
494	John Brown	W. E. Flanagan	09/16/29
495	George Braxton	W. E. Flanagan	10/03/29
496	Sarah Willis	W. E. Flanagan	09/18/29
503	Christine Redmond	Flanagan & Parker	10/12/29
508	Stanley Hardy	Flanagan & Parker	11/26/29
517	Stillborn	Ellis Langley, Acting	12/12/29
519	Stillborn	Ellis Langley, Acting	12/24/29
527	Stephen Davis	Flanagan & Parker	11/15/29
533	Stillborn	J. I. Baker	02/21/29
535	Stillborn	Ellis Langley, Acting	06/16/29
536	Stillborn	J. I. Baker	08/20/29
537	Sarah Grimes	Flanagan & Parker	10/08/29
538	Stillborn	J. I. Baker	04/01/29
539	Stillborn	J. I. Baker	05/28/29
541	Henry Langley	Flanagan & Parker	01/16/29

Vol. 17, 1930

435	Stillborn	Ellis Langley, Acting	01/22/30
437	Eli Langley	W. E. Flanagan	01/22/30
448	John H. Daniel	W. E. Flanagan	02/15/30
459	Henry Wooten	Flanagan & Parker	02/12/30
460	Washington Mayo	Flanagan & Parker	02/14/30
461	Maymie May	Flanagan & Parker	01/14/30
462	Annie Jefferies	Flanagan & Parker	02/04/30
466	Emmerlizer Moring	Flanagan & Parker	03/08/30
489	Thaddeus Norris	W. E. Flanagan	04/21/30
494	Marina Randolph	W. E. Flanagan	03/17/30
499	Fannie Hines	Flanagan & Parker	04/18/30
500	James F. Moore	Flanagan & Parker	05/09/30
516	Jesse Moye	Flanagan & Parker	06/15/30
520	Edith Brown	Ellis Langley, Acting	07/24/30
521	Julia Payton	Flanagan & Parker	07/16/30

527	Viola Patrick	Flanagan & Parker	07/09/30
534	Marcellus Reddick	Flanagan & Parker	08/12/30
546	Geo. W. Thomas	Flanagan & Parker	09/01/30
565	Pauline Sparkman	Flanagan & Parker	09/14/30
577	Mary Lewis	Flanagan & Parker	08/06/30
568	Emma L. Harris	Flanagan & Parker	11/08/30
595	Olivia Johnson	Flanagan & Parker	12/28/30
596	Clara Coward	Flanagan & Parker	01/02/31

Vol. 18, 1931

365	Sherman Foreman	Flanagan & Parker	11/11/30
367	Magnolia Gray	Flanagan & Parker	01/14/31
379	Josephine Whitfield	Pitt County Welfare	01/06/31
380	Willie Sparkman	Flanagan & Parker	01/26/31
381	Nell Clark	Flanagan & Parker	01/24/31
388	Talbert Porter	Flanagan & Parker	02/21/31
390	Willie B. Edwards	Flanagan & Parker	12/31/31
392	Martha Eaton	Flanagan & Parker	12/13/31
393	Blount Carr	Flanagan & Parker	12/16/30
398	Ivery Speight	Pitt County Welfare	03/02/31
406	Charles Gorham	Flanagan & Parker	03/05/31
407	George Mason	Flanagan & Parker	03/07/31
416	Emma Norcott	Flanagan & Parker	03/19/31
419	Rosa Scott	Flanagan & Parker	03/25/31
426	Maggie Langley	Flanagan & Parker	03/30/31
435	Alvania Clark	Flanagan & Parker	04/02/31
440	Lucinda Whichard	Flanagan & Parker	04/25/31
441	William Green	Flanagan & Parker	04/29/31
461	Willie Smith Turnage	Ellis Langley, Acting	06/19/31
467	Infant	Flanagan & Parker	06/26/31
476	Mary J. Allen	Flanagan & Parker	06/12/31
478	Eliza Peoples	Flanagan & Parker	07/07/31
479	Francis Williams	Flanagan & Parker	07/12/31
485	Henry Daniel	Flanagan & Parker	07/21/31
487	John Amos Glenn	Flanagan & Parker	07/27/31
491	Sarah Hemby	Flanagan & Parker	07/22/31
500	Mattie Smith	Flanagan & Parker	10/09/31
511	Robert G. Hodges	Flanagan & Parker	11/29/31
515	Lucy Daniels	Flanagan & Parker	12/04/31
517	Haven Gorham	Flanagan & Parker	12/05/31

Vol. 19, 1932

409	Walter Gooden	Flanagan & Parker	02/26/32
410	Annie West	Flanagan & Parker	02/29/32
413	Julia Sutton	Flanagan & Parker	11/01/28
414	Mary Bobbett	Flanagan & Parker	04/04/32
416	Stillborn	J. I. Baker	03/22/32
419	Amos Moye	Flanagan & Parker	03/28/32
423	Louise Mays	Flanagan & Parker	01/18/32
425	Boston N. Boyd, Sr.	Flanagan & Parker	02/12/32
428	Haywood Nettles	Williams Funeral Parlor	06/05/29
441	Ernestine T. Shillie	Flanagan & Parker	05/07/32
442	Gus Smith	Flanagan & Parker	05/24/32
444	Premature	Flanagan & Parker	04/04/32
448	Mack Neil	Flanagan & Parker	04/30/32
449	Henry Peele	Flanagan & Parker	05/11/32
450	Roberta Hines	Flanagan & Parker	05/12/32
451	Henry Reaves	Flanagan & Parker	05/20/32
460	Lillie Bruce Teele	Flanagan & Parker	06/06/32
461	Rhonda Small	Flanagan & Parker	06/10/32
462	Lonnie Wadell	Flanagan & Parker	06/18/32
472	Cliffie E. Vines	Flanagan & Parker	07/09/32
474	Bert Leggett, Jr.	Flanagan & Parker	07/18/32
478	Charlie Eaton	Flanagan & Parker	07/17/32
479	Amos Elks	Flanagan & Parker	07/24/32
485	Will Smith	Flanagan & Parker	08/04/32
493	Grace Belcher	Flanagan & Parker	08/23/32
501	Victoria Jones	Flanagan & Parker	09/30/32
505	Luke House	Flanagan & Parker	10/02/32
516	Lillie May Jordan	Flanagan & Parker	11/19/32
521	Wm. Redmond	Flanagan & Parker	10/25/32
534	Oscar Forbes	Flanagan & Parker	12/06/32
535	Mary Lucy Mooring	Flanagan & Parker	12/08/32
536	Willie Jordan	Flanagan & Parker	12/14/32
537	Sophia Haven	Flanagan & Parker	12/18/32
544	Eliza Anderson	Flanagan & Parker	10/07/32
545	Susan Adams	Flanagan & Parker	11/05/32
546	Florence D. Edmonds	Flanagan & Parker	12/28/32
548	Elbert Dixon	Flanagan & Parker	12/24/32

Vol. 20, 1933

285	Mozella Boyd	Flanagan & Parker	12/27/32
287	Melissa Dupree	Flanagan & Parker	01/07/33
295	Emma Jackson	Flanagan & Parker	02/17/33
296	Duffie Wiggins	Flanagan & Parker	02/25/33
298	Lucy Sutton	Flanagan & Parker	02/27/33
301	Joe Gray	Flanagan & Parker	04/06/33
305	Luther Savage	Flanagan & Parker	03/31/33
310	Richard Hardy	Flanagan & Parker	04/16/33
326	Hattie Powell	Flanagan & Parker	06/13/33
327	William Huereband	Flanagan & Parker	07/02/33
328	Lillie Adams	Flanagan & Parker	07/03/33
331	Malissa Wilson	Flanagan & Parker	07/29/33
332	Alfred Sumrell	Pitt County Health Dept.	08/01/33
338	Alice Carr	Flanagan & Parker	08/24/33
348	Hugle Willis	Flanagan & Parker	08/03/33
349	George Adams	Flanagan & Parker	09/08/33
362	Neal Farmer	Flanagan & Parker	11/16/33
363	Miles Copeland	Flanagan & Parker	10/29/33
376	David Price	Flanagan & Parker	11/17/33
378	Bessie Nobles	Flanagan & Parker	12/02/33
379	Rosa Wilson	Flanagan & Parker	12/15/33
380	James Sneed, Jr.	Flanagan & Parker	12/17/33
381	Mary Sueetle	Flanagan & Parker	10/18/33
387	Julius Johnson	Flanagan & Parker	12/27/33
392	Mollie Locke	Flanagan & Parker	12/06/33

Vol. 21, 1934

475	John Graves	Flanagan & Parker	02/05/34
481	Bettie Barnhill	Flanagan & Parker	03/04/34
484	No Name	Flanagan & Parker	01/18/34
490	Georgeniee Hulls	Flanagan & Parker	02/08/34
493	Maggie Whitley	Flanagan & Parker	12/14/34
495	Roxie Kinley	Flanagan & Parker	02/24/34
503	Obbie Batts	Flanagan & Parker	04/02/34
512	Clarence Williams	Flanagan & Parker	04/26/34
514	Laura Johnson	Flanagan & Parker	05/14/34
517	Luratea Staton	Flanagan & Parker	05/25/34

520	Louise Ellis, (Infant)	Flanagan & Parker	05/27/34
522	Janice Turner	Flanagan & Parker	06/05/34
530	Chas. R. Barrett	Flanagan & Parker	06/13/34
533	Sudie Batts	Flanagan & Parker	06/20/34
534	John Eaton	Flanagan & Parker	07/02/34
544	Cherry Atkinson	Flanagan & Parker	06/23/34
545	Julia Cherry	Flanagan & Parker	07/17/34
546	Aza Barnhill	Flanagan & Parker	06/03/34
551	Sheppard Barned	Flanagan & Parker	06/15/34
556	Frank Bradley	Flanagan & Parker	06/23/34
557	Dillon O. Langley	Flanagan & Parker	08/06/34
558	Fred Harris	Flanagan & Parker	08/04/34
572	Herman Nick Hines	Flanagan & Parker	07/30/34
577	Elnia Moore	Flanagan & Parker	10/09/34
578	Daniel Langley	Flanagan & Parker	09/14/34
589	Robert Baules	Flanagan & Parker	10/07/34
591	Hansen Foreman	Flanagan & Parker	11/19/34
594	Abner Gorham	Flanagan & Parker	12/12/34
604	Ella Wilson	Flanagan & Parker	11/22/34
621	Stillborn	Flanagan & Parker	06/08/34
630	Stillborn	Flanagan & Parker	10/31/34

Vol. 22, 1935

285	Leatrice J. Reans	Flanagan & Parker	09/25/34
289	Will Hardy	Flanagan & Parker	01/28/35
295	John Barnes	Flanagan & Parker	01/28/35
299	Annie May Moye	Citizens Funeral Home	03/09/35
309	Rita Tucker	Flanagan & Parker	03/02/35
310	Hardy H. Ward	Flanagan & Parker	03/05/35
311	Luther Cobb	Flanagan & Parker	02/22/35
325	James Cherry	Flanagan & Parker	04/14/35
326	Mary Simms	Flanagan & Parker	04/26/35
333	James Sheppard	Flanagan & Parker	05/03/35
336	Estella Hairaham	Flanagan & Parker	05/03/35
347	Eunice Evans	Citizens Funeral Home	06/21/35
349	Geneva Best	Citizens Funeral Home	06/14/35
353	Wm. Stanley Ebron	Citizens Funeral Home	07/10/35
356	Nora Lee Green	Flanagan & Parker	07/13/35
360	George Brown, Jr.	Citizens Funeral Home	07/26/35
363	Callie Hines	Flanagan & Parker	08/16/35

370	Killbrew Hemby	Flanagan & Parker	08/15/35
372	John Vines	Flanagan & Parker	08/13/35
373	Rebecca Williams	Flanagan & Parker	08/03/35
375	Nicole Teel	Flanagan & Parker	09/05/35
376	James Brown	Flanagan & Parker	08/31/35
391	Mary Louise Hill	Flanagan & Parker	09/27/35
395	George Lynch	Flanagan & Parker	10/26/35
396	George Lang	Flanagan & Parker	05/25/35
437	Andrew Jones	Flanagan & Parker	11/01/35
442	Julius Jenkins	Flanagan & Parker	12/26/35

Vol. 23-24, 1936-1937

315	Rosa Lee Blackwell	Flanagan & Parker	11/20/35
316	Emma Fleming	Flanagan & Parker	01/02/36
319	Emma Williams	Flanagan & Parker	01/10/36
323	Caswell Johnson	Flanagan & Parker	01/13/36
326	Davis May Spells	Flanagan & Parker	01/04/36
328	Allen Carr	Flanagan & Parker	01/23/36
337	Josephine Peoples	Flanagan & Parker	03/04/36
341	Laura Early Meadows	Flanagan & Parker	01/13/36
357	Bill Johnson	Flanagan & Parker	02/17/36
360	Henry Coburn	Flanagan & Parker	02/17/36
369	Zeno Price	Flanagan & Parker	03/01/36
389	Henry Porter	Flanagan & Parker	02/09/36
390	Jessie Hines	Flanagan & Parker	04/27/36
413	Lila Tucker	Flanagan & Parker	06/15/36
430	Bea Price	Flanagan & Parker	08/21/36
440	B. J. Clemmons	Flanagan & Parker	08/05/36
480	Martha Ryan	Flanagan & Parker	11/19/36
481	Mary Miller	Flanagan & Parker	11/01/36
484	Mariale Brown	Flanagan & Parker	10/21/36
503	Mollie Godette	Flanagan & Parker	08/20/36
509	Mack Whichard	Flanagan & Parker	12/14/36
511	Burner Williams	Flanagan & Parker	09/01/36
512	Carl Funchuss	Flanagan & Parker	11/29/36
513	John Kittrell	Flanagan & Parker	09/24/36
514	Alfred Barnhill	Flanagan & Parker	12/02/36
516	Martha Langley	Flanagan & Parker	12/02/36
278	James A. Barnes	Flanagan & Parker	09/24/36
279	Isaac Tatum	Flanagan & Parker	12/12/36

280	Samuel White	Flanagan & Parker	12/09/36
287	Andrew Maye	Flanagan & Parker	01/08/37
297	Mamie R. Chapman	Flanagan & Parker	02/20/37
303	John S. Kearney	Flanagan & Parker	05/02/37
309	Jasper Barnes	Flanagan & Parker	06/06/37
318	Mary E. Vines	Flanagan & Parker	06/04/37
345	Richard Wychee	Flanagan & Parker	08/30/37
346	Curtis Neal	Flanagan & Parker	09/01/37
347	Puck Joyner	Flanagan & Parker	09/14/37
366	Bridget L. Cardon	Flanagan & Parker	08/31/37
369	Elexandy Stokes	Flanagan & Parker	09/19/37
370	George Robert Mayo	Whitehead Funeral Home	10/01/37
373	Jasper Cooper	Flanagan & Parker	10/09/37
388	Martha Whitehead	Flanagan & Parker	11/12/37
389	Tynie Oliver	Flanagan & Parker	11/14/37
390	Henry Roden	Flanagan & Parker	11/15/37
393	John C. Dyer	Flanagan & Parker	11/12/37
397	Willie James	Citizens Funeral Home	12/01/37
401	John Donaldson	Flanagan & Parker	11/23/37
403	Cleo Carr	Flanagan & Parker	03/13/32
408	Emma G. Hemby	Flanagan & Parker	10/04/37
416	Bertha Mitchell	Flanagan & Parker	10/09/37

Vol. 24, 1938

317	Charlotte Smith	Flanagan & Parker	01/06/38
320	Wilbur Dixon, Jr.	Flanagan & Parker	01/04/38
345	Jennie Harris	Flanagan & Parker	03/13/38
347	Martha Ann Lumsford	Flanagan & Parker	02/17/38
361	Lee Thomas	Flanagan & Parker	04/17/38
378	Jessie Lee Gray	Flanagan & Parker	01/12/37
464	Addie Hollaway	Flanagan & Parker	10/01/38
504	Fred Gray, Jr.	Stokes & Congleton	12/15/37

Vol. 25, 1939

288	Eula Mae Alford	Flanagan & Parker	01/13/39
410	Glars Jean Edwards	Flanagan & Parker	07/15/39
455	Charlie F. Worthington	Flanagan & Parker	12/02/39

Table 4.4. Alphabetized List Of 454 Names on Death Certificates Of Individuals Buried In The Greenville Or City Cemeteries, Including Those Buried at Cooper Field.

Adams, George
Adams, Little
Adams, Mable
Adams, Susan
Alfred, Eula
Allen, Mary J.
Anderson, Eliza
Anderson, Mardecia
Atkinson, Cherry
Barber, Jimmie
Barnard, Fannie
Barned, Sheppard
Barnes, Gettrude   Cooper Field
Barnes, James A.
Barnes, Jasper
Barnes, John
Barnhill, Alfred
Barnhill, Aza
Barnhill, Baby
Barnhill, Betty
Barrett, Charles R.
Batts, Obbie
Batts, Sudie
Baules, Robert
Belcher, Grace
Best, Geneva
Blackwell, Rosa Lee
Bland, Edward
Blount, Caesar
Bobbett, Mary
Boyd, Boston B. N.   Cooper Field
Boyd, Hattie
Boyd, Mozella
Boyd, Plato   Cooper Field
Bradley, Frank
Bradley, Joseph F.   Cooper Field
Bradley, Julia   Cooper Field

Branch, Silver Bell
Braxton, Cherry
Braxton, Ed.
Braxton, Elizabeth
Braxton, George
Brown, Edith
Brown, Fannie
Brown, George, Jr.
Brown, James
Brown, John
Brown, Mariale
Brown, Ransome   Cooper Field
Bryant, Paulette
Burton, Bradshaw
Burton, Margaret Shine
Cardon, Briget I.
Carr, Alice
Carr, Allen
Carr, Blount
Carr, Cleo
Carr, Cleopatra   Cooper Field
Carr, Gladys
Chapman, Mamie R.
Cherry, Dora
Cherry, Etta   Cooper Field
Cherry, Flaura A.   Cooper Field
Cherry, James
Cherry, Julia
Cherry, Paula   Cooper Field
Clark, Allie   Cooper Field
Clark, Alvania
Clark, Hettie   Cooper Field
Clark, Nell
Clark, Wiley   Cooper Field
Clemmons, B. J.
Cobb, Luther
Coburn, Henry
Coburn, J. H.   Cooper Field
Collins, Mary
Cooper, Celia
Cooper, Jasper

Copeland, Miles	
Coward, Clara	
Daniel, Henry	
Daniel, John H.	
Daniel, Robert	
Daniels, Lucy	
Davis, Celia	Cooper Field
Davis, Stepen	
Dixon, Elbert	
Dixon, Moses	Cooper Field
Dixon, Rosa	Cooper Field
Dixon, Wilbur	
Donaldson, Charrie L.	Cooper Field
Donaldson, George	Cooper Field
Donaldson, John	
Donaldson, Mary	Cooper Field
Donaldson, Slade	Cooper Field
Dudley, George E.	Cooper Field
Dupree, Mamie	
Dupree, Melissa	
Dupree, Queen	
Dyer, John C.	
Eaton, Charles	
Eaton, John	
Eaton, Martha	
Ebron, Jarves	Cooper Field
Ebron, Lois Ann	Cooper Field
Ebron, Nellie B.	Cooper Field
Ebron, Peter C.	Cooper Field
Ebron, Wm. Stanley	Cooper Field
Edmonds, Ann	Cooper Field
Edmonds, Eliza	
Edmonds, Florence	
Edwards, Amos	
Edwards, Charles	
Edwards, Glavs Jean	
Edwards, Willie	
Elks, Amos	
Ellis, Louise	
Evans, Annie	Cooper Field
Evans, Eunice	

Farmer, Neil	
Fleming, Ann	Cooper Field
Fleming, Annie	Cooper Field
Fleming, Augusta	Cooper Field
Fleming, Emma	
Fleming, Maggie	Cooper Field
Fleming, Redmond	Cooper Field
Fomas, Edmond	
Forbes, Charity	Cooper Field
Forbes, Cherry	
Forbes, Claud	
Forbes, Elnora	Cooper Field
Forbes, Lizzy	Cooper Field
Forbes, Lucy	Cooper Field
Forbes, Marshall	Cooper Field
Forbes, Mayer	Cooper Field
Forbes, Oscar	
Forbes, Ouida Belle	Cooper Field
Forbes, Richard	Cooper Field
Foreman, Hansen	
Foreman, John S.	
Foreman, Sherman	
Funchuss, Carl	
Garfield, Cordena	
Gart, Gilbert	
Glenn, John Amos	
Godette, Mollie	
Gooden, Walter	
Gorham, Abner	
Gorham, Charles	
Gorham, Haven	
Gorham, Ruth	
Graham, Baby	Cooper Field
Graham, Bebie	Cooper Field
Graham, Moses	Cooper Field
Graves, John	
Gray, Emma	
Gray, Fred, Jr.	
Gray, Jessie	
Gray, Joe	
Gray, Magnolia	

Gray, Shade	Cooper Field
Green, Alifort	
Green, Ida	Cooper Field
Green, John F.	
Green, Nora Lee	
Green, William	Cooper Field
Greene, Mattie	
Griffin, William	Cooper Field
Grimes, James E.	Cooper Field
Grimes, Sarah	
Grimes, Slade	
Hard, Fenner	Cooper Field
Hard, Henry	Cooper Field
Hardee, James H.	
Hardy, Little Susan	Cooper Field
Hardy, Noah	
Hardy, Richard	
Hardy, Stanley	
Hardy, Will	
Harraham, Estella	
Harrington, Joe	Cooper Field
Harris, Charlie	Cooper Field
Harris, Edward	Cooper Field
Harris, Emma	
Harris, Ernest	
Harris, Fred	
Harris, Jennie	Cooper Field
Harris, J. J.	Cooper Field
Harris, Lena	Cooper Field
Harris, Mollie	Cooper Field
Haven, Sophia	
Hemby, Emma	
Hemby, Hattie	
Hemby, Kellbrew	
Hemby, Sarah	
Henrahand, Charlie	Cooper Field
Henrahand, Violet	Cooper Field
Herohan, Violette	
Hill, Mary Louise	
Hines, Callie	
Hines, Fannie	

Hines, Herman Nick
Hines, Jessie
Hines, Roberta
Hines, Viola
Hodges, Robert G.
Holloway, Addie
Hopkins, Arthur   Cooper Field
Hopkins, Jennie
House, Luke
Huereband, William
Hull, Georgeniee
Humphrey, Ella
Humphrey, S. P.   Cooper Field
Hunter, Mary C.   Cooper Field
Isler, Rhoda   Cooper Field
                                   Death Certificate SHBC

Jackson, Annie Lee
Jackson, Charlie   Cooper Field
Jackson, Emma
James, Harriett
James, Willie
Jefferies, Annie
Jenkins, Julius
Johnson, Bill
Johnson, Caswell
Johnson, Dink
Johnson, Jackson
Johnson, Julius
Johnson, Laura
Johnson, Linnie
Johnson, Olivia
Johnson, S. J.   Cooper Field
Johnson, Sam P.   Cooper Field
Johnson, Samuel R.   Cooper Field
Johnston, Dorsie
Jones, Andrew
Jones, E. D.   Cooper Field
Jones, Victoria
Jordan, John   Cooper Field
Jordan, Lillie May
Jordan, Willie

Joyner, Irvin	Cooper Field
Joyner, Puck	
Kearney, John S.	
Keel, William Jessie	Cooper Field
Kinley, Roxie	
Kittrell, John	
Lang, George	
Langley, Bettie	Cooper Field
Langley, Daniel	
Langley, Dillon O.	
Langley, Eli	
Langley, Esther	Cooper Field
Langley, Henry	
Langley, James	Cooper Field
Langley, Kathleen	Cooper Field
Langley, Maggie	
Langley, Mamie	
Langley, Martha	
Latham, James	
Latham, Jane	Cooper Field
Latham, Peter	
Legette, Bert, Jr.	
Lewis, Mary	
Locke, Mollie	
Lumsford, Moses	
Lumsford, Martha Ann	
Lynch, George	
Marable, John	Cooper Field
Mason, George	
May, Joseph	Cooper Field
May, Josephine	
May, Mame	Cooper Field
May, Maymie	
May, Tom	
Maye, Louise	
Mayer, Andrew	
Mayo, George	
Mayo, Hattie	
Mayo, Washington	
McDonaldson, Mary	
Meadows, Laura Early	

Miller, Mary	
Mills, Abraham	Cooper Field
Mitchell, Bertha	
Moore, Annie	Cooper Field
Moore, Arthur	Cooper Field
Moore, Eliza	
Moore, James	
Moore, Lillie May	
Moore, Maria	Cooper Field
Moore, Theodore	Cooper Field
Moore, Walter	Cooper Field
Mooring, Mary Lucy	
Mooring, Wm. Ernest	
Moring, Emmerlizer	
Moye, Annie May	
Moye, Jesse	
Neil, Curtis	
Neil, Mack	
Nettles, Haywood	
Nettles, Walter	Cooper Field
Nixon, Rees	Cooper Field
Nobles, Bessie	
Nobles, Frank	Cooper Field
Norcott, Emma Moye	Cooper Field
Norcott, Martha	Cooper Field
Norcott, Olivia	
Norris, Thaddeus	
Obey, Marion	
Obey, Sam	Cooper Field
Oliver, Tynie	
Ormond, Harriett	Cooper Field
Parker, Laura	
Patrick, Almyra	
Patrick, Charlie	
Patrick, Viola	
Payton, David	
Payton, Julia	
Payton, Nettie	Cooper Field
Peele, Henry	
Pender, Annie	
Peoples, Eliza	

Peoples, Josephine	
Pergkans, Mary	Cooper Field
Poindexter, Julia A.	Cooper Field
Porter, Henry	
Porter, Talbert	
Powell, Hattie	
Price, Bea	
Price, David	
Price, Zeno	
Randolph, Marion	
Reans, Leatrice	
Reaves, Henry	
Reddick, Marcellus	
Redmond, Christine	
Redmond, Wm.	
Reeves, Nixon	Cooper Field
Richardson, Daniel	Cooper Field
Richardson, David	Cooper Field
Robinson, Pattie	Cooper Field
Roden, Henry	
Ryan, Martha	
Savage, Luther	
Scott, Martha	
Scott, Rosa	
Selby, Alex	Cooper Field
Sheppard, Henry	Cooper Field
Sheppard, James	
Sheppard, Maggie	Cooper Field
Shillie, Ernestine T.	
Shivers, Isabella	Cooper Field
Simms, Mary	
Simon, Iva Beatrice	
Small, Andrew	Cooper Field
Small, Rhonda	
Smith, Charlotte	
Smith, Gus	
Smith, Mattie	
Smith, Walter	Cooper Field
Smith, Will	Cooper Field
Smith, Willie	Cooper Field
Sneed, James, Jr.	

Sparkman, Pauline	
Sparkman, Willie	
Spear, Hannah	Cooper Field
Speigh, Ivery	
Spell, Davis May	
Staton, James	Cooper Field
Staton, Laura	Cooper Field
Stokes, Elexandy	
Suettle, Mary	
Sumrell, Alfred	
Sutton, Julia	Cooper Field
Sutton, Lucy	Cooper Field
Sutton, Oscar	
Swittle, Ernestine	
Taft, John	Cooper Field
Taft, Mary J.	Cooper Field
Taft, Sally	
Tatum, Isaac	
Teel, Nicole	
Teele, Bruce	
Thomas, George W.	Cooper Field
Thomas, Lee	Cooper Field
Thompson, Annabell	
Tucker, Lila	
Tucker, Lula	Cooper Field
Tucker, Lydia	Cooper Field
Tucker, Pauline	Cooper Field
Tucker, Rita (Retha)	
Tucker, Sarah	Cooper Field
Turnage, Willie Smith	
Turner, Janice	
Vines, Cliffie E.	Cooper Field
Vines, John	
Vines, Mary E.	
Vines, Tabahia	Cooper Field
Wadell, Lonnie	
Walker, Sarah	
Ward, Hardy H.	
Watts, Eugene	Cooper Field
Wells, Eva	Cooper Field
West, Annie	

Whichard, Luinda
Whichard, Mack
Whitaker, Francis   Cooper Field
Whitaker, Irene   Cooper Field
Whitaker, Louis   Cooper Field
Whitaker, Richard   Cooper Field
White, Samuel
Whitehead, Martha
Whitehead, Richard   Cooper Field
Whitehurst, Heber   Cooper Field
Whitehurst, Lamb   Cooper Field
Whitfield, Josephine
Whitley, Della   Cooper Field
                            Death Certificate SHBC

Whitley, Maggie
Wiggins, Duffie
Wiggins, John   Cooper Field
Wilcox, Alton   Cooper Field
Williams, Albert   Cooper Field
Williams, Bruner
Williams, Carmella
Williams, Clarence
Williams, Dora
Williams, Edward L.   Cooper Field
Williams, Emma
Williams, Francis
Williams, George   Cooper Field
Williams, Mack   Cooper Field
Williams, Maria   Cooper Field
Williams, Mary   Cooper Field
Williams, Maua
Williams, Moses   Cooper Field
Williams, Rebecca
Williams, Thomas H.   Cooper Field
Willis, Hugle
Willis, Sarah
Wilson, Alonza   Cooper Field
Wilson, Ann Bradley   Cooper Field
Wilson, Ella
Wilson, Malissa
Wilson, Mary

Wilson, Rosa
Wooten, Cynthia   Cooper Field
Wooten, Helen
Wooten, Henry
Wooten, Lillie
Worthington, Charlie F.
Wychee, Richard   Cooper Field

SUMMARY

A dearth of administrative management documents precludes any hard evidence to show that the Greenville Negro community established or operated an independent or an adjacent cemetery next to what might be called the Slave Burying Ground or old Colored Cemetery. Evidence shows that by 1914, black citizens were being buried in the Colored Cemetery, later known as the Cooper Field Cemetery, in contrast to the Old Cemetery or the Slave Burying Ground (Map 3.1). Of approximately 451 death certificates listed in the Register of Deeds Office at the Pitt County Courthouse as being buried in the City Cemetery, 149 of these bodies were buried at Cooper Field. Mrs. Colleen Sicley, in a memo on April 24, 2012, stated that ". . . we have no information on them [about 250 grave plots on the 1941 Colored Cemetery map] because the city didn't own or operate the cemetery until October 1939."[112]

From on-site grave inspections and map evidence, these graves are clearly within the boundaries of the newly purchased Brown Hill Cemetery property. Given the abundance of headstones at Cooper Field, surely some of these 451 sites once had headstones. In all probability, records and memorials once existed, but over time have been misplaced, destroyed, or lost.

The culture of officially naming the site Brownhill Cemetery was problematic. Names define people, places, and things. Animate names honor people, while inanimate ones define locations. The etiology of the Brown Hill Cemetery originated from the property's former owners. The "hill" part of the name is designated by the elevation of the land, about 60 feet above sea level. It is higher than the elevation of the Cherry Hill Cemetery, about 50 feet above sea level, while the Sycamore Hill Baptist Church Cemetery is about 48 feet above sea level.[113]

Bessie Brown stated that the "W. B. Brown Estate would raise no objections whatsoever in using the family name for this cemetery . . . . At present, (it was

---

[112] Sicley. Ibid, April 24, 2012.
[113] Sam Barber. Christian Lockamy. Interview, 2011.

decided) to name the colored cemetery BROWNHILL."[114] Brown Hill is a two-part word and should be represented as such. The decision to spell the name of the cemetery "Brownhill" instead of "Brown Hill" perhaps misrepresents and dishonors the intent of the Brown family. Additionally, Brown Hill is sequential and in conformity with the names of the Sycamore Hill Baptist Church and the Cherry Hill Cemeteries.

When one visits the Visitors and Convention Bureau in Greenville, especially foreigners, one might be surprised to learn that after almost 250 years of the founding of the town of Greenville, it has no official historical sites for its Afro-American citizens. History tells us that Negroes, Blacks, or Afro-Americans played no marginal influence in the growth and development of Greenville and made it into the "hub" of eastern North Carolina.[115] To erect statues of selected Negroes and place them in strategic locations around the city, as well as to reconstruct the Bell Tower destroyed by an arsonist's torch at the Sycamore Hill Baptist Church, would be an impressive beginning and would shatter the "illusion of inclusion" myth of Negroes by many of its citizens.

When the Southside Group invited me to do a presentation, the invitation was deferred to Dr. Shelva Davis. Her presentation was outstanding. Confident that my services would no longer be needed, my interests became diversified. However, persistence from the chair and her friends persuaded me to reconsider. Reflecting on my experience while exploring some possibilities for upgrading the Greenwood Cemetery in New Bern, NC (Mrs. Mary Peterkin, Director), my attention focused on the Brown Hill Cemetery, a cemetery in need of much attention. My initial vision was to encourage the group to partner with the Public Works Department to help upgrade and to beautify the Brown Hill Cemetery. However, further investigation suggested that the Southside Group would benefit the citizens more by motivating and galvanizing the City Council to establish and develop four contiguous properties as historical sites on Howell Street. And even though there is a marker at the Downtown Common area where black folks lived, worked, and died, the current marker makes no reference to a black presence in the area and is blocked by huge shrubs. It merely says "Town Common." So, as soon as this generation of blacks dies off, and if no historical records have been chronicled, future generations of Greenvillians, especially blacks, will have lost a vast and rich historical past.

---

[114] J. O. Duval, City Clerk. "Naming of the Brown Hill Cemetery." *Minutes of City Council*, Greenville, NC, January 31, 1943, Book 6, p. 440.

[115] Thomas W. Young, Staff Correspondent. "Greenville's Spirit of Community Enterprise Has Counter-Part Among Negroes in Hub of Eastern Carolina." JOURNAL AND GUIDE, Norfolk, VA, August, 10, 1929, p. 9.

Now that the city has committed itself to upgrade Norris Street, a short contiguous street connecting Skinner and the Brown Hill Cemetery, at a cost of about $35,000,[116] it is conceivable that this area just might survive.

To create a partnership between the Southside Senior Group and the Public Works Department could be a herculean leap and a mutual benefit and healing process to long simmering race relations problems. There are, of course, some immediate major improvements that should be done with dispatch to help bridge this gap:

- Uppermost is to map the Slave Burying Ground of the few remaining markers at the Colored Cemetery, and the Cooper Field Sections of the Brown Hill Cemetery.

- Urgent attention should be to replace the cow-pasture gate with an aesthetically pleasing entrance and gate. The entrance and entrance marker should display and reflect historical data of the cemetery's origin and honorees. A similar marker should be placed at the Cherry Hill Cemetery as well.

- Immediate attention should be directed to retooling the borders around the grave plots. The original numbers from 1942 are invisible and in great need of retooling. With laser or imaging technology, the Southside Group can be of great help in locating family members to get permission to retool headstones as well as replace deteriorating vaults and broken headstones in need of urgent repair.

Even with these improvements, mourners will experience an even greater pain, discomfort, and distress when faced with huge mounds of unsightly dirt, rocks, concrete, debris, trucks, and many pieces of heavy-duty equipment stored in full view of the cemetery at the City's Public Works operating center. The City can bring great comfort and relief to the mourners and the black citizens alike by constructing a retaining wall between the cemetery and the Public Works property.

Southside Senior Citizens, with the 250th Anniversary celebration of the founding of the City of Greenville only a few years away, do your part to make sure some black Greenvillians are represented in this important celebration. With much work to be done and only a short time in which to do it, as the adage goes, "*a mind is a terrible thing to waste.*"

---

[116] Bowers, Ibid, 2012.

Despite many years of progress, remember the veil is being slowly lifted but it still has quite a distance to go. It is incumbent upon each of us to do our part in confirming Moses's powerful and passionate instructions to the Israelites: "Remember the days of old, consider the years of many generations: ask the father, and he will show thee, thy elders, and they will tell thee." AMEN!!

APPENDIX I

Post Script to the Brown Hill Cemetery

One of the seminal and fascinating aspects of research is to unearth unexpected yet rich troves of heretofore unexplored bodies of knowledge. An exciting excursion during this project unveiled the legislative authority, political savvy, quasi-intellectual skills, and disingenuous intimidation imposed on Negro citizens during this enforced and legal period of segregation in Greenville. Without the addition of three important appendices to this project, we would be less the wiser of the painful experiences Greenville Negroes encountered and endured during this period.

Since the founding of Greenville in 1771, the Sycamore Hill Baptist Church (SHBC) was the only acknowledged and recognized historical landmark for Negroes in Greenville. The church pictured in (Figure A 1.1) stood at the same location for over 58 years. Like most churches of its day, there was an attached cemetery on the property. The Gateway to the City's Central Business District from the North passed the church, and legend has it that this route inflamed the consciousness of City officials, especially when dignitaries visited the City. We may recall the same sense of embarrassment generated when the City Aldermen proposed putting a Colored Cemetery in what some citizens called the Gateway to the City from the East during the late '30s and early '40s.

When Democratic Presidential nominee John Fitzgerald Kennedy visited the City on Saturday, October 15, 1960, the first sight he saw after crossing the Tar River Bridge was a crowd of Negroes cheering in front of the SHBC.

For the candidate to witness this spectacle must have been a powerful statement for democracy in action, but perhaps embarrassed the sensibilities of Mayor West and his minions. With a vision for a redevelopment program already in progress, officials might have viewed the SHBC and cemetery as no longer a welcoming presence near the Central Business District and were determined to eliminate them at any cost and by any means.

Figure A 1.1. Presidential nominee John F. Kennedy visits Greenville in October, 1960.

Presidential candidate John F. Kennedy's motorcade passes Sycamore Hill Baptist Church, First and Greene Streets.

A rich trove of extant documents supports the lack of accountability and transparency by local officials not only in the decision to build a new Colored school on the south side of the City, but also in other areas, especially in the urban renewal area. Records retrieved from diverse sources such as City Council *Minutes*, THE DAILY REFLECTOR, letters and reports in the Special Collection and the Carolina Room at the East Carolina University, an East Carolina University Master's Thesis, and personal eye witness accounts from former on-site individuals and others tell a story of government that served powerful special interests.

Truncated excerpts of actual communications and events that include the Board of Education, the City Council, the Shore Drive Rehabilitation Commission, and the Sycamore Hill Baptist Church Pastor and Board of Trustees tell a tale of government in the shadows. The process to recreate these facts was challenging, educational, fascinating, and extraordinarily illuminating. To witness and to review the behavior of public officials' reliability and integrity when sworn to uphold the public trust of accountability and transparency in dealing with tax-payer dollars was, indeed, troubling, irresponsible and baffling. Perhaps because of the culture of distrust among politicians, public trust among City officials is no less problematic today. The process of collecting data for this project developed in stages and took a few years for completion.

Noteworthy, is how Negro citizens were disregarded, disrespected, and uninformed for generations before the Kennedy visit. When building a school and a gymnasium, among other decisions, on designated cemetery property specifically purchased for burying blacks in southwest Greenville, City officials bent laws, policies and processes to fit their plans. Cemeteries, churches and schools were revered institutions within the black community. And albeit needed, many citizens saw the process of constructing a school and a gymnasium on designated sacred property for a cemetery as sacrilege and a disregard for an eternal peaceful resting place after lives spent in suffering.

As may be seen from a 1939 resolution, the designated and specific purpose for purchasing the Brown Hill Cemetery was to bury colored citizens. Therefore, many in the black community viewed the action taken by the Aldermen as violating the human dignity and sacred purpose of the land and the trust of the colored citizens by constructing a school and a gymnasium on this special piece of cemetery property.

That resolution states:

> . . . The Board of Aldermen of the City of Greenville in regular session on the 22nd day of June, 1939 authorized and empowered the Cemetery Committee of said Board to purchase a site for a Negro Cemetery from the heirs of W. B. Brown for a price not to exceed $3,000.00 . . . .[117]

The Brown Hill Cemetery property surfaced as early as 1946 as an appropriate place to build a school. In that year, the Board of Education approached the City about donating a portion of the cemetery for constructing a school to reduce student overcrowding on the City's south side. On December 3, 1946, less than a decade after the City purchased the Brown Hill Cemetery for the express purpose of burying colored citizens, *Minutes* of a regular Board of Education meeting record:

---

[117] J. O. Duval, City Clerk. "Purchase of Brown Hill Cemetery." *Minutes of City Council,* Greenville, NC, July 6, 1939, p. 94, par. 5.

It was brought to the attention of the Board [of Education] by the superintendent that three grades were now being taught in the auditorium of the C. M. Eppes School and that some additional space must be provided. He pointed out the fact that there is no school building for negroes in the southern part of Greenville and furthermore that the town owns thirteen (13) acres of land bought for playground purposes in South Greenville (Brown Hill Cemetery property) and that it is a possibility that a building could be built there. The Board took this matter under advisement and consideration. It took no action at this time.[118]

But planning for the land did not end with the school board's decision not to act. In 1947, City Council passed an ordinance that stated: "No mausoleum, tomb, building or other structures of any kind shall be erected on any lot within said cemetery; [Greenwood] . . . under penalty of the law."[119]

Perhaps the Greenwood Cemetery property was perceived as being pure and Holy. One would assume that since the Brown Hill Cemetery was owned and the latest acquisition by the City, officials would have respected the sacredness of Brown Hill Cemetery and applied the same ordinance as was applied to the Greenwood Cemetery. The implication being that we can defile the Brown Hill Cemetery with impunity but not the Greenwood Cemetery. The City seems to have violated the spirit of its own 1939 resolution (which has lower legal standing than an ordinance) when constructing the school on the Brown Hill property. By constructing a school and a gymnasium on the Brown Hill Cemetery, apparently the Brown Hill resolution and the sacred ground were sacrificed for the convenience or control by the City and the Board of Education.

By owning the Brown Hill Cemetery property on the Greene Place in southwest Greenville where many Negroes lived, worked, died, and were buried, the City apparently had little or no respect for the colored people's sacredness for the cemetery but viewed ownership as the legal right to "take" the property for the "greater good" to build a colored school.

At the time, there were no Negroes on the Board of Education. Whether this information was circulated among the Negro citizenry to build a Negro school in the southern part of the City is unknown. But there was some discussion about building a Negro school in the southern part of the City among the Board

---

[118] J. H. Rose. "School Building for Negroes." *Minutes of the Board of Education*, Greenville, NC, December 3, 1946, Book 2, p. 215.

[119] J. O. Duval, City Clerk. "An Ordinance Adopting, Rules and Regulations for the Control of Greenwood Cemetery and Providing Penalties Thereto." *Minutes of City Council*, Greenville, NC: June 17, 1947, Book 7, Section 7, p. 248.

of Education and City officials. On April 29, 1948, in an effort to address the overcrowding condition in the Negro school.

> ... the [School] Board visited the site in south Greenville across from the negro cemetery, which site is owned by the City of Greenville and used as a playground for negroes. The Board inspected this site for the purpose of determining whether or not an elementary school for negroes should be built on this site. After considerable discussion it was moved and passed unanimously that the City Council be asked for permission to erect an elementary school on the site mentioned above.

> The superintendent brought up the matter of employing an architect to study the needs of the Greenville Schools and began to make temporary plans. He reported that the local architect, Mr. James W. Griffith, wished to talk to the Board and Mr. George R. Berryman, the architect who built all the Greenville Schools, likewise wished to talk to the Board about employment. There was some discussion then as to whether or not the Board was under any obligation to Mr. Eric Flanagan. It was then decided to have these architects appear at a School Board meeting on May 13.[120]

The school board moved quickly. On May 6, 1948, "Mr. Rose asked that the city approve the building of a six-room school on the Brown Hill land for a primary school for negro children."[121]

By February, 1949, the School Board's efforts to eliminate the shortage of classroom space for Negro students brought further activity:

> The Board, accompanied by the architect and superintendent of schools, first went to the Cooper Field site in south Greenville which is the proposed site for the new elementary school for negroes. At this point the Board looked at the site and the plans drawn by the architect. The architect told them that this unit was the first unit of a three-unit building to be placed on the fourteen-acre site. The superintendent stated that this building was to take care of children from the fifth grade down, living in the southern part of Greenville,

---

[120] Duval, Ibid, p. 225.
[121] J. O. Duval, City Clerk. "Build a School for Negro Children." *Minutes of City Council,* Greenville, NC, May 6, 1948, Book 7, p. 507.

and that this building, when completed, will take the pressure off the C. M. Eppes School where three classes are now taught in the auditorium. The superintendent stated that this was the most urgent program in the entire school system . . . . Money would come from . . . bonds which were issued in 1940.[122]

On April 8, 1949, bids for school construction were announced in THE DAILY REFLECTOR. According to the Board's *Minutes*, "The lowest bid went to O. W. Godwin for $75,444 to construct the elementary school."[123]

Evidently, however, there were legal problems with the proposed use of the 1940 bond funds. State intervention became necessary because, according to the *Minutes*:

> . . . the Supreme Court of North Carolina had rendered a decision on the question of the validity of the $250,000 in bonds voted in 1940. . . . The Court held that the Bonds could now be issued, provided that they were used for the purpose of erecting new buildings and purchasing new sites therefor.

> The superintendent reported that the Greenville School District would receive $51,000 from the $25,000,000 appropriation by the State of North Carolina for the school buildings and that the State Board of Education had also approved a loan of $30,000 to the Greenville School, making a total of $81,000 available for building a new south Greenville elementary school in case the bond issue money is delayed. Today is contract signing day for the new building at a cost of $75,444. It was moved and passed that the chairman is authorized with the architect to execute all the contracts for the new building:

General Construction, O. W. Godwin	$64.887.00
Electrical Wiring, Hub Electric	$1,672.00
Plumbing, R. E. Deans	$4,537.00
Heating-Taking ALT, #1, W. M. Wiggins	$4,348.00
Total	$75,444.00[124]

---

122 J. H. Rose. "Architect and Superintendent to Cooper Field." *Minutes of the Board of Education*, Greenville, NC, February 9, 1949, Book 2, p. 233.

123 Rose, Ibid, April 8, 1949, Book 2, p. 237.

124 Rose, Ibid, Book 2, p. 239.

A perceived unlawful and untrustworthy act by Board attorneys prompted the following response: "Board challenged the bills submitted by Mr. S. B. Underwood, Jr., and Mr. Lee, County and City attorneys for securing bond issue money for City schools." It was moved and passed unanimously that the School Board "...meet on January 11, 1950, in the High School library for the purpose of receiving bids on furniture and equipment for the South Greenville Negro Elementary School."[125]

At that meeting:

> After a long discussion with the representatives of the various companies followed by a discussion with the teachers present the Board authorized the purchase of the following equipment for the South Greenville Elementary School.

> From Universal Equipment Company $3049.50 and from A. D. Whitney Company, Inc., $1144.00 worth of furniture was purchased.[126]

> With the South Greenville Elementary School construction in an advanced stage,

> The superintendent reported that the South Greenville School would be ready for occupancy on the first day of May and wished permission to move in at that time. It was then moved and passed unanimously that the South Greenville School be occupied on May 1 provided the architect would make an agreement in writing with the contractors as to the unfinished portion of the building.[127]

Confirmation for the opening of the South Greenville Elementary School was recorded in the Board Minutes on April 27, 1949:

> The superintendent reported that the South Greenville School would be ready for occupancy on Monday, May 1, and that the architect had gone over the building with the superintendent and the contractors and reached an agreement whereby the building could be occupied by that time although not entirely complete and

---

125 Rose, Ibid, December 15, 1949, Book 2, p. 249.
126 Rose, Ibid, Book 2, p. 251.
127 Rose, Ibid, Book 2, p. 255.

that permanent payment would be withheld until such time as the architect reported the building entirely complete. It was then moved and passed unanimously that the building be used on Monday, May 1. The superintendent requested that the members of the Board be present on Monday, May 1, for the opening of the new school.[128]

Another story from the 1960s illustrates a lack of local government transparency and cultural violence against Greenville's Negro citizens. As the story unfolds, some citizens of the community and City Council members were persuaded that a slum area next to the Central Business District where Negroes lived, worked, died, and buried their dead needed to be redeveloped. Under the name of the Shore Drive Rehabilitation Project, former residents ultimately concluded that the project was really a surreptitious way to move colored citizens away from the Downtown area, which was only less than a half-mile from the Central Business District.

An examination of archival documents and conversations with former Downtown residents offer convincing evidence that the Shore Drive Rehabilitation Project Commission's rationale was unreasonable and a very poor reason to advance the project. Therefore, they believe that the action taken by the City, especially with the Commission, deserves further scrutiny and inquiry. Based on the passing of time and the extant documentation, many former residents believe they were betrayed and welcome an investigation and re-evaluation of the story. Former residents also believe that to uncover the true story of the Shore Drive Rehabilitation Project Commission in tandem with City officials will bode well for history and for future generations.

In 1949, Title I of the Housing Act of the Housing Urban Development Authority was established by the Federal government for the purpose of helping cities provide better housing conditions for its citizens. In 1958, Mayor S. Eugene West was elected Mayor of the City of Greenville. He firmly believed that the City could benefit from an Urban Renewal program. With dispatch, he appointed a Commission with the authority to investigate, study, and submit a proposal to the Housing Urban Development Authority for an Urban Renewal Project Grant. The City Council action reads:

> On December 18, 1958, the Greenville City Council called a special meeting . . . to appoint a Commission to establish a Greenville Urban Renewal Program. The City authorized and activated a Development Commission, named the Shore Drive Redevelopment Commission and the Greenville Housing Authority to implement plans for the

---

128   Rose, Ibid, Book 2, p. 259.

federally funded program. The Commission consisted of: H. L. Hodges, Jr., F. Badger Johnson, J. H. Rose, M. E. Cavendish, and J. D. McGloan.[129]

In establishing the Commission,

> ...The committee requested and received technical and organizational support from Federal and private agencies such as Mr. T. V. Connerat and Mr. Austin, Representative of the Federal Housing Administration of the Urban Renewal Program. These individuals came to Greenville to get the Urban Renewal Program organized.[130]

Additional advisors were used to support the committee:

> ...The committee requested and received high-powered, pre-eminent, top-shelf, expert technical and organizational support from Federal and private agencies. Mr. Earl Stapleton, a Field Service Director of the National Association of Real Estate Boards met to inform the Pitt County Board of Realtors and the Commission on how to survey property. Mr. Dean W. Dittmer, Executive Secretary of Build America Better Council, came and met with Greenville officials. Also, Mr. Paul Guthery of Charlotte Build America Council along with an official of the Housing and Home Finance Agency Regional Office of Atlanta jointly addressed public meetings in Greenville.[131]

Many other consultants made appearances and or advised the Commission through verbal and written communications. From the evidence, City Council members requested and received an inordinate amount of professional advice from a variety of sources, including advice from the Commissions at Norfolk, VA, and Goldsboro, NC.

In spite of all the expert professional knowledge and experience assembled by the Commission, faith and trust in God, the Power of Prayer and the Holy Spirit empowered Reverend B. B. Felder and the SHMBC Trustees to ultimately

---

129 H. H. Duncan, City Clerk. "Special Meeting to Appoint an Urban Renewal Commission." *City Council Minutes,* Greenville, NC, December 18, 1958, Book 8, p. 520.

130 H. H. Duncan, City Clerk. "Urban Renewal Program of Greenville." *City Council Minutes,* Greenville, NC, December 4, 1958, Book 8, p. 520.

131 Duncan, Ibid.

prevail in the struggle to confront the challenges and experts of government officials. On the face of being sworn City officials, Rev. Felder and the Board of Trustee's trusted their public officials to be honorable and upright men in exercising their sworn public trust to carrying out their legislative duties on behalf of all citizens. As Christians and as religious leaders, they should have followed God's Command to, "Trust No Man," but "Trust but Verify," man's every utterance.

By the 1960s, the Sycamore Hill Baptist Church Cemetery had become an impediment to the growth and development in the designated Shore Drive Rehabilitation Project area. The SHBC Cemetery figured prominently in the obstruction of this progress. The edict that 42 identified bodies at the SHBC Cemetery must be re-interred at the Brown Hill Cemetery or another location within Pitt County became "gospel" within the Commission, City government, and federal Housing and Urban Development (HUD) officials. With the purchase of the Brown Hill Cemetery in 1939, the specific language in a resolution passed by members of City Aldermen sworn to uphold and carry out the Laws of the State of North Carolina stated: "WHEREAS, the Board of Aldermen of the City of Greenville has agreed to purchase a site for a Negro Cemetery from the Heirs of W. B. Brown ..."[132]

As may be seen from the resolution, the designated and specific purpose for purchasing the Brown Hill Cemetery was to bury colored citizens and not to construct a building. Even so, forces within the city were at work to push development no matter what. During the Shore Drive Rehabilitation Project of the 1960s, SHBC was torched by an unknown and still unidentified arsonist on February 13, 1969.

Forty-two bodies were later re-interred to the Brown Hill Cemetery in October, 1969. With mission accomplished and with grandiose plans for the rehabilitation project already in progress to revitalize and redevelop the area with residential, commercial, and municipal improvements, the project outcome was a disappointing disaster. The area became a wasteland whose designers squandered thousands upon thousands of tax-payer dollars.

In contrast to the membership on the Board of Education that pushed the desecration of the Brown Hill Cemetery in the 1950s, three Negroes were on the Shore Drive Rehabilitation Project Commission. Transparency and accountably were completely jettisoned when applying for a HUD grant to support the project. The practices were so bad in the City that one writer stated that the Greenville officials and the Shore Drive Commission created a legacy of distrust

[132] J. O. Duval, City Clerk. "Purchase of Colored Cemetery." *Minutes of City Aldermen.* Greenville, NC, July 6, 1939, Book VI, p. 94.

that has plagued Greenville to this day. The Board of Education's aggressive move to abort the designated purpose of the Brown Hill Cemetery and the Shore Drive Rehabilitation Commission's disingenuous behavior exercised when executing the "NOT TO BE ACQUIRED AGREEMENT" (NTBA) with the SHBC compelled an appendix to this project, expanding it far beyond the boundaries of its intended purpose.

A close examination of the available documents covering the Board of Education and the Shore Drive Rehabilitation Project's machinations revealed an alarming and disturbing pattern of abusive use of procedures, especially the Shore Drive Rehabilitation Commission and the City of Greenville officials. In all probability, honest and open discussions about the SHBC and Brown Hill Cemetery could have very well been avoided or even eliminated the hostile environment that was created. A representative sampling of archival records strongly suggests that the controversy and tensions created between the Shore Drive Commission and the SHBC resulted from the disingenuous position taken by Commissioners and City officials when executing the NTBA with SHBC officials. Although no official application of the Shore Drive Rehabilitation Commission submitted to Housing and Urban Development Authority (HUD) has surfaced, the *First and Second Annual Reports* of the Project, N.C.R-15, show detailed and specific plans obviously contained in the HUD application, but omitted from the September 16, 1963, document NTBA signed and attested to by the SHBC officials.

Unfortunately, the faith and trust church officials put in man were betrayed by the Commission and City officials when the Commission defaulted on the NOT TO BE ACQUIRED AGREEMENT signed and attested to by the SHBC. The church was blindsided when the Commission in 1968 authorized construction of a retaining wall blocking the entrance to the church without church officials' knowledge or authority.

Figure A 1.2. Construction in front of Sycamore Hill Baptist Church in 1968

Shore Drive Rehabilitation Commission authorized construction of a retaining wall blocking the entrance to the church without church officials' knowledge in 1968.

Despite the myriad of professional and governmental support provided to the Shore Drive Commission, it did not lessen the confusion and ineptness of the Commission when navigating HUD's complex administrative maze. Therefore, it is not surprising that several official reports concluded that the Redevelopment Commissioners remained ill-prepared to understand and carry out the complex administrative duties required by HUD. One special publication specifically charged, targeted, and singled out Greenville Commissioners as an example of a group of unprepared Commissioners unable to meet the challenges of federal funding requirements:

> . . . Many Commissioners lacked an understanding of local problems and that misinformation given by local politicians who tried to panic people against urban renewal along with other major problems. But at times it looked like it (rehabilitation) would never happen, but it has—Greenville's hotly fought Shore Drive Project went into execution in October 1963.[133]

---

[133] Ruth L. Mace. *Urban Renewal Program in North Carolina.* Chapel Hill, NC: Institute of Government Press, 1962.

Indeed, the Urban Renewal program in Greenville was a hotly contested one. An article in The DAILY REFLECTOR stated, "It is true that the issue (urban renewal and slum clearance) proved to be one of the most controversial public questions ever to face the citizens of Greenville."[134] Several groups opposed urban renewal. The two most vocal opponents were the Property Owners Association headed by Mr. Charles Cobb and Mr. John Grier and the Neighborhood Group led by Mr. J. J. Perkins and Dr. John Wooten.[135] Mayor S. Eugene West led a group of adamant citizens committed to redeveloping, destroying, and displacing Downtown citizens' homes, businesses, and the SHBC.

On December 20, 1960, Mayor West called a special meeting—perhaps a pre-public hearing of citizens—to approve Notice of Authorizing for a Public Hearing to be set for January 5, 1960.

A petition signed by 43 residents for the purpose of Creating a Housing Authority in the City of Greenville, was read by Mayor West. The petition read:

> We, the undersigned residents of the City of Greenville, North Carolina, file this petition under and pursuant to the 'Housing Authority Law' of the State of North Carolina (Chapter 456, Public Laws of North Carolina, 1935), and hereby represent and state that insanitary and unsafe dwelling accommodations exist in the City of Greenville, North Carolina, that there is a lack of safe and sanitary dwelling accommodation in said City available for all the inhabitants thereof and particularly for person of low income, and that there is need for a Housing Authority to function therein.
>
> WHEREFORE, in attestation of the above and foregoing, we have hereunto subscribed our names and set opposite the same our places of residence in the City of Greenville, North Carolina, this 17th day of December, 1960.

134 "Greenville Has Made the Decision." THE DAILY REFLECTOR, Greenville, NC, May 4, 1961, p. 4.
135 Alvin Taylor. "Brand New City Public Housing Authority Appointed and Sworn." THE DAILY REFLECTOR, Greenville, NC, May 5, 1961, p. 1.

	Names	Address
1.	Thad Leggett	114-B W. 10th St.
2.	Dennis Lee	1404 Chestnut St.
3.	W. C. Taylor, Jr.	233 Pineview Dr.
4.	A. E. Murrell	401 Nash St.
5.	Mrs. A. E. Murrell	401 Nash St.
6.	W. H. Davenport	1407 W. 4th St.
7.	George S. Coffman	1801 Forrest Hills Dr.
8.	J. D. McGlohon, Jr.	315 Rutledge Rd.
9.	Grover C. Fowler, Jr.	1207 S. Overlook Dr.
10.	Leon L. Moore, Jr.	E. 5th St.
11.	Douglas Allen	2403 Dickerson Ave.
12.	William Hadden, Jr.	1042 W. Rock Springs Rd.
13.	Andrew Best, M. D.	1208 W. 4th St.
14.	Dr. C. Rudolph Graves	101 E. First St
15.	W. E. Flanagan	1026 W. 5th St.
16.	Ellis Brown	202 Reade St.
17.	Mrs. Amelia S. Capehart	109 S. Greene St.
18.	D. D. Garrett	611 Albemarle Ave.
19.	Mrs. Thelma Shepard	201 Ford St.
20.	Mrs. Odessa Johnson	301 Reade St.
21.	Edward M. Hagan	109 Boyd St.
22.	Mrs. Lillie Shiver	614 Clark St.
23.	Mrs. Maebell King	1404 B Green St.
24.	Mrs. Mary P. Smith	416 Bonners Lane
25.	Mrs. Annie Pugh	1415 W. 6th St.
26.	Mrs. Annie F. Little	1108 A. Pitt St.
27.	J. C. Taylor	1722 Longwood St.
28.	William H. Wallace	307 Evans St.
29.	Robert E. Cramer	1408 Evergreen St.
30.	Mamie Barnhill	213 S. Reade St.
31.	John B. Smith	415 Cadillac St.
32.	Mrs. R. L. Kearney	614 Clark St.
33.	Mrs. Vivian K. Shiver	614 Clark St.
34.	Richard M. Ottoway	495 E. 5th St. Apt. 1 E
35.	John W. Drake, Jr.	406 E. 4th St.
36.	Alberta C. Speights	1208 W. 4th St.
37.	Sarah A Mumford	1208 W. 4th St.
38.	John S. Whichard	411 Elm St.
39.	Mrs. Mary L. Butler	113 N. Greene St.
40.	Miss Hattie L. Porter	113 N. Greene St.

41. W. C. Sapp   1311 W. 4th St.
42. Johnnie L. Mitchell   614B Tyson St.
43. Ruth M. Staton   1206 Colonial Ave.[136]

It is believed many of these citizens volunteered to attend the meeting with the intent of signing the petition for the purpose of determining the need for a Housing Authority in Greenville, not to give the City the authority to use eminent domain to destroy, dismantle, and redevelop the beloved Downtown area. Apparently the objective of the plan suggests yet another disingenuous way City officials avoided accountability and transparency.

Another public meeting was held to feel the pulse of community support for an Urban Renewal and Slum Clearance Project before a referendum held on May 2, 1961. At the hearing, the urban renewal and slum clearing plans were met with disappointment. But since the Mayor was adamant about starting an Urban Renewal Movement, the success of the citizen groups apparently drove Mayor West to initiate an aggressive and hard-fought campaign to win the hearts and minds of the citizens to approve the Urban Renewal and Slum Clearance Project. This initiative consisted of full, half and quarter page ads in THE DAILY REFLECTOR, numerous commercials on radio and television, the use of bull horns in many neighborhoods, and many Town Hall-type meetings around the City. This aggressive move thwarted the momentum of the citizens' groups. Despite the strong due diligence efforts and persuasive appeal by these groups, the Urban Renewal programs won voter approval on May 2, 1961 by only a narrow margin. Mayor West, however, to his dismay, was defeated by Charles M. King. The voter tabulations were as follows:

FOR:	URBAN REDEVELOPMENT AND SLUM CLEARANCE	1,974
AGAINST:	URBAN REDEVELOPMENT AND SLUM CLEARANCE	1,872
FOR:	CREATING A HOUSING AUTHORITY	1,989
AGAINST:	CREATING A HOUSING AUTHORITY	1,598[137]

---

[136] W. N. Moore, City Clerk. "Special Meeting Authorizing for Public Hearing." *Minutes of City Council,* Greenville, NC, December 20, 1960, Book 7, p. 429-431.

[137] S. Eugene West, City Council. "Canvass of Election Returns." *Minutes of City Council,* Greenville, NC, May 3, 1961, Book 7, p. 466-466A.

At the caucus;

> Councilman Harvey was very much concerned ... that ballots were thrown out due to undecided choice of the voters, and since this election was the largest in Greenville's history, he requested a re-count ... to determine the needs for Public Housing, due to 'human error' possibility. Mr. James W. Lee and Mr. Milton Williamson advised the Council that (they) were present and helped in the tabulation of the ballots and felt it was satisfactory and a re-count was not necessary.[138]

With the Redevelopment Commission established by voter approval, the Commission prepared and submitted a proposal to HUD characterizing the targeted area as the "Tenderloin District"[139] of the City. A number of former Downtown residents were outraged, in total disbelief, and visibly shaken to learn that the Shore Drive Commission had characterized their beloved Downtown community in this way. Ironically, perhaps, three Commission members who orchestrated and prepared the HUD application were from the black community, namely, Dr. Andrew A. Best, physician; Mr. M. Donovan Phillips, a mortician and funeral director; and Mr. John H. Bizzell, a Trustee of the SHBC.[140] There is no evidence to suggest that these men opposed the insulting characterization of the Downtown area. Several residents stated that the Downtown community was a very close-knit one whose sole objectives were to educate and to empower their children to become responsible, productive, and moral citizens.

The Chamber-Merchants Association also pushed for the renewal: "Downtown merchants faced with increasing competition from shopping centers, realized something had to be done to make downtown Greenville attractive."[141] With the Common only a quarter of a mile from the Downtown area and given that most or all of the citizens shopped or worked for the merchants, uprooting them from their community was a slap in the face for the loyalty they had given to the Downtown merchants.

Although religious activities were hegemonic within the community, as in all communities and for some citizens, secular activities sometimes trump

138 Ibid, p. 466.
139 Cole, Jenest & Stone. "Past-A Brief History." Greenville, NC, December 7, 2009, p. 1.
140 Reverend W. J. Hadden, Chairman. "First Annual Report by the Redevelopment Commission of the City of Greenville, 1960-1961." p. 4.
141 "Greenville Decided to Revamp its Downtown in Major 1965 Action." THE DAILY REFLECTOR, February 25, 1967, p. 10.

sacred ones. Several former residents openly verbalized their disbelief that City officials characterized the Downtown area as the "Tenderloin District." If such characterization was to be believed, then, they cite that much of the blame lay squarely in the face of white men whose daily visits to the pleasure houses in the area set the standard. There were at least two widely known pleasure houses, one on Third Street, and the most popular and preeminent one was located at 102 Side Street. The property was owned by Ms. Margaret Tucker, (white) since 1933, and was rented and operated by Ms. Lillian G. Barrett, (white) aka Ms. Elizabeth.[142]

The process of submitting an application to HUD for federal dollars was long, arduous, detailed and complex. Perhaps to impress, to garner support, and to strengthen the proposal as a blighted area, the Redevelopment Commission's Proposal, accompanied by several photos of horrific slum conditions which were perhaps not taken within the area, included the following:

- Widespread building dilapidation—85% substandard to warrant clearance;
- Streets inadequate to meet local traffic needs, as well as downtown traffic;
- Residences mixed with commercial uses, producing an undesirable environment for dwelling uses and also limiting commercial expansion;
- Conversion of residential structures to commercial use;
- Lots with inadequate width and depths for proper use;

This 57.4-acre slum area conditions were described in 1961:

- 3.7% of City population;
- 4.6% of City dwelling units;
- 8.8% of dwelling fires in City;
- 6.0% of police complaints in City;
- 5.0% of police arrests in City;
- 2 TB cases of 54 in County;
- 17 TB cases of 137 from 1951-1960;
- 17 cases of venereal diseases of 264 in County;
- 1 case of infant mortality of 64 in County;
- 7 cases of illegitimacy of 292 in County;

---

[142] H. Ernest Miller, ed. *The Greenville North Carolina City Directory*. Ashville, N.C.: The Piedmont Press, 1965, p. 345.

- 13.5% (and $33,814 per year) of those receiving public assistance in City;
- Only $3,251 in City real estate taxes, but
  -garbage collection for area cost City: $2,930;
  -fire protection for area cost City: $7,090;
  -police protection for area cost City: $10,086;

(THIS IS AN ANNUAL LOSS OF $16,855 TO THE CITY, OR $60 PER DWELLING UNIT.)[143]

Based on its market analysis, the REDEVELOPMENT PLAN further spelled out in specific terms:

- Recreation of the old Town Common as a public recreational park;
- Increased rights-of-way to provide for new street widening;
- Improved sanitary and storm sewers and water distribution system;
- Underground utilities in this downtown area in keeping with existing policies and trends;
- 1,454 off-street and on-street parking spaces to serve this and the downtown area; this compares with 1,118 in the remainder of the Central Business District;
- Areas for new private luxury and efficiency apartments close to downtown and East Carolina College;
- Downtown motel and restaurant;
- An entire block for a department store;
- Areas for new commercial and office development;
- A program to maintain and protect private and public investments in the area from recurrence of the blight that exists today.[144]

The estimated cost for the Shore Drive Redevelopment Project was $2,858,055, with the City responsible for 25% and the Federal Government 75% of the cost. HUD approved the Shore Drive Project in October, 1963.[145]

---

[143] Badger F. Johnson. "Second Annual Report, Shore Drive Redevelopment Project N.C.R-15." Greenville, NC, September, 1962. p. 3-4.

[144] Ibid, p. 5.

[145] Ibid, p. 7.

With an approved HUD grant, the Commission now had the authority to acquire property in the area by either outright purchase or condemnation that was supposed to pay a fair selling price. Officials and members of the Sycamore Hill Baptist Church chose the NOT TO BE ACQUIRED Agreement with the confidence that the church would not be taken.

The "Restriction Agreement" in the NTBA between the Shore Drive Commission and the Sycamore Hill Baptist Church officials is instructive:

> THIS AGREEMENT, made and entered into this 16 day of Sept, 1963 by and between Trustees of the Sycamore Hill Baptist Church, H. F. Foust, Chairman, Alfred Barnhill, David Barnhill, W. H. Davenport, Clarence Bradley, and John W. May, (hereafter called the Property Owners) and the Redevelopment Commission).

> WITNESSETH THAT,

> WHEREAS, The City of Greenville has adopted a Redevelopment Plan prepared by the Redevelopment Commission, pursuant to authority granted it by sections 160-454 et. seq. of the General Statues of North Carolina, for renewal of the area known as the Shore Drive Redevelopment Project in the City of Greenville, including that property in Block 6, Lot 4, owned by the property owners, described as follows:

> In the City of Greenville, Pitt County, North Carolina, and

> BEGINNING at the point of intersection of the Northern property line of First Street with the Eastern property line of Greene Street and running thence Northwardly along the Eastern line of Greene Street 200 feet to the Daniels Southwest corner; running thence Eastwardly and parallel with First Street, a distance of 132 feet to a stake; thence Southwardly and parallel with Greene Street, a distance of 200 feet to the Northern property line of First Street; thence Westerly along the Northern property line of First Street 132 feet to the point of BEGINNING' and

> WHEREAS, the above described property is presently used or will be used substantially in accordance with the Redevelopment Plan as it is expected to exist, and if the continued use of the property in conformity with the Redevelopment Plan can be insured, the

property will not need to be acquired as a part of the Shore Drive redevelopment project (hereafter called "the Project"); and

WHEREAS, the property owner is desirous of retaining the property and benefiting from the enhancement value flowing from the successful completion of the Project; and

WHEREAS, the Redevelopment Commission is willing for the property owner to retain, develop, and use the property, substantially in accordance with the Redevelopment plan for the Shore Drive Redevelopment Project:

NOW, THEREFORE, IN CONSIDERATION of the Redevelopment Commission's carrying out the redevelopment of the Project and enforcing the provisions and restrictions applicable to the balance of the real property in the Shore Drive Redevelopment Project, as set forth in the final Redevelopment Plan for that area during the time that such provisions and restrictions are to be in effect pursuant to said final Redevelopment Plan, the parties agree as follows:

1. The property owner agrees and covenants that the above-described property owned by it shall continue to be used as a church, and for no other purpose, without the written consent of the Redevelopment Commission or it successors, and also agrees and covenants to observe and abide by the provisions as to time of development and restrictions contained in the Redevelopment Plan as to off street parking and loading space, rehabilitation, etc., reference to such Redevelopment Plan is made for a more complete recital of all said restrictions.

2. The Redevelopment Commission agrees not to acquire the above-described property, and to afford the property owner all of the assistance available to owners whose property is acquired so far as legally permissible.

3. This restriction of use shall remain in effect for such time as the provisions and restrictions applicable to the Shore Drive redevelopment Project remain in effect pursuant to the final Redevelopment Plan for that area.

4.   This restriction Agreement shall be a covenant running with the land and shall be binding on the successors in office and assigns of the parties hereto.

5.   The property owner agrees to execute such other documents for recordation as may be necessary for giving effect to the terms of this Restriction Agreement.

6.   The property owner represents that the undersigned own the property hereinabove described in fee simple and no other person, firm, or corporation holds or owns any interest therein, legal or equitable.

IN WITNESS WHEREOF, this instrument has been executed in duplicate by the parties thereto.

SYCAMORE HILL BAPTIST CHURCH
BY _____ (SEAL)
H. F. Foust, Chairman
BY _____ (SEAL)
Alfred Barnhill, Trustee
BY _____ (SEAL)
David Barnhill, Trustee
BY _____ (SEAL)
W. H. Davenport, Trustee
BY _____ (SEAL)
John W. May, Trustee
BY _____ (SEAL)
Clarence Bradley

REDEVELOPMENT COMMISSION OF THE CITY
OF GREENVILLE, NORTH CAROLINA

BY   F. B. Johnson, Jr.
Chairman

ATTEST:
A. E. DUBBER
Secretary[146]

As previously noted, Mr. Bizzell, Trustee at the SHBC; Mr. Phillips, a respected funeral director; and Dr. Best, physician, were members of the Negro community and members of the Board of the Shore Drive Commission that submitted the HUD application. There is no evidence that any of the three alerted the SHBC family of the horrific language in the application. Councilman Charles M. King, the newly elected Mayor, wanted to appoint Rev. J. A. Nimmo to the Commission Board, but rejected him because Rev. Nimmo and the SHBC had fought the establishment on the Urban Renewal Program.[147] The willful deceit communicated in the application by the Commission completely blindsided the SHBC membership when the Commission built a wall on the Greene Street side of the church and completely closed off the entrance to the church in 1968. (Figure A 1.2). By signing the NOT TO BE ACQUIRED AGREEMENT on September 16, 1963, the Sycamore Hill Baptist Board of Trustees, the Pastor, and church members felt secure in the knowledge that the church would remain untouched and outside of the Shore Drive Redevelopment Project.

Several documents necessary for a fuller understanding of the specifics of the HUD proposal were perhaps culled from the collection and are presumed lost or destroyed, especially the application. Attempts to obtain a copy from the Atlanta and District of Columbia HUD offices were unsuccessful. This missing document precludes any effort to ascertain an accurate and true assessment of the NOT TO BE ACQUIRED AGREEMENT and an assessment of the transparency and accountability of the "plan" by the Commission to the SHBC. What can be ascertained is the misrepresentation and misleading facts resulting in confusion, anger and a horrific hostile environment that has lasted until this day.

SHBC officials viewed the Commission's construction of the retaining wall in front of the church as a betrayal of trust and a default of the NOT TO BE ACQUIRED AGREEMENT. To the Commission's credit and before the referendum on May 1, 1961, an article appeared in THE DAILY REFLECTOR

[146] A. E. Dubber, Secretary for the Redevelopment Commission. "Restriction Agreement." Preliminary Inventory of the Greenville Urban Renewal Files, 1959-1977. http//digital.lib.ecu.edu/special/ead/finding aids/0674/Box 32.

[147] Alvin Taylor. "Brand New City Public Housing Authority Appointed and Sworn." THE DAILY REFLECTOR. Greenville, NC, May 5, 1961, p. 1.

noting that ". . . new street patterns would be developed (it is assumed that this pattern would also include widening) . . . ."[148] The Commission telegraphed the plan several times to the SHBC (perhaps verbally) and included it in the Annual Reports, but omitted the plan from the Agreement with the SHBC.

Had the discussions by the Shore Drive Commissioners and City officials been fully accountable and transparent during the initial stages when executing the NTBA with the SHBC pastor and officials regarding the location of the church, the resulting cemetery controversy, in all probability, might have been avoided. The historic records confirm that the controversy and tensions created resulted from detailed and specific plans obviously contained in the HUD application, but omitted from the September 16, 1963, NTBA signed and attested to by the SHBC officials.

Excerpts, however, of the missing original plans are contained in the *Second Annual Report* prepared by the Shore Drive Rehabilitation Commission and submitted to HUD in September, 1962.

> The Redevelopment Commission completed all plans for the Shore Drive Redevelopment Project and submitted them to the Urban Renewal Administration for review. Private development of several sites took more definite plans . . . the Sycamore Hill Baptist Church . . . had agreed in writing, to have their property conform to the proposed Redevelopment Plan for the area. In some cases, this will mean demolishing existing, non-compatible structures, allowing for new street widening, etc. In other cases, such as the church and the radio tower site, they will remain `as is' and will not be acquired so long as the present use remains, and as such, conform to the Plan.[149]

With no original plan or signed written statement to review, it is difficult to know the exact language of those agreements. But it is clear that the plan noted that the Commission would demolish existing and non-compatible structures and would allow for new street widening.

As noted, no reference in the NTBA document with the SHBC contains specific details citing new street patterns, widening of streets, realignment or street improvement or underground utility work due to the location of the church. Yet, the *Second Annual Report* makes it abundantly clear that "street widening

---

[148] Alvin Taylor. "Record Turnout of City Voters Expected To Take Place Tuesday." THE DAILY REFLECTOR, Greenville, NC, May 1, 1961, p. 1.

[149] F. Badger Johnson. *"Second Annual Report, Shore Drive Redevelopment Project N.C.R-15."* Greenville, NC, September, 1962, p. 1-2.

and realignments" were cited in the HUD application. The church membership was apparently uninformed of the plan and was completely blindsided by the Commission's actions.

Archival records show that the church was built in 1916[150] with the approval of City officials and remained in the same location until 1968 without blocking or obstructing City traffic. The two-lane bridge, another rationale for widening the street, was constructed in 1929,[151] well after the church was built. Despite change and growth patterns within the City, former residents said that neither the location of the church nor the construction of the bridge was a logical rationale to obstruct the church entrance. They believed the main rationale for blocking the church entrance and disrupting a way of life for the neighborhood's residents was to relocate Negro citizens as far away from the Central Business District as possible.

With the signing of the NTBA on September 16, 1963, the Board of Trustees and church membership felt secure and confident that the church would remain untouched. This security remained firm until about 1967. But there are no project records extant in the ECU archival collection for the entire year of 1966 and less than a dozen documents, including comments from the Chamber of Commerce in THE DAILY REFLECTOR. Evidence suggests, however, that the Commission contacted church officials several times about rescinding the NTBA during 1967. No action was taken by the church.

It is believed that HUD officials pressured the Shore Drive Commissioners to remain committed to the original "plan" as submitted or else default on the contract. By February 28, 1967, local pressure to sell the church intensified as seen in a request by the Commission to have the church property appraised:

> From the inception of our Shore Drive Project (N.C.R-15) the Sycamore Hill Baptist Church property (acquisition Parcel 6-4) has been 'NTBA.' The reason for accepting this parcel, while valid and reasonable in the beginning, are outweighed by existing project objectives and the future development pattern of the City of Greenville.
>
> Shown on the attached map [not found] is the unavoidable traffic pattern of the City, insofar as it affects and is affected by the Church's location. Greene Street, as shown in blue, will be a one-way South. It is a State Highway, and its necessary widening will put its west curb

---

[150] Lester E. Turnage, Jr. "Property of Sycamore Hill Baptist Church Parcel 4 6." *Minutes of City Council,* Greenville, NC, February 23, 1968, p. 1.

[151] City Historical Marker.

---

against the Church building, without adequate sidewalk. First Street, as shown in red, is the principal East-West thoroughfare in this part of the City. Its widening will leave the Church building protruding so as to constrict First Street and violate our line-of-sight requirements.

There is little doubt that the Church will move. The congregation and board are entirely willing to abandon the structure (which is sound, architecturally good, and aesthetically better than could be financed in these days). But the members no longer live near the Church, adequate parking space cannot be provided, and even if the obstruction to traffic which it creates could be tolerated, access will be extremely difficult when Greene and First Streets are improved in accordance with the development plans.

However, although the Church is free of debt, they have very little capital and are wary of assuming an insuperable obligation in financing a new structure in another part of the City. Most important, and perhaps the only obstruction to the Church's request that the NTBA be abandoned, is our inability or restriction to tell them how much they will probably receive for the land and structure if included in Project N.C.R-15, and how fully they can be reimbursed for unavoidable property loss (furnishings, furniture, etc.) peculiar to the existing structure.

We are certain that the present structure will be abandoned and that with our and the City help a satisfactory site for the new structure can be found. The Church also will readily agree to the removal of the graves on Parcel 6-4 to the nearby municipal cemetery. The Church will not, however, take any positive action unless we can appraise the property and tell them its present fair market value. And, while we must proceed with site improvements and street widening can be removed while our site improvements are in work.

Because of the unusual situation we face in this situation, it is most earnestly requested that we be permitted to have parcel 6-4 formally appraised.[152]

---

[152]   A. E. Dubber. "Assistant Regional Administration, Department of Housing and Urban Development." Greenville, NC, February 28, 1967.

Early on, the Commission appears to have been at odds with City Council over the proposed condemnation. As late as mid July, 1967, THE DAILY REFLECTOR reported:

> Redevelopment commissioners yesterday decided to recommend acquiring the Sycamore Hill Baptist Church at First and Greene Streets, but the City Council balked at the move pending a conference between city councilmen and church officials.[153]

It is believed that sometime by the middle of August, 1967, the Council agreed with the Commission's plan to condemn the SHBC property. A City Resolution states:

> WHEREAS, the redevelopment plan for the Shore Drive Redevelop ment Project, duly established by the Redevelopment Commission of the City of Greenville in conformance with applicable State and Federal Laws after the required public hearing and approved by the City Council of the City of Greenville as required by the general statutes of North Carolina after the required public hearing, contemplated that the property at the Northeast corner of First and Greene Streets in the City of Grenville, owned and occupied by the Sycamore Hill Baptist Church, would not be acquired by the Redevelopment Commission if the continued use of the property in conformity with said redevelopment plan could be insured, and
>
> WHEREAS, every effort has been made by the City and the Redevelopment Commission to provide the necessary widening and realignment of First and Greene Streets without disturbing the church property, and it is reluctantly concluded that the necessary street widenings and realignment cannot be carried out so as to insure the safety and convenience of the citizens of Greenville without removal of a significant portion of the church property, and
>
> WHEREAS, the Church cannot conform to the established and approved provisions of the redevelopment plan for the Shore Drive project:

---

[153] "Councilmen, Church Members to Meet; Sycamore Hill Church decision Still Pends." THE DAILY REFLECTOR, Greenville, NC, July 14, 1967, p. 3.

> NOW THEREFORE BE IT RESOLVED that the City Council approve the exercise by the Redevelopment Commission of its authority contained in the redevelopment plan for the Shore Drive Project to include the ACQUISITION OF THE Sycamore Hill Baptist Church property.[154]

Without the benefit of documentation, heightened activity in 1967 likely signaled the beginning of an intensified move by HUD to hold the Commission responsible to the original plans. It is believed that if the City defaulted, then it would lose thousands of taxpayer dollars. In the meantime, the SHBC became the sacrificial lamb of the Commission's actions. By signing the NTBA, the church unwittingly sounded its death knell by becoming part of suspected longer-run plans to eliminate the neighborhood.

Increased communications were exchanged by the various authorities beginning in March, 1967.

On March 19, 1967, for example, Mr. John T. Edmonds, HUD's Acting Assistant Regional Administration for Renewal Assistance

> . . . authorized you to have the parcel appraised for acquisition . . . . Before we give final approval for acquisition of the parcel, it will be necessary for you to furnish evidence that the graves can be lawfully relocated and furnish information as to the procedure to be followed.[155]

On April 10, 1967, the Department of Housing and Urban Development wrote:

> . . . owners of all NTBA properties have agreed to subject their properties to the controls of the Plan, including the Sycamore Hill Baptist Church, parcel 6-4. However, Item 8 in the Code A609 indicates that the agreement with the church has been revoked. Apparently the parcel will be acquired. Therefore, the Urban Renewal

---

[154] W. N. Moore. "Resolution to Condemn Property." *Minutes of City Council.* Greenville, NC, August 1967, Book 11, p. 466. Greenville Urban Renewal Files. Collection No 674. East Carolina Manuscript Collection, no date.

[155] John T. Edmonds, Acting Assistant Regional Administration for Renewal Assistance. Atlanta, GA, March 10, 1967. From the Greenville Urban Renewal Files, Collection No 647. Greenville, NC: East Carolina Manuscript Collection, J. Y. Joyner Library, East Carolina University.

Plan and affected maps should be changed to show parcel 6-4 as an acquisition parcel.[156]

On May 23, 1967, unable to contact church officials in person or by phone, it is believed that pressure on Mr. Dubber from HUD forced him to send a copy of a letter to the church office requesting that church officials contact him by 5:00 P.M. on May 24, 1967. The letter stated:

> This is not an attempt to bring pressure to bear upon you or any other member of the Sycamore Hill Church or upon that Church as a congregation, but events are moving so rapidly that immediate personal communication is essential.[157]

On June 6, 1967, a desperate communication stated:

> On September 16, 1963, an agreement was signed by the officials of your church and this Commission agreeing that the church property in our Shore Drive Redevelopment Project would not be acquired by the Commission and that the church would conform to all the restrictive covenants and requirements required of developers in the project Area. Since this agreement was signed, however, we have been approached several times unofficially of including the church property in the Project.
>
> Since this church is a "Not To Be Acquired" property, we have no funds or authorization to appraise the church property in order to establish its full market value. When we finally did get authorization from the Department of Housing and Urban Development to appraise this property in order to be able to let you know what we could pay, you refused to allow us to have the property appraised. We would like to be clearly understood that the purpose of this appraisal was not to put any pressure on the church to sell to us but only as a basis for a more intelligent discussion as to the possibilities of the sale. We feel we have a moral obligation to the church to ask you once more whether or not the church desires to remain as is or sell to the Commission. We feel

---

156 Thomas C. Malone, Acting Chief, Processing Control Renewal Assistance Office, "Mr. A. E. Dubber, Executive Director, Greenville Redevelopment Commission." Atlanta GA, April 10, 1967.

157 A. E. Dubber. "Chairman of the Board of Trustees, Sycamore Hill Baptist Church." Greenville, NC, May 23, 1967.

---

it our duty to point out that if you do sell to us we will pay you the fair market value of the land and improvements, pay for all moving expenses, and arrange for the relocation of the graves to the Cherry Hill Cemetery at no expense to the church. We will also assist you in every way possible to find a new location for the church.

Since we must award contracts for street work and other site improvements within the next 30-45 days, time is of the utmost importance and it is necessary that you tell us, in writing, immediately and finally whether you intend to move or remain. If you would like for me or our Chairman to meet with you to answer questions concerning this matter, we will be happy to do so.[158]

An indirect response to Mr. Dubber stated:

I am advised, this date by Chief Henry Lawson that, at a recent quarterly meeting of the Baptist Hierarchy in Pactolus, the powers that be turned down our offer on the relocation of the Sycamore Hill Baptist Church. Mr. Lewis advised Chief Lawson that they think they will get a better offer in the form of a more desirable location.[159]

In a desperate attempt to convince the church to rescind the NTBA, Mr. Dubber solicited the support of Rev. J. A. Nimmo to encourage the SHBC to sell. He wrote:

We have been talking with several members of the Sycamore Hill Baptist Church about including the Church in the Shore Drive Redevelopment Project. It has been suggested to us, by some of the members of the Church that you might be of some help in guiding the Church with this problem.[160]

Mr. Nimmo responded, but it is doubtful whether his support influenced the membership.[161]

---

[158] A. E. Dubber. "David Barnhill, Chairman, Board of Trustees, Sycamore Hill Baptist Church." Greenville, NC, June 6, 1967.

[159] Harry E. Hagerty. "Colonel A. E. Dubber, Executive Director Redevelopment Commission." Greenville, NC, July 5, 1967.

[160] A. E. Dubber. "Rev. J. A. Nimmo." Greenville, NC, June 30, 1967.

[161] Rev. J. Allen Nimmo. "Mr. A. E. Dubber." Camden, NJ, July 19, 1967.

On July 13, 1967, the City Council

> ...proposed a resolution authorizing the Redevelopment Commission to include the acquisition of the Sycamore Hill Baptist Church in the Shore Drive Project.

> The Council stated they feel that every effort should be made to encourage the officials ... to willingly relocate before such a resolution is adopted. Councilman Cox stated that it was his understanding in the beginning of Urban Renewal that this church would not be acquired. Mr. Messick ... stated that the church signed a 'not to be acquired' agreement in which they agreed to conform to the Redevelopment plans ... Several meetings and individual conferences have been held with the Deacons but no agreement has been reached.[162]

On July 31, 1967

> The City Council met with members of the Board of Deacons and Board of Trustees of the Sycamore Hill Baptist Church on Monday July 31, 1967 at 7:30 P. M. in the Church Sanctuary. Those present were: Mayor S. Eugene West, Councilmen Percy R. Cox, Frank G. Fuller, and City Manager Harry E. Hagerty. Members from Sycamore Hill Baptist Church included: Deacons: Pearlie W. Moore, I. A. Artis, Sr., Norman Barnhill, J. W. Maye, J. S. Alexander, Harrison Bradley and Alfred Barnhill. Trustees present included: Andrew Dupree, Warren G. Barnes, Leroy James, George Jackson, David Barnhill and Monty G. Frizzell.[163]

A newspaper story on July 14, 1967, stated, "Commissioners approved a resolution requesting withdrawal of the 'not to be acquired' designation for Sycamore Hill Baptist Church at First and Greene Streets."[164]

---

[162] W. N. Moore. "Resolution To Accelerate the Implementation of the Shore Drive Project (Removal of Sycamore Hill Baptist Church)." *City Council Minutes*, Greenville, NC, July 13, 1967, Book 11, p. 155.

[163] Mayor S. Eugene West. "Meeting of City Council Members with Members of Deacon Board and Board of Trustees of the Sycamore Hill Baptist Church." *City Council Minutes*, Greenville, NC, July 31, 1967, Book. 11, p. 159-161.

[164] "One Parcel of Land Unacquired For Shore Drive." THE DAILY REFLECTOR, Greenville, NC, July 14, 1967, p. 1.

Another story on the same day stated:

> Redevelopment commissioners . . . decided to recommend acquiring the Sycamore Hill Baptist Church at First and Greene Streets but the City Council balked at the move. Officer John Messick explained that the `not to be acquired' designation carried with it a stipulation that the property conform with the overall redevelopment plan.
>
> He said the church building could not be made to conform since widening of the streets would be prohibited if the building stays where it is.
>
> Both Greene Street, in front of the church, and First Street, on the side, must be widened.
>
> If the church is acquired the Redevelopment Commission would offer a price based on appraisals. If church representatives did not agree to the price, a fair selling price could be established through legal proceedings.

The Redevelopment Commission would also assist the church in relocation.[165]

The Commission recommended church sites at The Tar Riverfront,[166] six acres of land at Moyewood,[167] land at the southeast corner of Fifth Street and Memorial Drive,[168] and an area south of the present Pitt County Garage.[169]

On June 13, 1968, the church suggested to the Commission that it was willing to rescind the NTBA and sell the church property for $150.000.00.[170] The Commission countered by requesting that the church furnish two certified

[165] "Sycamore Hill Church Decision Still Pends." THE DAILY REFLECTOR, Greenville, NC, July 14, 1967, p. 1.

[166] Rev. B. B. Felder. "Col. A. A. Dubber." Greenville, NC, December 31, 1967.

[167] James Sutton, City Clerk. "Trustee Board, Sycamore Hill Baptist Church." Greenville, NC, January 9, 1968.

[168] A. E. Dubber. "The Sycamore Hill Baptist Church." Greenville, NC, March 18, 1968.

[169] Matthew T. Lewis. "The Greenville Redevelopment Commission." Greenville, NC, February 25, 1968.

[170] A. E. Dubber. "Mr. Julius LeVonne Chambers, Attorney at Law." Greenville, NC, June 13, 1968; September 18, 1968.

appraisals before the suggestion could be presented to HUD for authorization.
Several appraisals were submitted to the Commission:

Jack Wallace	August 21, 1967	Land:	$14,000.00
		Improvements	$72,000.00
		Total:	$86,000.00
Lester Turnage	March 12, 1968	Land:	$24,000.00
		Improvements:	$53, 160.00
		Total:	$77,160.00
W. Edward Jenkins	June	Land:	$34,848.00
		Improvements	$65, 700.00
		Total:	$100,548.00
Jack Wallace	August 12, 1968	Total:	$50,000.00
	(Revised After Sale of 8th Street Church)		
Lester Turnage	August 21, 1968	Total:	$51, 500.00
Daniel O. Hennigan	January 17, 1969	Land:	$66,600.00
		Improvements:	$188.000.00

At this stage of the negotiations, the church and the Commission had not
rescinded the NTBA.

In contrast to the absence of documents in the collection for 1966, there are
more than 30 for 1968. Except for documents pertaining to appraisals, finding
a suitable relocation site for the church and rescinding the NTBA, the most
intriguing exchanges were between Mr. Dubber and attorney Julius LeVonne
Chambers, lawyers for the opposing parties.

Pressure on the church to rescind the NTBA gained momentum in early
January, 1968. Mr. Patterson and Mr. Godard of HUD's Regional Administration
Office visited Greenville to encourage the church to rescind the NTBA citing
the attitude of the church board as "fickle." [171] Mr. Dubber already had solicited
the support of Rev. Nimmo to help persuade the church to comply with the
Commission's request to rescind the NTBA. Rev. Felder and the SHBC Board
of Trustees refused.

---

[171] A. E. Dubber. "Edward H. Baxter, Regional Administration of HUD." Greenville,
NC, January 22, 1968.

More direct communication to sell the church came on May 13, 1968:

> Nearly two months ago we sent to you an offer to sell the Church property....This letter is not in any way urging you to sell the property to this Commission, and to remind you that this Commission and the City Council have promised you that the property will not be condemned. The purpose . . . is to remind you that the progress of the site improvements in the Shore Drive area have reached the stage where the intersection of First and Greene Streets must be closed. The work will unavoidably close the two streets at their intersection and for a block in all directions . . . . It may well be that this temporary routing will have to be in use for a matter of weeks, and while we regret the inconvenience this will cause you, it cannot further be delayed.

> From your discussion with the City, I am sure you realize that the portion of the Greene Street entrance to your church which is within the right of way to Greene Street, will be lost in the Greene Street widening.[172]

This communication prompted the SHBC to stop negotiating and retain legal services of Attorney Julius LeVonne Chambers of Charlotte, N.C. Attorney Chambers wrote to the Commission Chair, Billy B. Laughinghouse:

> I have been retained by the SHMBC to represent the church in connection with the acquisition of the church property by the Redevelopment Commission of the City of Greenville.

> I have also received a copy of your letter to the church of May 13, 1968, regarding the closing of First and Greene Streets and closing of the Greene Street entrance to the church. While your letter does not indicate that you immediately contemplate instituting condemnation proceeding, I am sure that you agree that the effect of the closing of the streets will deprive the church members of the use of the church and, in effect, constitute a taking. Because of the action that has been taken

---

[172] Billy B. Laughinghouse. "Sycamore Hill Baptist Church." Greenville, NC, May 13, 1968.

by the Commission, the church has found it necessary to acquire other properties in order to carry on the ministry.[173]

The Commissioner's attorney responded to Mr. Chambers' letter on June 13, 1968, with what seems to be lecture:

> In framing a reply to your letter, it is important that you understand something of the background of this problem and the present legal position of the Commission and the Church. When this project was undertaken prior to September, 1963, the Church officially requested that its property be excluded from the redevelopment project. This request was consented to, and the Commission and the Church executed a 'not to be acquired agreement', on September 16, 1963. This agreement has not been altered, rescinded or modified and presently is in full force and effect. Therefore, no part of the Church property is within the bounds of the project, and the Commission has no jurisdiction whatsoever in this matter.
>
> Approximately six months ago, the Commission was approached by officials of the Church with regards to rescinding the 'not to be acquired agreement', of September 16, 1963, coupled with an inquiry pertaining to the inclusion of the Church property in the redevelopment project by way of amendment.
>
> Since the Church itself elected to withhold its property from the project, but now wishes for reasons satisfactory to itself to change its position, it is difficult to see the Redevelopment Commission of the City of Greenville is under any legal or moral burden with regard to the request of the Church.
>
> The temporary closing of Greene Street, referred to in the Commission's letter dated May 13, 1968, will not deny access to the Church. On the contrary, the Commission and the City will make every effort to see the access to the Church is impaired as little as is possible in accomplishing the necessary improvements to the streets upon which the Church property abuts. As the Church was reminded in the Commission's letter

---

[173] Julius LeVonne Chambers, Attorney at Law. "Mr. Billy B. Laughinghouse, Chairman, Redevelopment Commission of the City of Greenville." Charlotte, NC, June 5, 1968.

dated May 13, 1968, a portion of the steps leading to the Greene Street entrance to the Church are in the street right-of-way and will have to be removed in the scheduled improvement of Greene Street. The First Street entrance to the Church is not affected by the street improvements and the sidewalk along the Church property on First Street will not be disturbed.

Finally, we cannot agree that this Commission has done anything which would require the Church to acquire other property to carry on its ministry. The Commission stands ready, willing and able to assist the Church in any way it can. However, you understand, I am sure, that it is a public body discharging a public trust and responsibility, which it is endeavoring to perform within the framework of the rules and restrictions of the Federal Agencies and local agencies involved.[174]

On July 10, 1968, Mr. Chambers responded:

. . . Church had requested that this agreement be resended, that the agreement to resend had been signed by all the members of the Board of Trustees . . . and had been approved by the Redevelopment Commission of the City of Greenville.

In view of the fact that the Church did not realize at that time that it executed the agreement the extent to which the streets were to be developed . . . [this move] will involve taking of property from the Church.[175]

On July 16, 1968, Attorney Hite wrote:

I think it only fair to advise you that the Church officials were fully advised at the inception of its negotiations for the "not to be acquired agreement" that street work would be done at Greene and First Streets, the grades lowered, and the streets widened and the Commission is fully satisfied that the street grade work has no bearing whatsoever

---

[174]   Kenneth G. Hite, Attorney at Law. "Mr. Julius Levonne Chambers, Attorney at Law." Greenville, NC, June 13, 1968.

[175]   Julius Levonne Chambers. "Mr. Kenneth G. Hite and James and Hite Attorneys at Law." Charlotte, NC, July 10 1968.

on any position the Church takes with regards to this action being a "taking" of its property.[176]

Whenever the Shore Drive Commission negotiated with the SHBC in any way, the Commission always cited the NTBA signed by the SHBC on Sept 16, 1963 as "gospel." No place in that "gospel" document does it specify or point out any details of the claims made by the Commission such as to:

1. Street work
2. Lowering grades
3. Street widening
4. Building a retaining wall on Greene Street
5. Building a wood retaining wall by the cemetery
6. Closing the entrance to the church
7. Portion of the church blocking the flow of traffic
8. Church steps abating the widening of the street
9. Completely destroying and removing the church or
10. Constructing utility lines

Since the September 16, 1963 document does not specify the claims referenced by Attorney Hite, the SHBC officials were correct to challenge the Commission on these points as a "taking."

It is unconceivable and outright ludicrous to believe that of the six men on the SHBC Board of Trustees who signed the NTBA, that none understood or could interpret the terms of the NTBA. The qualifications of the Board members were:

- Mr. H. F. Foust, Chairman, Teacher at Eppes High School
- Mr. Alfred Barnhill, Custodian at Fleming School
- Mr. David Barnhill, Teacher at Eppes High School
- Mr. W. H. Davenport, Principal of Eppes High School
- Mr. John W. Maye, Principal of W. H. Robinson High School
- Mr. Clarence Bradley, Employee at Greenville Utilities

The "taking" resulting from the street widening and retaining wall prompted SHBC officials to purchase the Eighth Street Christian Church for $40,000.00

---

[176] Kenneth G. Hite, Attorney at Law. "Mr. Julius Levonne Chambers, Attorney at Law." Greenville, NC, July 16, 1968.

as the new location to worship.[177] The church moved to the new site on Sunday, June 9, 1968.[178]

With the purchase of the Eighth Street Church, Mr. Dubber, in correspondence with Lester E. Turnage on August 13, 1968, noted the move meant that the church now needed revenue and stated that it ". . . appears to us that it should be assumed that they probably are a willing seller."[179]

Meanwhile, communications between Attorney Chambers and Attorney Hite were continuing. In an exchange on August 12, 1968, Attorney Chambers told Attorney Hite:

> . . . The church is in the process of meeting to adopt resolutions agreeing to rescind the agreement between the Commission and the church of September 1963 and requesting . . . that the church site be included in the project and be acquired by the Commission.
>
> I have been advised by the church that the street improvements around the church site have prevented any meetings or use of the church.
>
> I am sure that you are aware the church has acquired another site and has moved the church services to the new site. I am also sure that you are aware that the church needs funds in order to complete the purchase of the new property and to make whatever improvements are needed. Funds for the purchase of the new church site and the improvements were anticipated to be derived from the sale of the old church site.[180]

Confident that the church would sell, Mr. Dubber stated in a letter to HUD on August 16, 1968:

> The enclosed letter indicates that the Sycamore Hill Baptist Church is coming to the point of selling the church to this Commission at its fair market value. This Commission agrees with you that the

---

177   Jack Wallace. "Development Commission." Greenville, NC, August 12, 1968.

178   "Sunday Is Moving Day For Church Members." THE DAILY REFLECTOR, Greenville, NC, June 7, 1968, p. 11.

179   A. E. Dubber. "Lester E. Turnage." Greenville, NC, August 13, 1968.

180   Julius LeVonne Chambers, Attorney at Law. "Mr. Kenneth G. Hite, Attorney at Law." Charlotte, NC, August 12, 1968.

purchase of the property and the removal of the church is essential to the attainment of the project objectives.[181]

Finally, the SHBC agreed to sell the Church property to the Commission on August 17, 1968. "The total price shall be $100,548.00. [The offer stated that] loss or damage to the property by fire or casualty shall be at the risk of the seller until title has been conveyed to the Commission."[182] In retrospect, inclusion of this standard legal clause turned out to be a tragic mistake when an arsonist torched the church in February, 1969.

On August 27, 1968, Mr. Dubber responded to the church's offer to sell the property by stating:

> . . . [Appraisers] believe that the Sycamore Hill Church property is now worth $51,500 at most. As you know, we fixed the acquisition price of this property, based on two separate, competent appraisals, at something over $78.000.
>
> Using Mr. Jenkins' unit price, . . . his estimate of the value of the Church is $76,304, approximately $2,000 less than our established acquisition price.
>
> A very material consideration has developed. In order to secure the structural safety of the Sycamore Hill Church property, we have constructed a concrete retaining wall along the Greene Street side of the building and secured the Greene Street side of the graveyard from erosion. This work is costing us in the neighborhood of $5,000. Because the Church prevents the construction of the north side of First Street in a straight line, it has been necessary for the Greenville Utilities Commission to spend some thousands of dollars in the construction of their new utilities lines around the Church. This cost to the Greenville Utilities Commission cannot be claimed under the City's no cash grant-in-aid contribution to the project and therefore represents some thousands of dollars loss to the City.

---

[181] A. E. Dubber. "Renewal Assistance Administration." Greenville, NC, August 16, 1968.

[182] Sycamore Hills Baptist Church. "Memorandum. Offer of Land Sale, Project No. N.C.R.-15, Parcel No. 6-4." Greenville, NC, August 17, 1968. Preliminary Inventory of the Greenville Urban Renewal Files, 1959-1977 (manuscript Collection #674) http:// digital. Lib.ecu.edu/special/ead/findingaids/0674.

I believe that you would be perfectly safe in informing Mr. Chambers that even in view of the facts above this Commission will stand by its established acquisition price for the property when we have in hand the properly executed offer of sale of land at our established acquisition price of $78,960. And I think that the HUD Regional office will still concur in that price. I call to your attention the letter dated October 11, 1967, from Mayor of the City of Greenville (copy furnished herewith), which could indicate that the City will not agree to . . . the change in our development plan to rescind the Not To Be acquired Agreement covering the Sycamore Hill Church property.[183]

Mr. Dubber's assessment of the situation seems to contradict the Mayor's intent in a letter dated October 11, 1967:

Based on this letter, I would like to request that the Redevelopment Commission proceed immediately with the Shore Drive project, leaving the Church property as is and adjusting the north side of the street so that the street will be narrow in this block as compared with the width in the other blocks. I believe that we can eliminate parking on both sides and by doing so, adequately take care of the movement on traffic in a successful way.[184]

On August 29, 1968, Attorney Hite wrote Attorney Chambers:

I trust you are aware that your client, Sycamore Hill Baptist Church, has recently concluded the purchase of the Church building formerly occupied by Eighth Street Christian Church and are now conducting services in the purchased premises . . . . It is also a fact that the purchase price paid by Sycamore Hill Baptist Church to Eighth Street Christian Church for these premises was $40,000.00.

. . . Mr. Jenkins' unit price will total the [Sycamore Hill] Church property at $76,304.00.[185]

---

183   A. E. Dubber. "Sycamore Hill Baptist Church." Greenville, NC, August 27, 1968.

184   S. Eugene West, Mayor. "Redevelopment Commission." Greenville, NC, October 11, 1967.

185   Attorney Kenneth G. Hite. "Mr. Julius Levonne Chambers." Greenville, NC, August 29, 1968.

Attorney Chambers' response reflected the difference in measurements. Attorney Chambers requested the Commission rescind the NTBA agreement and "… that the Church site be included in the project and that the Church be paid a total of $100,548.00 for the premises."[186]

Up until the time of the fire in February, 1969, records strongly suggest the absence of transparency and accountability on the part of the Shore Drive Rehabilitation Commission. Therefore, the Pastor, the Board of Trustees and the church members of the Sycamore Hill Baptist Church refused to acquiesce to the pressures of the Shore Drive Commission.

On September 18, 1968, correspondence shifted back to the appraisal aspirations of the SHBC. Mr. Dubber wrote to Attorney Chambers:

> We cannot too strongly emphasize that our figures are not 'estimates.' The boundaries of the land have been properly established by a certified land surveyor, and we hold his certificate plat of the premises. The building has also been accurately measured, and we hold drawings showing the exact gross, or outside, dimensions of the church building. The plat of the property also indicates, so far as can be determined, the amount of the Church's land which is encumbered by graves.
>
> I am sure that you and the Church Board understand that this Commission is not trying to secure the Church's property and certainly not trying to beat the Church down on the price. I must point out, however, that if the Church's offer is corrected and if my Commission looks with favor upon the Church's request for the property to be included in the Shore Drive Project and if the City concurs and if RAA approves, it will take us a matter of several months to secure the necessary funds with which to purchase the Church property. We have gone to the not inconsiderable expense of constructing a concrete wall along the Greene Street side of the Church building and a wood retaining wall along the Greene Street side of the graveyard in order to protect the Church's property. And the City has gone to some considerable expense in routing utility lines around the Church's property and adapting the obstruction the Church offers to the street pattern.[187]

---

[186] J. LeVonne Chambers. "Mr. Kenneth G. Hite." Charlotte, NC, September 4, 1968.

[187] A. E. Dubber. "Julius Levonne Chambers." Greenville, NC, September 18, 1968.

Some of the last communications about negotiations addressed the final appraisals and the crucial problem of removing the graves from the SHBC Cemetery to the Brown Hill Cemetery. On January 17, 1969, Mr. David Hennigan wrote:

The site is divided into two sections: (1) church site and (2) gravesite with 42 existing graves on it. The value of the land and building in the final value estimate is as following:

1. Land $2.90 per sq. ft. @ 25,846 sq. ft. Less $8,400.00 for existing graves	$66,600.00
2. Sanctuary after depreciation	$188,000.00
Final value estimate of land and sanctuary	$254,600.00[188]

HUD officials questioned the Hennigan appraisal and concluded ". . . it is our feeling that this appraisal is not well supported and has serious appraisal flaws."[189]

Attorney Chambers and Mr. Dubber exchanged letters again. On February 11, 1969, Attorney Dubber wrote:

We are deeply concerned about the Sycamore Hill property because we and the City have spent so much money working around the property, arranging street pavements, utilities, etc., that we have come to more or less accept the Church as remaining a permanent serious impediment to traffic on Greene and First Streets as well as being an obstruction on the historic Town Common.

We fear that further delay will cause us and the City, perforce, to abandon any idea of acquiring the property, and this would deny the congregation any hope of disposing of it; certainly at anything approaching the price we have offered.[190]

---

[188] David O. Hennigan, Appraiser. "Sycamore Hill Baptist Church." Greenville, NC, January 7, 1969.

[189] Francis D. Anderson. "Mr. A. E. Dubber, Executive Director Greenville Redevelopment Commission." Atlanta, GA, February 5, 1969.

[190] A. E. Dubber. "J. LeVonne Chambers." Greenville, NC, February 11, 1969.

On February 11, 1969, Mr. Hennigan gave a detailed description of the land, building and of the graves. The graves, although benign at this point, became the focal point of discussions about the church property:

> The site is a corner lot 194.4 feet on North Greene Street and 132.9 feet on West First Street. This site is divided into two sections. The first is 95 x 132.9 and is denoted by the existence of a church building. The second consists of a grave yard 99.4 x 132.9 in size. There is a discrepancy with regard to the amount of land used for these two purposes as shown on the surveyors report drawn by William W. Shaw, R. L. S. on August 1967 which divides the land as indicated above and that of Rivers and Associates dated May 26, 1967. [Neither of these reports is available for inspection.] The Rivers map exhibited as Parcel No. 1B, Shore Drive Project No. N.C. R-15 indicates division as following 165 x 132 as the church site and a tract 20 x 126.93 consisting of graves.

> While none of these reports indicate the number of graves in the area the pastor of the church, Rev. Felder, verified that there are 42 in the area. The West side of the graveyard is fenced and hedges have been planted by it.

> The church edifice was built in 1916 and consists of 13,140 square feet of floor space. This church will seat 450 to 500 persons on the . . . and in floor and balcony area.

> The appraiser notes that in addition to the easements granted to serving utilities companies as provided by the State of North Carolina there are 42 graves which may constitute rights in reality by the families or heirs of the deceased.

> For a visual picture of the graveyard see Exhibit C lodged in the Addenda section. [not found] The effective date of this appraisal is December 2, 1968.

> Due to the existence of 42 graves and the cost factor of $200.00 per grave to remove these graves, purchase new graves, and to bury the removed remains, the site is penalized $8,400.00. The remaining value being $66.600.00.

The subject property suffers no penalty for economic obsolescence inasmuch as no serious evidence of loss of income or membership is evidenced as a result of blight.

The estimated reproduction cost of the Sycamore Hill Baptist Church less depreciation is $188.000.00 as indicated by the local cost index or the approach to value labeled in this report as A.

Total final value estimate of land and building: (1) Land: $66,600.00 Building: $188.600.00.[191]

On February 13, 1969, tragedy struck the Sycamore Hill Baptist Church. THE DAILY REFLECTOR reported:

The old Sycamore Hill Baptist Church building at the intersection of First and Greene Streets was gutted by fire early today.

The fire was reported at 12:04 a. m . . . . The building burned today was constructed in 1917. It replaced a wood-frame church building that also burned.
The Rev. B. B. Felder, pastor of the church, said electricity to the building had been cut off and oil furnace was not in operation. When asked his opinion of how the fire might have been started, Rev. Felder said, 'From the construction of the building, and the fact that there was no electric service in the building,' 'it had to be arson.'

Fire fighters also said arson may have been the cause of the fire, although the cause could not be immediately determined.

Fire Chief Ray Smith did say, however, that the first firemen reaching the scene found a partially melted bottle behind the church and found grass behind the building ablaze indicating Molotov cocktails may have been used to start the fire.

Rev. Felder said appraisers last week set the value of the building at $149,000 and value of the contents at $39,000.[192]

---

191   Daniel O. Hennigan. "Shore Drive Commission." Greenville, NC, December 2, 1968.
192   Stuart Savage. "Arson Suspected In Costly Loss: Old Sycamore Hill Church Burns." THE DAILY REFLECTOR, Greenville, NC, February 13, 1969, p. 1.

There is no doubt that the arsonist's actions altered the negotiations and damaged the SHBC case and financial position. Below are appraisals after the church fire of February 13, 1969:

Jack Wallace	February 18, 1969	Land: without graves	$38,796.00
		with graves	$19,398.00
Lester Turnage	February 20, 1969	Land: without graves	$ 50,000.00
		with graves	$ 24,000.00

At a special meeting held by Commissioners on February 20, 1969, the following action was taken:

Moseley motion	$25,157.90 with graves
Cavendish second	$45,000.00 graves removed

Church to remain

$3,150 amount included under relocation grant for removal of 42 graves

Commissioners voted:

Land: with graves	$25,264.90
Without graves	$45,000.00[193]

Many citizens of Greenville believed that students demonstrating for civil rights in Greenville might have set the church on fire. THE DAILY REFLECTOR stated the marchers:

> . . . were forced out of Greenville by police Wednesday morning. They did return around 9 p.m., went without incident, to Mount Calvary Church in West Greenville to spend the night in the church basement, They were milling around the church shortly before midnight.[194]

Obviously, a police presence kept a vigilant eye and a dragnet around the area where the students were housed for the night.

---

[193] "Tabulation Sheet. Sycamore Hill Baptist Church."
[194] Roy Hardee. "Marchers Hauled Out of Greenville." THE DAILY REFLECTOR, Greenville, NC, February 13, 1969, p. 1.

A final investigation of the fire was never completed, and fire fighter Bryan Oliver stated that ". . . the files for the years 1968-1971 were missing from the Department files."[195]

The fire changed the whole attitude of the Commissioners and the appraisers with regards the purchase price of the Sycamore Hill Baptist Church. A special meeting was called by the Commissioners on February 20, 1969, for the express purpose

> . . . to consider reappraisals and set new acquisition price on the Sycamore Hill Church property.
>
> The Chairman informed the Commissioners that the Sycamore Hill Church had been destroyed by fire on the night of Wednesday, February 12, 1969; hence, we have asked our appraisers to give us their opinion of the value of the property since the fire. He asked the Director to read the appraisals. Jack Wallace stated that in his opinion the property is worth what it was worth before the fire excluding the building, which is worth nothing. Lester E. Turnage, Jr., informed us that in his opinion the land is worth just what is was worth before the fire and the building is now worth nothing.
>
> After considerable discussion and due consideration of all features, Commissioner Mosley moved that the acquisition price which the Commission would pay for the Sycamore Hill Church property if the Church offered it to us, in view of their previous request to cancel the Not To Be Required Agreement should be $25,157.90. He further moved that the price be $45, 000 if the graves are moved by others than the Commission. Commissioner Cavendish seconded the motion, and upon the call for a vote, all Commissioners present voted 'Aye.'
>
> The Chairman declared the motion carried and the price established. He instructed the Director to see that our records are documented accordingly. He further cautioned all present that no word of this action is to go beyond our office and files.[196]

---

[195] Sam Barber. Bryan Oliver. Interview. Greenville, NC, June 13, 2011.

[196] Redevelopment Commission of the City of Greenville, N.C. "Special Meeting of the Commissioners." *Minutes of a Special Meeting* . . . . Greenville, NC, February 30, 1969.

With the Commissioners' decision not to talk with Rev. Felder, on April 24, 1969, Rev. Felder penned the following:

The following is an agreement in principal concurred by officials of the church, but before the same could be binding would have to have the approval of the church congregation:

1. The Church land will be sold to the Redevelopment Commission of the City of Greenville at a price of $60,000.00, to be paid within sixty days after settlement is signed. All debts and encumbrances against the land will be removed by the Church.
2. The historical bell will be removed in good condition to 126 W. 8th Street and that the brick will be removed to place or places designated by the Church within a five mile radius of City of Greenville and further that anything of value will be removed to present Church site by the Redevelopment Commission.
3. The City will cooperate with the Sycamore Hill Baptist in removing the remains from the Sycamore Hill Baptist Church Cemetery located at corner of First and Greene Streets to Brown Hill Cemetery and other designated places by next of kin. The Redevelopment Commission and City of Greenville, North Carolina will provide grave sites only in Brown Hill Cemetery.

The Redevelopment Commission will reimburse the Sycamore Hill Baptist Church at the rate of $200.00 per grave total cost $8,400.00 within ten days after removal of bodies. The above Church will provide Funeral Director and professional services in removing the remains head stones, digging graves, re-committing the remains with Christian burial according to laws of North Carolina.

This proposal can be reduced to a formal agreement, but requires prompt action on part of both parties and we request you consider the same without delay and give us a reply at your very earliest convenience.[197]

---

[197] B. B. Felder. "Redevelopment Commission of the City of Greenville." Greenville, NC, April 24, 1969.

A response to Rev. Felder's letter on April 24, 1969 suggests it "... opens an entirely new area and I will take this up with the Commissioners in our regular meeting on May 31 because it must be seriously considered."[198]

On April 29, 1969, Mr. Laughinghouse responded:

> The Commissioners met at noon today, and after considerable and thorough discussion we can give you the following answer ... regarding the possible acquisition of the Sycamore Hill Baptist Church property.
>
> Since the Church building was destroyed by fire, we have had the property informally appraised in order to establish informally its present fair value.
>
> After due deliberations and consideration this morning, the Commissioners have authorized me to inform you that if the City and the Redevelopment Assistance Administration will concur, we will agree to cancel the Not To Be Acquired Agreement if the property can be acquired for the sum of $45,000.00 total after the bodies have been removed from the property.
>
> We cannot offer more than $45,000 after the Church has removed the bodies from the property. We would be willing at our expense to remove the bell. We are unwilling to enter into any further condition regarding the brick or other material remaining in the ruin of the Church.
>
> If we should acquire the Church, we will make a contract with a reputable wrecker to demolish what is left of the structure, grade the whole site after you have removed the graves, fill in the basement cap all utilities, etc. If the Church wants the brick remaining in the structure, the brick or any other materials would have to be secured from the wrecking contractor.[199]

---

[198] Billy B. Laughinghouse. "Rev. B. B. Felder." Greenville, NC, April 28, 1969.
[199] Billy B. Laughinghouse. "Reverend Mr. B. B. Felder." Greenville, NC, April 29, 1969.

A follow-up letter from Mr. Laughinghouse was dated April 30, 1969, and stated:

> The Commission cannot be responsible for the removal of the graves and head stones and must limit itself severely with regard to the salvage. We, therefore, make a counterproposal.
>
> 1. The Commission will pay for the property the sum of $45,000.00 provided the graves have been removed at the expense of Sycamore Hill Baptist Church.
> 2. The historic Church Bell will be removed from the bell tower in its present condition and loaded on a vehicle selected by the Church at the site, in condition the same has been moved.
> 3. The Commission feels that it can take no legal position with regard to the brick and salvage that may result when the present structure is demolished.
>
> The Commission has instructed me to make its decision known to you promptly, so you will have an opportunity to consider this proposal with the proper 3 Church officials and further to emphasize that its decision is contingent upon approval of the City of Greenville and appropriate federal agencies and this proposal is not binding unless approvals can be obtained from these bodies.[200]

From the beginning of the Town, City Officials have been very careful to enact ordinance to protect cemeteries. As early as 1841, the General Assembly of the State of North Carolina enacted a law stating:

> That every person who shall willfully or maliciously remove any monument or Wood, Stone, or other durable material, erected for the purpose of designating the spot where any dead body is interred, or of preserving or perpetuating the birth, age, death or memory of any dead person in any public or private Burying ground or Church or who shall willfully or maliciously deface or alter any such monument, or the marks or letters, or any inscription upon any such monument, made and erected as aforesaid, for the purpose aforesaid, or who shall willfully deface any part of any Church or other Building devoted to the service of Almighty God, shall upon conviction in any Court of

---

[200] Billy B. Laughinghouse. "Rev. B. B. Felder." Greenville, NC, April 30, 1969.

record, be adjudged guilty of a misdemeanor, and fined or imprisoned at the discretion of the Court.[201]

Local ordinances of 1910, 1928, and 1947 reflect this point of view. Except for the Memorial Baptist Church and City conflict around 1920, and before the purchase of the Brown Hill Cemetery, City cemetery operations were basically benign. A pattern of opaque transparency and accountability with the Memorial Baptist Church perhaps set the tone for the toxic climate experienced by the Sycamore Hill Missionary Baptist Church regarding the re-interment procedures in 1969 with the Brown Hill Cemetery.

Around 1919, the City insisted on expanding the Central Business District and needed the Memorial Baptist Church property at Fourth and Greene streets. The church, as many did during that time, had a graveyard attachment on the property. The church planned to enlarge the church and stated: ". . . by a vote of its members, the graveyard of said church was abandoned for the purpose of enlarging the present church . . . in order to erect on said site a new church."[202]

Experiencing opposition from the church to sell the property and with an eagerness to expand the Central Business Area, City Aldermen contacted, encouraged and tried to persuade the General Assembly to enact a law giving them authority to force the Memorial Baptist Church to abandon its property and to re-inter the graves to the Cherry Hill Cemetery at the church's expense.

The Private Laws passed by the General Assembly at its Session of 1919 held in Raleigh on Wednesday, The Eighth Day of January, A.D. 1919, specifies:

> That the board of the town of Greenville shall have the power and the authority, and they are hereby authorized to remove any said and all graves in the town of Greenville, Pitt County, North Carolina, and to remove the bodies, bones or dust, with the stones and monuments erected thereto, from said graves to some other graveyard or cemetery in Pitt County, the site and location to be designated and provided by the said board of aldermen.[203]

---

[201] North Carolina General Assembly. "Churches." Raleigh, NC: W. R. Gales, printer to the Legislature (Office of the Raleigh Register), January 12, 1841, p. 10.

[202] Rex L. Farmer, City Clerk. "Abandon Graveyard." *Minutes of City Aldermen,* Greenville, NC, March 8, 1920, Vol. III, 1-202, p. 35.

[203] North Carolina General Assembly. "An Act to Allow the Board of Aldermen of the Town of Greenville in Pitt County to Remove Certain Graves in Said Town." March 8, 1919. *North Carolina Private Laws passed by the General Assembly at its Session of 1919.* Raleigh, NC: Edward and Broughton Printing Co., 1919, p.100.

The language of the Private Laws passed by the General Assembly was clear.

> At an adjourned meeting of said Board, on Monday night, March 8, 1920, that the said ordinance heretofore enacted pursuant to Chapter 76 of the Public Acts of 1919, be amended, as follows, to wit; 'That the graveyard of the Memorial Baptist Church in the Town of Greenville be and the same is hereby declared abandoned pursuant to Chapter 136 of the Public Acts of 1919, and to that end it is hereby directed that all remains in the graves in said yard be disinterred, ... together with the monuments standing and enclosures erected on any of the plots in said graveyard be removed to Cherry Hill Cemetery ... and all expenses incident to the execution of said ordinance as herein amended to be borne by the Memorial Baptist Church.[204]

However, in an effort to force the Memorial Baptist Church to re-inter the bodies on the church property to the Cherry Hill Cemetery at the church's expense, it appears that the Greenville Aldermen amended the Private Laws of 1919 without authority from the General Assembly.

Instead of negotiating with the City Aldermen as did the SHMBC with City Council in 1969, the Memorial Baptist Church ". . . served the Board of Aldermen with an injunction to stop the Town from removing the bodies from the Memorial Baptist Church yard."[205]

Accordingly, the City Aldermen dropped their case with the Memorial Baptist Church. But in 1945 when the church decided to build an education wing, ". . . the church, with authorization from the Greenville Mayor, removed the bodies, bones or dust, with the stones and monuments erected thereto to the Greenwood Cemetery at the church's expense."[206] Incidentally, the Memorial Baptist Church, located at Fourth and Greene streets and established in 1872, was only three blocks south of the Sycamore Hill Baptist Church established in 1865.

Correspondence dated 1957 alerted the City Council and Commissioners of the authority and power to relocate graves within Pitt County. Why the City officials and the Commissioners were determined to intimidate the SHMBC

---

[204] North Carolina General Assembly. Ibid, p. 100.
[205] North Carolina General Assembly. Ibid, p. 34.
[206] Hugh Wease. *A Journey of Faith*. Nashville, TN: Baptist and Heritage Society and Fields Publishing, Inc., 2002, p. 90.

into moving the graves at the church's expense to the Brown Hill Cemetery is unknown. As with the Memorial Baptist Church, Rev. Felder refused to comply with the request and sought counsel from Attorney Jerry Paul:

> The Reverend B. B. Felder requested that the City Council relocate these graves at City expense. It was pointed out that according to Article 1, Section 1 and Section 2 of the Code of the City of Greenville, North Carolina dated 1957, the Council of the City of Greenville has the power and authority to [e]ffect such relocation.[207]

During the second half of 1969, an intense series of communications was circulated among the Commission, SHMBC, the attorneys, and the City of Greenville.

On June 24, 1969, Attorney Hite wrote:

> The City of Greenville cannot legally or financially pay any sums with regards to this proposed purchase. I have, however, gotten them to look with favor on the giving of sufficient space in Brown Hill Cemetery for the re-interment of the remains in the Church cemetery without cost to the Church.[208]

On July 3, 1969, Mr. Messick informed the Shore Drive Redevelopment Commission that:

> Mr. Lewis stated that the Board of Trustees of the Church turned down our offer of $45.000.00 for the Church property but he felt the members were anxious to sell and would be willing to consider a higher offer. Mr. Lewis and Mr. Artis felt they could persuade the Board to sell the property for $50.000.00 provided the Commission moved the 42 graves at Commission expense.
>
> Col. Dubber suggested that Mr. Lewis and Mr. Artis discuss this with the Commission Chairman. He also indicated he felt the Regional

---

[207]   Harry E. Hagerty, City Manager. "Relocation of the Sycamore Hill Baptist Church Cemetery." *Minutes of City Council,* Greenville, NC, August 6, 1969, p. 1.

[208]   Kenneth G. Hite, Attorney. "Mr. James E. Ferguson, Attorney. Sycamore Hill Baptist Church." Greenville, NC, June 24, 1968.

Office of HUD and the City might go along with a total price of $45,000 to $50.000.[209]

A letter to Mr. Leroy James, Chairman of the Trustees Board of the SHMBC, noted:

> . . . Concerning the inclusion of the church property in the Shore Drive Redevelopment Project N.C. R-15 . . . the Commission has been successful in persuading the Department of Housing and Urban Development to concur in a price of $50,000.00 for the church property. The price, however, is for land only, free and clear of all encumbrances. We will be willing to purchase the property with the ruins of the church building left but all graves must be removed before acquisition.

> As Mr. Messick discussed with you, Section 1. Of Article I of the Code of the City of Greenville authorizes the City to remove graves and monuments in the City of Greenville to some other graveyard or cemetery in Pitt County. You may be able to persuade the City to move the graves at City expense. As I stated before, the graves will have to be moved before we can purchase the property for $50,000.00.[210]

A response (not found) prompted Mr. Leroy James to write a letter to Mayor Frank M. Wooten (draft only). He told the Mayor:

> It appears that the Sycamore Hill Baptist Church has about reached an agreement with the Redevelopment Commission to include the church property . . . in the Shore Drive Redevelopment Project. The Commission had made the church an acceptable offer, but the offer is for the land free and clear of all encumbrances. As you know, there are approximately 42 graves on the property and they must be moved before the property can be acquired by the Commission.

> Article I, section 1 of the Code of the City of Greenville authorizes the City to remove graves and monuments in the City of Greenville to

---

[209] John A. Messick. "Shore Drive Redevelopment Project. Sycamore Hill Baptist Church." Greenville, NC, July 3, 1969.

[210] A. E. Dubber. "Mr. Leroy James, Chairman, Board of Trustees, Sycamore Hill Missionary Baptist Church." Greenville, NC, July 14, 1969.

some other graveyard or cemetery in Pitt County. We hereby made a formal request that the City remove all the graves from the cemetery on Greene Street to the Brown Hill Cemetery.[211]

Of interest in the resolution to move graves from the church property, the SHBC officials signed the NTBA with the Shore Drive Redevelopment Commission an entire month (September 16, 1963) before the Commission entered into a contract with the U.S. Government (October 17, 1963) for funds under Title I of the Housing Act of 1964:

> Enclosed is a resolution passed by our Commission on July 17, 1969 establishing fair market value of Parcel 6-4 of the Shore Drive Redevelopment Project, N.C. R-15 at $50.000. Your office had previously concurred in acquisition price of $78,000 for this parcel, but the building . . . was destroyed by fire after your concurrence.

> The Board of Trustees of the church have made an agreement with the City Council for the City to move the graves from the church property at no expense to this Commission. This would be done before transfer of a deed to the Commission.

> Since the Commission and the church have agreed on a purchase price of $50,000 . . . we request your concurrence.

RESOLUTION

> WHEREAS, the Redevelopment Commission of the City of Greenville, N.C. entered into a contract with the U. S. Government on October 17, 1963, for financial and technical assistance as provided for under Title I of the Housing Act of 1964, as amended, for the redevelopment of an urban renewal project known as the Shore Drive Redevelopment Project, N.C. N-15; and

> WHEREAS, the Commission entered into an agreement on September 16, 1963, with the Sycamore Hill Baptist Church, owners of Parcel 6-4 in the N.C. R-15 project area, whereby the Commission

---

[211] Leroy James, Chairman, Board of Trustees, Sycamore Hill Missionary Baptist Church. "Mayor Frank M. Wooten." (draft) Greenville, NC, July 15, 1969.

agreed not to acquire Parcel 6-4 if the owners could and would comply with the Urban renewal Plan for the project; and

WHEREAS, the Board of Trustees of Sycamore Hill Baptist Church requested an appraisal of the church property to determine the fair market value which could be paid by the Commission should Parcel 6-4 be taken into the project; and WHEREAS, the independent appraisals were made of Parcel 6-4 and the Commission by formal resolution on March 19, 1968, established the Fair market value to be $78,960.00; and

WHEREAS, on March 29, 1968, the Regional Office of the Department of Urban Renewal concurred in an acquisition price of $78.960.00 for Parcel 6-4; and Inc.[212]

In an effort to get tax earned concessions from the City, Rev. Felder requested that the City Council relocate the bodies from the Sycamore Hill Baptist Church Cemetery to the Brown Hill Cemetery:

The Reverend B. B. Felder requested that the City Council relocate these graves at City expense.

. . . Article 1, Section 1, and Section 2 of the Code of the City of Greenville, North Carolina dated 1957, the Council of the City of Greenville has the power and authority to affect such relocation.

Reverend Felder advised . . . that the Church and the Redevelopment Commission of the City were negotiating an agreed price for the property now occupied by the Church and the cemetery and that the Redevelopment Commission desires to acquire the land unencumbered by the cemetery. Therefore, the Sycamore Hill Baptist Church requests the City to exercise its rights and authority to relocate these graves.

Agreement:

a.   A letter will be formulated by the Board of Trustees requesting that the City Council of the City of Greenville arrange to

---

[212]   A. E. Dubber. "Regional Assistance Association." Greenville, NC, July 18, 1969.

relocate all graves from the Sycamore Hill site to the Brown Hill Cemetery or to scattered sites within Pitt County.

b. It was further agreed that this letter be accompanied by a plot plan of the existing cemetery showing the identification of the remains contained thereon and the present position in the existing cemetery. Further, this letter will be accompanied by a plot plan of the lots to be used in the Brown Hill Cemetery indicating which remains are to be buried in which lots.

c. Upon receipt of the letter request and the designations of graves and grave sites, the City Manager will secure firm proposals from selected registered undertakers to relocate there remains as indicated providing proper removal and re-burial procedures and materials and affording these remains respectful treatment expected by all Christian burial rites.[213]

After quoting the law, Rev. Felder found it difficult to convince the City fathers to honor its own laws, so consequently, he retained the services of Attorney Jerry Paul to accompany him and the Board of Trustees to a special meeting called by the Redevelopment Commission and City officials:

Meeting called by Mr. Paul, attorney for the Sycamore Hill Baptist Church . . . to clarify the proposed purchase of the Sycamore Hill Baptist Church property by the Redevelopment Commission.

The City is not a party to any contract between the Redevelopment Commission and the Sycamore Hill Baptist Church. The City was not a party to the Not-To-Be-Acquired Agreement. The City has no control over the acquisition of the parcel but does have the authority to consent or deny consent to the Church in the development plan necessary to include the Church property in the Shore Drive Project.

The latest conference between Board of Trustees and City Council on August 6, 1969. Attached is a memorandum prepared by the

---

[213] Harry E. Hagerty, City Manager. "Relocation of the Sycamore Hill Baptist Church Cemetery." *Minutes of City Council*, Greenville, NC, August 6, 1969. Notes from memorandum, p. 1-2 (Section CC Lots 41 through 70 Burial Plots).

City manager summarizing the matters discussed and the decisions reached in that conference.

The Redevelopment Commission has offered to rescind the Not-To-Be-Acquired Agreement and pay the Church $50,000 for the property with the provision that the graves must be removed from the property before the purchase is made.

The City has not guaranteed to move the graves at no expense to the Church but appears to be willing to do so. The Redevelopment Commission is not a party to any agreement between the City and the Church.

MEMORANDUM

1. Rev. B. B. Felder requested that the City Council relocate these graves at City expense.

2. Rev. Felder advised those present that the Church and the Redevelopment Commission ... were negotiating an agreed price for the property ... and the cemetery and that the Redevelopment Commission desires to acquire the land unencumbered by the cemetery. Therefore, the Sycamore Hill Baptist Church requests the City to exercise its rights and authority to relocate these graves.

3. Rev. Felder requested that the brick resulting from the demolition ... be deposited on two lots in West Greenville to be designated for that purpose.

4. Rev. Felder advised ... that the Redevelopment Commission ... has agreed to salvage the church bell ... and deliver it to the location selected in Greenville by the Church.

After lengthy discussion, it was agreed as follows:

a. A letter be formulated by the Board of Trustees requesting that the City Council ... arrange to relocate all graves from the Sycamore Hill site to the Brown Hill Cemetery or to scattered sites within Pitt County.

b.   That the City . . . be requested to arrange for the unprocessed brick to be deposited on the two lots located in West Greenville to be designated by the Board of Trustees.

It was further agreed that this letter be accompanied by a plot plan of the existing cemetery showing the identification of the remains contained thereon and present position in the existing cemetery. Further, this letter will be accompanied by a plot plan of the lots to be used in the Brown Hill Cemetery indicating which remains are to be buried in which lots.

c.   Upon receipt of the letter request and the designation of graves and grave sites, the City manager will secure firm proposals from selected registered undertakers to relocate these remains as indicated providing proper removal and re-burial procedures and materials and affording these remains respectful treatment expected by all Christian burial rites. The Redevelopment Commission . . . will be requested to make provisions in a contract with the demolition firm employed to remove the old Church from the Church site to deposit the unprocessed old brick on the two lots in West Greenville to be designated.

d.   The City Council . . . being provided all the facts will make a decision and advise the Board of Trustees of the Sycamore Hill Baptist Church of its decision promptly.[214]

The local paper published an article stating that the "Larger job of locating old graves sites remains."[215]

On October 8, 1969, the Board of Trustees and Deacons of the Sycamore Hill Missionary Baptist Church agreed to sell the church property to the Redevelopment Commission. The Resolution Stated:

---

[214]   Harry E. Hagerty, City Manager. "Meeting of the Development Commission of the City of Greenville and the Board of Trustees of the Sycamore Hill Baptist Church at 7:30 P. M. on August 12, 1969. *Minutes of City Council,* Book 11 p. 1-2.

[215]   "Larger Job of Locating Old Graves Sites Remains." THE DAILY REFLECTOR, Greenville, NC, September 5, 1969, p. 6.

> RESOLVED: That the trustees of Sycamore Hill Missionary Baptist Church Incorporated, pursuant to the authorization and instructions of the Church congregation, hereby agree to sell to the Redevelopment Commission of the City of Greenville, and or the City of Greenville, the Church site located at First and Greene Streets, Greenville, North Carolina for the agreed price of $50,000.00 and any such other further considerations which the Redevelopment Commission, and or the City of Greenville may offer.[216]

With the support and presence of legal counsel, the Sycamore Hill Missionary Baptist Church succeeded in reaching an agreement with the City to re-inter the graves from the SHBC Cemetery to the Brown Hill Cemetery.

WITNESSETH

> WHEREAS, the party of the first part is desirous of assisting the party of the second part in the removal of graves presently located at the Sycamore Hill Baptist Church Cemetery located in the City of Greenville; and

> WHEREAS, the party of the second part is in the process of negotiating and consummating transfer of title of the property whereon said cemetery is located to the Redevelopment Commission of the City of Greenville; and

> WHEREAS, it is necessary in order to consummate to said sale that the removal of all graves located in said cemetery be effected
> NOW, THEREFORE, we the parties agree as follows:

> FIRST, that the party of the first part agrees to pay to the party of the second part the sum of five thousand dollars ($5,000.00) as a contribution toward the cost of removal of said graves. Said sum of five thousand dollars ($5.000.00) shall be paid as follows: two-thousand five-hundred dollars ($2,500.00) upon the execution of this agreement and two thousand five-hundred ($2,500.00) upon receipt of written notice from the party of the second part stating that the removal of said graves has been completed.

---

[216] Charles M. Dickens. "Agreement to Sell Church Property to the Redevelopment Commission." Greenville, NC, October 8, 1969.

SECOND, it is understood and agreed that the removal of said graves will be done and performed exclusively by the party of the second party. That the party of the first part agrees to make available to the party of the second part one (1) backhoe and one (1) front end loader, plus the services of an operator for the said equipment to assist the part of the second part in the necessary excavation work to be done in the removal of said graves,

THIRD, the party of the second part agrees and assumes by the execution of this agreement all legal responsibility for the removal of said graves to save harmless the party of the first part from any and all liability growing out of the removal of said graves in any manner whatsoever.

FOURTH, the party of the first part agrees to convey to the party of the second part grave lot numbers 41 through 70 of Section CC of the Brown Hill Cemetery located in the city of Greenville for the purpose of receiving the remains which are presently located in the said Sycamore Hill Baptist Church Cemetery.[217]

On October 30, 1969, a letter from Harry E. Hagerty to Mr. Leroy James confirmed the agreement to relocate the SHBC Cemetery graves to the Brown Hill Cemetery:

You are advised that the City Council of the City of Greenville ... on October 9, 1969, approved the resolution of cooperation in the matter of relocation of the Sycamore Hill Baptist Church Cemetery from its present location to the Brown Hill Cemetery.

I am authorized to make the first payment to the Church at the time removal operations commence and to complete the agreed payment upon completion of the move. I am also authorized to instruct the City Clerk to deed to the Church the section of the Brown Hill Cemetery sufficient to accommodate all graves displaced therein.[218]

---

[217] Frank M. Wooten, Mayor. "Contract No 97 between The City of Greenville and the SHMBC." *Minutes of City Council,* Greenville, NC, October 9, 1969, Book 12, p. 117-118.

[218] W. N. Moore, City Clerk, City Manager. "Mr. Leroy James, Chairman, Board of Trustees." *Minutes of City Council,* Greenville, NC, October 14, 1969, Book 12, p. 117.

Another confirmation letter about moving the graves from Mr. Dubber to Mr. Leroy James on October 30, 1969, stated:

> The Redevelopment Commission has offered to rescind the Not-To-Be-Acquired Agreement and pay the church $50,000.00 for the property . . . provided the graves be removed from the property before the purchase is made . . . . the Redevelopment Commission has agreed to remove the bell from the church, assuming no responsibility for the condition of the bell, and deliver it to the Eighth Street location of the church.

> Enclosed . . . is an Offer of Sale of land which will be effective and should be executed in triplicate as soon as you have certified to the City that the graves have been removed. The Not-To-Be-Acquired Agreement will be rescinded when we have this offer properly executed.[219]

On November 6, 1969, City Council noted: "Removal of graves from the Sycamore Hill Baptist Church Cemetery to Brown Hill Cemetery was reported to be completed under the agreement with the Council on October 9, 1969."[220]

On November 26, 1969, Attorney Kenneth G. Hite, communicated with the Redevelopment Commission stating:

> According to the records of Pitt County, the record title to the land is the Trustees of Sycamore Hill Baptist Church. However, in May 1968, this church was incorporated under the name of Sycamore Hill Missionary Baptist Church, Inc. and presently conducts its affairs under this corporate name.

> My examination revealed that the property was encumbered by a mortgage in favor of Wachovia Bank and Trust Company in the original principal amount of $40,000.00.

---

[219] A. E. Dubber, "Mr. Leroy James, Chairman, Board of Trustees." Greenville, NC, October 30, 1969.

[220] Harry E. Hagerty, City Manager. "Removal of Graves." *Minutes of City Council,* Greenville, NC, November 6, 1969.

It is also a matter of common knowledge that there was a church cemetery on the grounds, but the certificate of removal of graves appears on record in Book V-38, page 53, of the Pitt County Registry, a copy of which has been furnished the Commission as a part of the offer of sale.

This transaction was closed in my office this date, the deed received, and the purchase price delivered.

I also observed a small irregularity in that the corporate seal of the church does not bear the identical corporate name. However, it appears that it is the officially adopted seal of the corporate church, and in preparation of the deed, I indicated that the church was sealing the deed with its "adopted seal". I believe this is an inconsequential matter and will not affect the validity of the transaction.

Relying, therefore, upon the certificate of removal of the church graves from the church site, it is my opinion that the deed executed by Sycamore Hill Missionary Baptist Church, Inc. to the Commission effectively conveys fee simple title to the church property at the northeast intersection of First and Greene Streets.

Church property is not subject to taxation."[221]

On the same date, Attorney Hite wrote to Rev. Felder, informing him:

The Redevelopment Commission . . . last night called a special meeting for the purpose of considering your request to salvage the boiler and the remains of the church organ from the old Sycamore Hill Baptist Church.

It was the unanimous decision of the Commission that in view of the perilous condition of the remains of the building and possible liability on the Commission in the event of an accident which might occur during any salvage operation, that the Commission could not consider giving permission to any person to enter the remains of the building for any purpose whatsoever.

---

[221] Kenneth G. Hite. "Redevelopment Commission of the City of Greenville." Greenville, NC, November 26, 1969.

At last evening's meeting, the Commission emphasized its position that was reached at the joint meeting of the Church Board and the Commission held several weeks ago; and that no change in this position had been authorized by the Commission with regard to its commitment to the disposition of the salvage. Because of the danger involved in working around the weakened building, it must categorically refuse to permit any one to conduct any operation in the remains of the building except a salvage operator, and that any further arrangements with regard to any salvageable materials at the site, exclusive of the brick and bell, will have to be taken up with the wrecking company.[222]

On December 11, 1969, Mr. Laughinghouse wrote to the Church, stating:

In connection with the impending demolition of the remains of the old Sycamore Hill Baptist Church . . . and after examination of the proposed sites for the deposits of the debris contained in our original agreement, we have both agreed that these sites are not suitable for the deposit of the debris and another deposit area must be identified.

After consultation with you, it has been agreed that the brick in debris form as removed from the church site will be delivered and dumped at 110 West Moore Street.

The demolition contractor will be required to use care in the removal of the historic church bell from the bell tower and deliver the same in as good condition as possible to the church premises on Eighth Street.

We will . . . require written consent of the owner of the land at 110 West Moore Street that the debris may be dumped at this site.[223]

A response and confirmation letter from Mr. Jackson stated:

My wife and I hereby consent and grant permission to the Redevelopment Commission . . . to have the brick from the old

---

[222] Kenneth G. Hite. "Rev. B. B. Felder." Greenville, NC, November 26, 1969.
[223] Billy B. Laughinghouse. "Sycamore Hill Missionary Baptist Church, Inc." Greenville, NC, December 11, 1969.

Sycamore Hill Baptist Church dumped as debris in the designated area at 110 West Moore Street. [224]

Finally, the Settlement Sheet for the Sale of the Church Property revealed:

Sale of property located northeast corner First and Greene Streets, Greenville, North Carolina, by Sycamore Hill Missionary Baptist Church, Inc. to Redevelopment Commission of the city of Greenville, November 25, 1969.

Purchase price $50.000.00

Paid as follows:

Wachovia Bank and Trust Co., Greenville, N.C.
To retire mortgage indebtedness $44,821.33
Paid Sycamore Hill Missionary Baptist
Church, Inc., balance purchase price $5,178.67

TOTAL $50,000.00

The foregoing is correct and the same is hereby approved:

Sycamore Hill Missionary Baptist Church, Inc.
By: Leroy James

Redevelopment Commission of the City Of Greenville
By: Lawrence D. Hart
Kenneth G. Hite
Attorney[225]

The final entry of the collection states that the Sycamore Hill Baptist Church property had been acquired:

City manager advised that the Sycamore Hill Church at the corner of First and Greene Street has been acquired and makes it possible for

---

[224] Mr. and Mrs. George O. Jackson. "Redevelopment Commission of the City of Greenville." Greenville, NC, December 12, 1969.
[225] Kenneth H. Hite. "Settlement Sheet." Greenville, NC, November 25, 1969.

the project to be completed according to the original plan. First Street will be widened and sidewalks and curb and gutter will be installed.[226]

To confirm that all graves were moved to the Brown Hill Cemetery, a certified copy of the move was recorded with the Register of Deeds at the Pitt County Courthouse, the Commission requested to check Book V-8, p. 53 in the Pitt County Register's Office.[227]

Mr. Hagerty pointed out:

As stated, with legal assistance from Attorney Paul, with faith, prayers and the persistence of Rev. B. B. Felder and the Sycamore Hill Missionary Baptist Church members, the contentious struggle to get an agreement from the city to relocate the graves in the SHBC to the Brown Hill Cemetery at the City's expense was successful.[228]

To mitigate inflamed hostilities and anger, Rev. Felder requested and the city offered church members the opportunity to purchase the unused plots at reduced prices. The idea was for selected members to be buried in the same location as their love ones.

The Council approved the request with the requirement that a contract be secured with the church stipulating that individual church members would not have to pay more for a grave site than the church paid the city.[229]

However, Ms. Ellis Brown, Director of the Flanagan Funeral Home and an eyewitness to the removal and selling of the plots, stated that the Church sold the plots for $40.00 each.[230] The designated plots in Section CC are numbered

[226] W. N. Moore, City Clerk. "Site Improvement Work in Shore Drive Project, Sycamore Hill Missionary Baptist Church Property." *Minutes of City Council,* January 7, 1970, Book 12, p. 152.

[227] Pitt County Register of Deeds. "Removal of Graves." Greenville, NC, October 19, 1968, Book V-8, p. 53.

[228] Harry E. Hagerty, City Clerk. "Relocation of the Sycamore Hill Baptist Church Cemetery." *Minutes of City Council,* August 6, 1969, p. 1

[229] "Local Church Requests Graves Sites Together." THE DAILY REFLECTOR, Greenville, NC, February 10, 1974, p. B-3.

[230] Sam Barber. Ms. Ellis Brown. Interview. September 27, 2012.

41 to 70. Each number represented four grave plots, making a total of 120 plots (Table A 1.1).

Table A 1.1 Grave Plots in Section CC for Sycamore Hill Missionary Baptist Church

TOTAL PLOT NOS.	FULL	UNFILLED	TOTAL
41-50	18	22	40
51-60	28	12	40
61-70	29	11	40
TOTAL	75	45	120

In a chart prepared by Deacon Matthew Lewis, Head Deacon at SHMBC for more than 50 years and submitted to the Chair of the Public Works Department on February 28, 1994, the 19 identified bodies and the 23 unidentified bodies don't align with the chart. Although incomplete, the numbered chart does not give any names of individuals, so reconstructing the list has been a challenge. By combining the Kittrell list, the on-site grave inspection, and the work by Denton, we get a more complete idea of the re-interred individuals from the Sycamore Hill Baptist Church Cemetery.[231]

Since only numbers are assigned to the chart, we can assume that the 19 identified bodies and the 21 unidentified bodies are included somewhere within these numbers. An on-site inspection does not show 19 headstones transferred from the SHBC Cemetery. And those headstones reflective of that period are juxtaposed among contemporary ones.

Kittrell accounts for three headstones that were perhaps moved from the SHBC Cemetery. They are:

Ransome Brown, b. 6/12/1826-d. 9/25/1905; John Marable b. 5/8/1887-d. 8/17/1905; and Sarah Tucker, b. 2/26/1892-d. 6/6/1908 (mm/dd/yy).

---

[231] Denton, Ibid; Kittrell, Ibid; Barber. On-Site Inspections.

On-site grave inspections account for only seven headstones of an earlier period: Hettie Clark, b. 1866-d. 1913; S.P. Humphrey, b. 5/5/1847-d. 2/27/1912; Jane Latham, b. 5/13/1841-d. 11/8/1924; Rhonda (illegible inscription) d. 4/20/1899; Thelma, (illegible inscription) b. 1909-d. 1910; George Williams, b. 3/4/1834-d. 8/14/1918. Denton accounts for one: George V. Donalson, b. 2/3/1892-d. 1/5/1909.

Given that Rev. Nimmo testified to the Commission that there were more than 200 bodies in the cemetery during his 33 years as pastor at the church, and given that only 42 bodies were identified to be moved, the numbers don't add up. The Register of Deeds accounts for 51 death Certificates buried at the SHBC Cemetery between 1913 and 1951 (Table 1).

By only moving 42 bodies from the SHBC Cemetery, it appears that many bodies were bulldozed, plowed over, and entombed at the Town Common site for eternity. G.S. No. 14-148 and G.S. No. 14-149 of the North Carolina Laws and Statutes outlines the penalties for desecrating gravesites and for plowing over or covering up graves.[232] The evidence suggests that the site was probably desecrated during the Shore Drive Rehabilitation Urban Renewal Project in 1969. Now that the City has plans to develop residential and commercial property on the same site, it would be wise to monitor the excavation process for bones and headstones. An even better suggestion would be to alert the North Carolina Department of Cultural Resources about the City's plans. The CHRONICLE reports that SHBC's "...cornerstone was laid in 1916, and in July 1917, Reverend William Andrew Taylor delivered the dedication sermon."[233] Certainly, assuming this report is accurate, the cornerstone of the church is buried on the location and if unearthed, could reveal the name and date of the long-sought-after architect for the SHBC.

Final closure to the SHBC Cemetery and the Brown Hill Cemetery resulted from a myopic view and a lack of vision on the part of the City fathers. Vivid memories of former generations stealing away in the night and current memories of worshiping under bush harbor tents apparently motivated and inspired the following individuals to take action to organize the Colored Religious Society, later the First Baptist Church and then the SHBC.

---

[232] North Carolina General Assembly. "Laws and Statues Regarding Cemeteries, Article 12, Section 14-149, Desecrating, Plowing Over or Covering Up Graves: Desecrating Human Remains." Raleigh, NC: North Carolina General Statues, p. 13.

[233] Elizabeth H. Copeland, comp. *Chronicles of Pitt County* #125. "Sycamore Hill Baptist Church." By Mrs. Lena B. Brown, Mrs. Beatrice C. Maye, and Mr. Monte G. Frizzell. Winston-Salem, NC: Hunter Publishing Company, 1982.

Ruth Armond	Daniel King
Sarah Cherry	Moses King
Annie Daniels	Virginia King
Lucy Eaton	Cathrine Knox
Jennie Elks	Bettie Moye
Sally Forbes	Tom Moye
Adelaide Foreman	Phoebe Nobles
Madison Foreman	Alfred Payton
Jane Hardy	Jane Powell
Lena Harris	Martha Simmons
Bettie King	Percy Williams[234]

These twenty-two founders struggled to secure and maintain a permanent location for the church and a permanent resting place for the dead, not only for themselves, but for future generations. With the destruction of the SHBC on February 13, 1969, the most prominent and acknowledged memorial representing a black presence in Greenville was destroyed by an arsonist's torch. The destruction of that architectural gem and the "taking" of the Brown Hill Cemetery property in the 1950s for the construction of a school and a gymnasium resulted in reducing the size of the cemetery. Space shortages forced the city to purchase the Homestead Cemetery in 2003 as an expansion cemetery for all, but predominantly for its black citizens. These two major events altered the face and landscape of Greenville's black presence and closed the final chapter on both of these historic black institutions.

Sadly, there are no extant documents to support the claim that local churches, fraternities, sororities, social and civic community organizations, Negro professionals, local pastors, teachers, and the community at large offered support to keep the SHBC at First and Greene Streets. Only the dogged faith, prayers and persistence of Rev. Felder guided the church membership to press forward.

The only evidence for support to preserve the SHBC was from Mr. John C. Atkinson, a professor at East Carolina University. He expressed his strong support for the preservation of the church in a letter to Mr. Dubber on September 18, 1968:

> While I am no real architectural critic, I have long been an admirer
> of the Sycamore Hill Church, located at First and Green Sts. It has,

---

[234] Sycamore Hill Missionary Baptist Church. "Our Journey of Faith, 1860-2010." Greenville, NC.

for me, a certain strength of design lacking in most of the other structures in the City of Greenville. This was not always apparent until the structures previously surrounding the church were removed. Now, the more that I see the church, the more I become convinced that Sycamore Hill Church merits salvation.

The question, of course, is what to do with the building to justify its existence, leaving aside the argument that some things need no justification beyond their existence, let me suggest one or two possibilities.

East Carolina University or the Greenville Art Society might be able to use the building as an art gallery. Certainly, for this purpose, little real change in the building would be necessary.

The Greenville City Council has recently been cramped for room. The entire building could be made into one of the more unique city council chambers in the United States. Virtually no-change other than general renovation would be necessary to use the building as a council chamber with plenty of room for those interested citizens to attend meetings. The remainder of the building could be utilized for individual offices for the council members and for such secretarial or clerical assistance as they might need. The Greenville Chamber of Commerce might find it to be a very useful building.

The point to be stressed is the very fact that the architecture is interesting and the building is old but not beyond use. It would be a unique setting for many organizations. Granted, it might not blend with the more modern architecture going up in the area but it would constitute a break in the sameness of the more modern mode.

I believe that saving Sycamore Hill Church is worth the effort. At the rate that we Americans are going, there will be nothing left of our past for our future to see and that would be a lasting shame.

Sincerely,
John C. Atkinson, Jr.[235]

---

[235] John C. Atkinson, Jr. "Mr. A. E. Dubber, Executive Director." Greenville, NC, September 18, 1968.

Mr. Dubber responded on September 18, 1968, stating that the SHBC had expressed a repeated interest in the church being acquired by the Commission:

> My dear Mr. Atkinson,
>
> Your interest in the physical appearance of Greenville and its component is very commendable, and I have told our Commission of your interest in the Sycamore Hill Church. We can have no opinion in this matter, nor can we take any action, because the Sycamore Hill Church property is not in the Shore Drive Project. The church requested and this Commission agreed that the Sycamore Hill Church property not be acquired.
>
> We understand that the Sycamore Hill Church has purchased and moved to the building on Eighth Street, which formerly was occupied by the Eighth Street Christian Church. And it may be that the old church building on the corner of First and Greene Streets is available for purchase by any of the organizations you mentioned in your letter to us dated September 18, 1968.
>
> Very truly Yours,
A. E. Dubber
>
> AED: eem
> CC: City of Greenville[236]

---

[236] A. E. Dubber. "John C. Atkinson, Jr." Greenville, NC, September 19, 1968.

APPENDIX II

Undertakers

Funerals, cemeteries, churches, and schools have long been sacred and cherished institutions within the black community. From the beginning of the funeral service and embalming profession in 1901,[237] the funeral service business has been beset by aggressive and competitive struggles. From the 1920s to the 1940s, the competition, as seen in (Table 3.4), was so fierce that more than 40 undertakers or their minions buried folks at the Cooper Field Cemetery.

Final rites, especially up to the 1940s, were marked by sacred dignity, simplicity and affordability. Today, final rites are stylized and expensive, marked by pomp, pageantry, and reflective of the high liturgical dramas of pristine years. Despite improved facilities and calculated marketing strategies, fierce competition pervades the profession until this day. Today, there are nine black and two white funeral establishments serving Greenville.

The two towering funeral establishments in Greenville during the 1920s to the 1940s were the S. G. Wilkerson Funeral Home, (white) and the W. E. Flanagan Funeral Home (black). During the early days of established funeral services, both funeral directors buried folks at Cooper Field. Wilkerson did a thriving business among black folks for many years. Not only was he a funeral director, he was also the Pitt County coroner. It is reported that when folks died, black and white, Mr. Wilkerson would pronounce them dead one day and bury them the next or sometimes even the same day.[238]

When Walter E. Flanagan started his funeral business in Greenville, it was noted that he had a very difficult time attracting black folks to use his services. Early in his practice, it is reported that he stood on the bridge at the county lines

---

[237] North Carolina State Board of Embalmers. *Proceedings of North Carolina State Board of Embalmers Organized at Morehead City, N.C., July 6, 1901*, p. 1.

[238] Sam Barber. Elliot Futrell. Interview and Email exchanges. Goldsboro, NC, 2011-2012.

of Lenoir and Pitt counties on Highway 11 soliciting black business.[239] It has been suggested that Mr. S. G. Wilkerson helped set up Flanagan in business at the corner of Second Street.[240] There is little evidence to support that claim. Mr. Flanagan moved his services to its present site at 1026 W. 5th Street in 1963.

In the mid-twenties, with the funeral business downsizing and with a large family for which to provide, Mr. Wilkerson quit the undertaking business to work for a casket company.[241] Apparently in 1932, with increased deaths during the early years of the Great Depression, Mr. Wilkerson, along with his sons, re-established his funeral business.[242] Evidence, however, does support the claim that Mr. Monty Cherry and later Mr. David Parker became partners/agents with the Flanagan Funeral Home to advertise its services.[243] By the late twenties, Flanagan Funeral Home was the dominant black undertaker in Greenville. After he died in 1984, the funeral home was ultimately eclipsed by competing funeral homes. The nine active black funeral homes serving the Greenville area are listed in Table A 2.1:

[239]   Sam Barber. Louise Russell. Interview. Kinston, NC, March 21, 2011.
[240]   Sam Barber. Stan Little. Interview. Greenville, NC, April 25, 2012.
[241]   Elizabeth H. Copeland, comp. *Chronicles of Pitt County*. Winston-Salem, NC: Hunter Publishing Company, 1982.
[242]   Copeland. Ibid.
[243]   Sam Barber. On-Site inspection of Headstones at the Brown Hill Cemetery, 1924-1940.

Table A 2.1. Black Funeral Homes Serving the Greenville Area

Blake Phillips Funeral Services
103 Raleigh Avenue
Greenville, NC 27834
252-551-5921

Mitchell's Funeral Home
1000 Howell Street
Greenville, NC 27834
252-353-5111

Boris Barrett Funeral Service Licensee
111 Larkin Lane
Greenville, NC 27834
252-758-0860

Phillips Brothers Mortuary
1501 W. 14th Street
Greenville, NC 27834
252-752-2536/752-5177

Congleton Memorial Mortuary
3205 East 10th Street
Greenville, NC 27858
252-355-9995

Tri-County Funeral Services
5420 Front Lane
Ayden, NC 28513
252-746-6070

Don Brown Funeral Home
497 2nd Street
Ayden, NC 28513
252-746-3133

Roundtree Family Mortuary
315 W. 2nd St.
Greenville, NC 27835
252-757-2067
www.rfm.com

W. E. Flanagan Memorial Funeral Home
1926 W. 5th Street
Greenville, NC 27834
252-752-3530

On February 14, 2011, each funeral director was invited to participate in this project. Only the Don Brown Funeral Home responded to the invitation.

DON BROWN FUNERAL HOME, INC.

In June, 1999, Don Brown established the Don Brown Funeral Home, Inc. at 497 Second Street, Ayden, North Carolina 28513, (Phone: 252-746-3133, Fax: 252-746-9676). Email: dbfuneralhome@aol.com; Website: www.donbrownfuneralhome.com.

Within a decade, the Don Brown Funeral Home evolved and eclipsed all of the black funeral homes in the Greenville vicinity. Presently, it is the premier black funeral home in the area. The mission of the home is simple: Committed to the communities we serve. The home offers a full-service funeral package consisting of embalming, a floral shop, full cosmetics services, a cemetery and crematory services at competitive yet affordable prices. The full-time staff consists of Mr. Charles Edwards, licensed funeral director; Mrs. Cathy Venable, secretary/receptionist; and Mr. Keith Goddard, cemetery supervisor. The staff prides itself in doing quality work for all people all of the time; always performing at a high level of expectation; exuding respect for themselves, for the leader, and for the community; and above all, instilling pride in all they do for the Don Brown Funeral Home's operations both in Ayden and the surrounding areas.

Don apprenticed under the supervision of Mr. Gratz Norcott of the Norcott Funeral Home in Greenville and Ayden and earned a bachelor's degree at Fayetteville State University in Fayetteville, NC. Later, he received his associate degree in funeral service from the Fayetteville Technical Community College, Fayetteville, NC.

Don is characterized by his winning and relaxed personality. These traits have earned for him membership in several professional organizations, including the National Directors and Morticians of Georgia and North Carolina. He was chairman of the Board for the State of North Carolina Funeral Directors and Morticians Association, president of the Epsilon Nu Delta Mortuary Fraternity, and president and a voting delegate for the National Funeral Directors and Morticians Association House of Representatives.

For Don's distinguished and unselfish service to the Ayden community and the state of North Carolina, he received the North Carolina Funeral Directors and Morticians Association Business Achievement Award in 2000, a certificate of recognition from the town of Ayden in 2008, and the Annie M. Brown Community Service Award of Ayden in 2011. Don has also been featured in the North Carolina Mutual Life Insurance magazine for his outstanding contributions to the funeral service profession and his community.

Don is married to Mrs. Clarissa Edwards Brown and they are the proud parents of two beautiful children, Dontario and Kierra Brown. Dontario is a student at the North Carolina A & T State University in Greensboro, North Carolina. They are also blessed with two godsons, LaQuon Rogers and Perry Smith.

S. G. WILKERSON AND SONS

With Mr. S. G. Wilkerson's decision to return to the funeral business with his sons in 1932, the funeral business grew stronger and is now the dominant white funeral establishment in Greenville. In August 2011, the Smith Funeral and Home Cremation Services (white), 605 Country Club Drive, Greenville, NC 27834, (252-272-2121) became the most recent partner in Greenville to join the S. G. Wilkerson and Sons funeral service family.

Profiles of the two dominant funeral directors, Mr. Stephen George Wilkerson Sr. (white) and Mr. Walter Esmer Flanagan (black), are chronicled for contrast and comparison.

Figure A 2.1 Founder of the S. G. Wilkerson & Sons Funeral Home

S. G. Wilkerson, Sr., 1882-1948

Reared on a farm in Person County several miles outside of the City Limits of Roxboro, NC, Mr. Stephen George Wilkerson was the son of Mr. Josiah L. and Sallie Rogers Wilkerson. He was born March 3, 1882. He died at the Pitt County Hospital on August 26, 1948, at the age of 66. His interest in undertaking surfaced when he moved to Roxboro. Also, it was in Roxboro that he met his wife, Mattie Mitchell, a high-spirited, bright young 'belle' who played the piano and wore big hats and long skirts. He worked for his uncle, but his interest was focused on a pair of handsome draped gray horses used by the local undertaker to pull the ornately carved hearse with its glass panels and brass lamps.

Mr. Wilkerson married Miss Mitchell on December 31, 1904, before they moved to Lexington, NC, where their first son, Edwin Mitchell, was born. While in Lexington, Mr. Wilkerson completed a correspondence course with the Cincinnati College of Embalming (OH) and spent six weeks of practicum in Cincinnati to acquire a diploma. It is also believed that the family's other children—Stephen Lindsey, Charles Vestal, and Ida Christine—were born while he resided in Lexington.

After acquiring his diploma, the record states that Mr. Wilkerson accepted a position in Virginia, and moved with his family to Emporia, where he sold furniture and operated an undertaking establishment. The family stayed in Emporia long enough to have their fifth child, George Wilbur. The family then moved to Farmville, NC. There, Mr. Wilkerson operated an undertaking establishment for the Farmville Furniture Company. In 1916, the family moved from Farmville to Greenville, where Mr. Wilkerson purchased the funeral business of the John Flanagan Buggy Company. Brother E. G. Flanagan operated the business at that time. The last three of the Wilkersons' eight children were born in Greenville: Herbert Mosley, Joseph Louis, and Norman Warren. In Greenville, Mr. Wilkerson partnered for a time with Mr. Edward S. Williams to form the Wilkerson and Williams Undertaking Company.

With eight children and troubled financial times, Wilkerson sold his business interest to his partner and became a representative for a casket manufacturer. By 1932, the decision was made to reopen the funeral business with his sons. By 1947, S. G. Wilkerson and Sons had opened a funeral home in Robersonville, NC. In 1958, the firm opened the Pinewood Memorial Park in Greenville, and in 1975 moved into their present establishment on East Fifth Street. Another facility was opened in Vanceboro, NC, in 1980.[244]

---

[244] "S. G. Wilkerson Dies in Hospital." THE DAILY REFLECTOR, Greenville, NC, August 26, 1948, p. 1; "S. G. Wilkerson Rites to be Held Saturday." THE DAILY REFLECTOR, Greenville, NC, August 27, 1948, p. 2; Copeland. *Chronicles of Pitt County North Carolina.* 1982.

Walter Esmer Flanagan

Service of Triumph and
Memorial for the
Homegoing
of

Mr. Walter Esmer Flanagan

Saturday, July 14, 1984 — 1:00 P.M.
Sycamore Hill Baptist Church
Greenville, North Carolina
Rev. Howard Parker, Pastor

Mr. Walter E. Flanagan was born March 4, 1898, and reared on a farm near Wooten Crossroad in the Vance Township of Lenoir County. Wooten Crossroad is about ten miles north of Kinston on North Carolina Highway 58. With the passing of his parents, Calvin and Ida Flanagan, he was raised by his grandmother, Mrs. Dollie Flanagan. Mr. Flanagan died in Greenville at the Pitt County Memorial Hospital in 1984 at the age of 86 years.[245]

Mr. Flanagan received his early education at the Post Oak School, a two-room school affiliated with Post Oak Free Will Baptist Church near Wooten Crossroad. The school and community were so rural at the time that the Lenoir County Board of Education rendered them nameless. Board *Minutes* of February 2, 1914, considered the school to be one of the three nameless colored schools located in Vance Township of Lenoir County. Despite any supposed lack of identity, the

---

[245] Flanagan, Walter E. *Obituary. Service of Triumph.* Greenville, NC. 1984.

Post Oak School produced Mr. Walter Esmer Flanagan, perhaps the only black millionaire ever to come out of the Lenoir County School System.[246]

To break the cycle of sharecropping in the Flanagan family, Mr. Flanagan taught himself to cut hair. In order to perfect his barbering skills, he apprenticed under Mr. William "Will" Whitehead at the Whitehead Barber Shop in Kinston. Not only did Mr. Whitehead own and operate a barbershop, but he was a licensed embalmer and a funeral director. In addition, Mr. Whitehead, along with board members Rev. Emmanuel Hill, Rev. Peter Hood, and Mr. William E. Webb operated the Whitehead Mutual Burial Association of Kinston.[247] While working at the barbershop and witnessing Mr. Whitehead's funeral operations, "Walter seized the opportunity to pursue an embalming/funeral directing career, to make some money, and, most importantly, to leave the farm."[248],[249]

During the Jim Crow era of our history, some educational institutions defied the strict laws of segregation and accepted black candidates in their schools. Such a school was the Brown School of Embalming of the Brown Funeral Home in Raleigh, NC. The Brown Funeral Home, established in 1836, was North Carolina's oldest funeral home and remains the oldest continuous business in Raleigh.[250]

Evidence shows that during the late 1800s or early 1900s, courage, bravery and an egalitarian humanitarian spirit propelled the Browns to establish an embalming school as a service to any interested citizen in Raleigh and surrounding areas,

---

[246] Incredibly, Post Oak School today is still not recognized, and is perhaps the only two-or three-room school building still standing in Lenoir or surrounding counties today. Bringing the Post Oak School building's existence to the attention of the Lenoir County School officials was a shock and mind-boggling experience. Administrators were unaware of the school's existence and were rather suspicious of my insistence that, indeed, the school existed. Fortunately, and to everyone's surprise, after over a century, the Post Oak School survives in a very good state of preservation. Lenoir County Board of Education administrators are now aware of this school's existence and have promised to correct the omission with recognition in the next printing of the *Survey of the Public Schools of Lenoir County*. A debt of gratitude is offered to Mrs. Christine Sutton Gray for sharing this invaluable piece of information. And to her parents, Mr. and Mrs. Marcuff Alton Sutton of the Wooten Cross Road Community, in the Vance Township of Lenoir County, a debt of gratitude for their vision to preserve the school will long be remembered. Sam Barber. Christine Gray. Interview at home. Kinston, NC, March 29, 2011.

[247] Sam Barber. Clemmie Mills. Phone Interview. Kinston, NC, March 18, 2011.

[248] Sam Barber. Louise Russell. Interview at Home Health Care Provider Center. Kinston, NC, March 21, 2011.

[249] Sam Barber. Blanchie Morgan. Interview at Home Health Care Provider Center. Kinston, NC, March 21, 2011.

[250] Lynne Belvin; Harriette Riggs. *The Heritage of Wake County North Carolina*. Winston-Salem, NC: Hunter Publishing Company, 1983, p. 14-15.

---

including other states. Despite enforced legal segregation, Mr. Fabius Brown, the son of Henry L. Brown, founder of the business in 1836, replaced his father as president upon his death. Along with Professor Ed. S. Brown, the grandson of the founder and professor of embalming, they exercised a bold and aggressive humanitarian move to accept two "colored" students as early as 1911. Walter E. Flanagan, another Negro, matriculated at the school in 1924.[251] Of note is that Mr. E. G. Flanagan (white) and Mr. Ed. S. Brown passed the State Board of Embalming Test on the same date.

A 1911 newspaper story cites all twelve students by name. The colored students were Charles F. Cain of Tarboro and Mrs. W. F. Kelsey of Salisbury. The story continues:

> "Prof. Ed. S. Brown, of the Raleigh (Brown) School of Embalming, will carry with him to High Point his class of twelve to take the examination of the [embalming] association. In the class are ten white young men, one colored man and a colored woman."[252]

With an unwavering desire to dispel the notion by contemporary funeral directors that the Brown School of Embalming was just a myth, many emails, faxes, letters and telephone calls were exchanged daily with institutions and individuals in Raleigh and vicinity, including Ms. Saundra Cropps of the Olivia Raney Library, Raleigh; Ms. Delia Little, Wake County Register of Deeds, Raleigh; Mr. John Scarborough of Scarborough Funeral Home, Durham; Mr. Bob Wynne of Brown-Wynne Funeral Home, Raleigh; Mrs. Dorathy Chance, librarian, Edenton Street Methodist Church, Raleigh, Ms. Elizabeth Hayden, North Carolina Archives, Raleigh; Mr. J. T. Willoughby, Hemby-Willoughby Funeral Home, Tarboro; Mr. P. M. Burke, North Carolina Association of Funeral Directors, Raleigh; Mr. Bruce Lightner of Lightner Funeral Home, Raleigh; and Mr. Elliott Futrell, President of Evergreen Memorial Services, Goldsboro. Mr. Futrell, a former member of the North Carolina Funeral Directors' Board, confirmed that the common practice for Negroes interested in an embalming career was to go North for certification or to work under a licensed embalmer outside of one's hometown.[253] At that time, most black embalming students either trained under

---

[251]   *Raleigh North Carolina City Directory.* Richmond, VA: The Hill Directory Press, 1925, p. 827.

[252]   "Meet in High Point-Funeral Directors and Embalmers There Next Month." RALEIGH-TIMES, Raleigh, NC, April 26, 1911, p. 8.

[253]   Sam Barber. Elliott Futrell, Interview at Evergreen Memorial Gardens. Goldsboro, NC, March 3, 2011.

a local or regional licensed black embalmer or attended the McAllister School of Embalming in New York or Eckles College of Embalming in Philadelphia, PA.[254] A few candidates went South to the Meharry School of Medicine in Nashville, TN.

Mr. "Will" Whitehead undoubtedly referred Mr. Walter Flanagan to Mr. James Guess, Sr. of Goldsboro. Mr. Guess was highly respected and well-known. He was a major influence in the development of his three sons' as well as Mr. Flanagan's embalming skills and career. Mr. Flanagan was perhaps 20 or 21 years old when he moved to Goldsboro to apprentice with Mr. Guess. The Board of Embalmers policy stated "Resolved that all applicants for license to practice embalming shall have had at least one year of practical experience under some licensed embalmer in this state or some other state."[255]

The Fourteenth US 1920 Census lists Mr. Flanagan in the household of his parents at the age of 19.[256] He must have been a quick study for on May 9, 1921, at the age of 23, and unlike so many of his colleagues, Mr. Flanagan passed the North Carolina State Board of Examiners funeral directors' test on the first take.[257]

Before moving to Greenville, it is reported that Mr. Flanagan, along with Mr. James Guess, Sr., and Kenon Guess, the son, all worked at night for the Seymour Funeral Home, the leading white funeral home in Goldsboro.[258] From the 1920s to the 1940s, black embalmers who worked for white funeral homes were only paid $15 per body, while white embalmers were paid $20 per body. Because black embalmers would work mostly at night, worked longer hours and were cheaper than white ones, between 1921 and 1949, Mr. Bill Seymour hired mostly black embalmers on a case-by-case basis.

By 1922, Mr. Flanagan moved to Greenville to establish his own practice.[259] Evidence of his deft intellectual and frugal skills surfaced at an early age. According to his cousins, Walter purchased his own transportation, make and model unknown, at a very young age.[260] Some have suggested that Mr. S. G. Wilkerson set Mr. Flanagan up in business at a Second Street office. Because Mr. Wilkerson was struggling to support a large family and with the economy in free fall in the

---

[254] Barber. Futrell Interview. Ibid.

[255] North Carolina State Board of Embalmers. *Proceedings of the Annual Meeting of the North Carolina State Board of Embalmers, May 9, 1921.* Salisbury, NC, p. 1.

[256] United States. Bureau of the Census. *Fourteenth Census of the United States. 1920 North Carolina Population Schedules, Vance Township. Lenoir County, North Carolina.* (Lenoir Co., EDs 54-70). https://archive.org/details/14thcensusofpopu1308unit.

[257] North Carolina State Board of Embalmers, Ibid, p. 1.

[258] Sam Barber. Elliott Futrell. Interview, 2011.

[259] Flanagan Obituary, 1984.

[260] Sam Barber. Russell. Interview, 2011.

years just after World War I, it would be highly unusual for a business man to help set up his competition in troubled times. Documented evidence shows that with a decline in business and with eight children and a wife to support, Mr. Wilkerson sold off his business and worked for a casket company.[261]

Official death certificates show that Mr. Flanagan buried his first body, Mr. William J. Gardner who died on November 5, 1922, and was buried on November 6 in the Cooper Field Cemetery. On December 24, 1922, Mr. Flanagan buried his second body, Ms. Elizabeth Smith, who died on December 22. She was buried at the Cherry Hill Cemetery. Although Ms. Smith's birth date is not listed on the official death certificate, her age is given as 28. (Faulty or late reporting might lead one to think that this is the same Ms. Elizabeth Smith listed in Ms. Ross's *Grave Description Report*. Ms. Ross identifies a Mrs. Elizabeth Smith who was born June 8, 1896, and died in December, 1922.)

By 1924, Mr. Flanagan had partnered with Mr. Monty Cherry. They buried at least 17 bodies at Cooper Field and several bodies at other locations throughout Pitt County. White funeral directors dominated the funeral business from the late teens to the early 1920s. Even after Mr. Flanagan opened his Greenville practice, black folks were still suspect of his services and continued to use the services of Mr. Wilkerson and other white undertakers.

Failure was not an option for Mr. Flanagan. With a resolve and a passion to become successful, Mr. Flanagan partnered with both Mr. Cherry and later with Mr. David Parker to recruit business within the black community. His business accelerated so rapidly that in 1924, Mr. Flanagan saw the need for additional training. He then matriculated at the Brown School of Embalming in Raleigh, NC.[262]

Before entering the Brown School of Embalming, Mr. Flanagan met and married Ms. Charlotte Foxhall, a young attractive nurse at Pitt Memorial Hospital from Washington, NC. No children were born to this union.[263]

Mr. Flanagan's business succeeded far beyond all expectations. By the 1940s, with his business firmly established, Mr. Flanagan turned his attention to real estate. Over the years, he acquired a vast amount of property from Philadelphia to Florida. It is reported that he owned more than 200 pieces of property in Raleigh alone,[264] more in Wilson and Rocky Mount, and a substantial number

---

[261]   Elizabeth H. Copeland, comp. *Chronicles of Pitt County North Carolina*. No. 1318, 1319. Winston-Salem, NC: Hunter Publishing Company, 1982, p. 729-730.

[262]   Flanagan Obituary, 1984.

[263]   Flanagan. Obituary, 1984.

[264]   Sam Barber. Charles G. Irving, Jr, Phone Interview with Retired Book Publisher. Raleigh, NC, March 31, 2011.

of pieces in Greenville.[265] During the 1950s and 1960s, slumlords dominated ownership of real property in the downtown area. Accounts from the Shore Drive Redevelopment Project in the 1960s show that of 118 identified dwellings in the downtown area, only 29 were owned by Negroes. In contrast to the Shore Drive Report in 1963, more than 40 downtown property owners petitioned the Urban Development Commission to practice conservation rather than to take their property by eminent domain (Table A 2.2).

Table A 2.2. Homeowners Who Petitioned the Greenville Urban Development Commission to Practice Conservation Instead of Demolition.[266]

Helen Brooks	Mrs. Helen D. Scott	Mrs. Kate Gorham
Maggie Cherry	R. I. Hardy	Emma N. Kincaid
Eleanor Hagans	E. R. Dudley	Celia Little
James Hagans	Robert Lee Tucker	Odessa Johnson
Selena S. Lang	Mrs. Lola C. Taft	C. L. Daniels, Jr.
Mrs. Martha Jones	Arthur L. Norcott	Lemon C. Little
Earnest C. Adams	Bettie Tucker	Mrs. Eleanor Hussey
Mrs. Mattie Huffine	Jane Lang	Marion Norcott
Mrs. J. E. Nobles	Mrs. Virgil Meekins	William H. Lilley
Mrs. J. B. Smith	Mrs. Sallye Streeter	Mrs. Della Lilley
R. W. Hardy	Mattie Webb	Milton Carr, Jr.
Arthur Johnson	Mrs. Mary Hymon	Mrs. Pauline Carr
Jimmie Skipper	Mrs. Martha Boyd	Francine Carr
Dora Harvey	Thad Barnhill	Linda Carr
Elias Carr	Mrs. Ferdinano Barnhill	Bertha E. Savage
Pearline Mitchell	Mrs. Frances B. Frenches	Joseph Savage
John O. Mitchell	Mrs. Alvania Clark	Wiley P. Norcott
Mrs. Lottie Harris	Christine B. Clark	Alice Sheppard
Mrs. Bessie J. Askew	Willie T. May	J. S. Alexander
Mrs. Ella Wood	Mrs. Sindia D. May	George Foreman
Mrs. Mattie Lloyd	Hinton D. Barnhill	
Mrs. Alvaine Watson	I. A. Artis, Sr.	

---

[265] Sam Barber. Ellis Brown. Interview with Retired Funeral Home Director. Greenville, NC, 2011-2012.

[266] W. N. Moore, City Clerk. "Public Hearing of the Urban Renewal Plan." *City Council Minutes,* Greenville, NC, June 27, 1963, Book 10, p. 27.

Heartbroken, the pleas of the petitioners went unheeded, and the records at the Register of Deeds Office show that by 1975, at least fifteen of the petition signers had gone on to glory. Their death records are in Table A 2.3:

Table A 2.3. Death Records of Homeowners Listed on Petition to the Greenville Urban Development Commission.

NAME	DEATH DATE*	CERTIFICATE BOOK	PAGE
Artis, Isaac	11/28/73	59	616
Barnhill, Fredinando	01/15/65	51	441
Barnhill, Thad	11/07/73	49	893
Boyd, Martha	01/07/71	57	166
Carr, Milton, Sr.	11/14/62	48	587
Cherry, Maggie	02/27/69	55	235
Clark, Alvania F.	11/13/63	49	884
Frenches, Francis B.	07/05/64	50	833
Gorham, Kate	08/05/63	49	771
Jones, Martha	02/01/62	48	294
Kincaid, Emma	02/06/71	57	240
May, Willie T.	03/22/66	52	400
Norcott, Arthur Lee	10/03/75	61	547
Norcott, Wiley P.	01/14/69	55	208
Taft, Lola Cherry	02/29/70	56	306

Dates in tables are in mm/dd/yy format.

Further evidence of ownership recorded on Sheet 2, Chart 5 of the *Urban Renewal Manual* states that there were 261 dwelling units in the downtown area and 15% were owner-occupied.[267] About 39 families were homeowners.

With a long and successful funeral director's career, the legacy of Mr. Flanagan is indisputable. He was characterized as being a compassionate, a loving, gentle, fair, just, dedicated, and a personable man with a herculean humanitarian spirit. He treated his employees and citizens in the community with decency and the utmost respect. Consequently, for many years, he maintained a loyal staff who provided excellent service both to him and to the community.

---

[267] Mace. *Urban Renewal Programs in North Carolina.*

Service of Triumph and
Memorial for the
Homegoing
of

Mr. Walter Esmer Flanagan

Saturday, July 14, 1984- 1:00 P.M.
Sycamore Hill Baptist Church

Greenville, North Carolina

Rev. Howard Parker, Pastor

Mr. Flanagan died on July 10, 1984, at the Pitt County Memorial Hospital. His funeral was held on July 14, 1984, at his beloved Sycamore Hill Missionary Baptist Church.[268] Interment was at the Brown Hill Cemetery, where he buried so many of his friends, colleagues, and community folks.[269] With no wife or children, Mr. Flanagan started early to reduce his property holdings and gave or sold much of it to many impoverished citizens affected by the Shore Drive Rehabilitation Project at no or little cost with no interest.[270], [271] Before his death, he bequeathed (no Last Will and Testament found) the remainder of his earthly belongings to his cousins, Mrs. Louise Russell and Blanchie Morgan; to his loyal staff, Ms. Ellis Brown, Mrs. Louise Anderson, Mr. Clinton Mills, Mr. David Hammonds and to his church, The Sycamore Hill Missionary Baptist Church.[272, 273, 274, 275]

It is encumbered upon each of us to "Remember the days of old, consider the years of many generations: ask thy father, and he will show thee, thy elders, and they will tell thee,"[276] the final passionate farewell instructions spoken by Moses to the new generation of Israelites waiting with eager anticipation to enter into the promise land. That powerful call resonates as loudly today as it did for the Israelites of Moses' day. Disobedience to God's Word results in calamitous consequences and precludes His people from receiving His promised bountiful blessings.

The powerful words of Moses should resonate with definitive clarity not only to the few remaining Flanagan loyalists, but to all of Greenville's African American community who benefited so handsomely from Mr. Walter Esmer Flanagan's gift. Even though this was a different generation of church folks, courtesy and respect are not limited by generations. On June 28, 1942, the Sycamore Hill Baptist Church ". . . observed a Memorial for Colonel Edward G. Flanagan for his expert advice and matters of business and for donating the first one hundred dollars on the pipe organ."[277] This memorial took place twelve

---

268   Flanagan Obituary, 1984.

269   Ibid.

270   Sam Barber. Ellis Brown. Interviews. 2011-2012.

271   Sam Barber. Charles Gatlin. Interviews with Church Member of Mr. Walter Flanagan. Greenville, NC, 2011-2012.

272   Sam Barber. Russell. Interview. 2011.

273   Sam Barber. Morgan. Interview. 2011.

274   Sam Barber. Brown. Interviews. 2011-2012.

275   Sam Barber. Gatlin. Interviews. 2011-2012.

276   Nelson, *Holy Bible*, 1998.

277   "Colored News: Resolution of Respect." THE DAILY REFLECTOR, Greenville, NC, June 29, 1942, P. 6.

years after the event. The unveiling of the organ actually took place on January 5, 1930. The citation reads, "The unveiling of a newly installed Kimball pipe organ took place at Sycamore Hill Baptist Church Sunday, January 5, amidst impressive services."[278]

The church and community at the time, or at any time in fact, of Mr. Walter E. Flanagan's passing should have been no less responsive. The entire black community should *remember*, unquestioningly, that it owes Mr. Flanagan a tremendous debt of gratitude beyond measure for his compassion, his generosity, his liberality, and his humanitarian spirit. A special tribute of *celebration* and *remembrance* should be an annual public event of his passing.

---

[278] "Unveiling Services of Pipe Organ Held Greenville Church." NORFOLK JOURNAL AND GUIDE, Norfolk, VA, January 11, 1930, p. 13.

Appendix III

Professor Charles M. Eppes

Figure A 3.1 Professor of C. M. Eppes High School

Charles Montgomery Eppes

Charles Montgomery Eppes, 1858-1942

Archival evidence is offered for a deeper understanding and better appreciation of Professor C. M. Eppes' background, character, personality, courage, and resolve:

- Charles Montgomery Eppes, educator, principal, writer, scholar, diplomat and beloved citizen, was born a slave on December 25, 1858, in Halifax, N.C., to Mr. Henry and Luvinia Eppes. Charles was the third of seven children. One source cites that Professor Eppes' parents had twelve (12) children.[279] Albeit born a slave, Charles was favored with many entitlements. Professor Eppes' father was for twenty years a State Senator of North Carolina. His mother was an avid reader and house wife and perhaps Charles' earliest teacher.[280]

- Professor Eppes began school when he was six years old and, along with his mother, attended a school established by Methodist Missionaries for Freemen.[281]
- Charles attended public school in Halifax County. He later attended the Episcopal School in Raleigh, NC.[282]
- In 1873, at the age of 15, Mr. Eppes began 'school keeping . . .' in a log hut of one room. The children were seated to rotate around the heater. Due to farm duties and responsibilities, the school term was only four months. All teachers were paid the same salary.[283]
- Professor Eppes attended but did not graduate from Shaw Collegiate Institute (University), Raleigh, NC,[284] and A&T (College) State University, Greensboro.[285]
- In 1882, emphasis was placed on giving the colored race an education and to the credit of whites, the matter was fully considered and supported. A large school for the negro was erected at Princeville, another at Battleboro, a third school at Whitakers, and others at other places in the county. C. M. Epps, a negro teacher, received support from the white people and accomplished good until he was debarred from the negro schools by the negroes themselves, who declared he was a Democrat. During the fusion era he was persecuted by his race. He later

[279] Special to the *Journal and Guide*. "Venerable Educator, 84 Dies." NORFOLK JOURNAL AND GUIDE, Norfolk, VA, August 8, 1942, p. 1.; United States Census. "Halifax Township, Halifax North Carolina." Washington, D.C. Government Printing Office, June 18, 1880.
[280] *Who's Who in Colored America: A Biographical Dictionary of Notable Living Men and Women. Eppes, Charles Montgomery.* New York: Who's Who in Colored America Corp., 1927, p. 178.
[281] Special to the *Journal and Guide*, p. 1.
[282] Roger Kammerer. "Charles M. Eppes: Noted Black Educator and Civic Leader." GREENVILLE TIMES, Greenville, NC, October 18-21, 1993, p. 8.
[283] Special to the *Journal and Guide*, p. 1.
[284] Special to the *Journal and Guide*, p. 1.
[285] Chester Walsh. "Hold Funeral for C.M. Eppes." THE DAILY REFLECTOR, Greenville, NC, August 3, 1942, p. 6.

left Edgecombe County, and was appointed assistant superintendent of the Colored Normal School at Plymouth.

- He served as principal of schools in Wilmington, and Wilson, NC,[286] and was Superintendent of the State Normal School, Plymouth, NC,[287] before coming to Greenville in 1903.
- As a pioneer in the cause of early education for Freemen . . . Professor Eppes ranks among the North Carolinians whose names are synonymous with the genesis of free education for colored people.[288]
- He assumed the mantle of leadership for the education of black youths in Greenville from 1903 until his death on July 31, 1942. During his 39-year tenure, he exerted a profound influence on black youths and the black community. He was honored by the Greenville Board of Education on May 30, 1941, in a meeting naming the Greenville Industrial High School to The C.M. Eppes High School. Contrary to a lot of famous individuals, this honor was bestowed on Professor Eppes while he was still alive.[289]

Local and contiguous county principals who provided support, encouragement, and cooperation to Professor Eppes were Mr. G. R. Whitfield, Pitt County Training School (1916), school named in his honor in 1945 after his death, Grimesland, NC; Professor John Thomas Barber, West Street High School, New Bern, NC, school named in his honor in 1944 after his death. (Professor J. T. Barber was the second cousin to the writer.) Professor W. C. Chance, Parmalee High, Parmalee, NC; Professor J. W. Willie, Jones County Training School, Pollocksville, NC; Professor Julian A. Prince, Greene County Training School (1925) Snow Hill, NC; Professor J. T. Kerr, Georgetown High School, Jacksonville, NC; and Professor C. C. Franks, Trenton High School (1936), Trenton, NC.

Being legally prohibited from any state-supported education for centuries, in 1899 with the beginning of public education in North Carolina for all students and in Greenville in 1903, the leap from a rudimentary elementary education to the beginning of a high school education by 1922, by any account, was a momentous challenge and a leap of faith and resolve on behalf of Professor Eppes, his teachers, his staff, his students, the parents, and the community. Although the

---

[286] Walsh, Ibid.; J. Kelly Turner; J. C. Bridges, Jr. *History of Edgecome County School.* Raleigh, NC: Edward and Burough Press, 1990, p. 378.

[287] *Who's Who in Colored America*, p. 178.

[288] Special to the *Journal and Guide*, p. 1.

[289] J. H. Rose. "Special Meeting of the Board of Education." Greenville, NC, Board of Education, May 30, 1941, Book III, p. 103.

high school was labeled as an industrial school, mostly non-industrial subjects were taught. The subjects taught were academic in nature and without academic preparation, the students accepted the daunting challenge with aplomb and alacrity.

A flood of misinformation circulating about the genesis of the high school in Greenville for colored children lends itself to pause and clarification. The paucity of recorded data in the Board of Education *Minutes* does not help to clarify this misinformation. The *Minutes* are extremely parsimonious about recording any information about the academic progress of the colored schools. They are limited to some citations about a few fiscal practices such as the cost of a new school building and money spent on persistent repairs and leaks at the colored schools.

To trace the origin of the Negro public high school, one needs only to track the origin of the white public high school. Both races attended private high schools before the North Carolina Public Act of 1899. The record shows that "...in 1915 the first four-year (white) high school class graduated."[290] But because the Negro schools could not meet the standards set by the state, the record shows that "... before 1921 and the establishment of the Negro Division of Education, no Negro school (high school) could comply with the standard."[291]

Once the white high school started, a colored high school was sure to follow. Therefore, we can, with a degree of certainty, agree that the high school for Negro students actually began in Greenville in 1922. Albeit the annual principal's report to the North Carolina Department of Public Instruction records in Raleigh show no graduates until 1926, we can infer that in 1922-1923, the eighth grade was added; in 1923-1924, the ninth grade; in 1924-1925, the tenth grade; and in 1925-1926, the first graduating class recorded one male student, no females.

Professor Eppes made the acquisition of an education the core principle of Greenville's Negro community. The following *Annual Progress Reports* from the State Department of Education are instructive:

---

[290] Scott E. Power. *The Historic Architecture of Pitt County, North Carolina.* Greenville, NC: The Pitt County Historical Society, Inc., 1991, p. 66.

[291] Hugh Brown. *A History of the Education of Negroes in North Carolina.* Raleigh, NC: Irvin-Swain Press, 1961, p. 61.

Table A 3.1 Progress Reports on Greenville's Public Education System, 1922-1944. (Copied directly from the "Annual Principal's report to the North Carolina Department of Public Instruction, State Archives, Raleigh, NC)

Annual Principal's Report to the North Carolina Department of Public Instruction

1922- 1923	No Report
1923- 1924	No Report
1924- 1925	No Report
1925- 1926	First Graduating Class

The Industrial School, Greenville, NC: C. M. Eppes, Principal

Teachers

Elliott, Margaret	Shaw Univ	Bio, Latin Lit, Eng., Algebra
Peace, Annie E.	Bennett & Clark Col.	Hist & Latin Lit
C. M. Eppes	Shaw Univ	Hist, Math, Algebra, Civ, Geo

Graduates

1 Boy   0 Girls

Cornelius Forbes

1926-1927

Industrial High School, Greenville, NC: C. M. Eppes, Principal

Teachers

Davis, Bessie M.	Howard Univ	Latin, History/Bio
Johnson, Vivian	Howard Univ	Comp, Phys Ed, Lit
Eppes, C. M.	Shaw Univ	Hist, Geo/Civ

Graduates

1 Boy   3 Girls

William Ralph Peele   Thelma Lanier
                                         Hernie Lee Peel

Lucile Daniel

1927-1928

Industrial Graded and High School, Greenville, NC: C. M. Eppes, Principal

Teachers

McComas, R. A.	Howard Univ	Eng., F. language
Bynum, C. H. Jr.	Lincoln Univ	Eng
C. M. Eppes	Shaw Univ	Hist, Civ
(B. C. Donnell)	Missing	

Graduates

3 Boys	12 Girls
Rosher Johnson	Odessa Chapman
Henry Turnage	Violet B. Cherry
Charles Williams	Avania Clark
	Betty Dudley
	Porcia Dudley
	Annie M. Ford
	Virgil Gorham
	Mary Gorham
	Olivia Gorham
	Thelma Lang
	Fannie Parker
	Bernice West

1928-1929

Industrial and Graded School, Greenville, NC: C. M. Eppes, Principal

Teachers

Davenport, W. H.	Union Univ	Alg, Geo, Bio, Chem
McComas, Ruby	Howard Univ	English, F. Lan
Donnell, Bertha C.	Nat'l Tng. School,	Home Economics
Eppes, C. M.	Shaw Univ	Hist (A. M. & Modern)

Graduates

1 Boy   7 Girls

Milton Daniels   Davenport, Ruby
                                         Forbes, Hattie V.
                                         Grimes, Annie
                                         Price, Viola
                                         Thompson, Martha Lee
                                         Levies, Lizzie
                                         Brown, Wilson Susie

1929- 1930

Industrial High School, Greenville, NC: C. M. Eppes, Principal

Teachers:

McComas, R. A.	Howard Univ	Eng & F. Lan
Davenport, W. H.	VA. Union	Sci, Math, Coach
Reed, E. Ridley	Shaw Univ	Eng, Hist, F. Lan
Donnell, B. C.	Nat'l Tng. School	Home Economics
Eppes, C. M.	Shaw Univ	Hist, Civ, Geo

Graduates

1 Boy   11 Girls

Milton Carr Junius   Melba Cherry
                                         Garrett, Naomi
                                         Mary Alice Williams
                                         Christine B. Johnson
                                         Lena Odessa Bradley
                                         Inez Butler
                                         Mason, Anna
                                         Moore, Halese
                                         Rosebury, Sudie
                                         Vines, Ruby
                                         Armstrong, Beulah

1930-1931   No Report

1931 -1932

Industrial High School, Greenville, NC: C. M. Eppes, Principal

Teachers

C. M. Eppes	Shaw Univ	History
McComas, Ruby A.	Howard Univ	
Battle, Olga Lee	Talladega	History, A & Medieval
Davenport, W. H.	VA. Union	Sci & Math
Donnell, Bertha	Durham Nat. Tng. Sch.	Home Economics

Graduates

3 Boys   9 Girls

Claude Edwards	Merle Daniel
Chas. Daniel, Jr.	Mamie Lee Norris
G. Peacock (Un-reported 1931)	Annie E. Ebron
	Pauline Fleming
	Willie F. Fleming
	Clydia Long
	Thelma Smith
	Lucile Rich
	Melba C. McKinnie

1932-1933

Industrial Graded and High School, Greenville, NC: C. M. Eppes, Principal

Eppes, C. M.	Shaw Univ	Hist, Civ, Geo
McComas, R. A.	Howard Univ	Eng & F. Language
Davenport, W. H.	VA. Union	Science
Battle, Olga Lee	Talladega	Eng, F. Lan, History
Donnell, Bertha	Nat'l Tng. Sch.	Home Economics
	(Now NC College)	

Graduates

6 Boys	10 Girls
Brown, Samuel	Moore, Amelia
Hester, W. H.	McIver, Janet
Hopkins, James W.	McIver, Juliet
Jenkins, Hugh M.	McClinton, Marion C.
Lang, Joseph J., Jr.	Harris, Evelyn
May, John	Gorham, Fannie Ruth
	Harrington, Alice
	Joyner, Ethel Rush
	Hopkins, Rosa Lee
	Mary Whitley

None to College on Account of Money

1933-1934

Industrial & High School, Greenville, NC: C. M. Eppes, Principal

Teachers

Eppes, C. M.	Shaw Univ	Hist, Civ, Geo
Battle, O. L.	Talladega	Eng, Hist. A&M
Davenport, Willie H.	VA Union	Science
McComas, Ruby A.	Howard Univ	Eng, F. Language
Donnell, Bertha C.	NC College	Home Economics

Graduates

6 Boys	7 Girls
Barnhill, Howard	James, Essie M.
Myers, Wm. H.	Carvey, Mamie
Revis, Charles R.	Latham, Mabel
Javen, Leonard	Dupree, Mabel
Javen, Charles	Daniel, Ollie
Whitfield, Roscoe	Vines, Cliffie
	Savage, Sudie

To College: 2   To Trade School: 3

1934-1935

Industrial High School, Greenville, NC: C. M. Eppes, Principal

Teachers

Battle, O. L.	Talladega	Latin, Eng, Hist
Davenport, W. H.	VA Union	
Eppes, C. M.	Shaw Univ	Hist, Geo/Civ
McComas	Howard Univ	

Graduates

6 Boys   9 Girls

Aston, Tumma	Boston, Virginia
Thomas, Alfred Melrose	Barrett, Charlotte
Hemby, Samuel	Bernard, Mary
Forbes, Herman L.	Tucker, Mary
Tucker, Joseph	May, Niva
Winston, John	May, Bernice
	Hemby, Martha
	Ethel Wooten
	Carrie Wooten

To College: 2   To Tech School: 4   To Business College: 1

1935- 1936

Industrial High School, Greenville, NC: C. M. Eppes, Principal

Teachers

Eppes, C. M.	Shaw Univ	Hist. Gov, Geo, Eng,
McComas	Howard Univ	F. Language, Sci
Davenport, W. H.	VA Union	Math
Battle	Talladega	Eng, Hist, F. Lan.
Donnell	Nat'l Tng. School	Home Economics
Mabry, C. G.	Tuskegee	Sci/Chem, Vocation

Graduates

9 Boys	17 Girls
Brown, Noah	Brown, Novella
Barnhill, David	Burke, Jessie Marie
Fleming, Joseph	Donnelson, Emily
Atkinson, Robert	Foreman, Mildred
Mann, Jack,	Glover, Annie
Moore, Lawrence	Gray, Louise Thelma
Lang, Raymond	Harris, Beatrice Marie
Hopkins, Arzon	Harris, Laura Lee
Hopkins, Milton Jones	Hopkins, Arzrow
	James, Beatrice Bettie
	James, Melvin Hettie
	Jones, Jesse Mae
	Langley, Mavis
	Miller, Cora
	Price, Lillian Mae
	Pugh, Lillian Bezonia
	Sherrod, Odella Melda

1936-1937

Industrial High School, Greenville, NC: C. M. Eppes, Principal

Teachers

C. M. Eppes	Shaw Univ	Hist, Geo, Civ
McComas, R. A.	Howard Univ	Latin, French, Soci
Battle, O. Lee	Talladega	
Davenport, W. H.	VA Union	
Donnell, Bertha C.	Nat'l Tng. School	Home Economics
Mabry, C. G.		

Graduates

9 Boys	7 Girls
Cherry, Charles	Gorham, Magnolia
U. S. Grant Bell	Forbes, Blanche

Herbert Miller
Norman B. Barnhill
Dennison Garrett
Cherry, Ernest
Alfred B. Barnhill
Franklin, Bradley
Keyes, James

Jordan, Alberta
Braswell, Yvette
Hemby, Lucy
Irma Maye
Brown, Laura

1937-1938

Industrial High School, Greenville, NC: C. M. Eppes, Principal

Teachers

Bertha C. Donnell	N. C. Col. (Durham)	Home Economics
Olga L. Battle	Talladega	Hist, Eng, Latin
Curtis G. Mabry	A&T	lnd Arts, Coach/SS
Ruby A. McComas	Howard	Eng, Latin, French
Willis H. Davenport	VA Union	Math, Biology
C. M. Eppes	Shaw Univ	Hist, Civ

Graduates

6 Boys

9 Girls

Cherry, Alonza W.
Edwards, Griffin
Harris, Southie, Jr.
Hopkins, Nelson
Pitt, Ernest
Wilkins, William

Barnett, Lula
Edwards, Virgie
Jenkins, Ruth Thelma
Little, Christine
Rasburg, Emma O.
Spain, Annie Mae
Spence, Vivian
Whitfield, Mary E.
Wooten, Cleopatra

To College: 1

To Technical School: 8

1938- 1939

Fleming Street School, Greenville, NC: C. M. Eppes, Principal

Teachers

C. M. Eppes	Shaw Coll, Inst.	History
W. H. Davenport	VA Union	Math & Sci
C. G. Mabry	A&T	Sci & Man, Trg Eng,
O. L. Battle	Talladega	Hist, Latin, English
E. C. Johnson	Hampton	& French
B. C. Donnell	NC Col. College	Home Economics

Graduates

7 Boys   17 Girls

7 Boys	17 Girls
Bradley, Boston	Barnhill, Dorothy
Foreman, Thomas	Cherry, Dora B.
Maye, George	Cherry, Lula C.
Jones, Charles	Corey, Lillie Dill
Smith, Alexander	Dawson, Clementine
Spain, Willie	Daniels, Marion
Wadell, David	Eaton, Hymen
	Ennett, Myrtle
	Gorham, Lue Etta
	Jenkins, Myrtle
	Jordan, Willie Mae
	League, Marie B.
	Moore, Mary E.
	Morris, Doris M.
	Sharpe, Barbara
	Smith, Sylvia
	Taylor, Sara

1939-1940

Industrial High School, Greenville, NC: C. M. Eppes, Principal

Teachers

Eppes, C. M.	Shaw Univ	Hist & Civ
Myers, Olga		Hist & Eng
Mabry, C. G.		Ind Arts/Math/Chem
Davenport, W. H.		Math & Bio

Haith, Cora M.   Eng.
Donnell, Bertha C.   French, Home Economics

Graduates

6 Boys   17 Girls

Daniel, Percy Lennon	Atkins, Maverly Olivia
Godette, Joseph	Bell, Ira Dell
Jones, William Ernest	Banks, Lena Roberta
Nobles, James Ernest	Braxton, Lassie Bell
Teele, Willie	Corey, Connelia
Williams, Melvin H.	Clark, Onedia Virginia
	Dupree, Mary Elizabeth
	Godette, Winifred F.
	Hall, Mildred Louise
	Mitchell, Jessie Mae
	Pettaway, Ethel Mae
	Short, Amanda
	Spain, Lillie Queen
	Spence, Thelma Louise
	Saunders, Lucille
	Tyre, Helena
	Wooten, Earlean

1940- 1941

C. M. Eppes Industrial High School, Greenville, NC: C. M. Eppes, Principal

Teachers

W. H. Davenport	Gen Math
Bertha Donnell	H.Eco
Chester Bradley	Algebra
C. M. Eppes	
Olga G. Myers	World Hist
A. B. Williams	Shop/SciNoc
Cora M. Haith	Eng

Graduates

17 Boys   14 Girls

Marvin Anderson   Mabel Barnes
Douglas Barnhill   Mammie Corey
Charles Eaton   Frances Flood
Alfert Hill   Annie Forbes
Douglas Gorham   Lina Mae Hill
Charles Glenn   Mary House
Albert Hill   Ethel Moore
Fred Jones   Sally Mae Norcott
Elsworth A. Langley   Mary Ruffin
Herbert Lee   Hazel Taft
Clifton Morris   Beulah Whitfield
James A. Nimmo   Othalia White
James Syms   Willie Mae Woodard
Robert Shivers   Jennie Willoughby
Robert Teele
Henry Tyner
James Vines

1941 -1942

C. M. Eppes Industrial High School, Greenville, NC: C. M. Eppes, Principal

Teachers

Chester Bradley
Willis H. Davenport
Selina L. Davenport   French, Eng/Hist
Eva DeJournette   Phs., Math/G. Sci
Bertha C. Donnell
Charles M. Eppes
Irma L. Joyner   Eng
Olga Myers

Graduates

9 Boys

23 Girls

Travis Banks
James Clarke
Wm. Collins
Howard Cherry
Luke Hemby
David Richardson
William Streeter
Thomas Churchill
Frank Wilson

Jean Askew
Edna Braxton
Ruth Ellington
Melba Forbes
Ruby Gibbs
Evelyn Gorham
Myrtle Hooks
Helen Joyner
Elma Langley
Iris Langley
Lillie Moore
Cryena Moore
Elsie Moore
Hazel Mitchell
Sudie Monk
Inez Nimmo
Ivery Outterbridge
Beulah Sherrod
Louise Sherrod
Mable Shirley
Mammie Taylor
Ella Weatherington
Ella Wilcock

1942- 1943

C. M. Eppes High School, Greenville, NC: Willis H. Davenport, Principal

Teachers

David Barnhill
Chester Bradley
Bernice Brett
Selina Davenport
Willis Davenport, Principal
Bertha Donnell (Deceased)
Estelle Forest

Eng/Math/Com
Chem/Bio/G. Sci
SS & Library
French/SS
Math, H.Ec
H. C.
Eng

Irma Joyner	SS
E. Louise McConnell	Math/Sci
Willie J. Small	Eng/Hist/Sci
Mildred Thompson	

Graduates

11 Boys	15 Girls
Geo. L. Cherry	Ethel G. Barnhill
Kelly L. Darden	Queen E. Bartelette
Geo D. Garrett	Mary L. Blow
Willie J. Gorham	Mary A Garrett
Cannell Grimes	Doris M. Hill
Emmerson C. Hardy	Carrie E. Johnson
Talmadge D. Hill	Hazel O. Jones
Geo J. Jenkins	Loretta McLone
Jousha Jones	Mary Maye
James U. Stokes	Harriett V. Norcott
Earl E. Williams	Mary B. Robinson
	Curlie M. Spell
	Curlie L. Spell
	Laura M. Ward
	Minnie L. Wiggins

1943-1944

C. M. Eppes High School, Greenville, NC: Willis H. Davenport, Principal

Teachers

David Barnhill	
Chester Bradley	
Bernice Brett	Library & SS
Selina Davenport	
Willis H. Davenport	
Olga B. Myers	
Louise McConnell	SS
Hattie F. Robinson	Home Ec
Willie V. Small	Math & Sci
Majorie Townes (Resigned)	Home Ec
Mildred Thompson	Eng/SS/Sci

Graduates

5 Boys   14 Girls

Hebra Anderson   Audrey Mae Artis
Charles Ackinson   Bernice Atkinson
Marvin Barrett   Mavis Barnes
Leonard Forbes   Leah Bynum
Vernon Dawson   Mary H. Chapman
                                          Eunice Oneil Forbes
                                          Edna Earle Garrett
                                          Ophelia Marie Jones
                                          Laura Mae Langley
                                          Dorothy Hall Murrell
                                          Melba Halese Norris
                                          Mary Dorothea Rogers
                                          Claudia Louise Shepard
                                          Martha Doris Williams

     Another bit of misinformation circulating about the colored high school in Greenville is its name. From the beginning of the colored school in 1903 to 1941, the school underwent several name changes. From 1903 to 1922, but for few exceptions, most of the colored students attended public elementary school. However, according to reports submitted to the North Carolina Department of Public Instruction in Raleigh from 1925 until 1944, the school underwent a series of name changes from Industrial School, Industrial Graded and High School, the Fleming Street School, the C.M. Eppes Industrial High School, the Fifth Street Negro School, and finally the C.M. Eppes High School.[292] Although the name *Industrial* implies a mostly manual track of instruction, as stated, there were very few non-academic subjects taught. Widely recognized locally and throughout the State of North Carolina and the nation as the Dean of Negro Education in Greenville, the colored school or Fifth Street Negro School was officially named for C.M. Eppes on May 30, 1941. The Greenville City Schools Board of Education *Minutes* state:

[292] North Carolina Department of Public Instruction. [C.M. Eppes]. *Annual Principal's Report to the North Carolina Department of Public Instruction.* Raleigh, NC: North Carolina Archives, 1923-1944.

A Special Call Meeting with the following Board members present: Mr. E. G. Flanagan, Mr. J. L. Little, Mr. Joe Taft, Mrs. E. W. Harvey, Mr. W. E. Hooker, Mr. J. B. James, and Mrs. D. M. Clark. This meeting was called for the purpose of discussing the advisability of naming the FIFTH STREET NEGRO SCHOOL for the present supervising principal of Negro schools, C. M. Eppes.

After some discussion, the following resolution was made by Mr. Taft, seconded by Mr. Hooker, and passed unanimously:

Resolved that the Board of Trustees of the Greenville City Schools desire to show their appreciation to C. M. Eppes, supervising principal of the Negro schools in Greenville for thirty-eight years, beginning in 1903. Therefore, in recognition of the faithful and efficient service over these thirty-eight years, it is hereby ordered that from henceforth the name of the FIFTH STREET COLORED SCHOOL be changed to that of the C. M. Eppes High School.

Signed: J. H. Rose[293]

It is an anomaly for a school to be named for a living recipient, especially a black one. So we know that Professor Eppes had to be an extraordinarily exceptional individual to receive such an honor during his life time.

The record shows that Mr. Eppes worked faithfully and dutifully until the very end of his long and illustrious career. He signed the 1941-1942 annual principal report in May and died July 31, 1942. Despite Professor Eppes' long tenure in the Greenville schools, he undoubtedly suffered some serious health issues. On his last trip to Raleigh and after fifteen days of treatment by a physician, on July 31, 1942, Professor Eppes succumbed to prostate cancer.[294] He is buried in the Brown Hill Cemetery.[295]

Despite the honor bestowed on Professor Eppes in 1941 and after thirty-nine years of longevity with The Greenville Board of Education and a lifetime of

---

[293] J. H. Rose, Secretary. "Naming of High School." *Minutes of Board of Education*, Greenville, NC, May 30, 1941, Book III, p. 103.

[294] North Carolina State Board of Health. "Certificate of Death: Eppes, Charles M." Raleigh, NC, July 31, 1942, # 30.

[295] C.M. Eppes Cultural Center. "Greenville Industrial C. M. Eppes High School Alumni Association." Greenville, NC.

exemplary service and sacrifice, one would expect a well-deserved public profile of Professor Eppes' career in the local paper by the Board of Education on Professor Eppes' passing. Several articles in the *DAILY REFLECTOR* outside of the *COLORED NEWS COLUMN*, acknowledged the death of Professor Eppes. Noted were: *DEATH CLAIMS CHAS. M. EPPES*, July 31, 1942; an editorial, *CHARLES M. EPPES*, August 1, 1942; and *HOLD FUNERAL FOR C. M. EPPES*, by Chester Walsh, August 3, 1942. In the *COLORED NEWS COLUMN* two articles were cited: *RESOLUTIONS OF RESPECT* by Mrs. L. R. Taylor, August 5, 1942, and *TO THE COLORED CITIZENS OF GREENVILLE* by J. B. Taft, August 10, 1942. Missing from these articles was an official Profile from the Greenville Board of Education. A brief Editorial Tribute to Professor Eppes published in the *DAILY REFLECTOR* on Saturday, August 1, 1942, merits attention:

CHARLES M. EPPES

Professor Eppes is dead but the accomplishments of his thirty nine years of service as head of our Negro schools will live on for years to come, to the enrichment of the people of his own race and to the community. He was an outstanding negro educator and his full realization of that accord and cooperation between the races was necessary if our community was to go forward, was a driving force that caused him to put uppermost in his endeavors an effort at all times to see to it that there was complete understanding between our people. Under his guidance our Negro schools have made much progress and in appreciation for his fine service our city board last year paid him a deserved tribute by naming the Negro high school for him. Eppes was truly the white man's friend and the friend of his own race, and in his death our community has lost a valuable citizen.[296]

Also, noteworthy was the RESOLUTION OF RESPECT in the COLORED NEWS COLUMN published by the faculty at the C. M. Eppes High School acknowledging Professor Eppes' passing. It reads:

RESOLUTION OF RESPECT

The following are resolutions as written and read by Mrs. L. R. Taylor at the last rites for Professor C. M. Eppes.

---

[296] "Charles M. Eppes." DAILY REFLECTOR, Greenville, NC, August 1, 1942, p. 4.

In as much as God in His all wise power and His infinite love and wisdom has seen fit to call from this earthly life our own dear principal and co-worker Professor Charles Montgomery Eppes, and inasmuch as the departed has meant so much good to the lives of generations of people both young and old, we the faculty of the Negro schools of this city wish to submit the following resolutions:

1. Be it resolved that we are in deepest sympathy with the family,
2. That his was a noble life, a life of sacrifice and service and worthy of emulation,
3. That the work that he so nobly established shall stand out in the days and years to come as a monument to his memory,
4. That as he worked for quiet, peace, love and contentment among the different groups of people in our city, county and state, that we as a group continue to work to that end,
5. That his presence and work shall be missed by all people of Greenville, Pitt County and of North Carolina,
6. That the school that he established 39 years ago continue to hold up the high standards of morals for which he so nobly fought,
7. Finally, that a copy of these resolutions be sent to the family, a copy placed in the school files, and a copy to the daily papers.

Respectfully submitted: The Faculty of the Negro Schools of This City.[297]

A 1942 DAILY REFLECTOR editorial stated that "Eppes was truly the white man's friend." That statement speaks volumes as to Professor Eppes' personality and character. But what did it say about his relationship to the Negro community? It is a widely held truism that Professor Eppes' service to the black community is legendary. But at what cost?

On May 12, 1931, an extra meeting was called by the Board of Education for

> . . . the purpose of hearing protest on reelection on the Principal of the Negro School by the Negro Welfare Association. The following negroes appeared before the Board. Dr. Battle, Dr. J. S. Shaw, Joe Taft. Dr. Battle acted as spokesman for the group and stated that he represented a large group of negro people, and that he opposed the

---

[297] Mrs. L. R. Taylor. "Resolution of Respect." DAILY REFLECTOR, Greenville, NC, June 29, 1942, p.6.

election of the negro principal, solely on the grounds that C.M. Eppes at the present time was too old, was not progressive and thinks in terms of the past. He further stated that there might be things that could be said against the administration of C.M. Eppes, but that the main protest he would like to make was on account of his age, he asked that the Board of Trustees give them a principal in keeping with the times.[298]

On May 16, 1931 Professor Eppes appeared before the Board and presented his side of the controversy:

Professor Eppes appeared with a number of volumes of reports, and clippings and reviewed in detail the history of his life and the part he played in the struggle between the blacks and whites in the early North Carolina history. He called to the attention of the Board his work in Greenville over a period of twenty-eight years and reviewed the struggles of certain negro factions in this town during that time. He furthermore stated that the Welfare League fell out with him because he insisted that all negro relief funds be handled by the white people, and further that they were jealous of his appointment by the Governor on the State Employment Commission. He further stated that there were numbers of negro men in North Carolina who were older than he was and who were still actively engaged in work, and that his age did not bar him if he was active.[299]

The selection of the Negro principal resurfaced in July 12, 1934. The *Minutes* state:

The Board took up the matter of election of the principal for negro schools .... The (Board) agreed to hear from the Pitt County Welfare and Community League before the election of the principal. However, the secretary stated that since that time, he had received a petition from certain members of the League, and that the petition took the place of a hearing .... Petition read but not included in the minutes. The Board discussed the matter at great length, then it was moved and passed that C. M. Eppes be re-elected as principal for the ensuing year.[300]

---

[298] J. H. Rose, Secretary. "Extra Meeting, Board of Education." Board of Education, Greenville City Schools, Greenville, NC, May 12, 1931.

[299] Ibid. May 16, 1931.

[300] Ibid. July 12, 1934.

Conservatism served Professor Eppes very well and for the next 10 years he was rewarded for his loyalty. No other queries about Professor Eppes' retirement surfaced until May 14, 1942. At that time:

> The Superintendent reported that it was necessary for the School Board to determine whether or not C.M. Eppes, principal of the colored schools, should be retained as active principal or be retired and be made principal emeritus. The secretary was authorized to write C.M. Eppes a letter asking him to reply in writing whether or not he would like to be retired or whether he would like to retain his position as principal of the school.[301]

On June 11, 1942, a reply from Professor Eppes

> ...requesting that he be kept in service for another year that he did not wish to retire, and asked the School Board to ask the State Retirement Commission to permit him to remain in the service for another year. It was moved by Mr. Taft and seconded by Mr. James that the School Board request the Retirement Commission to allow C.M. Eppes to remain in service for another year.[302]

The last entry in the Board's *Minutes* about Professor Eppes' tenure was on August 11, 1942:

> The Superintendent reported that since the last meeting of the Board C.M. Eppes, supervising principal of the Negro schools since 1903 (the organization date of the graded schools of Greenville), had died in Raleigh on Friday, July 31, 1942. The Superintendent also reported that in cooperation with the Mayor and the City engineers and the leading Negro citizens of Greenville they had seen to it that a beautiful lot was provided as a last resting place for this faithful public servant, and that all details for the funeral had been worked out with the leaders of the Negro race and the relatives of Professor Eppes, and that proper respect had been shown in every way by the school and the School Board. It was moved and passed that proper resolutions of appreciation for the life and work of Professor Eppes in

---

[301] Ibid. May 14, 1942, p. 133.
[302] Ibid. June 11, 1942, p. 135.

the community be drawn to be spread upon the records of the school (not found).

The Superintendent reported that it was necessary for the Board to elect a successor to Professor Eppes, and that he had talked with the leaders of the Negro race in Greenville and they were of the opinion that W.H. Davenport was the man to succeed Professor Eppes because (1) he had been schooled under Professor Eppes for thirteen years and professor Eppes believed in him; (2) he was a safe, conservative man who desired to do the right thing; (3) he had a good educational background and would receive his Master's degree from Hampton Institute the latter part of August 1942; (4) a petition bearing the names of several hundred good Negro citizens of Greenville had been presented asking for his election.

Professor Davenport was then called before the Board, and the Board talked with him at length asking questions. After a time he was excused. It was moved and passed unanimously that W.H. Davenport be elected supervising principal of the Negro schools for a term of one year.[303]

---

[303]   Ibid. August 11, 1942, p 139.

APPENDIX IV

Document Concerning
Re-interred Bodies Found

A recently discovered document certifying 97 identified and 7 unknown names of re-interred bodies from the Sycamore Hill Baptist Church Cemetery to the Brown Hill Cemetery is the defining moment for the lack of accountability and transparency accompanied by a disingenuous and woefully disrespectful behavior displayed by Greenville City officials and the Shore Drive Rehabilitation Commission, already commented on several times throughout this book. As reported earlier, City officials and the Rehabilitation Commission reported only 42 bodies were re-interred from the SHBC Cemetery to the Brown Hill Cemetery in 1969. Of these 42 bodies, 23 were unidentified and 19 identified.

In comments gleaned from a DAILY REFLECTOR article by the Rev. J. A. Nimmo, pastor of the church for more than 33 years, we learned that "200 or more bodies" were buried on the cemetery grounds. Intense research on the church's long history of owning and operating a private cemetery, along with personal discernment, influenced my decision to conclude that there were more than 42 bodies buried at the SHBC Cemetery. My conclusion was completely validated when I discovered this rare, important and powerful document. The document, certified by C. A. Holliday, Chief Engineer for the City of Greenville, dated October 21, 1969, identifies 97 named individuals, 7 unknown individuals, and 16 unfilled plots in Section CC of the Brown Hill Cemetery.

Section CC of the Brown Hill Cemetery was specifically designated gratis and deeded to SHBC by the City for the re-interment of bodies moved from the SHBC Cemetery. Section CC consists of double plots numbered 41 through 70, a total of 120 spots for single graves. Sixteen plots, (numbers 49, 50, 59, and 60, with four plots each) were unfilled; seven spots were unknown, and 97 spots were identified with full names. No birth or death dates were included. Consequently, identifications without death and birth dates led to an on-sight grave inspection. The on-sight inspection showed no evidence of 97 headstones moved to the Brown Hill Cemetery. Therefore, seeing no evidence of headstones, the big question is, what happened to the headstones? Were they discarded, buried, broken into pieces and used to improve potholes, to pave sidewalks and walkways or like many bodies of black citizens before this public cemetery, thrown into the Tar River?

Due diligence prevailed to locate the list of re-interred bodies from the Coroner's office, both the City and County Boards of Health, the State Archives in Raleigh, NC, the Pitt County Register of Deeds office, the Sycamore Hill Missionary Baptist Church, and Ms. Esther Hammonds of the W. E. Flanagan Memorial Funeral Home, all proved abortive. Divine intervention led to the discovery of this extraordinary rare and valuable document. The North Carolina General Statutes require that all individuals re-interred from one cemetery to another must fill out completely State Form 1673 and file it with both local and State agencies. All efforts to locate these forms proved abortive. Consequently, local and state laws were totally ignored and broken when officials failed to comply with the State mandate.

The results of this lawlessness in failing to file the appropriate forms resulted in some of the 120 plots designated by the City and Commission officials to re-inter bodies from the SHBC Cemetery to the Brown Hill Cemetery being sold to select members of the Sycamore Hill Missionary Baptist Church. A lack of accountability and transparency resulted in multiple bodies being buried on top of each other. That was/is an unacceptable practice in Greenville and many surrounding communities. With churches, schools and cemeteries being the anchor within the Black community, that practice is considered a sacrilege. In 2004, the Greenville City Council specifically passed an ordinance specifying that only one body per grave will be acceptable in City cemeteries.

Because of the late discovery of this extraordinary document, a Fourth Appendix has been added to this book, but it is not indexed. The original document will appear in Table 4. 1 and an enlarged copy for easy reading will appear in Table 4. 2 and Table 4. 3.

Table 4. 1-- A list of Bodies Moved from the Sycamore Hill Baptist Church to the Brown Hill Cemetery. Certified Copy by Mr. C. A. Holliday, City Engineer, filed with the City of Greenville, NC on October 21, 1969.

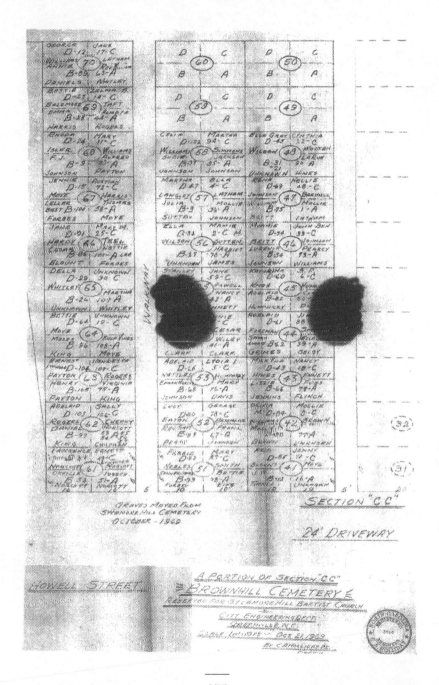

TABLE 4.2-- TOP PART OF TABLE 4.1 (ENHANCED)

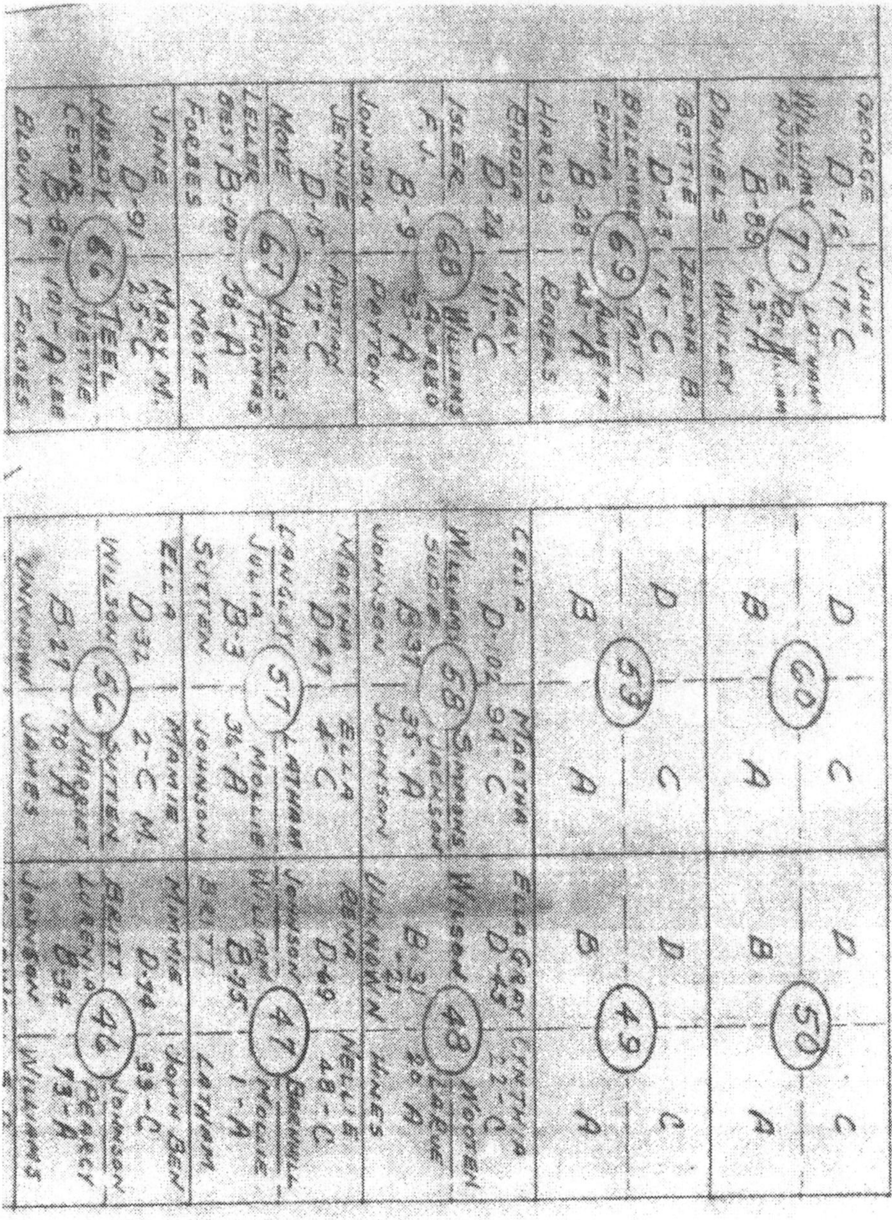

(Handwritten table, rotated. Best-effort transcription of circled entry numbers and legible names.)

GEORGE JANE D-12 17-C	WILLIAMS ROSIE B-89 (70) RAY LATHAM 63-A	DANIELS HURLEY	BETTIE ZELMA B. D-23 11-C	BALLINGER EMMA B-28 (69) JEFF 13-A ROGERS
HARRIS	BROOK MARY D-24 (68) WILLIAMS B-9 ALFRED 31-A PERTON	ISLER F.J.	JOHNSON	MORE (67) HARRIS LELLER THOMAS BEST B-100 38-A MOVE
JENNIE AUSTIN D-15 17-C	JANE D-91 (66) MARY M. HARDY TEEL 25-C CESAR B-86 NETTIE 101-A LEE	FOEBES	BLOUNT FOEBES	

D C	B A	D C (59) B A	D C (60) B A	D C
CELIA D-02 94-C JOHNSON	WILLIAM (58) SANDERS SUE B-37 JACKSON 35-A	MARTHA D-47 JOHNSON	ELLA 4-C JOHNSON	MARTHA
LONGLEY (57) LATHAM JULIA MOLLIE B-3 WILLIS 36-A JOHNSON	MARTIN MAMIE D-47 2-C M. SUTTEN	ELLA D-32 SUTTEN	WILSON (56) HARRIET B-27 70-A	UNKNOWN JAMES
ELLA GRAY D-45 (50) CYNTHIA 22-C A	MOOREN LADUE 26-A	RENA D-49 UNKNOWN HINES	NELLIE 48-C JOHN BEN	BAGWELL (47) MOLLIE 1-A LATHAM
MARTHA WILSON (48) LADUE B-3 31-A	BELL D-34 33-C JOHNSON	BRITT (46) LUTENIA B-34 PERACY 73-A JOHNSON	WILLIAMS	

TABLE 4.2-- BOTTOM PART OF TABLE 4.1 (ENHANCED)

Graves Plotted From Shoreacre Hill Cemetery
October - 1969

BIBLIOGRAPHY

Books

Barnett, Marguerite Ross, et al. *Public Policy for the Black Community*. New York: Alfred Publishing Co., 1976.

Belvin, Lynne; Harriette Riggs. *The Heritage of Wake County North Carolina*. Winston-Salem, NC: Hunter Publishing Company, 1983.

Brandon, Levi. Branson's North Carolina Business Directory, Raleigh, NC: 1867/68-1897

Brown, H. V. *A History of the Education of Negroes in North Carolina*. Raleigh, NC: The Irvin-Swain Press, Inc. 1961.

Copeland, H. Elizabeth. *Chronicles Of Pitt County North Carolina*. Winston-Salem, NC: Hunter Publishing Company, 1982.

Cotter, Michael, ed. *The Architectural Heritage of Greenville, NC*. Greenville, NC: Greenville Area Preservation Association, Inc., 1988.

Insurance Maps of Greenville, NC: Green Run Mill. New York: Sanborn Publishing, 1916.

Kittrell, William "Bill". *Cemetery Survey of Pitt County, North Carolina*. Greenville, NC: Pitt County Historical Society, Inc., 2008.

Mace, Ruth L. *Urban Renewal Programs in North Carolina* Chapel Hill, NC: Institute of Government, 1962.

Miller, H. Ernest, ed. *Greenville North Carolina City Directory*. Asheville, NC: The Piedmont Press, 1916-1917; 1937-1938; 1944-45.

Power, Scott E. *The Historic Architecture of Pitt County, North Carolina*. Greenville, NC: The Pitt County Historical Society, Inc., 1991.

Nelson, Thomas ed. *Holy Bible*. Nashville, TN: Thomas Nelson Publishers, 1988.

North Carolina State Board of Embalmers.
> *Proceedings of North Carolina State Board of Embalmers Organized at Morehead City, NC:* July 6, 1901.
> *Meeting of State Board of Embalmers*. Raleigh, NC September 23, 1901.
> *Proceedings of the Annual Meeting of the North Carolina State Board of Embalmers*. Salisbury, NC: May 9, 1921.

Raleigh North Carolina City Directory. Richmond, VA: The Hill Directory Press, 1925.

Shipman, M. L. *Annual Report of the Department Of Labor and Printing.* Raleigh, NC: E. M. Uzzell and Company, State Printers and Binders, 1912; 1913; 1914; 1916.

Shipman, M. L.; Geo. B. Justice. *Twenty-Sixth Annual Report of the Department of Labor and Printing of the State of North Carolina.* Raleigh, NC: Edwards and Broughton Printers and Binders, 1912.

Turner, J. Kelly; J. C. Bridges, Jr. *History of Edgecome County School.* Raleigh, NC: Edward and Burough Press, 1990.

Tyson, J. C., City Clerk. *Ordinances of the Town of Greenville, North Carolina.* Greenville, NC: *The Daily Reflector* Company Publishers, 1910.

Wease, Hugh. *A Journey of Faith.* Nashville, TN: Baptist and Heritage Society, Fields Publishing, Inc., 2002.

Who's Who In Colored America: A Biographical Dictionary of Notable Living Men and Women. Eppes, Charles Montgomery. New York: Who's Who in Colored America Corp., 1927.

Newspaper Articles

THE DAILY REFLECTOR:
August 16, 1898; April 16, 1938; April 18, 1938; June 19, 1942; June 29, 1942; August 1, 1942; August 6, 1942; August 26, 1948; August 27, 1948; April 29, 1961; May 2, 1961; May 4, 1961; July 14, 1967; February 13, 1969; June 1969; September 5, 1969; February 10, 1974; July 30, 2009.

"Colored News." June 29, 1942, p. 6.

"Charles M. Eppes." DAILY REFLECTOR, Greenville, NC, August 1, 1942, p. 4.

"Greenville Decided to Revamp its Downtown in Major 1965 Action." THE DAILY REFLECTOR, February 25, 1967, p. 10.

"This House of God Will Be Destroyed Under Urban Redevelopment." THE DAILY REFLECTOR, Greenville, NC, April 29, 1961, p. 7.

"Sunday Is Moving Day For Church Members." June 7, 1968, p. 11.

Taylor, Alvin. "Record Turnout of City Voters Expected To Take Place Tuesday." May 1, 1961, p. 1.

Taylor, Alvin. "Brand New City Public Housing Authority Appointed and Sworn." May 5, 1961, p. 1.

Taylor, Mrs. L. R. "Resolution of Respect." June 29, 1942, p. 6.

Walsh, Chester. "Hold Funeral for C.M. Eppes." August 3, 1942, p. 6.

EASTERN REFLECTOR:
"Negroized take over of Greenville." THE EASTERN REFLECTOR, Greenville, NC, November 18, 1898, p. 2.

GREENVILLE TIMES:
Kammerer, Roger. "Pitt County's Five Courthouses." Greenville, NC, GREENVILLE-TIMES, September 18-October 1, 1985, p. 5.

Kammerer, Roger. "Charles M. Eppes: Noted Black Educator and Civic Leader." October 18-21, 1993, p. 8.

Kammerer, Roger. "Undertakers and Funeral Homes in Greenville." October 18-21, 2009.

NORFOLK JOURNAL AND GUIDE:
August 10, 1929

Special to the *Journal and Guide*. "Venerable Educator, 84 Dies." August 8, 1942, p. 1.

"Unveiling Services of Pipe Organ Held Greenville Church." January 11, 1930, p.13.

Young, Thomas W., Staff Correspondent. "Greenville's Spirit of Community Enterprise Has Counter-Part Among Negroes in Hub of Eastern Carolina." JOURNAL AND GUIDE, Norfolk, VA, August, 10, 1929, p. 9.

RALEIGH-TIMES:
"Meet in High Point-Funeral Directors and Embalmers There Next Month." RALEIGH-TIMES, Raleigh, NC, April 26, 1911, p. 8.

Interviews and Correspondence

Barber, Sam.

Brown, Ellis, former director of the Flanagan Funeral Home. Interviews. Greenville, NC. January 2011-February 2014.

Futrell, Elliot, owner of the Evergreen Memorial Gardens and former member of the Board of North Carolina Embalmers Association, Goldsboro, NC. Interviews and Emails. 2011-2012.

Gatlin, Charles, former church member with Walter E. Flanagan. Interviews. 2011-2014.

Gray, Christine M., homemaker. Interview. March 21, 2011.

Grimsley, Johnny and Keith Heiffner. Interview. Greenville, NC. November 29, 2012.

Grimsely, Johnny, former director of the Brown Hill Cemetery Department and now supervisor of grounds. Interviews. May 8, 2012, November 29, 2012.

Irving, Charles, Jr., retired book publisher, Raleigh, NC. Interviews and correspondence. 2011-2012.

Little, Stan, administrative assistant and restoration specialist of the Eastern Office State Historic Preservation Office, Greenville, NC. Interview. 2012.

Lockamy, Christian, map specialist for the City of Greenville, NC. Interviews and Office Visits. 2011-2012.

Mills, Climmie, owner of Mills Funeral Home, Kinston, NC. Interview. October 2011.

Morgan, Blanche, co-owner of In God We Trust Senior Care, Kinston, NC. Interviews. March 21 and June 30, 2011.

Morris, Connie, deaconess, Sycamore Hill Missionary Baptist Church, Greenville, NC, Interview. May 8, 2012.

Oliver, Bryan, archivist for the Greenville Police Department, Greenville, NC. Interview. 2011.

Russell, Louise, co-owner of In God We Trust Senior Care, Kinston, NC. Interviews. March 21 and June 30, 2011.

Unpublished Documents

Anderson, Francis D. "Mr. A. E. Dubber, Executive Director, Greenville Redevelopment Commission." Atlanta, GA, February 5, 1969.

Atkinson, John C. Jr. "Mr A. E. Dubber, Executive Director." Greenville, NC, September 18, 1968.

Barber, Sam. *The Choral Style of the Wings Over Jordan Choir.* DMA Dissertation. Cincinnati, OH: University of Cincinnati Conservatory of Music, 1978.

Bowers, Wayne, Director of Public Works. "Ervin Mills Memorandum." Greenville, NC, February 17, 2012.

Brown, G. A. "Last Will and Testament of Willie Brown." Register of Deeds, Greenville, NC, July 26, 1886, Book 8, p. 167.

Carsparphen, W. H., Mayor. "Council Memorandum no. 26." Greenville, NC, 1973.

Chambers, Julius LeVonne, Attorney at Law.
    "Mr. Billy B. Laughinghouse, Chairman, Redevelopment Commission of the City of Greenville." Charlotte, NC, June 5, 1968.
    "Mr. Kenneth G. Hite and James and Hite Attorneys at Law." Charlotte, NC, July 10, 1968.
    "Mr. Kenneth G. Hite, Attorney at Law." Charlotte, NC, August 12, 1968.
    "Mr. Kenneth G. Hite." Charlotte, NC, September 4, 1968.

C.M. Eppes Cultural Center. "Greenville Industrial C. M. Eppes High School Alumni Association." Greenville, NC.

Cole, Jenest & Stone. "Past-A Brief History." Greenville, NC, December 7, 2009.

Cox, Percy R., Mayor. "Donovan Phillips." Greenville, NC, April 11, 1978.

Denton, Ernest L. *Cooper Field Cemetery*. Raleigh, NC, 1940.

Dickens, Charles M. "Agreement to Sell Church Property to the Redevelopment Commission." Greenville, NC, October 8, 1969.

Dubber, A. E., Executive Director, Greenville Redevelopment Commission
> "Assistant Regional Administration, Department of Housing and Urban Development." Greenville, NC, February 28, 1967.
>
> "Chairman of the Board of Trustees, Sycamore Hill Baptist Church." Greenville, NC, May 23, 1967.
>
> "David Barnhill, Chairman, Board of Trustees, Sycamore Hill Baptist Church." Greenville, NC, June 6, 1967.
>
> "Rev. J. A. Nimmo." Greenville, NC, June 30, 1967.
>
> "The Sycamore Hill Baptist Church." Greenville, NC, March 18, 1968.
>
> "Edward H. Baxter, Regional Administration of HUD." Charlotte, NC, January 22, 1968.
>
> "Mr. Julius LeVonne Chambers, Attorney at Law." Charlotte, NC July 13, 1968, Sept 18, 1968, and February 11, 1969.
>
> "Lester E. Turnage." Charlotte, NC, August 13, 1968.
>
> "Renewal Assistance Administration." Greenville, NC, August 16, 1968.
>
> "Sycamore Hill Baptist Church." Charlotte, NC, August 27, 1968.
>
> "Julius LeVonne Chambers." Greenville, NC, September 18, 1968.
>
> "John C. Atkinson, Jr." Charlotte, NC, September 19, 1968.
>
> "J. LeVonne Chambers." Greenville, NC, February 11, 1969.
>
> "Mr. Leroy James, Chairman, Board of Trustees, Sycamore Hill Missionary Baptist Church." Greenville, NC, July 14, 1969.
>
> "Regional Assistance Association." Greenville, NC, July 18, 1969.
>
> "Mr. Leroy James, Chairman, Board of Trustees." Greenville, NC, October 30, 1969.

Duncan, H. H., City Clerk.
> "Urban Renewal Program of Greenville." *City Council Minutes*, Greenville, NC, December 4, 1958, Book 8, p. 520.
>
> "Special Meeting to Appoint an Urban Renewal Commission." *City Council Minutes*, Greenville, NC, December 18, 1958, Book 8, p. 520.

Duval, J. O., City Clerk.
> "Black Fireman's Petition." *Minutes of Aldermen*, Greenville, NC: February 7, 1924, Book III, p. 379.
>
> "Purchasing the Greenwood Cemetery." *Minutes of City Aldermen*, Greenville, NC, April 1, 1924, Book III, p. 546.

"Promissory Note to James and Elvira Brown." *Minutes of City Aldermen*, Greenville, NC, November 8, 1924, Book III, p. 451.

"Developing a Cemetery in West Greenville." *Minutes of City Aldermen*, Greenville, NC, April 1, 1926, Book 6, p. 546.

"Resolution for Proposed Colored Cemetery." *Minutes of City Aldermen*, Greenville, NC, April 6, 1939, Book 6, p. 32.

"Purchase of Brown Hill Cemetery." *Minutes of City Aldermen*, Greenville, NC, April 6, 1939, Book 6, p. 32.

"Blocked Proposed Colored Cemetery." *Minutes of City Aldermen*, Greenville, NC, April 26, 1939, Book 6, p. 38.

"Resolution to Purchase of Cemetery Known as Cooper Field." *Minutes of City Aldermen*, Greenville, NC, May 4, 1939, Book. 6, p. 44.

"Dr. Battle's Approval of Brown Hill Cemetery." *Minutes, of City Aldermen*, Greenville, NC, June, 1, 1939, Book 6, p. 51.

"Sale of Brown Land for Colored Cemetery." *Minutes of City Aldermen*, Greenville, NC, June 1, 1939, Book 6, p. 53.

"Purchase of Colored Cemetery." *Minutes of City Aldermen*. Greenville, NC, July 6, 1939, Book VI, p. 94.

"Purchase of Brown Hill Cemetery." *Minutes of City Council*, Greenville, NC, July 6, 1939, p. 94, par. 5.

"Resolution to Purchase Brown Hill Cemetery." *Minutes of City Aldermen*, Greenville, NC, October 5, 1939, Book 6, p. 136.

"Price of Lots for the New Colored Cemetery." *Minutes of City Council*, Greenville, NC, Book 6, June 6, 1940, p. 194.

"Notice of Public Renting of Farm Land." *Minutes of City Aldermen*, *Greenville*, NC, December 5, 1940, Book 6, p. 252.

"Naming of the Brownhill Cemetery." *Minutes of the City Council*, Greenville, NC, January, 21, 1943, p. 440.

"Request from Boston Boyd's Daughter to Take Over Maintenance of the Cooper Field Cemetery." *Minutes of City Council*, Greenville, NC, September 2, 1943, Book 6, p. 508.

"An Ordinance Adopting, Rules and Regulations for the Control of Greenwood Cemetery and Providing Penalties Thereto." *Minutes of City Council*, Greenville, NC, June 17, 1947, Book 7, Section 7, p. 248.

"Build a School for Negro Children." *Minutes of City Council*, Greenville, NC, May 6, 1948, Book 7, p. 507.

Edmonds, John T. "Acting Assistant Regional Administration for Renewal Assistance." Atlanta, GA, March 10, 1967.

Farmer, Rex L., City Clerk. "Abandon Graveyard." *Minutes of City Aldermen*, Greenville, NC, March 8, 1920.

Felder, B. B., Rev. "Col. A. A. Dubber." Greenville, NC, December 31, 1967.
   "Redevelopment Commission of the City of Greenville." Greenville,
   NC, April 24, 1969.
Flanagan, Walter E. "Obituary. Service of Triumph." Greenville, NC, 1984.
Hadden, W. J. Reverend, Chairman. "First Annual Report by the Redevelopment
   Commission of the City of Greenville, 1960-1961."
Harry E. Hagerty, City Manager
   "Cooper Field Cemetery." *Minutes of City Council,* Greenville, NC,
      June 9, 1966.
   "Colonel A. E. Dubber, Executive Director Redevelopment
      Commission." Greenville, NC, July 5, 1967.
   "Relocation of the Sycamore Hill Baptist Church Cemetery."
      Minutes of City Council, Greenville, NC, August 6. 1969.
   "Meeting of the Development Commission of the City of Greenville
      and the Board of Trustees of the Sycamore Hill Baptist Church
      at 7:30 P. M. on August 12, 1969." *Minutes of City Council,*
      Greenville, NC, August 12, 1969.
   "Removal of Graves." *Minutes of City Council,* Greenville, NC,
      November 6, 1969.
Hennigan, David O., Appraiser
   "Shore Drive Commission." Greenville, NC, December 2, 1968.
   "Sycamore Hill Baptist Church." Greenville, NC, January 17, 1969.
Hite, Kenneth G., Attorney at Law
   "Mr. Julius Levonne Chambers, Attorney at Law." Charlotte, NC,
      June 13, 1968, July 16, 1968, and August 29, 1968.
   "Mr. James E. Ferguson, Sycamore Hill Baptist Church." Greenville,
      NC, June 24, 1968.
   "Mr. Julius Levonne Chambers, Attorney at Law." Greenville, NC, July
      16, 1968.
   "Mr. Julius Levonne Chambers." Greenville, NC, August 29, 1968.
   "Settlement Sheet." Greenville, NC, November 25, 1969.
   "Redevelopment Commission of the City of Greenville." Greenville,
      NC, November 26, 1969.
   "Rev. B. B. Felder." Greenville, NC, November 26, 1969.
   Jackson, George, Mr. and Mrs. "Redevelopment Commission of
      the City of Greenville" Greenville, NC, December 12, 1969,
      Greenville, NC.
James, Leroy, Chairman, Board of Trustees, Sycamore Hill Missionary Baptist
   Church. "Mayor Frank M. Wooten." (draft) Greenville, NC, July 15, 1969.
Johnson, F. Badger. *Second Annual Report, Shore Drive Redevelopment Project
   N.C.R-15.* Greenville, NC, September, 1962.

Laughinghouse, Billy B., Chairman, Redevelopment Commission of the City of Greenville
 "Sycamore Hill Baptist Church." Greenville, NC, May 13, 1968.
 "Rev. B. B. Felder." Greenville, NC, April 28, 1969.
 "Reverend Mr. B. B. Felder." Greenville, NC, April 29, 1969.
 "Rev. B. B. Felder." Greenville, NC, April 30, 1969.
 "Sycamore Hill Missionary Baptist Church, Inc." Greenville, NC, December 11, 1969.
Lewis, Matthew T. "The Greenville Redevelopment Commission." Greenville, NC, February 25, 1968.
Malone, Thomas C. Acting Chief, Processing Control Renewal Assistance Office. "Mr. A. E. Dubber, Executive Director, Greenville Redevelopment Commission." Atlanta, GA, April 10, 1967.
Messick, John A. "Shore Drive Redevelopment Project. Sycamore Hill Baptist Church." Greenville, NC, July 3, 1969.
Moore, W. N., City Clerk
 "Special Meeting Authorizing for Public Hearing." *Minutes of City Council,* Greenville, NC, December 20, 1960, Book 7, p. 429-431.
 "Public Hearing of the Urban Renewal Plan." *Minutes of City Council,* Greenville, NC, June 27, 1963, Book 10, p. 27j.
 "Resolution To Accelerate the Implementation of the Shore Drive Project (Removal of Sycamore Hill Baptist Church)." *City Council Minutes,* Greenville, NC, July 13, 1967, Book 11, p. 155.
 "Resolution to Condemn Property." *Minutes of City Council.* Greenville, NC, August 1967, Book 11, p. 466.
 "Site Improvement Work in Shore Drive Project, Sycamore Hill Missionary Baptist Church Property." *Minutes of City Council,* January 7, 1970, Book 12, p. 152.
Moore, W. N., City Clerk, City Manager. "Mr. Leroy James, Chairman, Board of Trustees." *Minutes of City Council,* Greenville, NC, October 14, 1969, Book 12, p. 117.
Nimmo, J. Allen, Rev. "Mr. A. E. Dubber." Camden, NJ, July 19, 1967.
North Carolina General Assembly. "An Act to Allow the Board of Aldermen of the Town of Greenville in Pitt County to Remove Certain Graves in Said Town." March 8, 1919. *North Carolina Private Laws passed by the General Assembly at its Session of 1919.* Raleigh, NC: Edward and Broughton Printing Co., 1919.
North Carolina General Assembly. "Churches." Raleigh, NC: W. R. Gales, printer to the Legislature (Office of the Raleigh Register), January 12, 1841.

North Carolina General Assembly. "Laws and Statues Regarding Cemeteries, Article 12, Section 14-149, Desecrating, Plowing Over or Covering Up Graves: Desecrating Human Remains." Raleigh, NC: North Carolina General Statues, p. 13.

North Carolina State Board of Health. "Certificate of Death: Eppes, Charles M." Raleigh, NC, July 31, 1942, # 30.

North Carolina Department of Public Instruction. [C.M. Eppes]. *Annual Principal's Report to the North Carolina Department of Public Instruction.* Raleigh, NC: North Carolina Archives, 1923-1944.

Phillips, Donovan, Co-Owner, Phillips Brothers Mortuary. "Mayor Percy R. Cox." Greenville, NC, March 31, 1978.

Pitt County Clerk of Court, Wills and Testimonies.

> "Sale of Negro Girl." Superior Court, Greenville, NC, Vol. R, 1810, p. 366.

> "Sale of Negro Man." Superior Court, Greenville, NC, Vol. R, 1809, p. 224.

Pitt County Clerk of Courts. "Special Proceedings Document: Bessie Brown." Superior Court, 1939, Book 6, p. 468.

Pitt County Register of Deeds

> "Colored Section of Cherry Hill Cemetery." Deed Book V, April 5, 1872, p. 59-61.

> "Higgs Bros to Col School Dist No 46." Deed Book F-6, May 12, 1897, p. 190.

> "Colored Christian College." Deed Book M-8, January 17, 1907, p. 447.

> "W. B. Brown and Nancy Lee." Book S-8, January 17, 1907, p. 447.

> "Colored Christian College." Deed Book R-9, October 17, 1910, p. 415.

> "The Tar River Industrial and College Institute." Deed Book A-11, 1910, p. 376.

> "Death Certificates, 1913-1940."

> "The Tar River Industrial and College Institute." Deed Book R-9, 1914, p. 415.

> "Tar River Industrial and Collegiate Institute Certificate of Incorporation." Book 2, October 8, 1915, p. 447.

> "Oak City Live Stock Company, Inc." Book W 14, November 21, 1923, p. 124.

> "George Greene to Charles Greene Bill of Sale." Book CC, November 25, 1923, p. 129.

> "Foreclosure Deed." Deed Book X-21, January 11, 1937, p. 331.

> "Tucker, A. C." Deed Book J-13, June 23, 1939, p. 201.

"Bessie R. Brown." Deed Book V-22, October 12, 1939, p. 556.

"Purchase of the Cemetery known as Greene Place or Cooper Field." Deed Book V-22, October, 12, 1939, p. 556.

"Removal of Graves." Greenville, NC, October 19, 1968, Book V-8, p. 53.

"Certificate for Removal of Graves." Deed Book V-38, October 9, 1969, p. 53.

Redevelopment Commission of the City of Greenville, NC. "Special Meeting of the Commissioners." *Minutes of a Special Meeting* . . . . Greenville, NC, February 30, 1969.

Rivers, Henry. "Colored Cemetery Map." Greenville, NC, 1941.

Rodman, W. C. "Property of Greenville Spinners, Inc." Map. Greenville, NC, October, 30, 1946.

Rose, J. H., Secretary, Board of Education.

"Extra Meeting, Board of Education." Board of Education, Greenville City Schools, Greenville, NC, May 12, 1931.

"Special Meeting of the Board of Education." Greenville, NC, Board of Education, May 30, 1941, Book III, p. 103.

"Naming of High School." *Minutes of Board of Education.* Greenville, NC, May 30, 1941, Book III, p. 103.

"Building a Negro School." *Minutes of the Board of Education*, Greenville, NC, December 3, 1946, Book III, p. 245.

"School Building for Negroes." *Minutes of the Board of Education*, Greenville, NC, December 3, 1946, Book 2, p. 215.

"Architect and Superintendent to Cooper Field." *Minutes of the Board of Education*, Greenville, NC, 9 February 1949, Book 2, p. 233.

"School Ready for Occupancy." *Minutes of the Board of Education*, Greenville, NC, April 27, 1950, p. 259.

Sicley, Colleen, Secretary of the Brown Hill Cemetery Department. "Memorandum: Cooper Field Cemetery." Greenville, NC, April 24, 2012.

South Side Gymnasium. "Plaque." Greenville, NC, 1957.

Sutton, James, City Clerk. "Trustee Board, Sycamore Hill Baptist Church." Greenville, NC, January 9, 1968.

Sycamore Hill Missionary Baptist Church. "Our Journey of Faith, 1860-2010." Sycamore Hill Missionary Baptist Church, Greenville, NC.

Tabulation Sheet. "Sycamore Hill Baptist Church."

Turnage, Lester Jr., Appraiser. "Property of Sycamore Hill Baptist Church Parcel 4-6." *Minutes of City Council,* Greenville, NC, February 23, 1968.

Tyson, James C. "Provide Lights to the Greenville Cooperage and Lumber Company." Minutes of the *Greenville Utility Commission*, November 12, 1912.

United States Census. June, 5, 1860. Washington, DC, U.S. Govt. Printing Office.

United States Census. "Halifax Township, Halifax, North Carolina." Washington, D.C. Government Printing Office, June 18, 1880.

United States Bureau of the Census. "Fourteenth U.S. Census Report of 1920 State of North Carolina, Greenville Township, Sheet No. 8, Enumeration District No. 52. Washington, DC.

Wallace, Jack. "Development Commission," Greenville, NC, August 12, 1968.

West, S. Eugene, City Council. "Canvass of Election Returns." *Minutes of City Council.* Greenville, NC, May 3, 1961, Book 7, p. 466-466A.

West, S. Eugene, Mayor.
"Meeting of City Council Members with Members of Deacon Board and Board of Trustees of the Sycamore Hill Baptist Church." *City Council Minutes,* Greenville, NC, July 31, 1967, Book. 11, p. 159-161.
"Redevelopment Commission." Greenville, NC, October 11, 1967.

Wooten, Frank M., Mayor
"Agreement." Minutes of *City Council,* Greenville, NC, October 9, 1969, p. 2.
"Contract No 97 between The City of Greenville and the SHMBC." *Minutes of City Council,* Greenville, NC, October 9, 1969, Book 12, p. 117-118.

World Wide Web

Angelfire, *INTERESTING TIDBITS ABOUT THE PITT COUNTY COURTHOUSE, 1858-1910 WWW.ANGELFIRE.COM/ART2/1910COURTHOUSE/COURT.HTML*

Cooper, Lewis, Lewis G. Cooper Papers, Lewis Cooper, LEWIS G. COOPER PAPERS, 1922-1950 http//digital.lib.ecu.edu.special/ead/review.aspx/id=0304&q-cooper.(n.d.).L. G. Cooper Files. File Folder.

Dubber, A. E., Secretary for the Redevelopment Commission. "Restriction Agreement." Preliminary Inventory of the Greenville Urban Renewal Files, 1959-1977. http//digital.lib.ecu.edu/special/ead/finding aids/0674/Box 32

Johnson, A., "Life in a Southern Mill Village." Greenville, NC, 2005. www.ecu.edu/cs-lib/reference/instruction/millvillages.cmf.

Michalak, Russell, African American Newspapers in North Carolina, 2009. http://www.lib.unc.edu/ncc/ref/study/africanamericannewspapers.html.

Rootweb-Achiever>NC-PCFR>2009-1271259851229

Ross, Elizabeth, "The Cherry Hill Cemetery Gravestone Inscriptions, 1990." www. rootsweb.ancestry.com/~ncpcfr/pChrHill.htm.

Sycamore Hills Baptist Church. "Memorandum. Offer of Land Sale, Project No. N.C.R.-15, Parcel No. 6-4." Greenville, NC, August 17, 1968. Preliminary Inventory of the Greenville Urban Renewal Files, 1959-1977 (manuscript Collection #674) http:// digital. Lib.ecu.edu/special/ead/findingaids/0674.

United States Bureau of the Census. *Fourteenth Census of the United States, June 9, 1920. Vance Township. Lenoir County, North Carolina.* (Lenoir Co., EDs 54-70). https://archive.org/details/14thcensusofpopu1308unit.

On-Site Grave Inspections

Barber, Sam.

ABOUT THE AUTHOR

Sam Barber, inspired by his family, teachers, church, and community to love and appreciate the joys of learning, is the ninth and last of thirteen children born to the parents of Celia Ann Brown Barber and Augustus "Gus" Barber, Sr., on the family -owned farm of his great, great-grandparents, Peter and Hulda Barber. The family has owned the farm, which is in a suburb of Trenton, Jones County, North Carolina, since 1873.

Graduating salutatorian from the Trenton High School, he earned the degrees of bachelor of music education from Howard University, Washington, D.C.; the master's of music education from the Chicago-Conservatory of Music, Roosevelt University, Chicago, Illinois; and the doctor of musical arts from the College-Conservatory of Music, University of Cincinnati in Cincinnati, Ohio.

His professional career spanned a period of over thirty-seven years. His travels included ten European countries, Canada, Mexico, Jamaica, and Haiti. Twenty-three years of active and inactive military service concluded with the rank of major in the U.S. Army.

Sam is the definitive authority on the life and career of the Reverend Glenn Thomas Settle, founder of the once internationally famous Wings Over Jordan Choir. For seven years, the Wings Collection was on loan at the Southern Historical Collection at the University of North Carolina, Chapel Hill, North Carolina. And later, the Collection was on loan at the Collins-Callaway Library at Paine College, Augusta, Ga.

Albeit a lifetime member of the Hill's Chapel Missionary Baptist Church, Trenton, North Carolina, regular on-site religious participation includes Anderson Chapel A. M. E. Church, Chicod, North Carolina; Sycamore Hill, St. Mary, Hayes Chapel, Philippi-Simpson, and Cornerstone, all Missionary Baptist churches in Greenville, North Carolina. Professional organizations include the Alpha Phi Alpha and the Phi Mu Alpha fraternities, the NAACP, the American Legion, and the Reserve Officers Association.

He married and later divorced Margaret Walker of Cincinnati, Ohio. No children were born of this union.

BOOK REVIEW

Greenville's Visitors and Convention Bureau lists no official historical sites for Afro-Americans. Afro-Americans have lived in Greenville since 1771.

The Southside Group should promote the installation of historical sites on Howell Street and the Town Common. Without records, generations of blacks will have lost a vast and rich historical past.

Immediate attention can be devoted to mapping unmapped graves, replacing the cow-pasture gate with an aesthetically pleasing one, placing historical data on the entrance sign or gate, retooling grave borders and headstones, replacing deteriorating vaults and broken headstones, and building a retaining wall to hide the Public Works workstation in full view of the cemetery.

Reveals the Sycamore Hill Baptist Church and the Brown Hill Cemetery Connection.

Profiles the lives of Messrs S. G. Wilkerson, Walter E. Flanagan and Professor Charles M. Eppes.

With Greenville's 250th Anniversary celebration approaching, Southside Seniors can use their energy and resources to ensure black representation. A mind is a terrible thing to waste.

Implementation of Moses's instructions can be a challenge to all:

Remember the days of old, consider the years of many generations:
ask thy father and, he will show thee, thy elders, and they will tell thee.[304]

---

[304] Thomas Nelson, ed. *Holy Bible.* Nashville, TN: Thomas Nelson Publishers, 1988, p. 350.

SUMMARY

A dearth of administrative management documents precludes any hard evidence to show that the Greenville black community established or operated an independent or a cemetery adjacent to what might be called the Slave Burying Ground or old Colored Cemetery. Evidence shows that by 1914 black citizens were being buried in what Mr. Henry Rivers, City of Greenville Engineer, mapped as the Colored Cemetery, later known as the Cooper Field Cemetery, in contrast to the Old Cemetery or the Slave Burying Ground. (See 1941 map by Henry Rivers, City of Greenville Engineer [Rivers, 1941].) Of the approximately 451 death certificates listed in the Register of Deeds office at the Pitt County Courthouse as being buried in the City Cemetery, 149 of these bodies were buried at Cooper Field. Mrs. Colleen Sicley in a memo on April 24, 2012, states that ". . . we have no information on them [the c.250 grave plots on the 1941 Colored Cemetery map] because the city didn't own or operate the cemetery until October 1939."[305]

From on-site grave inspections and map evidence, these graves are clearly within the boundaries of the newly purchased Brown Hill Cemetery property. The boundaries represent bodies buried in the Brown Hill Cemetery after the city purchased it. And given the abundance of headstones at Cooper Field, surely some of these 451 sites had headstones. In all probability, records and memorials once existed, but over time have been misplaced, destroyed or lost.

The culture of officially naming the site Brownhill Cemetery was problematic. Names define people, places, and things. Animate names honor people, while inanimate ones define locations. The etiology of the Brown Hill Cemetery originated from the property's former owners. The Hill part of the name is designated by the elevation of the topography of the land, about 60 feet above sea level. It is about 50 feet above sea level and higher than the elevation of the Cherry Hill Cemetery, while the Sycamore Hill Baptist Church Cemetery is about 48 feet above sea level.[306]

---

[305] Sicley. Ibid, April 24, 2012.
[306] Sam Barber. Christian Lockamy. Interview. 2011.

Bessie Brown stated that the "W. B. Brown Estate would raise no objections whatsoever in using the name of Brown's in naming this cemetery . . .at present, (it was decided) to name the colored cemetery BROWNHILL."[307] Brown Hill is a two-part word and should be represented as such. The decision to spell the name of the cemetery "Brownhill" instead of "Brown Hill" perhaps misrepresents and dishonors the intent of the Brown family. Additionally, Brown Hill is sequential and in conformity with the names of the Sycamore Hill Baptist Church Cemetery and the Cherry Hill Cemetery.

When one visits the Visitors and Convention Bureau in Greenville, especially foreigners, one might be surprised to learn that after almost 250 years of the founding of the town of Greenville, it has no official historical sites of its Afro-American citizens. History tells us that Negroes, blacks, or Afro-Americans played no marginal influence in the growth and development of Greenville and made it into the "hub" of eastern North Carolina.[308] To erect statures of selected Negroes and place them in strategic locations around the city as well as to reconstruct the Bell Tower that was destroyed by an arsonist's torch at the Sycamore Hill Baptist Church would be an impressive beginning and would shatter the "illusion of inclusion" myth of Negroes by many of its citizens.

The request to make a presentation to the Southside Group was deferred to Dr. Shelva Davis. She gave a dynamic and outstanding presentation. Confident that my services would never be needed anymore, my attention turned to other interests. However, persistent endorsement from the chair and her colleagues persuaded me to reconsider. Reflecting on my experience while exploring some possibilities for upgrading the Greenwood Cemetery in New Bern, NC, my attention focused on the Brown Hill Cemetery, a cemetery in need of much attention. My initial vision was to galvanize the group to partner with the Public Works Department to help upgrade and to beautify the Brown Hill Cemetery. However, with some exploratory research, the conclusion to utilize the resources of the Southside Group more aggressively and productively to motivate and galvanize city council members to establish and develop three contiguous properties as historical sites along Howell Street, namely the Brown Hill Cemetery, the South Greenville School, the site of the former Tar River Collegiate and Industrial Institute on which the South Greenville School and the South Greenville Gymnasium site stands. And even though there is a marker

---

[307] Duval, J. O., City Clerk. "Naming the Brownhill Cemetery." *Minutes of the City Council*, Greenville, NC, January 21, 1943, p. 440.

[308] Thomas W. Young, Staff Correspondent. "Greenville's Spirit of Community Enterprise Has Counter-Part Among Negroes in Hub of Eastern Carolina." JOURNAL AND GUIDE, Norfolk, VA, August, 10, 1929, p. 9.

at the downtown TOWN COMMON site where black folks lived, worked, died and were buried, the Town Common marker makes no reference to a black presence. It just says "Town Common." So as soon as this generation of blacks dies off and if no historical records have been chronicled, future generations of Greenvillians, especially blacks, will have lost a vast and rich historical past.

Now that the city has committed itself to upgrade Norris Street, a short contiguous street connecting Howell and the Brown Hill Cemetery, at a cost of circa $35,000,[309] it is conceivable that this area just might survive.

To create a partnership between the Southside Senior Group and the Public Works Department could be a herculean leap and a mutual benefit and healing process for long simmering race relations problems. There are, of course, some immediate major improvements that should be done with dispatch to help bridge this gap.

- Uppermost is to map the Slave Burying Ground or the few existing markers before the Colored Cemetery and the Cooper Field Sections of the Brown Hill Cemetery.

- Urgent attention should be to replace the cow-pasture gate with an aesthetically pleasing entrance and gate. The entrance and entrance marker should display and reflect historical data of the cemetery's origin and honorees. A similar marker should be placed at the Cherry Hill Cemetery as well.

- Immediate attention should be directed to retooling the borders around the grave plots. The original numbers from 1942 are invisible and in great need of retooling. With laser or imaging technology, the Southside Group can be of great help in locating family members to get permission to retool headstones as well as replace deteriorating vaults and broken headstones in need of urgent repair.

Even with these improvements, mourners will experience an even greater pain, discomfort and distress when faced with huge mounds of unsightly dirt, rocks, concrete, debris, trucks, and many pieces of heavy-duty equipment stored in full view of the cemetery at the Public Works operating center. The City can bring great comfort and relief to the mourners and the black citizens alike by constructing a retaining wall between the cemetery and the Public Works property.

---

[309] Bowers, Ibid, 2012.

Southside Senior Citizens, with the 250th Anniversary celebration of the founding of the city of Greenville only a few years away, do your part to make sure that some black Greenvillians are represented in this celebration. There is much work to be done and only a short time to do it. *A mind is a terrible thing to waste.* In all you do and say, remember the *veil* of darkness is slowly but surely being lifted. It is encumbered upon each of us to do our part in confirming Moses' powerful and passionate instructions to the Israelites:

> *Remember the days of old, consider the years of many generations: ask the father, and he will show thee, thy elders, and they will tell thee.*

INDEX

A

299

CAREER

GLOW

UP

How to Own Your Ambition and Create the Career of Your Dreams

Jennifer Brick

ROCK
POINT

Dedicated to my Career Besties.

Brimming with creative inspiration, how-to projects, and useful information to enrich your everyday life, quarto.com is a favorite destination for those pursuing their interests and passions.

First published in 2022 by Rock Point, an imprint of The Quarto Group, 142 West 36th Street, 4th Floor, New York, NY 10018, USA
T (212) 779-4972 F (212) 779-6058 www.Quarto.com

Rock Point titles are also available at discount for retail, wholesale, promotional, and bulk purchase. For details, contact the Special Sales Manager by email at specialsales@quarto.com or by mail at The Quarto Group, Attn: Special Sales Manager, 100 Cummings Center Suite 265D, Beverly, MA 01915 USA.

10 9 8 7 6 5 4 3 2 1   ISBN: 978-1-63106-871-3

Publisher: Rage Kindelsperger
Creative Director: Laura Drew
Senior Managing Editor: Cara Donaldson
Editor: Keyla Pizarro-Hernández
Interior Design: Amy Sly

Printed in China

Contents

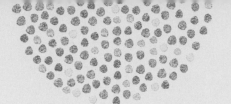

Introduction

As an ambitious woman intent on getting a promotion, I felt like the path to get to the next level was lined with booby traps. You've probably stumbled upon some (or all of them): being assertive but not abrasive, promoting yourself without being self-promotional, being likable but also knowing how to say no. For each of these traps, almost all the advice I read resided in there being two solutions, both of which ended up with me being less promotable. For example, you have to boast about your accomplishments if you want to advance your career, but no one likes a bragger, and you won't be promoted if you're not liked.

I knew there had to be a way around career traps. After all, there are women who defy the double standards, and gravity, and ascend the career ladder quickly. As an unapologetic career climber, I began to study them. I read books and spoke with mentors and powerful leaders (mostly women) who had risen the ranks with ease. I began testing things in my career. This is how I created the Career Glow Up System: I was subject zero. As I developed it, I rose from an entry level role to an executive level. I mentored others using this system, and they gained career success too. I became so passionate about this I ended up leaving my corporate job to focus on helping ambitious professionals implement the Career Glow Up System full time through my YouTube channel and training programs.

Stop being ordinary when you were born to be extraordinary.

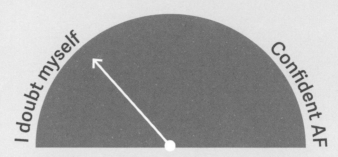

GLOW UP CONFIDENCE METER

That's what brings us here, to this workbook. Whenever I had a big challenge or an obstacle at work, I always turned to books. And since you're here, I assume you do too. I wanted to create a workbook for you that laid out the Career Glow Up System in a way that made it as simple to implement as possible. That's why this isn't your typical business book, this is your Career Success Plan. Over the next seven chapters, I am going to bring you through each step, and you will be implementing and taking action along the way.

As you move through the exercises in this book, you'll also see confidence check-in prompts to check in on your confidence in each step of the Career Glow Up process. This will bring awareness to areas where you feel less confident (focus on those exercises!) and you'll likely see your confidence growing. As you move through the Glow Up system and your confidence grows, you will also notice a few of the confidence check-in prompts change too.

Have a pen handy to do the exercises. If this all goes the way I planned it for you, and you do the work, you will have elevated and accelerated your career by the time you finish reading the last page. If you run out of space, feel free to use a blank journal or loose paper for any of the practices in this book.

And, if you want to go even deeper into your Career Glow Up, you can find even more resources by following the link in the Further Resources, on page 159, to my Career Glow Up Expansion Pack.

Career Glow Up Audit

The funny thing about progress is that we often don't notice it happening. Throughout this book, you'll complete this Career Glow Up Audit to see how you're doing career wise. Some of the sections or rows will change as you go through each chapter. You'll hopefully notice a difference in yourself after each chapter. Write a checkmark next to where you are, with 1 being the lowest rating and 5 being the highest.

	1 (I'm lost)	2 (I need help)	3 (Okay, I guess)	4 (Good but growing)	5 (I'm slaying this!)
I know what I want from my career.					
I am confident I will achieve my goals.					
I know why I am an invaluable asset to my company.					
I know how to identify priorities to spend my time on.					
I have a network that advocates for me.					
I feel confident networking.					
I am intentional about my professional brand.					
I know I will be successful in my career and life.					

Make Success Personal

1

- Create a Career Vision
- Your Success Plan

You are
the main
character in
your career.

From a very young age, the message of what your life is supposed to look like is clear: Go to school, get a job, make lots of money, put said money into a large vault and occasionally jump in and swim (okay, I think only fellow *DuckTales* enthusiasts have this vision), get married and settle down. At the same time, professional success has been defined in a specific way that you might not even be fully aware of, so let's start with uncovering the success archetype you have. Take a moment to do the exercise on the opposite page.

Without peering into your head, I can probably predict a few truths in what that vision looked like: It was probably a man. He was probably white. He was probably wearing a suit, sitting or power standing inside a corner office, or perhaps carrying around a briefcase. He is probably assertive and competitive, and you probably didn't envision him playing with his kids.

I know right now you're probably shook because I just read your mind through the page. And if your vision was wildly different, then I am oozing with admiration for you having already shaken this up.

There is the reason I can tell you the vision so clearly and so easily: It's the one we are bombarded from every which way on a daily basis. We can spend all day dissecting why this is true and how it impacts us, but you don't have all day and you probably have hobbies or Netflix, which are way more interesting. So, let's cut straight to the chase: Is your vision of a successful professional aligned with what you want in your career and life?

Getting clear on what you want your career and life to look like is crucial. If you skip this step, you'll struggle with motivation and end up with a career that not only makes you miserable but also leaves you with a wicked case of imposter syndrome. This is your permission slip: You are allowed to want what you want at work. Now we'll figure out what that is.

Define Success

Spend a few minutes envisioning a successful professional. Imagine as many details as possible.

What do they do?

_____

_____

_____

_____

What do they look like?

_____

_____

_____

_____

What clothes do they wear?

_____

_____

_____

_____

What is their personality like?

_____

_____

_____

Your Version of Success

It's time for you to define what success looks like for *you*.

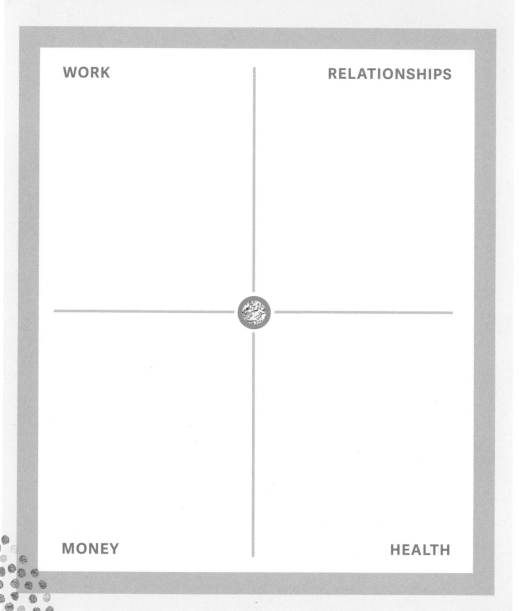

WORK

RELATIONSHIPS

MONEY

HEALTH

Create a Career Vision

If you're like I used to be, you might roll your eyes at the mention of a career vision or five-year plan. I don't know what I want to eat for lunch in an hour, how am I supposed to know what I want my career to look like half a decade from now?! However, taking the time to dig in and create this vision pays off in dividends.

Success does not happen by accident; it happens through intention. Think of it like this: You probably wouldn't get in a car to go on a road trip without knowing your destination. Your career vision is the destination you want to arrive at. Once you have it, your journey may still have construction, pit stops, and detours, but even when you get totally lost, you'll know the general direction to go in.

Feeling Visionless?

If you are early in your career, you might have drawn a blank for your career vision. Cue OMG-I'm-so-lost panic. While some people achieve clarity early on, others take a while. A Career Walkabout is basically the career sampler; you work in different roles and areas of the business to help you find the career path that excites you. Some companies offer new grad programs with rotations through the business, but you can also do a walkabout by working for a small company or startup where you get to do all of the things or by doing a bit of job-hopping.

Your Five(ish)-Year Career Vision

Which industry do you want to work in? (Circle one.)

Tech   Finance   Education   Health Care   Government

Nonprofit   Other _____

What level do you see yourself at? (Circle one.)

Individual contributor   Manager   Director   VP

C-suite   Other _____

What impact do you want to make?

_____

_____

_____

_____

_____

_____

_____

Now that you have answered the essentials, it's time to put everything together to determine your career vision. Complete this sentence:

In five years, I would like to be working in _____

as a _____ helping my company achieve _____

.

Your vision should be ambitious, but you want to make sure you can achieve what you want in the time line you're talking about. For example, if you want to be a Fortune 500 CEO and you just graduated, this isn't a five-year vision; it's more of a fifteen- to twenty-year vision. It's awesome if your vision goes that far out, but for the purpose of your Career Glow Up, zoom it in to focus on the next few years. Make sure it will be possible to achieve your career vision in the next five years.

Your Success Plan

There are so many things you can plot: your wardrobe, a trip, world domination. What we'll plan here is closer to the latter than the former: It's time to plan to succeed. Having your career vision is a big long-term thing. By design, it should always be out of your reach—and this is where good old goal-setting comes into play.

Set Slayable Goals

Start to chunk your career vision into progressive milestones. This is a great time to channel Sherlock Holmes because you are going to deduce goals from your overall career vision.

Starting with the vision, map the milestones that you need to achieve in order for that vision to happen. Once you have mapped your milestones, the first of these is going to be your next career goal. It should be something that you want to achieve within the next six to twelve months. This might be getting a new job, getting a promotion, completing a project, or getting a certification; in fact, you might be working to do more than one of these in the next year.

Setting a slayable goal is the start, but now you need to turn the goal into a plan. This is where you turn "I want this" into "This is how I'm going to get it," which will follow as you complete this workbook. The main catalyst for your career goal-getting will be based on knowing why you are uniquely awesome at what you do. In the next chapter you are going to get clear on what sets you apart (it's a game changer).

Creating Slayable Goals

Working from your vision, you'll determine the milestones you need to reach to achieve your goal.

Example: Maria's career vision is to become a manager in the next five years. She is currently an associate. In order to move up the ladder, she needs to be promoted to a senior associate, then team lead, and finally manager. Her time line might look like this:

- 1 year: Senior associate

- 3 years: Team lead

- 5 years: Manager

My career vision: _____

_____

_____

_____

_____

_____

_____

My milestones to get there: _____

_____

_____

_____

_____

_____

_____

Milestone (such as a job title)	Timeline

Based on your milestones, what do you want to achieve in the next six to twelve months? _____

_____

_____

_____

_____

_____

_____

_____

_____

_____

_____

_____

Glow Up Goal Ideas

Don't know where to get started with your goals? Here are some common career goals to give you ideas:

- Land a new job in the next ninety days that makes at least $60,000.

- Get promoted in the next twelve months.

- Be rated as "Greatly Exceeds Expectations" on my next performance review.

Where Are You Now?

Before you fully embark on creating the career you want, let's document and celebrate where you are now.

What is your job title (or target job title)? _____

_____

_____

_____

_____

_____

_____

_____

What level are you at?

_____

_____

_____

_____

Do you see yourself as a leader?

_____

_____

_____

_____

Do you see yourself as someone with high potential?

_____

_____

_____

_____

How confident are you that you can achieve your career goals?

_____

_____

_____

_____

Now that you have a clearer vision of your goals, we can move on to the next stage your Unique Awesomeness Quotient (UAQ).

Focus on Your Goal

Keep your actions aligned with your career goals. What career goal are you targeting right now?

_____

_____

_____

_____

Revisit Your Vision

Revisiting your career vision is important. Take a few moments to think about this, including your super-successful future self doing what you're preparing to do right now.

What did you envision? _____

_____

_____

_____

How did it feel? _____

_____

_____

_____

Do you feel closer to this version of you? _____

_____

_____

_____

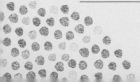

What You Love About You

One of the most important factors in success is confidence. Write down three reasons why you are awesome, to cultivate your inner confidence.

1. _____

2. _____

3. _____

Build a Success Habit

Gratitude is a game changer. A daily gratitude practice can improve relationships[1], help you maintain a positive outlook[2] needed to spot opportunities, and improve your overall mood[3]. Take a moment to be grateful (and reap the rewards!).

Who are you grateful for right now?	What are you grateful for?

GLOW UP CONFIDENCE METER

One Tiny Step to Success

The path to success is paved with tiny tasks and decisions. What can you do today that will get you closer to your goals?

_____

_____

_____

_____

_____

_____

_____

_____

_____

Moment of Awesomeness

What is one thing you are proud of right now?

_____

_____

_____

_____

_____

_____

_____

_____

Career Glow Up Audit

The funny thing about progress is that we don't notice it happening. Let's check in with where you are now.

	1 (I'm lost)	2 (I need help)	3 (Okay, I guess)	4 (Good but growing)	5 (I'm slaying this!)
I know what I want from my career.					
I am confident I will achieve my goals.					
I know why I am an invaluable asset to my company.					
I have a network that advocates for me.					
I know I will be successful in my career and life.					

Your Unique Awesomeness Quotient

2

- Excel with Ease
- Others Notice
- Your Interests
- Curate Your Unique Awesomeness Quotient
- Use Your Unique Awesomeness Quotient
- Your Unique Awesomeness Quotient in a Job Search

See your own potential and everyone else will follow.

There is one career success strategy that will help you land dream job offers, get onto the promotion fast track, earn you endless praise, and even boost your salary and bonuses. That strategy is knowing and owning your Unique Awesomeness Quotient (UAQ). It is so important that every step in your Career Glow Up that follows is based on your Unique Awesomeness Quotient or UAQ—plus it's going to save you time, stress, and maybe even a bit of drama at work.

Your UAQ is a combination of your natural talents, the skills you have developed, and your interests. Of course, in order to leverage your UAQ, you need to know what it is. You might be thinking, "I'm not sure if I have a UAQ," and I can assure you that you do. At every stage in your career, you have a UAQ that you can use to differentiate yourself. Over the next several pages, you will uncover yours and start bringing it to life.

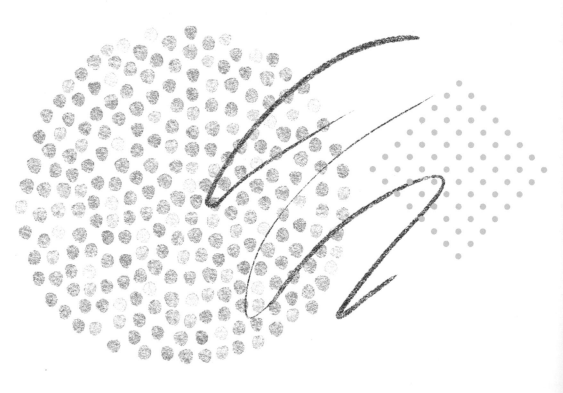

You've Got Skills

You are an exceptional and talented human with so many skills. We'll kick off this process of uncovering your Unique Awesomeness Quotient (UAQ) by acknowledging and celebrating all of your abilities and things you're proud of (bragging is expected).

Hard skills I have:	(Skills you have that are measurable. Examples: photo editing, coding in Python)
My soft skills are:	(Non-measurable subjective skills such as communication, leadership, and persuasion)
Things I've accomplished that I'm proud of:	I get excited anytime I get to do this at work:

Excel with Ease

One of the biggest missteps in the corporate world is an emphasis on getting better at the things you're not good at. What's much easier, and more aligned with your potential, is to focus instead on the things that come naturally to you. There are things that you excel at without you even trying. These don't have to be life-changing, career-making skills and abilities—in fact, most aren't. What most people find is that the things they already excel at are things that feel normal—so normal, in fact, that you might not even notice them.

Where You Excel

What are you already exceptional at? Write down *everything* related to your job (or the job you want) that comes easily to you or that you know you stand out for.

_____

_____

_____

_____

_____

_____

_____

_____

_____

_____

_____
_____
_____
_____
_____
_____
_____
_____
_____
_____
_____
_____
_____
_____
_____
_____
_____
_____
_____
_____
_____
_____
_____
_____
_____

A note for new professionals and career changers: It can be helpful to review
a few job postings or even conduct a few informational interviews to help you
understand the role. You bring skills to the table that will stage you for success,
even if it's your first job or you're trying to break into a new role.

Others' Notice

Here's the thing about talents: It's nearly impossible to keep them secret. Consciously or subconsciously, people around you notice the things you are great at, just like how you have observed the things others are good at. Think about a time you had a question about a process at work or needed input to get through a stuck point with a customer. You probably knew exactly who to ask. This brings us to the second area we'll explore to uncover your Unique Awesomeness Quotient (UAQ).

We'll start with the obvious: compliments you've gotten at work. This can be from your manager, a customer, or a colleague on another team. Perhaps a colleague pinged you to give you a virtual high five on an idea you had in a meeting (you outside-the-box thinker, you) or a customer remarked on your expertise.

That said, admiration isn't always obvious. As you work through the next exercises, you'll answer some questions that will help you find the things others notice.

What Others Notice

Recent Praise or Awards

What compliments have you gotten from a coworker, your boss, a customer, or a business partner?

_____

_____

_____

_____

_____

Have you received kudos or a thank you for your contributions on a project or
an initiative?

_____

_____

_____

_____

_____

_____

_____

_____

_____

What awards or public praise have you gotten?

_____

_____

_____

_____

_____

_____

_____

_____

continued

When You Are Asked to Help

What questions have colleagues asked you?

_____

_____

_____

_____

Is there a process or technology you are asked to train your coworkers on?

_____

_____

_____

_____

In what area do your coworkers point everyone to you for help with?

_____

_____

_____

_____

When You Are Asked for Input

What topics or areas do your coworkers ask to pick your brain on?

_____

_____

_____

_____

_____

What do your colleagues look to you to review and validate?

_____

_____

_____

_____

They Should Ask For . . .

What topics or areas do you wish your colleagues would ask for your input on?

_____

_____

_____

_____

What are you most eager to help with or add ideas on?

_____

_____

_____

_____

Your Interests

As you're listing your skills based on what you excel at and what others notice, you probably noticed something: some of what you listed are things that you love, while others you would put in a "not my favorite part of the job" list. On the flip side, there are probably areas that you are eager to grow in. How do you solve this predicament, you wonder? It's simple: You're going to create a list of things that you have a high level of interest in, perhaps even passion for (as cliché as it is).

Where Your Interests Lie

Use the following prompts to uncover relevant interests that may be part of your Unique Awesomeness Quotient (UAQ).

What skills are you most excited to develop (examples: leadership, negotiation, project management)?

_____

_____

_____

_____

What projects or tasks are you most excited to work on?

_____

_____

_____

_____

What topics do you wish your coworkers would ask you about?

_____

_____

_____

_____

The Nexus

Once you have created your lists, it's time to find where they overlap.
This is "the nexus." As you review the lists you created in the last few
exercises, write down the items that show up in two or three lists.

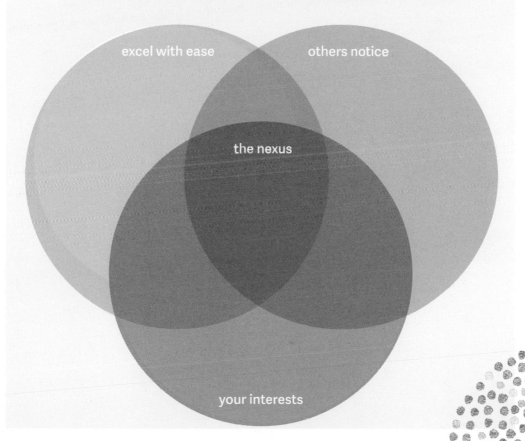

excel with ease

others notice

the nexus

your interests

Curate Your Unique Awesomeness Quotient

At this point you might still have a lengthy list, or you may have a short but respectable one. The final step to uncover your Unique Awesomeness Quotient (UAQ) is to curate it. Most people are not the top expert or authority in any one thing, but when you begin combining skills and capabilities in the nexus, your UAQ will emerge.

How can you curate it down, though? To begin, start by crossing off anything that doesn't excite you. Just because you're great at something doesn't mean that you should do it. Next, consider the needs of your current company or the company you want to work for. If you aren't sure what the company's priorities are, assume increasing profitability is the most important thing (because that's the core of all businesses). Finally, look at what's left and see how it fits together. It won't always come together perfectly, and it can be complex, but ultimately it will set you apart.

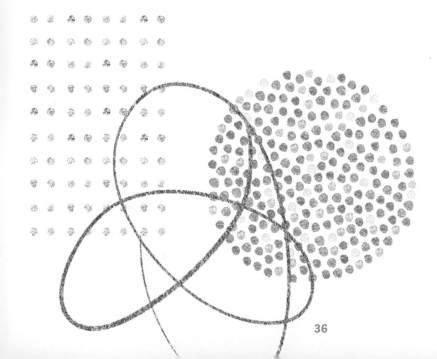

Determine Your UAQ

Review what you listed in pages 34 to 35. Which skills and talents excite
you most and are most applicable to your current work situation?
List them here.

_____

_____

_____

_____

_____

_____

_____

_____

_____

_____

_____

_____

_____

_____

_____

_____

_____

_____

_____

Use Your Unique Awesomeness Quotient

Now that you know your Unique Awesomeness Quotient, it is time to begin bringing it to life, starting with communicating it clearly and concisely. This is your new elevator pitch. Whether you're at a networking event, writing the headline of your resume, or meeting a new coworker, this is a powerful way to introduce yourself.

I know, I just put a lot of pressure on you, but I am going to make this easy by giving you a simple formula. Of course, you can make your own, but if you have no idea where to begin, then start with the following exercises.

Summarize Your UAQ

What is the simplest way you would explain your Unique Awesomeness Quotient?

_____

_____

_____

_____

_____

Examples:

- I build scalable learner-centric organizations.

- I create interactive digital experiences.

Why It Matters

To increase the wow factor, add what impact your Unique Awesomeness
Quotient makes to your summary statement.

_____

_____

_____

_____

_____

_____

_____

_____

_____

_____

_____

_____

_____

_____

_____

_____

_____

Examples:

- I build scalable learner-centric organizations that drive top-line revenue
  growth through service and product upsells.

- I create interactive digital experiences that reduce the cost of customer
  acquisition and increase client retention.

Your Unique Awesomeness Quotient in a Job Search

If you're actively looking for a job, or simply know it's time to give your resume and LinkedIn profile a makeover, your Unique Awesomeness Quotient (UAQ) should play a central role because it will differentiate you. Your UAQ should align with the company's needs; this means that your resume and interview should showcase elements of your UAQ that align with the opportunity. I've been on both sides of hiring decisions more times than I can count, and I can tell you this: The candidate who doesn't just check the basic boxes for the job but adds to it with their UAQ is the candidate who gets top-dollar offers.

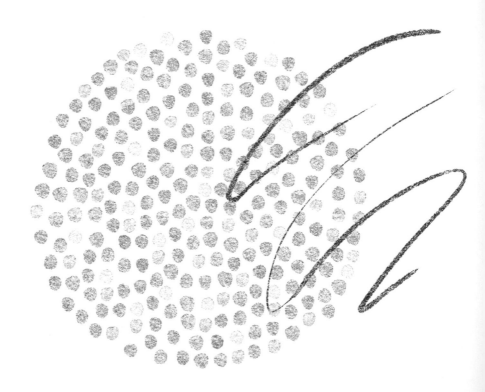

Checklist: Using Your Unique Awesomeness Quotient in a Job Search

Your UAQ will make you stand out in a sea of qualified candidates. Showcase it in your job search by doing the following:

☐ Resume

* Use your UAQ summary as your resume summary.

* Feature your UAQ and impact in bullet points in your experience section, using numbers whenever possible.

☐ LinkedIn Profile

* Feature your UAQ summary in your headline.

* Write a LinkedIn summary that tells the story of your UAQ.

* Add relevant skills in your profile.

☐ Interview

* To prepare, research the company and review the job description. Write down ideas of how your UAQ would positively impact the team and company.

* Identify stories that show how your UAQ uniquely qualifies you.

☐ Negotiations

* Research the market to ensure your expectations are competitive.

* Remember that you and your UAQ offer incredible value.

Let's be real—it's easy to make claims about your awesomeness. But what matters much more is integrating your UAQ into your day-to-day actions and impact. Your success squad is instrumental in helping you bring your UAQ to life through support, collaboration, and opportunity connection. In the next chapter you are going to discover who your success squad is and create a plan to cultivate a powerful network of advocates.

Focus on Your Goal

Keep your actions aligned with your career goals. What career goal are you targeting right now?

_____

_____

_____

Revisit Your Vision

Revisiting your career vision is important. Take a few moments to think about this, including your super-successful future self doing what you're preparing to do right now.

What did you envision? _____

_____

_____

_____

How did it feel? _____

_____

_____

Do you feel closer to this version of you? _____

_____

_____

GLOW UP CONFIDENCE METER

What You Love About You

One of the most important factors in success is confidence. Write down three reasons why you are awesome, to cultivate your inner confidence.

1. _____

2. _____

3. _____

Build a Success Habit

Gratitude is a game changer. Take a moment to be grateful.

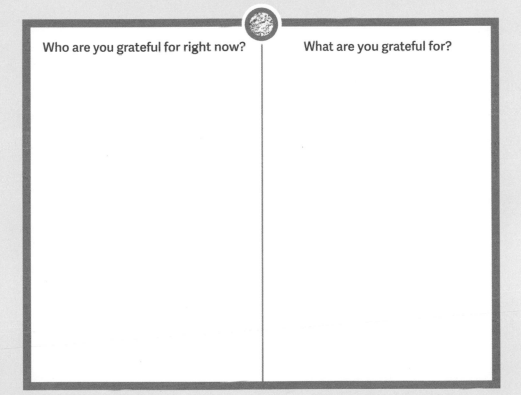

Who are you grateful for right now?	What are you grateful for?

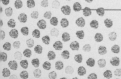

One Tiny Step to Success

The path to success is paved with tiny tasks and decisions. What can you do today that will get you closer to your goals?

_____

_____

_____

_____

_____

_____

_____

_____

_____

Moment of Awesomeness

What is one thing you are proud of right now?

_____

_____

_____

_____

_____

_____

_____

Career Glow Up Audit

The funny thing about progress is that we don't notice it happening.
Let's check in with where you are now.

	1 (I'm lost)	2 (I need help)	3 (Okay, I guess)	4 (Good but growing)	5 (I'm slaying this!)
I know what I want from my career.					
I am confident I will achieve my goals.					
I know why I am an invaluable asset to my company.					
I have a network that advocates for me.					
I know I will be successful in my career and life.					

Assemble Your Success Squad

3

- #Networking Goals
- Your Network of Advocates
- Value and Reciprocity
- How to Cultivate Relationships

Success is
not solitary.

No matter how good your work is and how awesome you are, if you don't have people of influence and authority advocating for you, then you will find your career growth struggling or stalling. You've probably heard this countless times: Mentors and sponsors are required to succeed. What's often overlooked is where to find them and other important people in your network.

This is why I want you to focus on cultivating a success squad. This is a collection of connections who will play varying roles in your career success, and hopefully you in theirs, because effective and long-lasting relationships are mutually beneficial. By the end of this chapter, you will have your success squad mapped, with a plan to expand your connections with precision.

To build your success squad, you will need to network. As you read this, you probably had a very specific reaction to the mention of "networking." To get started, it's important to understand your feelings and beliefs around networking. This will help you implement the next several steps in a way that is both comfortable and authentic to you.

What Type of Networker Are You?

1. How do you feel about networking?

   a. I love it.

   b. It's necessary.

   c. I hate it.

2. How good do you think you are at making new connections?

   a. I could write a book about it.

   b. I get to know the people I work with.

   c. It's something I struggle with.

3. When I think of networking, the image I get in my head is . . .

   a. Fun!

   b. Stuffy room with awkward conversations.

   c. Gross shmoozing and me hiding in the corner.

Mostly a's	Bold networker: You're the life of a party and can (and do) talk to anyone. You make a lot of connections, and this chapter will help you cultivate them strategically.
Mostly b's	Necessity networker: You get your networking on, and you're pretty good at it. This chapter will help you focus your networking and give you strategies to boost your confidence.
Mostly c's	Timid networker: You're shy and avoid networking at all costs. As a timid networker myself, I created the strategies I'm about to share specifically for you (even though they work for everyone).

#NetworkingGoals

Networking can be enjoyable and productive, no matter what type of networker you are, with precision networking. Unless you're just networking for the fun and potential of growing your connections, precision networking begins with setting a goal. Why are you doing this in the first place? This should be easy to answer: It should align with the career goals you set in chapter 1.

Set Networking Goals

There are lots of reasons to network. What are your goals?

_____

_____

_____

_____

_____

_____

_____

_____

_____

_____

(BTW: When I work with clients, some of them quite honestly give me a side-eye when we cover this step, but it's important! It is the beginning step in precision networking. If you're going to do this, I want you to do it well and with clarity.)

Your Network of Advocates

Wouldn't it be awesome if you had a collective of contacts who bragged about you, connected you with opportunities, and supported you in achieving your professional goals? This is exactly what your network of advocates does. Your network of advocates will talk you up when you are not in the room, recommend you for the job opportunity of your dreams, remove obstacles that get in your way, and be a source of inspiration and motivation.

Even better, you already have a network of advocates—at least the start of one. But who is in your network of advocates and who is missing? What role do they play in your career—and what role do you play in theirs?

The Decider

The decider is exactly who you think it is: the person who has the authority to give you what you want. They are the ones who decide whether you get hired, promoted, or assigned to that key project. You shouldn't have to look hard to find them; it will be the hiring manager, your boss, or the key stakeholder.

The Influencer

There are a lot of people who have the power to make introductions, recommendations, and have influence over deciders. Influencers can be at any rank in an organization, from entry level up to the executive who holds sway over the CEO. Being in the good graces of the influencer your decider turns to can be career changing. You can spot the influencer by answering the questions in the exercise on page 54.

The Connector

Some people just seem to know everyone, or at least know the people that you want to know. The great thing about connectors is they tend to already be in your network of advocates. Most people enjoy being able to make introductions and referrals. They enjoy helping others, and making valuable introductions makes them look good, so they are happy to help out friends.

The Supporter

Your network of advocates is rounded out by your supporters. Supporters are family, friends, colleagues, peers, and even your online career besties. These are the people who encourage you when you are discouraged, listen to you when you need to talk through an obstacle at work, and endlessly believe in you and your potential. Your supporters can also play a pivotal role in the rooms you are not in. They will sing your praises for a project you slayed (we'll come back to this in bragless self-promotion), recommend you for opportunities, and help you achieve your professional goals directly and indirectly. Ultimately, they are in your corner, and you should be in theirs too.

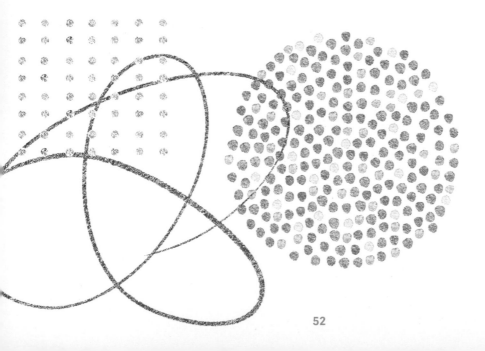

Who Are Your Deciders?

What is your main networking goal?

_____

_____

_____

Who is the decision maker for you to achieve this goal? (Tip: Use the organization chart or LinkedIn to be specific.)

_____

_____

Do you have a relationship with this person?

_____

_____

What's in it for them?

_____

_____

What's In It for Them?

One of the biggest mistakes I see professionals make is putting themselves in the center of the relationship. Put the other person in the center and be clear on what is in it for them. How will helping you make them look good and boost their career?

Who Are Your Influencers?

Who can grant you access to the decider?

_____

_____

_____

_____

Who does the decider look to for ideas or opinions?

_____

_____

_____

_____

_____

Who has a strong reputation with the decider?

_____

_____

_____

_____

What's in it for them?

_____

_____

_____

_____

_____

Who Are Your Connectors?

Who in your existing network can introduce you to deciders or influencers you don't have a relationship with?

_____

_____

_____

_____

Within your company?

_____

_____

_____

_____

At a different company?
(Tip: Use LinkedIn to look for second-degree connections.)

_____

_____

_____

_____

What's in it for them?

_____

_____

_____

_____

Who Are Your Supporters?

Make a list of your supporters.

_____

_____

_____

_____

Personal: Who do you call on a bad day, when you don't get a job, or when you make a mistake at work?

_____

_____

_____

_____

Professional: Which coworkers do you celebrate your ideas and successes with?

_____

_____

_____

_____

What is in it for them?

_____

_____

_____

_____

Value and Reciprocity

Lopsided relationships won't last. If you want to have a powerful and effective network of advocates (which obviously you do), the relationships you build need to be of mutual benefit. The fastest way to build a relationship with someone is to bring them value. This is the point where I know a lot of you will be scratching your head and wondering, "How can I add value to a decider?" The first thing you need to figure out is what role you play for your network of advocates. Just as your network fulfills one of these roles for you, you will fulfill one of these roles for them. This is how you begin to understand what is in it for them.

The Takers

You should give value without expectations. However, takers will, well, take advantage. While it's not always a 1:1 exchange, scenarios should in general be win-win. If your generosity isn't serving you both, this strategy is not for that relationship.

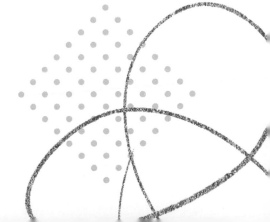

What's In It for Them?

Use this table to map key relationships with key people in your network of advocates.

Connection	Role They Play	Who Are You to Them?	Ideas to Add Value
Example: Deirdre	Decider	Connector	Needs to collaborate with the product team; I am close with the manager and can make introductions.

How to Cultivate Relationships

The thing I love about this modern world of ours is all the opportunities there are to build and maintain relationships. Back in the day, everything happened in person: bumping into key people in the elevator or getting to know people at a happy hour after work. Proximity can serve to get you on the radar of people you want to know by bumping into them or having your conversation overheard (careful with that).

However, these days being in person isn't a requirement. The virtual world gives unlimited opportunities to connect and grow relationships with almost anyone. You can use internal tools and messenger, public platforms like LinkedIn, or drop in a virtual networking mixer. Figuring out which approach to follow is simple: go where the people are that you want to meet and develop relationships with.

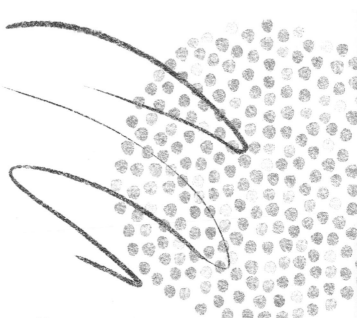

Relationship Development Plan

Now that you know whom you need to know and which relationships to cultivate, it's time to make a plan of action to meet and engage with your network of advocates.

Whom You Need to Know	How to Meet Them	Where You Can Engage with Them	How You Can Engage and/or Add Value
Example: Deirdre	I already know Deirdre	Slack, email, LinkedIn	I will send an instant message offering to introduce her to Mark in production

As great (and career changing) as it is to proactively cultivate connections, the next level is to get on their radar without your outreach. In the next chapter, you'll learn how to do that through creating an unignorable impact.

Whom You Need to Know	How to Meet Them	Where You Can Engage with Them	How You Can Engage and/or Add Value
Example: Deirdre	I already know Deirdre	Slack, email, LinkedIn	I will send an instant message offering to introduce her to Mark in production

Focus on Your Goal

Keep your actions aligned with your career goals. What career goal are you targeting right now?

_____

_____

_____

Revisit Your Vision

Revisiting your career vision is important. Take a few moments to think about this, including your super-successful future self doing what you're preparing to do right now.

What did you envision? _____

_____

_____

How did it feel? _____

_____

_____

Do you feel closer to this version of you? _____

_____

_____

GLOW UP CONFIDENCE METER

What You Love About You

One of the most important factors in success is confidence. Write down three reasons why you are awesome, to cultivate your inner confidence.

1. _____

2. _____

3. _____

Build a Success Habit

Gratitude is a game changer. Take a moment to be grateful.

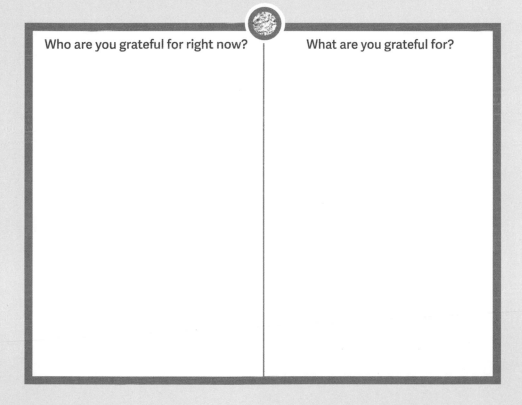

Who are you grateful for right now?	What are you grateful for?

One Tiny Step to Success

The path to success is paved with tiny tasks and decisions. What can you do today that will get you closer to your goals?

_____

_____

_____

_____

_____

_____

_____

_____

_____

Moment of Awesomeness

What is one thing you are proud of right now?

_____

_____

_____

_____

_____

_____

_____

_____

_____

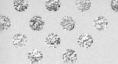

Career Glow Up Audit

The funny thing about progress is that we don't notice it happening.
Let's check in with where you are now.

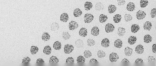

	1 (I'm lost)	2 (I need help)	3 (Okay, I guess)	4 (Good but growing)	5 (I'm slaying this!)
I know what I want from my career.					
I am confident I will achieve my goals.					
I know why I am an invaluable asset to my company.					
I have a network that advocates for me.					
I know I will be successful in my career and life.					

Unignorable Impact

Results speak louder than words.

You cannot stand out when you are doing the same thing as everyone else. In fact, that is a guaranteed way to blend in. Unfortunately, this is the approach I've seen too many ambitious professionals take. Just like in school, when they got high grades and did extracurricular activities to boost their applications and resumes, they bring that strategy into their careers. They end up working sixty-plus hours a week, waiting for someone to see their potential and struggling to get career-advancing opportunities. Then they get frustrated when their slacker coworker gets promoted ahead of them.

If you've been taking this approach—first off, don't worry. Most people (especially women) start out here. But if you'd like to stop working all of the hours for none of the praise, you're in the right place. By the end of this chapter you won't be waiting for an opportunity to fall into your lap—you will create your own. But first, there is something we need to take care of . . .

Where Are You Now?

What do you think you need to do to get ahead at work?

_____

_____

_____

_____

_____

_____

_____

_____

_____

How many hours do you work each week on average?

_____

_____

_____

_____

_____

_____

What work has gotten you noticed?

_____

_____

_____

_____

_____

_____

_____

_____

What tasks have you done that have gone unnoticed?

_____

_____

_____

_____

_____

_____

_____

Invent Time

We aren't going to add to your to-do list until we've added to your to-don't list. It might not seem like a big deal to volunteer to plan the team summit or say yes to that extra project when it's only a few hours a week. The problem is all hours add up, and suddenly you're working all the time, and not necessarily on things that will get you ahead. In fact, most often, my clients find they're spending a ton of time on things that don't map to their goals.

This is where you are going to look to invent time. Well, not invent, what you're going to do now is figure out the things you can either stop doing (ideal) or do the bare minimum on (I know, gasp, right!?). It starts with taking an inventory of the tasks you complete over a typical week at work (see the opposite page).

As you add tasks to your inventory, you might notice—yikes, there are a lot! This is where you become a curator. Begin by considering a simple question: Do you have to do that task? If it is part of your job description, performance reviews, and your boss's expectations, then you have to do that task. However, what you might notice is there are things that you don't really have to do that you do anyway.

Next, you'll consider whether each task is of consequence to the business and your career development. Consider the priorities of your boss, team, and overall company. Some tasks are mission critical to each. On the other hand, you may have taken on tasks and work assignments to stretch your skills and get closer to your career goals.

What Do You Do Daily?

Using the Inventing Time Machine worksheet on page 72, create a list
below of regular tasks you typically do daily and weekly.

Daily

_____

_____

_____

_____

_____

_____

_____

_____

_____

Weekly

_____

_____

_____

_____

_____

_____

_____

_____

Inventing Time Machine

Okay, it's a table, but you have to admit the Inventing Time Machine has a ring to it.

Task	Is It Necessary?	Is It of Consequence?	Stop, Settle, or Stellar

Is It Necessary?

Without judging yourself or your efforts, scan through the task list you created in the Inventing Time Machine on page 72 and honestly answer this question: Is it necessary?

_____

_____

_____

_____

_____

_____

_____

_____

_____

_____

_____

_____

_____

_____

_____

_____

_____

_____

_____

_____

_____

_____

_____

_____

_____

Is It of Consequence?

Scan through the list you created in the Inventing Time Machine worksheet and honestly answer this question: Does this matter to the business, my team, or my boss, or does it support my career goals?

_____

_____

_____

_____

_____

_____

_____

_____

_____

_____

_____

Armed with the answers to the questions on this page and page 73, the next step is to figure out whether you are going to stop, settle, or be stellar for each. Knowing you're ambitious, I'm guessing you are overachieving on pretty much everything. However, that also means you're probably also working all the time without the recognition you deserve. Some of these tasks you can stop doing or delegate to someone else. Others, you should settle and simply meet expectations on. For example, you will not get promoted for having the most organized expense report. Finally, there are tasks that will make you stand out when you are stellar (i.e., where you should be overachieving).

Stop, Settle, or Stellar

Using the table below, determine for each task you listed which you need to stop, settle and be stellar on.

Do I Have to Do It?	Does It Matter?	Your Approach Should Be
No	No	Stop
Yes	No	Settle
Yes	Yes	Stellar
No	Yes	Varies (e.g., stellar if it's a career-advancement opportunity)

Strategic High-impact Opportunities

With your calendar cleared up, it's time to create an unignorable impact. But how will you do that? It begins with identifying strategic high-impact opportunities. These opportunities allow you to flex your Unique Awesomeness Quotient (UAQ) to differentiate yourself, while increasing your visibility. Over the next few pages, you will uncover potential areas to focus your energy and effort to generate an unignorable impact.

Company Priorities

Chances are your company has goals they are trying to achieve this year. They're definitely thinking about revenue—even if you work in a nonprofit, dollars coming in the door matters. In addition, there are likely goals that focus on growing the business: new products, new markets, increasing internal efficiencies, and decreasing operating costs. If you work at an established company, your CEO and executive team probably have goals set that can be a great resource to review.

Leadership Priorities

The next consideration is what is important to your boss, and their boss. If your team has goals, what are they? Knowing what your boss is expected to achieve and what they are evaluated on will help you determine how you can make an unignorable impact. You can identify these by asking your boss, looking up their annual goals, or observing what they are focused on.

What Are Your Company's Priorities?

Write down the things you know your company is trying to achieve this year. Tip: When in doubt, always assume revenue growth.

_____

_____

_____

_____

_____

_____

_____

_____

For job seekers: If your target company is publicly traded, listen to their most recent earnings call. What priorities and challenges are mentioned?

_____

_____

_____

_____

_____

_____

_____

_____

What Are Leadership's Priorities?

What does your boss ask about or talk about often?

_____
_____
_____
_____
_____
_____
_____
_____
_____
_____

How is your boss's success measured?

_____
_____
_____
_____
_____
_____
_____
_____
_____
_____
_____

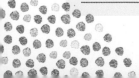

How could your Unique Awesomeness Quotient (UAQ) benefit?

_____

_____

_____

_____

_____

_____

For job seekers: Search for interviews or articles with leadership at your target companies. What are they talking about?

_____

_____

_____

_____

_____

_____

How would your UAQ help their priorities succeed?

_____

_____

_____

_____

_____

_____

_____

Make Them SHIP You

Your highest potential is in your Unique Awesomeness Quotient (UAQ), so naturally it needs to play a role in creating unignorable impact and identifying strategic high-impact opportunities. Looking through the lists you just created and your UAQ, ask yourself: How can my UAQ help my boss and company achieve their priorities? It's where these two things intersect that you will find a Strategic High-impact Project (SHIP). What is a SHIP idea? You could create a productized service, create templates for customer presentations, outsource content development to a third party, concept a partnership model for services, create a training that reduces onboarding time, and many more.

Your SHIP Ideas

What initial ideas do you have for your Strategic High-impact Project (SHIP)?

_____

_____

_____

_____

_____

_____

_____

_____

_____

_____

_____

_____

Four Types of Impact

At this point, the possibilities might seem endless—or you might be drawing a blank. No matter which camp you're in, it's important to know the types of impact that you can make. For each of these you'll write down a few ideas.

Improvement Impact

There is always an opportunity for improvement. There are probably things that you do on a day-to-day basis that could be done faster, cheaper, and better. In fact, you've probably noticed a ton of these in your work: a way to make a process smoother, a feature that would make a product more usable, or a more effective way to communicate key information. Improvement projects offer so many opportunities to proactively make an unignorable impact. This also has the benefit of not bringing problems forward but solutions, showing you are a proactive problem solver.

Upward Impact

The next type of impact is to look at the job you want and start to prove yourself in that role. For example, if you want to become a manager, ask how you can demonstrate leadership in the position you are in today. One thing I've observed is a growing trend where companies will promote you to the level at which you are already performing. I love this in practice, because it avoids Peter's Principle,[4] when people are promoted to the level of their incompetence. However, performing at the next level requires clarity on what that level is.

What Improvements Can You Make?

What ideas do you have to improve your team, product, or company?

_____

_____

_____

_____

_____

_____

_____

_____

_____

Which of these ideas can you make the most impact with using your Unique Awesomeness Quotient (UAQ)?

_____

_____

_____

_____

_____

_____

_____

_____

How Can You Make an Upward Impact?

How are responsibilities different in the job you want next versus the job you have?

_____

_____

_____

_____

_____

_____

_____

_____

_____

What tasks or responsibilities are handled by someone who does the job you want, that you could start doing now?

_____

_____

_____

_____

_____

_____

_____

_____

_____

_____

Visibility Impact

Other initiatives or projects you pursue are designed to get you outsized visibility to key people in your organization. This might mean knowing and focusing on stellar tasks you identified earlier or contributing to highly visible initiatives. This can accelerate your personal brand building and grow your network of advocates. For example, if there is a strategic project that an executive leader you want to know is sponsoring and will have their eyes on, it is a solid Strategic High-impact Project (SHIP) to jump on to raise your visibility and flex your UAQ.

How Can You Boost Your Visibility?

What big problems or initiatives are leaders talking about at your company (or at your target company)?

_____

_____

_____

How can your Unique Awesomeness Quotient (UAQ) uniquely solve the problem to create success?

_____

_____

What trends are emerging in your industry that intersect with your (UAQ) and that you can share expertise on?

_____

_____

Brand Impact

The final type of impact opportunity to consider for your Strategic High-impact Project (SHIP) is for your professional branding. This centers on your UAQ and establishing your reputation as the go-to person or the one with this unique set of skills. Obviously, this will be dependent on your UAQ, but don't forget how important it is to relate it to a company priority.

How Can You Advance Your Professional Brand?

What gaps or problems could you solve using your UAQ?

_____

_____

_____

_____

_____

_____

What opportunities do you have to demonstrate your UAQ?

_____

_____

_____

_____

_____

_____

Choose Your SHIP

Now that you have your Unique Awesomeness Quotient (UAQ), a list of your company and team priorities, and ideas of the types of impact you can make, it's time to choose a Strategic High-impact Project (SHIP). Reviewing your ideas, choose ones that intersect company needs and your UAQ.

List the SHIP Possibilities

Review your ideas, and write down the top three contenders for your Strategic High-impact Project (SHIP).

1. _____

_____

2. _____

_____

3. _____

_____

Before you run with it, though, you want to make sure it has the highest potential to raise your visibility and career trajectory. That's why the next thing you will do is use the SHIP feasibility validator to assess your SHIP, and choose the one with the most yeses.

_____

_____

SHIP Feasibility Validator

	✓ Or ✗
No Red Tape Requires no budget or resource approvals	
Quick Win Takes 90 days or less with minimal time investment	
Measurable Results are quantifiable in revenue, costs, or hours	
Highly Visible Likely to be noticed by your boss, and their boss	
Has Scale Can be widely implemented to your team or company	
Fulfillment You are excited to do the work	
Personal Brand Building It will boost your authority within your company, or your resume for your dream job	

Plan to Succeed

Once your Strategic High-impact Project (SHIP) is selected, it's time to make a plan for how you will bring it to life. Begin by mapping steps to make the SHIP happen. For example, if you have an idea for a process to streamline or automate, list what you need to do to test or implement it. Once you have the steps, block time in your calendar to make progress on your SHIP. The more you protect the time to focus on your SHIP, the quicker you can make an unignorable impact.

Plan Your SHIP

What steps are required to implement your Strategic High-impact Project (SHIP)?

1. _____

2. _____

3. _____

4. _____

5. _____

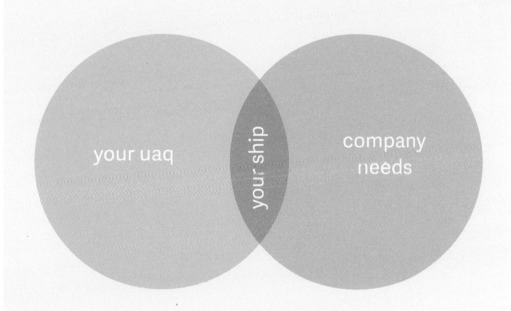

When will you work on your Strategic High-impact Project (SHIP)?

_____

_____

_____

_____

Can you complete each step in the next 90 days?

_____

_____

_____

_____

your uaq   your ship   company needs

A well-selected SHIP won't go without notice. This leads us to our next Career Glow Up task in the following chapter: shameless self-promotion in a non-gross way.

Focus on Your Goal

Keep your actions aligned with your career goals. What career goal are you targeting right now?

_____

_____

_____

_____

_____

Revisit Your Vision

Revisiting your career vision is important. Take a few moments to think about this, including your super-successful future self doing what you're preparing to do right now.

What did you envision?

_____

_____

_____

_____

_____

GLOW UP CONFIDENCE METER

How did it feel?

_____

_____

_____

_____

_____

_____

Do you feel closer to this version of you?

_____

_____

_____

_____

_____

_____

What You Love About You

One of the most important factors in success is confidence. Write down three reasons why you are awesome, to cultivate your inner confidence.

1. _____

2. _____

3. _____

Build a Success Habit

Gratitude is a game changer. Take a moment to be grateful.

Who are you grateful for right now?	What are you grateful for?

One Tiny Step to Success

The path to success is paved with tiny tasks and decisions. What can you do today that will get you closer to your goals?

_____

_____

_____

_____

_____

Moment of Awesomeness

What is one thing you are proud of right now?

_____

_____

_____

Career Glow Up Audit

The funny thing about progress is that we don't notice it happening.
Let's check in with where you are now.

	1 (I'm lost)	2 (I need help)	3 (Okay, I guess)	4 (Good but growing)	5 (I'm slaying this!)
I know what I want from my career.					
I am confident I will achieve my goals.					
I know why I am an invaluable asset to my company.					
I have a network that advocates for me.					
I know I will be successful in my career and life.					

Shameless Self-promotion

5

- Inventory of Awesomeness
- Bragless Self-promotion

Don't brag about yourself when others will do it for you.

No one likes a bragger, but you can't advance your career without boasting about your achievements. This leaves you with a choice: brag and be disliked and lose promotions over not being liked, or don't brag and lose promotions because no one knows the awesome impact you have made. I can't tell you how many career books I read when I was trying to figure this out that told me the problem (screwed either way), but not the solution.

The thing is, there is a third option: Get people to brag on your behalf. But how do you get people to do that? By the end of this chapter, you will have four ways to get your work on the radar of people who can move your career forward.

Inventory of Awesomeness

It's one thing to seek feedback to understand how you're perceived and even to identify strengths you didn't notice about yourself; it's another to have no idea why you're great at your job or what impact you're making. In the process of identifying your Unique Awesomeness Quotient (UAQ), you already inventoried achievements, but this needs to be an ongoing process. Enter the Inventory of Awesomeness. What is it, you ask? It's a living list you update (ideally weekly) of your achievements, impacts, and progress both big and small. As a bonus, not only will your Inventory of Awesomeness help you with bragless self-promotion, but it will also help you when you're preparing for a performance review, updating your resume, or preparing for an interview, and it will deepen professional confidence.

Begin Your Inventory of Awesomeness

Write down at least three things you have accomplished or are proud of.

1. _____

_____

2. _____

_____

3. _____

_____

Need some examples?

- Meeting or exceeding your key performance indicators

- Overcoming an obstacle

- Identifying your UAQ

- Completing a professional training class or certification

- Getting a customer compliment

Tip

Set a weekly reminder on your phone to add three achievements to your Inventory of Awesomeness.

Bragless Self-promotion

Now that you have a few things worth bragging about, it's time to learn the four strategies to brag without bragging. Let's dig into what each of these are and how to use them.

Ask for Input

There is no better way to get on someone's radar than to ask them for help. Asking for someone's advice or expertise gets them invested in the success of the problem or project you are seeking guidance on. Once they have contributed, they feel included and are more likely to talk about it themselves. More importantly, it is a way of communicating what you are working on and even progress you have made without boasting about yourself.

There are a few things you need to know to use this strategy effectively. First, the person whose input you are seeking should be someone you are trying to connect or engage with in your network of advocates. Next, approaching people to pick their brain generically won't bring you far. Instead, find a specific element where input would be helpful. For example, instead of approaching your boss and asking how to position a new product to prospects, you could ask for feedback on a pitch idea you had.

One more thing to note before we go on to the next strategy. Depending on the input you are seeking, this can also be a path to giving updates to this person. Following the example I mentioned in the previous paragraph, you could tell your boss how great the customer pitch went. This reinforces their involvement and shows respect for their expertise and contribution, and it gives them talking points to brag about you.

Getting Input

Who in your network of advocates do you want to engage?

_____

_____

_____

_____

What will you ask for input on?

_____

_____

_____

How is it relevant to them or their expertise?

_____

_____

_____

Will you implement their suggestion?   Yes   No

When will you follow up with them? (Remember to follow up so they know, and can brag about, the outcome.)

_____

_____

_____

Kudos Karma

When was the last time you bragged about a coworker or peer to your boss, their boss, or anyone else? If you can't remember, it's time to start boasting about other people. When you praise them publicly, their brain is automatically going to begin to look for ways to pay you back. For the purpose of self-promotion, this means the person you compliment is likely to return the compliment. You get bonus points when you praise someone for contributions they made on your Strategic High-impact Project (SHIP) or another high-impact task, as it raises visibility on your work at the same time. I'm not saying to do a shady brag in disguise; this needs to be genuine. But doing this strategically creates a win-win situation. No matter what, bragging about others will help create better working relationships.

Tip

When you receive compliments or kudos at work, save them to a folder. Then when you are preparing for your next performance review or applying for a promotion, they'll be at your fingertips!

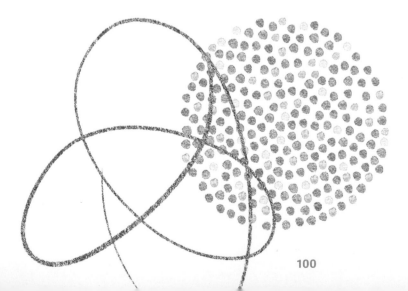

What Kudos Have You Received?

Have you received a compliment from another person?

_____

_____

_____

_____

What was the compliment?

_____

_____

_____

_____

How did it make you feel?

_____

_____

_____

_____

How did it impact your friendship or working relationship?

_____

_____

_____

_____

What Kudos Can You Give?

Who has helped you with something lately at work or in your job search?

_____

_____

_____

How did they help you?

_____

_____

_____

_____

What will you give them kudos for?

_____

_____

_____

_____

Who else should know how they helped you or the impact they had?

_____

_____

_____

Pass It Along

Have you ever gotten a "thank you" or "you're so awesome" note from a coworker or customer? If you have, chances are it totally made your day. But did you forward it to your boss? If you're like many ambitious professionals, you didn't because it felt weird, like a thirsty attempt to say, "Look how good I am at my job," or even worse, "Validate me!" So, you let the kudos you received sit secretly in an email folder that no one else will ever see.

Let's be clear: If someone vocalizes in speech or in email that you have done great work or helped them out immensely, it's because you have far exceeded their expectations. Assume they want the people who rate your performance to know, and that your boss would also like to know about it.

What Can You Pass Along?

Have you received a compliment from a coworker, customer, or business partner?

_____

_____

What was the compliment?

_____

_____

When did you receive it?

_____

_____

Advocate Amplifiers

This is the holy grail of bragless self-promotion: when others brag about you. To be clear, this isn't a case where you do one thing and all of a sudden you have people bragging about you to your CEO. It takes time. The good thing is you are not starting from square one. Cultivating your network of advocates is the first step. As you establish advocates, keep them informed of your brag-worthy accomplishments. For example, if you add a big accomplishment to your Inventory of Awesomeness, bring it up in your next discussion.

Who Are Your Advocate Amplifiers?

Which deciders, influencers, and connectors in your network of advocates have you established relationships with?

_____

_____

Who in your network of advocates is aware of or has given input on your SHIP?

_____

_____

Who is most likely to brag about you (other than your mom)?

_____

_____

Brag-worthy Updates

Referring to your Inventory of Awesomeness, what is your biggest recent accomplishment?

_____

_____

_____

_____

_____

_____

_____

_____

_____

_____

_____

_____

_____

_____

Is it relevant to the most likely advocate amplifier identified in the last exercise?
Yes   No

Do they know about it?   Yes   No

Now it's time to get clear on why your brag-worthy update is something that will make your advocate amplifier look good. Next, you'll commit to sending it to them.

Make Your Advocate Amplifier Look Good

How does the brag-worthy update relate to your advocate amplifier?

How does it benefit . . .

Them: _____

_____

_____

The team: _____

_____

_____

The company: _____

_____

_____

When will you send the update? _____

What people say about you when you're not in the room matters. While having a network of advocates bragging on your behalf is important, the true accelerator on all the strategies you have learned and implemented so far is something too many professionals overlook: their professional brand. In the next chapter, you'll start building this.

Focus on Your Goal

Keep your actions aligned with your career goals. What career goal are you targeting right now?

_____

_____

_____

_____

_____

_____

Revisit Your Vision

Revisiting your career vision is important. Take a few moments to think about your career vision, including your super-successful future self doing what you're preparing to do right now.

What did you envision?

_____

_____

_____

_____

_____

_____

GLOW UP CONFIDENCE METER

How did it feel?

_____

_____

_____

_____

_____

_____

Do you feel closer to this version of you?

_____

_____

_____

_____

_____

_____

What You Love About You

One of the most important factors in success is confidence. Write down three reasons why you are awesome, to cultivate your inner confidence.

1. _____

2. _____

3. _____

Build a Success Habit

Gratitude is a game changer. Take a moment to be grateful
(and reap the rewards!).

Who are you grateful for right now?	What are you grateful for?

Stop, Settle, or Stellar Sync

Take a moment to check in on your time-inventing progress.

I stopped ...	I've settled ...	I've focused on ...
I still need to stop ...	I'm struggling to settle ...	I still need to invent more time for ...

One Tiny Step to Success

The path to success is paved with tiny tasks and decisions. What can you do today that will get you closer to your goals?

_____

_____

_____

_____

_____

_____

_____

_____

_____

_____

Grow Your Inventory of Awesomeness

You're taking action, glowing up your career, and doing awesome work, which means it's time to add to your Inventory of Awesomeness. What three things are you proud of right now?

1. _____

2. _____

3. _____

Career Glow Up Audit

The funny thing about progress is that we don't notice it happening.
Let's check in with where you are now.

	1 (I'm lost)	2 (I need help)	3 (Okay, I guess)	4 (Good but growing)	5 (I'm slaying this!)
I know what I want from my career.					
I am confident I will achieve my goals.					
I know why I am an invaluable asset to my company.					
I have a network that advocates for me.					
I know I will be successful in my career and life.					

Build a Brand

6

- Professional Brand Basics
- Phases of Brand Building

Be present, not perfect.

I n 2012, I moved to the United States, leaving my life and job behind. When I got my work authorization, I struggled to get interviews. Meanwhile, my friends who worked at big-name tech companies had recruiters sliding into their DMs with high-paying job offers. I was jealous AF. I wanted jobs to come to me, so I made a commitment to myself: *I am going to become someone who companies headhunt.* But without being Ivy League alumni, having an MBA, or having any recognizable companies on my resume, I needed to figure out a way to get on recruiters' radar. That's when I discovered the power of personal branding. Within months, I had a dream job offer, and I established a reputation that helped me quickly advance from an entry level role to an executive role within a few years.

Personal branding doesn't mean you need to become an influencer. It simply comes down to managing your professional reputation and increasing your visibility with the right people. Since it plays a role at every juncture of your career success journey, let's get into it.

What Do You Think of Personal Branding?

When you hear the words personal brand, what image springs to mind?

_____

_____

How do you feel about personal branding? _____

_____

_____

Have you thought about your professional brand? _____

_____

_____

Professional Brand Basics

The first things that might have sprung to mind when I said "professional brand" are logos, color schemes, and maybe some campy photos. If you want any or all of those things, that's cool but not required. Your professional brand goes much deeper. In essence, your brand is what people say about you when you are not in the room. Whether you intentionally create it or not, you have a reputation. Personal branding at its core is being intentional about that reputation.

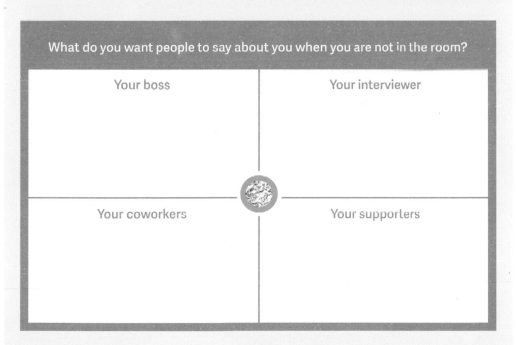

What Will Your Brand Be?

What do you want people to say about you when you are not in the room?

Your boss	Your interviewer
Your coworkers	Your supporters

Phases of Brand Building

With clarity on your Unique Awesomeness Quotient (UAQ) and the professional brand you want to build, it's time to get started. There are three phases to build your personal brand.

Phase I: In Real Life

You don't create an amazing professional brand by stating it. You create an amazing professional brand by living it and showing up in alignment with it every day. The good news is that most of the exercises in this book have been helping you do this up until this point. How you show up daily, and how your peers and leadership perceive you, impact your current job and future opportunities. Being mindful will help you act in alignment with the professional brand you want to build. Take a few minutes to answer the following prompts—and be sure to revisit them often.

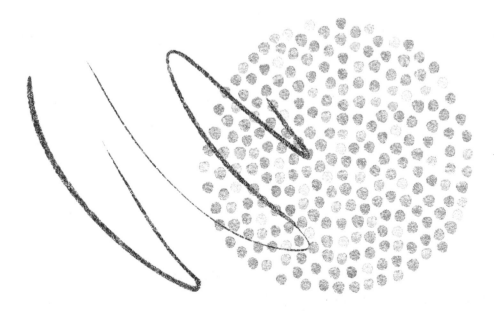

Acting in Alignment

Brainstorm ideas of how you can bring your professional brand to life on the regular.

How can you live your values?

1. _____

_____

2. _____

_____

3. _____

_____

Which activities or tasks align with your Unique Awesomeness Quotient (UAQ)?

1. _____

_____

2. _____

_____

3. _____

_____

Who has similar expertise to you or expertise in an area you want to grow in?

1. _____

_____

2. _____

_____

3. _____

_____

Phase II: Online

The next step to scaling your professional brand is to bring it online. Even if you have zero interest in being an industry influencer, this step is key to getting job opportunities, promotions, and recognition from your peers. These days no one gets a job offer without their future employer googling them and lurking their LinkedIn profile. Promotions are influenced by how you influence others (at your company and beyond). What you say online can give you authority in the real world. For the purpose of your Career Glow Up, right now you're going to begin with the essentials.

How Big Do You Want Your Brand to Be?

Building a professional brand doesn't mean you need to try to gain hundreds of thousands of followers. There are three levels of professional branding; which one do you aspire to?

1. Who do you want to be visible to?

    a. The people in your network only.

    b. People in your network and recruiters and hiring managers.

    c. Everyone within your industry.

2. How do you want your UAQ to be known?

    a. Obvious to your boss and people you work with.

    b. Discoverable by your extended network.

    c. Known and helping people in your industry.

3. **Where would you be most excited to have the opportunity to share your expertise?**

   a. A lunch and learn with your team.

   b. In a blog post and social media post.

   c. In podcast interviews, on conference stages—just hand you the microphone!

Mostly a's	Basic: You want your UAQ to be recognized by the people you work with and your professional community.
Mostly b's	Glowed up: You are ready to elevate your profile beyond your company and network and maybe a bit further.
Mostly c's	Authority: You want to make a name for yourself and make an impact in your industry—and you wouldn't mind having thousands of followers.

No matter which level of branding you aspire to, LinkedIn is essential for ambitious professionals. While it isn't as hot as other platforms, and I know LinkedIn can have library vibes sometimes, it has active professional communities and is the best place to grow your professional brand. You are likely connected with many (or all) of your coworkers, and it's a platform dedicated to professional networking and growth. More importantly, the vast majority of recruiters use it every day to find candidates. While you can grow an audience there, this option is functional for the purpose of your Career Glow Up.

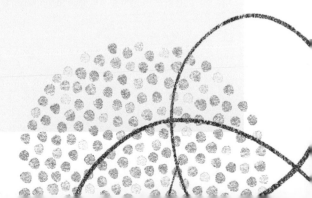

LinkedIn Profile Essentials

Here's how to prepare your profile.

1. Get a profile picture ready.

* Target vibe: _____

* What to wear: _____

* Where to take it: _____

2. Decide what you want people to know in these categories:

* Your most intriguing accomplishment: _____

* Your UAQ statement: _____

* Three things from your Inventory of Awesomeness:

  _____

  _____

  _____

3. Fill in your experience.

* Your most recent job: _____

* Top three accomplishments:

  1. _____   2. _____

  3. _____

4. Now, connect and grow.

* Who in business do you admire and can follow?

  _____

  _____

  _____

* Who has spoken at conferences related to your field?

_____

_____

* Who are the last five people you have met or interviewed with?

1._____   2._____

3._____   4._____

5._____

Professional Brand Expansion

If you want to expand your brand beyond LinkedIn, do so with intention.
Answer these questions to help you figure out where to invest your time.
Add a check mark to whatever applies.

Which social networks do you use for professional purposes?	Where do your deciders, influencers, and connectors hang out?	Where do you want to build your professional brand?
☐ LinkedIn	☐ LinkedIn	☐ LinkedIn
☐ Instagram	☐ Instagram	☐ Instagram
☐ Facebook	☐ Facebook	☐ Facebook
☐ TikTok	☐ TikTok	☐ TikTok
☐ YouTube	☐ YouTube	☐ YouTube
☐ Slack or Discord communities	☐ Slack or Discord communities	☐ Slack or Discord communities
☐ Other _____	☐ Other _____	☐ Other _____

No matter which platform you're using, people need to know about your Unique Awesomeness Quotient (UAQ). On the socials, there are two places where your UAQ must be on show. First, your profile is basically a banner to advertise your UAQ. Most people don't do this, missing a huge opportunity to spark intrigue. More importantly, the point of highlighting your Unique Awesomeness Quotient (UAQ) is to make sure anyone who lurks your profile not only knows what you do, but also why it matters. Don't expect anyone to connect the dots; spell out what is and why it matters. There are four types of posts that garner attention and allow you to showcase your UAQ.

Dos and Don'ts of Commenting

Online professional etiquette is important to ensure you make positive connections and you flex your UAQ. Follow these simple rules.

DO	DON'T
• Praise the poster ("Great point, Anne!")	• Tell people they're wrong (just scroll by)
• Include a supporting anecdote from your experience	• Drop links to your own posts
• Expand on their post	• Be unprofessional

Showcase Your UAQ with a Headline That Hooks

Headlines and bios are where so many professionals get stumped and end up boring people with bland information. Start by completing these three elements:

Your current or target job title	
Your top one to three skills	
Your UAQ summary statement	

Then assemble your headline based on your next career goal:

Job seeker	JOB TITLE	TOP SKILLS	UAQ
Thought leader	UAQ	JOB TITLE	TOP SKILLS
Trying to get a promotion	UAQ	TOP SKILLS	JOB TITLE
IDK what I'm doing here	JOB TITLE	UAQ	TOP SKILLS

There is no better way to flex your Unique Awesomeness Quotient (UAQ) on LinkedIn than creating posts. I know so many professionals get intimidated by this step. What if no one likes it and your coworkers snicker behind your back? If you can relate, remember: The goal isn't to go viral. It's to share your knowledge and demonstrate your awesomeness.

Fear of Posting

How do you feel about creating posts to showcase your Unique
Awesomeness Quotient (UAQ)?
(Circle all that apply.)

Nervous   Scared   Excited   Other _____

What's the best thing that could happen from posting? And if you circled nervous
or scared, what is the worst? _____

_____

_____

Will what you just wrote down matter a year from now? Five years? _____

_____

_____

What is the best-case scenario that could come from building your personal
brand online? _____

_____

_____

This brings us to what to post. The simplest thing to share is something
you recently learned. Sharing your observations as they relate to your
UAQ both broadcasts the work you are doing and offers value to others
who haven't learned the lessons firsthand. These don't need to be
revolutionary. Think of a time someone showed you a shortcut that
changed the way you work; it probably was something simple but the
person's knowledge impressed and helped you. Similarly, you want to
share insightful information.

Insightful Posts

Make a list of five topics, tips, or hacks around your UAQ that you can write a post about. Having trouble thinking of something? Common themes include mistakes people typically make, a step people often forget, simplifying a difficult task, or something you recently learned or are reminded of.

1. _____

_____

2. _____

_____

3. _____

_____

4. _____

_____

5. _____

_____

Fewer posts are harder to resist than a content piece made to celebrate something. The good thing is there is always something you can celebrate. You can celebrate yourself: Did you land a new job, complete a course, get an award? Share it in a shameless humblebrag post. You're not limited to celebrating yourself, though. You can also celebrate a coworker or exciting news your company just announced.

Celebration Posts

What accomplishments or milestones have you achieved recently?

_____

_____

_____

_____

Why is it so exciting?

_____

_____

_____

_____

Has your company or target company had any big announcements or news you can share?

_____

_____

_____

_____

Another type of post focuses on expressing gratitude. People like to be appreciated. Most particularly enjoy being appreciated in public. In chapter 5, we talked about kudos karma, and this is one way to practice it. When someone helps you accomplish a big achievement, let the world know. It helps build their professional brand and lets others know how awesome they are.

Gratitude Posts

Make a list of three people who have helped you recently.
How did they help you and why did it matter?

1. _____

_____

_____

_____

2. _____

_____

_____

_____

3. _____

_____

_____

_____

Yet another type of post features tips and hacks. Share ways that people who do the same job you do can make their lives easier. Undoubtedly, you have found ways to do your job more efficiently, more effectively, and more accurately. Whether it's putting your DMs on "do not disturb" for thirty minutes a day or a checklist you go through when preparing for a big presentation, this type of post both demonstrates your expertise and benefits the reader who implements it.

Tips and Hacks

What do you do that makes your day more efficient?

_____

_____

_____

Do you have a process you created that makes you better at an aspect of your job?

_____

_____

What did you learn at school that you applied at work or in an internship?

_____

_____

_____

Now you have a lot of ideas to work from. To get started, aim to share one to three posts per week. This gets you into the feed, and the more you create and the more conversations you have on the topics you write about, the more you'll get ideas, so keep adding to these lists.

Beware What You Share

Before posting, check out your company's social media guidelines. Make sure you don't share any confidential or proprietary information, such as talking about a product before it launches. And when it doubt, leave it out!

Phase III: Building Beyond

Depending on where you are in your career and in developing your professional brand, you may be ready to step beyond the online world and build your authority in your industry. In fact, as you build your professional brand, opportunities to expand beyond the online space might come to you. I won't overwhelm you with this advanced strategy, but you can start thinking about it.

Dream About the Future

What level of impact and influence do you want to have?

_____

_____

_____

_____

As your expertise expands, how do you see yourself sharing it?

_____

_____

_____

_____

_____

In order to be ready for the next level and to solidify your career glow up, there's something we need to talk about: the person who will get in your way (and what to do about it). When you're ready to find out who that is, and prepare for it, continue to the next chapter.

Focus on Your Goal

Keep your actions aligned with your career goals. What career goal are you targeting right now? _____

_____

_____

_____

_____

Revisit Your Vision

Revisiting your career vision is important. Take a few moments to think about this, including your super-successful future self doing what you're preparing to do right now.

What did you envision? _____

_____

_____

_____

_____

How did it feel? _____

_____

_____

_____

_____

GLOW UP CONFIDENCE METER

130

Do you feel closer to this version of you? _____

_____

_____

_____

What You Love About You

One of the most important factors in success is confidence. Write down three reasons why you are awesome, to cultivate your inner confidence.

1. _____

2. _____

3. _____

Build a Success Habit

Gratitude is a game changer. Take a moment to be grateful.

Who are you grateful for right now?	What are you grateful for?

Stop, Settle, or Stellar Sync

Take a moment to check in on your time-inventing progress.

I stopped . . .	I've settled . . .	I've focused on . . .
I still need to stop . . .	I'm struggling to settle . . .	I still need to invent more time for . . .

One Tiny Step to Success

Write down what you can do today that will get you closer to your goals.

_____

_____

Grow Your Inventory of Awesomeness

What three things are you proud of right now?

1. _____

2. _____

3. _____

Career Glow Up Audit

The funny thing about progress is that we don't notice it happening. Let's check in with where you are now.

	1 (I'm lost)	2 (I need help)	3 (Okay, I guess)	4 (Good but growing)	5 (I'm slaying this!)
I know what I want from my career.					
I am confident I will achieve my goals.					
I know why I am an invaluable asset to my company.					
I have a network that advocates for me.					
I know I will be successful in my career and life.					

Own Your Awesomeness

7

- Value Vectors
- Stop Hiding from Your Potential

Be
unapologetically
ambitious.

No one can get in the way of your career success more than you can. Self-sabotage is real, and I've seen everyone do it, from ambitious professionals just starting their careers to senior executives. You've done so much work already to uncover your awesomeness and glow up your career, so now it's time to make sure that you don't hinder your own potential. Get ready because you are about to prepare your value vectors and spot some potential hiding places, where too many professionals undermine or procrastinate their own success.

Career Glow Up Check-in

What is your current confidence level in your Career Glow Up? Make an x where you feel you fall on the scale below.

Not confident ————————————————————————— Confident AF

Value Vectors

There are three value vectors: pay, promotions, and praise. While one may be more important to you than the others, and which is most important may change over time, each is crucial to a rewarding career. The most important thing is you have clarity on what each of these is for you. I also suggest revisiting the next few exercises annually to make sure your value vectors are aligned with your career.

Your Value Vectors

While each of these is important, there is likely a vector that is most important to you. Take a few moments to write the things that are most important to you at work and in your career. Then, mark where you feel you fit in these value vectors.

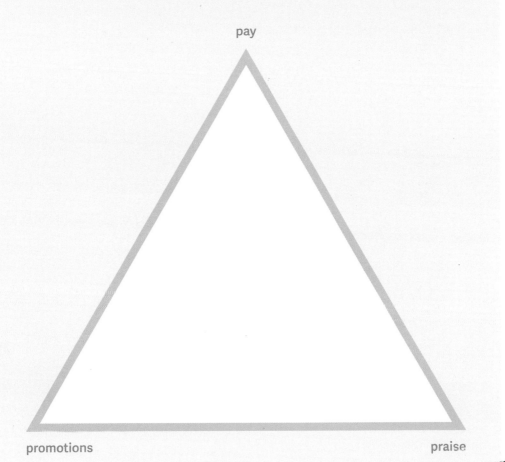

137

Pay

The easiest way a company can demonstrate they value you is to pay you competitive rates. For many women, this is a fact we have been shamed away from. However, unless you are volunteering, you are going to work to get paid. Otherwise, you'd probably be enjoying daytime television, long lunches with friends, and daily Pilates classes. We know there is a pay gap between women and men, and if you're a woman of color, it widens. While I could write an entire book on this and how to negotiate as a woman, right now I want to address the biggest issue I've seen with my clients when it comes to pay: You need to know what you should be paid in order to ask and negotiate for it.

Quick Tips to Negotiate with Confidence

Review your Unique Awesomeness Quotient (UAQ) and reflect on how valuable you are.

- Know your numbers.

- Don't ask for your target, state it.

- Refuse to feel guilt or shame for expecting to be fairly compensated.

Prepare for your next negotiation using the guide in the Career Glow Up Expansion Pack (see page 159 for the link).

Set Your Target Salary

Are you part of a professional association that conducts annual salary reports? If so, download the latest salary report, review the range for your role, and note it here. (Tip: Google "[your target job title] + salary report" to find it.)

What does the internet say? While not perfect, there are sites that compile data to establish ranges for your local market. For each of these sites, note the average salary and ranges.

	Average Salary	Salary Range
Payscale		
Glassdoor		
LinkedIn Salary		
Other		

Review the numbers above. Focusing on the averages, you can estimate the market standards.

Low	Middle	High

Now it's time to create your target salary based on the numbers you determined.

Your target salary: _____

Promotions

There is more to career satisfaction than getting paid. In fact, I know for many of you reading this, you likely prioritize growth and a good work environment above compensation. When you apply the Career Glow Up system to your career strategy, your career trajectory is going to rise. Unfortunately, the opportunities are not infinite at every company. You may encounter ceilings and limits that no amount of unignorable impact or stellar network of advocates can change. This is where the career trajectory review comes in. It is designed to help you determine when you are on track, and when you're getting stuck. Repeat this checklist a few times a year, and when making a decision about new job opportunities.

Career Trajectory Review

For each prompt, answer yes or no. If you answer mostly yes, you're likely to be on the right path. However, if you find yourself answering mostly no, it's time to figure out what needs to change.

	Yes	No
There are opportunities to use my Unique Awesomeness Quotient.		
I have opportunities to make an unignorable impact.		
My boss or another leader at my company is advocating for my career advancement.		
My professional growth is being supported.		
I can see an opportunity to get to the next level.		

Praise

Using unignorable impact and bragless self-promotion strategies, you should not have a shortage of praise. That said, sometimes praise doesn't come easily. Many managers struggle with giving meaningful feedback, both positive and constructive, to their teams. Unfortunately, in some circumstances, a manager may feel threatened or insecure by a top performer's achievements and give criticism instead. While you cannot resolve issues for them, you can get clear on what feedback is important to you, and what you need to thrive. Then have a conversation with your manager to let them know the answers to these questions. It will help them manage you and get you relevant feedback.

Getting Clear About Praise

What type of feedback do you want? _____

_____

_____

_____

Why is it important to you? _____

_____

_____

How often do you want feedback? _____

_____

_____

Stop Hiding from Your Potential

Maybe it's a fear of failure, a fear of success, or some other reason. There are many real-world obstacles to creating the successful career you deserve. I often see ambitious professionals find reasons not to succeed. Here are a few of the following that I often encounter.

I Need More Experience, Education, Etc.

Too many ambitious professionals undermine their awesomeness by thinking they need more degrees, experience, etc. Here's an example I see frequently with my clients: They graduated with a bachelor's degree, but as they start applying for jobs they feel like they need an MBA. But if they have an MBA, they think they need a PhD, then a post-doctorate or another master's degree. There will always be more experience to get, more education you could pursue. It's easy to hide behind artifacts that prove your worthiness, instead of evaluating yourself to uncover how uniquely qualified you are.

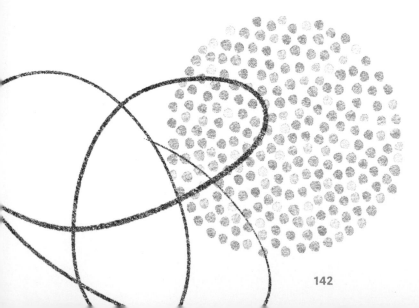

Do You *Need* More Experience or Education?

What do you think you need more of to achieve your next career goal? Circle one.

More experience   More education   Both

Is it possible to achieve your goal without more education and/or experience? Circle one.

Yes   No

What do you have that replaces the education/experience? _____

_____

_____

_____

_____

_____

_____

_____

_____

_____

_____

_____

Busywork and Procrastination

It's easy to get lost in the mundane tasks of the day-to-day. You get so busy answering emails, going to meetings, and doing the actual work that you don't have time for anything else. The thing is: busyness is a place you can hide. If you've been too busy to focus on your stellar tasks or fully take action on everything you've planned in this book, what you have is an invitation to explore. Let's see what's behind it.

Busy or Hiding?

Has something been holding you back from your stellar tasks (including implementing your Career Glow Up)? Circle one.

Yes   No

How would you categorize those tasks? Circle one.

Stop   Settle   Stellar

What makes you scared or uneasy of the stellar tasks? Circle or write your answer.

I'm afraid I'll fail miserably.   I'm terrified I'll succeed.

Other _____

_____

_____

_____

What specifically makes you afraid of failing or succeeding? (Example: I won't have time, people will think I'm not talented, etc.)

_____

_____

_____

_____

_____

_____

_____

_____

_____

What is the likelihood of that happening? Circle one.

Low   Medium   High

What is one small task you can do today to get started on your stellar tasks?

_____

_____

_____

_____

_____

_____

_____

_____

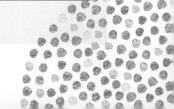

I Can't Succeed Where I Am

Hard truth: Sometimes this is true. Sometimes no matter how much great work you do, how strategic your impact is, and how much effort you put into establishing your network of advocates, there are greater forces at play that hold you back. Real barriers exist in the world, including the old boys club, systemic racism in hiring and promotions, and much more. But I don't want you to hide behind these obstacles. If your current boss or company is hostile, biased, or worse, you alone cannot change them—but you can choose to move on to a better opportunity.

Is It Time to Move On?

While no quiz or checklist can answer this for you, these questions can help you gain clarity on the next step for you. Circle your answers to the questions below.

Do you feel you are being treated well?　　　　　　　　　　　　　Y　　N

Is your professional growth being supported?　　　　　　　　　　Y　　N

Is the problem specific to your team?　　　　　　　　　　　　　　Y　　N

Have you spoken with your manager about the issue?　　　　　　Y　　N

Do you see a path to being successful and having job satisfaction?　Y　　N

What is your gut telling you? _____

_____

_____

_____

_____

It's Good Enough

How many times have you settled? From the B you got on that term paper you know was an A paper, to accepting a job offer that was just okay, over the course of your life, you have probably learned to accept things being fine. But you aren't glowing up your career for it to be fine. You went through the Career Glow Up process because you want your career to be exceptional (whatever that looks like for you is up to you). This brings us to the last step in your Career Glow Up, how to glow on from here, covered in the next chapter.

Focus on Your Goal

Keep your actions aligned with your career goals. What career goal are you targeting right now?

_____

_____

_____

_____

_____

_____

_____

_____

_____

_____

_____

_____

_____

_____

_____

Revisit Your Vision

Revisiting your career vision is important. Take a few moments to think about this, including your super-successful future self doing what you're preparing to do right now.

What did you envision? _____

_____

_____

How did it feel? _____

_____

_____

Do you feel closer to this version of you? _____

_____

_____

What You Love About You

One of the most important factors in success is confidence. Write down three reasons why you are awesome, to cultivate your inner confidence.

1. _____

2. _____

3. _____

GLOW UP CONFIDENCE METER

Build a Success Habit

Gratitude is a game changer. Take a moment to be grateful.

Who are you grateful for right now?	What are you grateful for?

Stop, Settle, or Stellar Sync

Take a moment to check in on your time-inventing progress.

I stopped . . .	I've settled . . .	I've focused on . . .
I still need to stop . . .	I'm struggling to settle . . .	I need to invent more time for . . .

One Tiny Step to Success

The path to success is paved with tiny tasks and decisions. What can you do today that will get you closer to your goals?

_____

_____

_____

_____

_____

_____

_____

_____

_____

_____

Grow Your Inventory of Awesomeness

You're taking action, glowing up your career, and doing awesome work. What are you proud of right now?

1. _____

2. _____

3. _____

Career Glow Up Audit

The funny thing about progress is that we don't notice it happening.
Let's check in with where you are now.

	1 (I'm lost)	2 (I need help)	3 (Okay, I guess)	4 (Good but growing)	5 (I'm slaying this!)
I know what I want from my career.					
I am confident I will achieve my goals.					
I know why I am an invaluable asset to my company.					
I have a network that advocates for me.					
I know I will be successful in my career and life.					

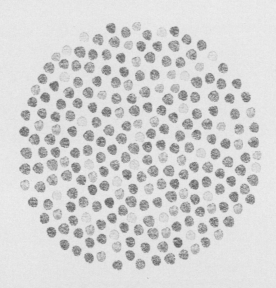

Glow On

At this point, you might be nervous. You're wondering, "Is this all it takes?" There is so much discussion around career success, especially for ambitious women (or really anyone who doesn't fit the typical corporate bro mold). Here's the thing about career success strategy: You are the main character in your career. There will be supporting characters, like those in your network of advocates, and even some antagonists along the way. But with the strategies you worked through in this workbook, you have everything you need to be the hero(ine) everyone is cheering for.

Be accountable to your possibilities.

Claim It

In big bold letters, claim your role by writing: I am the main character.

Now, where do you glow from here? This book is your career success guide, and as you grow, these exercises should be revisited. At least once a year, and whenever you start a new job or get a promotion, revisit the Career Glow Up process to refine your strategy to remain aligned with your career vision.

Refresh Your Glow

The most important thing you will do with this book is take action. You've done the work, and now you have all your potential laid out in front of you. Don't leave it on a shelf to collect dust. Implement these strategies every day. On days where it is hard, when you are discouraged, open these pages and review the work you have done to remind yourself of what you want and what you know you can do. Stepping back from the ambition you uncovered here would be settling—and that's not what you're here to do. Hold yourself accountable to your possibilities. They are truly infinite.

When will you repeat the Career Glow Up process?

Where Are You Now?

Before we fully embark on creating the career you want, let's document and celebrate where you are now.

What is your job title (or target job title)?

_____

_____

What level are you at?

_____

_____

Do you see yourself as a leader?

_____

_____

Do you see yourself as someone with high potential?

_____

_____

How confident are you that you can achieve your career goals?

_____

_____

Commit to Your Potential

I am an ambitious professional who has a vision to

_____.

I commit to using my Unique Awesomeness Quotient (UAQ)

_____,

to create a positive and unignorable impact, develop a network of

advocates who lift me up, and pay it forward whenever I can. I will

prioritize and honor my reputation and ability to achieve everything

I wrote down in this book.

Signed,

_____

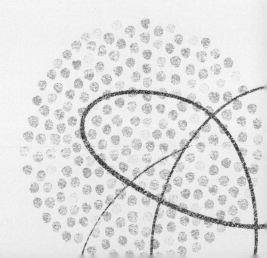

Acknowledgments

Success is not solitary, and there are so many people who have been part of my success squad that I need to acknowledge.

First, I like to share my gratitude for the team at Quarto. This workbook truly would not exist as it is (and it definitely wouldn't be nearly as fabulous). In particular, I want to thank Rage Kindelsperger for believing in my message, and Keyla Pizarro-Hernández for helping me refine this workbook into something impactful. A million thanks for all you have done, and the opportunity to create this book.

Over my career I was fortunate to have had leaders and mentors who helped me learn each of these lessons, and who saw potential in me even when I didn't see it myself. Arlene Lambert, Kj Kuipers, Troy Inman, and Danielle Du Toit, I'm endlessly grateful to have gotten to work for, learn from, and be inspired by each of you.

Another integral part of my own success squad has been my longtime friends. They've celebrated life stuff with me, given space for rants, been there through hard times, and most importantly been an endless source of laughs and love. Jenn, Cassandra, Heather, Darren, Sandra, Chelsea, and so many more (if I haven't named you it's because I'm over my word count by a lot already!). I also must give a shout out to my business besties Charlene Rymsha and Sarah Mac. This whole journey of starting a business would have been miserable if it weren't for you two.

To mom, Linda, who always believed in my ability as a writer from my first attempt at writing a book at the age of seven (it was a memoir, obvs); I hope you are looking down from the other side to know this dream of mine came true. My dad, Dennis, who I learned so much from personally and professionally, and who also has always held me to my potential, even when it scared me. My sister, Angela, for being the model of unapologetically ambitious in the best possible way. To my sons, Warren and Conrad, who thought it was no big deal I was writing a book because they write books all the time. You both brighten my life and being your mom is my favorite job ever.

To my husband, Jared. You encouraged me to be everything I am and gave me space to make this reality. The best decision I've ever made was marrying you. I love you extra much, and will never stop pinching myself because life with you is so wonderful.

Finally, I want to acknowledge all my Career Besties, but in particular you, dear reader. I truly believe when awesome and value-aligned people succeed at work, the better our workplaces (and world) will be. I hope this book helped you believe in yourself as much as I do.

About the Author

Jennifer Brick is your new career bestie. After climbing the career ladder in the technology industry, she discovered her true purpose in life was to help people succeed at work. In 2019, she started a YouTube channel that focused on everything from navigating career advancement to dealing with coworker drama and getting over a toxic job. Her audience has quickly grown to over 120k across platforms, and she is the creator of the Career Glow Up System and Toxic Job Detox. Her advice has also been featured in *Fast Company, Business Insider*, InHerSight, and many more.

For more resources, including examples of the concepts we covered in this book, a salary negotiation guide, and more, download your complimentary Career Glow Up Expansion Pack by visiting: careerglowupbook.com/bonus.

References

[1] Sara B. Algoe, Jonathan Haidt, and Shelly L. Gable. "Beyond Reciprocity: Gratitude and Relationships in Everyday Life." *Emotion* 8, no. 3 (2008): 425–429. https://www.ncbi.nlm.nih.gov/pmc/articles/PMC2692821.

[2] Robert A. Emmons and Michael E. McCullough. "Counting Blessings Versus Burdens: An Experimental Investigation of Gratitude and Subjective Well-Being in Daily Life." *Journal of Personality and Social Psychology* 84, no. 2 (2003): 377–389. https://whish.stanford.edu/wp-content/uploads/2018/11/GratitudeArticle.pdf.

[3] Philip C. Watkins, Kathrane Woodward, Tamara Stone, and Russell L. Kolts. "Gratitude and Happiness: Development of a Measure of Gratitude, and Relationships with Subjective Well-Being." *Social Behavior and Personality* 31, no. 5 (2003): 431-451. https://www.ingentaconnect.com/content/sbp/sbp/2003/00000031/00000005/art00001.

[4] Laurence J. Peter and Raymond Hull. *The Peter Principle*. New York: William Morrow & Company, 1969.

While I did not directly draw from these works, these books have had an impact on me and provided inspiration as I developed my career success strategies.

Shawn Achor. *The Happiness Advantage: The Seven Principles of Positive Psychology That Fuel Success and Performance at Work.* New York: Crown Business, 2010.

Dale Carnegie. *How to Win Friends and Influence People.* New York: Simon & Schuster, 2009.

Stephen R. Covey. (2004). *The 7 Habits of Highly Effective People: Powerful Lessons in Personal Change.* New York: Simon & Schuster, 2004.